The History and Topography of Harrogate, and the Forest of Knaresborough

GRAINGE'S HARROGATE.

Armitage & Ibbetson.   Bradford

CHRIST CHURCH AND THE STRAY, HIGH HARROGATE.

THE

History and Topography

OF

✦ HARROGATE, ✦

WITH NOTICES OF

Birstwith.	Haverah Park.	Rigton.
Blubberhouses.	Killinghall.	Scriven.
Castley.	Lindley.	Stainburn.
Clint.	Little Ribston.	Swinden.
Dunkeswick.	Menwith-with-	Thornthwaite-with-
Felliscliffe.	Darley.	Padside.
Fewston.	Norwood.	Thruscross.
Great Timble.	Pannal.	Weeton.
Hampsthwaite.	Plumpton.	

AND

The Forest of Knaresbro'.

BY

WILLIAM GRAINGE,

AUTHOR OF

"THE BATTLES AND BATTLE FIELDS OF YORKSHIRE;"
"THE CASTLES AND ABBEYS OF YORKSHIRE;"
"VALE OF MOWBRAY;" "NIDDERDALE;" ETC.

LONDON: SIMPKIN, MARSHALL, AND CO.
YORK: JOHN SAMPSON.
1882.

PREFACE.

———

THE district of which this volume treats was formerly known as the Royal Forest of Knaresborough, and of which no previous history can be said to exist. In this work a detailed account is given of each place, from the earliest known times to the present day, chiefly derived from materials never before published. Pedigrees are given of the principal landowners in the district—both ancient and modern; and pains have been taken to collect notices of eminent individuals and families connected with the district, some of which have been little known to the public. Besides what may be termed the political, civil, and ecclesiastical history of the district, sketches of the physical history and geology are given, principally derived from the author's personal observations, made during the last ten years.

To those who have ever undertaken the task of writing a local history, no apology is needed to explain the delay which has taken place in the production of this volume, as they well know the great variety of sources whence the materials must be drawn, and the difficulty of bringing together such a number of minute facts as are necessary to the making of local history.

By the residents within the Forest of Knaresborough, and also by those, in other places, connected with it by birth or association, I presume this book will be kindly received as the first attempt to give a regular and authentic history of the district. Along with its companion volume "Nidderdale" it forms a history and topography of more than three-fourths of the valley of the Nidd.

To the clergy and landowners my grateful acknowledgments are due, for the opportunities afforded me for the examination of their registers and other records, and for the information supplied from their private documents, not otherwise accessible. More particularly to the Messrs. Powell, of Knaresborough, for permission to inspect the Rolls of the Honour Court, deposited under their charge. To the kindness of my esteemed friend, R. H. Skaife, Esq., of the Mount, York, I am indebted for many and great favours—some of which are acknowledged, but many are not—so I here tender my sincere thanks for assistance which I can never expect to return.

A preface (always the last written portion of a book) perhaps cannot be better employed than by adding to the information which the book contains to which it is affixed, therefore I shall introduce here the census of the district taken in 1871, and a short account of the new baths at Harrogate, built in the same year, both of which events occurred too late to be introduced in their proper places.

POPULATION IN 1871.

	Mls.	Fms.	Total		Mls.	Fms.	Total
Bilton-with-Harrogate ..	3079	3686	6765	Clint	212	184	396
Pannal	920	973	1893	Hampsthwaite	207	241	448
Plumpton.............	88	85	173	Felliscliffe	164	157	321
Little Ribston..........	93	95	188	Birstwith	266	304	570
Dunkeswick	80	88	168	Menwith-with-Darley ..	307	268	575
Weeton................	148	165	313	Thornthwaite-with-			
Castley	37	36	73	Padside	185	187	372
Rigton	217	213	430	Fewston	231	168	399
Stainburn.............	102	95	197	Norwood	304	192	496
Lindley...............	327	115	442	Great Timble	109	78	187
Haverah Park..........	49	53	84	Blubberhouses	40	29	62
Killinghall	324	330	654	Thruscross	155	147	302

The New Victoria Baths adjoin the old baths of the same name, and extend eastward from Promenade Terrace to Cheltenham Square. The foundation stone was laid Feb. 4th, and the building formally opened to the public Aug. 24th, 1871. The water intended for the use of these baths is the surplus water of the Bog Wells, conveyed from them by means of glass tubes, and stored in five large underground reservoirs at the upper end of the building, so that the water can gravitate to the heating apparatus and the baths. The capacity of these reservoirs is upwards of 200,000 gallons. The building partakes largely of the Italian style, and is at once substantial, massive, and elegant. It consists of a centre and two wings; the former being two stories in height, the latter only one; while at each end is a swimming bath, which rises higher and projects further in front than the other parts of the wings, and adds much to the pictorial appearance of the building. Along the front, with the exception of the portions occupied by the swimming baths, extends a verandah of ornamental ironwork. That part of it in front of the centre and grand entrance projects across the carriage road, so that parties can drive up and enter the rooms under its shelter. On the upper part of this front is cut the name and date of the building—"Victoria Baths, 1871." Above the cornice of this front rises a colossal shield, on which is sculptured, in bold relief, the arms of the town, surmounted by a crown. The windows have circular heads and columns at the sides. The swimming bath at the west

end is twenty feet in height; lighted at each end by a window
of three lights, and on the front by two similar windows, each of
three lights. The east end swimming bath, owing to the slope
of the ground, is thirty-three feet in height; lighted at each end
by a window of three lights, and in the front by one of four
lights. On the top of a massive cornice, around the roofs
of the three elevated portions, runs a stone balustrade,
relieved at each corner by a square pedestal bearing a carved
urn; a pierced battlement runs along the front of the lower
portions of the wings. The roof and ridge are adorned with
ornamental ironwork. The grand entrance leads directly to the
manager's office, the front of which is circular, and built in such
a manner as to command a full view of each corridor. On each
side are waiting rooms; one for ladies the other for gentlemen.
The corridors run east and west, and are each two hundred feet
in length by eight feet in width, and lighted from above by
windows of stained glass. On each side are arranged the bath
rooms, eighteen in number, each measuring ten feet by eleven,
and sixteen in height. On one side of the corridor one dressing
room is attached to each bath room, and on the other, two;
in each of which is a water closet and lavatory. In each wing
provision is made for four shower and as many vapour baths.
The floors of the bath-rooms, dressing-rooms, and corridors
are boarded, and covered with linoleum. The sides of the walls,
to a certain height, are lined with Minton's tiles. Some of the
baths are also lined with tiles, and entered by white marble
steps; others are made of porcelain. The swimming bath at
the east end is 47 feet in length by 17 feet in width, and
the height from the floor line to the ceiling is 28 feet. The
bath is so arranged that the water at each end will be three
feet six inches deep, and the centre five feet deep. The bottom
is lined with white tiles, and also the sides up to the height

of five feet six inches, above which is a very pretty border in blue tiles. The roof is open, with moulded wall plates, boarded and stained. The west end swimming bath is similar in its arrangements, but larger, being 68 feet long by 18 feet wide. There is an ample supply of water closets, lavatories, and dressing-rooms, provided in all parts of the building.

The plans were prepared by Mr. John Richardson, surveyor to the Local Board; and the following were the contractors, with the amount of each contract—

		£	s.	d.
Construction of Reservoirs	W. Newsome, Leeds	1297	0	0
Masons' work	J. Stephenson, Harrogate	4700	0	0
Joiners' work	R. Raworth, Harrogate	1586	0	0
Slaters' work	Heavysides, Leeds	216	10	0
Plumbers' work	J. Marshall, Harrogate	760	0	0
Iron work	Heaps & Robinson, Leeds	694	10	0
Plasterers' work	R. Fortune, Harrogate	209	0	0
		£9343	0	0

This does not include the tiling and fitting of the baths, nor the cost of the heating apparatus.

With these remarks and additions this volume is consigned to the judgment of an impartial public.

W. GRAINGE.

Harrogate,
    Oct., 1871.

CONTENTS.

CONTENTS.

HARROGATE.

WATERS OF HARROGATE.

BATHS.

PUBLIC BUILDINGS.

THE STRAY. 1

STATISTICS.

TOPOGRAPHICAL SURVEY.

CONTENTS.

The Forest of Knaresborough.

SITUATION, PHYSICAL ASPECT, RIVERS, AND STREAMS.

THE Forest of Knaresborough is situate between the rivers Nidd and Wharfe, in the Wapontake of Claro, and West Riding of the County of York; and is about twenty miles in length, by eight in average breadth, comprising 100,000 acres of land, divided into twenty-four townships or places, of which three are ancient parish towns.

The physical aspect of this district is generally that of a region of undulations, a series of hills and valleys, none of them remarkably high or deep; both of them rounded and smoothed by the action of water. Here and there appear masses of rock which have resisted the action of the smoothing element—as in Great and Little Almes Cliff, Birk Crag, Swincliffe, Kexgill, and a few other places, where the masses of gritstone have been of too great bulk and hardness to yield to the torrent, but hard as they are they have not escaped— their softer parts have been washed away, and countless crannies and crevices cut into their flinty sides; they have evidently formed cliffs exposed to the action of sea waves, until at length, either the elevation of the land on which they stood, or the draining of the waters into some deeper sea bed, left them high and dry as we now behold them. The millstone grit is the

B

only rock which has survived the action of the watery element; all the softer beds have melted before it, and all their ridges and angles have been rounded down into gentle acclivities. The highest land is on the western boundary, and approaches closely to 1,600 feet above the sea level, while the lowest at Harewood bridge is only 98. The high lands are for miles upon miles, bleak and desolate—an undulating forest of ling, rushes and brackens; these heights form the watershed between the valleys of the Nidd and the Wharfe, into which two rivers all the surplus water of the Forest of Knaresborough eventually finds its way.

The Nidd first touches our district by its junction with Darley Beck, near the village of that name, and flows alongside of it until a short distance below Newbridge, when it runs entirely within it, dividing Clint from Birstwith and Hampsthwaite. On reaching the township of Ripley, it again forms the Forest boundary; after passing Killinghall bridge it touches a patch of yellow, marly, magnesian limestone on the left, while on the right is a quarry of strong gritstone. Near the railway viaduct it receives the waters of Oakbeck, and thence to the dam at Scotton mill it is a full quiet stream, the woods on both sides sloping grandly down to the water, the bordering rocks being gritstone and shale, until it reaches Gateshill, when it again meets the magnesian limestone. The scenery along its banks in passing Knaresborough is exceedingly varied and beautiful, as it winds along mid rocks, woods, fields and gardens, until it has passed Goldsborough mill, when the banks subside and the scenery becomes tamer; and in this manner it continues to form the boundary of our district until its junction with the Crimple, near Walshford bridge.

The Wharfe is a longer and larger stream than the Nidd, and first touches the Forest of Knaresborough at Castley, and forms its southern boundary down to Harewood bridge. The most interesting place upon its banks is Rougemont, the site of the mansion of the family of the Lords D l'Isle.

Among the hills and valleys of the high land between these rivers many fine streams have their origin ; none of them, however, attain to any great magnitude or length of course before they are swallowed by the bounding rivers.

On the southern side is the Crimple, which rises from many small runnels on the high land west of Beckwithshaw and north of Rigton. At Beckwith it falls into somewhat of a deep valley, and flows downward to Pannal amid some pretty scenery. Near Burn-bridge mill it receives a small stream from the right called Buttersike, and for the remainder of its course forms the boundary of the Forest, dividing it from Follifoot, Spofforth, and North Deighton. Passing Crimple hamlet and bleach works, and almost close to Spofforth village, it loses itself in the Nidd a short distance above Walshford bridge.

Oakbeck rises at the top of Haverah Park, down which it flows in a shallow thickly-wooded valley, receiving many small tributaries from the same district on either side. Quitting the park a short distance below Pot bridge, it receives a small affluent from Harlow Car, flows through the romantic glen of Birk Crag, and after receiving a small stream from the right, partly derived from the sulphur springs of Harrogate, it empties itself into the Nidd, a short distance above the North Eastern Railway viaduct of that name.

A small stream called Cockhill beck empties itself into the Nidd on the eastern side of the village of Hampsthwaite, which draws its waters from Graystone Plain and the high lands in that neighbourhood. At Rowden Lane, one of its tributaries has cut a deep gully into the shale and ironstone formation, which bears the name of Hell-hole.

Tang beck derives its waters from Kettlesing Head, and the slopes of Felliscliffe and Birstwith. These waters form a junction near the Kettlesing Wesleyan Chapel, and thence flowing eastward divide the townships of Birstwith and Felliscliffe; after passing Birstwith Hall and Hurst Grove, this stream enters the Nidd near Hampsthwaite Church.

Padside beck, or Darley beck, is another stream of the Forest, deriving some of its waters from Redlish and the southern slopes of Greenhow. Near Padside Hall it becomes the boundary of the Forest, dividing it from the township of Dacre; thence flowing downward past Thornthwaite Church and Darley village, it also enters the Nidd.

Kexbeck is another stream which has its origin on forest soil, on the high lands of Poxstones and Kexgill Moor. Unlike every other stream in the district, it flows towards the west, past Hazelwood and Beamsley Hall, and empties itself into the Wharfe a short distance below Bolton Bridge.

The largest, longest, and most important of all the Forest-born streams is the Washburn, which draws its first supplies from many different springs in the high region which extends from Greenhow Hill to Beamsley Beacon, generally in the parish of Fewston. These springs supply small runnels in the moorland hollows, their sides fringed with rushes, heath, and ferns; where the red grouse haunt and the black-faced sheep graze; in a region rarely trod except by the sportsman and the shepherd. The convergence of these small brooklets form larger, until at length they are all swallowed up by one master stream. These shallow valleys are not at all picturesque until they leave the moorlands, when they become wider and deeper, and their sides are in some places furrowed by rugged gills and in others improved by cultivation. At Bramley Head one of the tributaries is first interrupted for manufacturing purposes to turn the spindles of a flax mill. Four or five factories down the valley derive their motive power from this stream or its auxiliaries. Many murmuring streams during the summer

season creep down their gully-like courses hidden by native
foliage; in winter they are loud brawling torrents, dashing over
stony beds, and pouring their muddy waters into the main
stream. In a narrow part of the valley stands the parochial
chapel of Thruscross, almost close to the stream, and always
within hearing of its music. Descending the valley, many
a choice piece of scenery worthy the artist's pencil may be
found. Near the hamlet of Blubberhouses is a large manufactory known as Westhouse mill, the machinery of which is
driven by two gigantic water wheels. A small affluent here
enters from the right, which rises on Kexgill moor, and thence
tumbles down the wild, romantic, rugged glen through which
the turnpike road to Skipton passes. In its downward course
it next receives Gill beck and Thackerey beck from the right,
leaves Crag Hall and Fewston on the left, passes close to
Newhall, once the residence of Edward Fairfax the poet, when
it receives the waters of Whidrah beck, or Gill beck, from
the left; when turning south, it leaves Swinsty Hall on the
right, and Scough Hall and Jack hill on the left. Viewed
from either side, the valley at this point presents some fine
pictures of natural scenery—fields, farms, and cottages studding
the slopes as they rise from the wood-fringed banks of the
stream to the gorse and heath-clad hills above. A considerable
stream enters on the right from the hills of Snowdon, and
the moors of Askwith; after receiving this addition to its
waters the main stream bends easterly, enclosing a wooded
island, a short distance below which is Dog, or Dobb Park
mill, a lonely spot surrounded by woods and hills. On the
southern side of the valley, overtopping a large plantation of
larches, stand the ruins of Dobb Park Lodge, a lofty building
of Tudor architecture, four stories in height. It does not
appear to have been destroyed by time or tempest, but to
have been carefully pulled down in such a manner as to leave

a portion standing, but uninhabitable. There appears to have been four rooms in each storey, to which a winding stair in a projecting turret in the rear has formed the only means of access. One half of the south front yet remains, presenting square windows of two lights, each divided by a transom; over the lower is a cornice, supported by brackets, which are ornamented with armorial shields, each charged with two quoits or circular discs. In the centre has been a projecting semi-circular window, a part of which yet remains. When complete it has been a lofty and elegant building, and even yet, though ruinous and deserted, it forms a highly interesting feature in the sylvan landscape around. Of its history we know nothing.*

Below Dobb Park mill† the valley becomes in many places thickly wooded, interspersed with cultivated fields and farm houses. On the eastern skirt of a large patch of woodland stands Lindley Hall (now a farm house), overlooking a scene of exquisite natural beauty. Below this house the course of the Washburn bends to the southward, the banks sloping gently down to the level of the Wharfe, and finally between the pleasant sylvan villages of Farnley and Leathley, the two streams become united in one; or, as Polyolbion Drayton singeth—

    "Washbrook with her wealth her mistress doth supply."

The next stream which flows from our district is Stainburn beck, which has but a short course. From the high ground

*In the parish register of Fewston is the following entry.—"1658. Aprill. Mr. John Vavasour, of Dog Park, was buried the first day." This was probably one of the Weston family of that name who resided here at that time, when it was probably complete and inhabitable.

†"This river is subject to sudden floods. On the 4th of August, 1767, there were great floods in the Aire, the Wharfe, and the Washburn; about three o'clock in the morning the water rose upwards of two yards in the space of an hour. At Beamsley two houses were swept away, and the Dob Park and Lindley bridges on the Washburn destroyed; great numbers of cattle, horses, and sheep were carried down the streams, and much damage done to the corn lands."—*Annual Register*, 1767.

south of Little Almes Cliff, and the moors of Stainburn, it runs southward to the Wharfe, which it enters near Castley. In the lower part of its course it bears the name of Riffa beck.

Another small stream, called Weeton beck, enters the Wharfe near Rougemont.

Swindon Sike is but a small stream, worthy of notice only because it forms the boundary of the Forest on that side. It rises from a spring called Wareholes Well, near Walton Head, and flows into the Wharfe a short distance below Harewood bridge.

The following tabulated view of the height of different places in the Forest of Knaresborough above the average level of the sea is from Professor Phillips and the Ordnance Survey.

	feet.		feet.
Simon's Seat	1593	Fewston Church	564
Lord's Seat	1585	Beckwith Head	562
Poxstones Moor	1517	Birk Crag	550
Greenhow Hill	1441	Rigton	550
Black Fell	1341	Brackenthwaite	540
Roggan Hall	1318	Burnt Yates	520
Gaukhall Ridge	1100	Horn Bank	500
Lipperaley Pike	1068	Saltergate Hill	481
Jack Hill—Fox Crag	951	Swincliffe Top	450
Little Almes Cliff	837	Queen Hotel, Harrogate	406
Rocking Stone, in Thorn-		The Bogs, Harrogate	400
thwaite	810	Clint Hall	400
Timble Great	753	Bilton Church	339
Lindley Bents	750	Concert Room, Harrogate	329
Burscough Rigg	743	Bilton Hall	300
Great Almes Cliff	716	Knox Hill, Harrogate	300
Kettlesing Head	715	Starbeck	274
Dangerous Corner	688	Pannal Church	231
Hopper Lane Hotel	678	Hampsthwaite Bridge	200
John O'Gaunt's Castle	625	Plumpton Lake	175
Harlow Hill	600	Dropping Well, Knaresboro'	150
Thornthwaite Church	600	Harewood Bridge	98
Castle Hill, in Pannal	594		

BOUNDARIES.

As the most recent and authentic account of the Boundaries of the Forest, we give "A Return to a Commission for taking the general Boundaries of the Forest of Knaresborough, in the year 1767."

"In obedience to His Majesty's Commission, under the seal of his Duchy of Lancaster, bearing date the 15th day of July, in the seventh year of the king's Majesty's reign, and in the year of our Lord 1767; hereunto annexed, to us and others the commissioners therein named, directed; for perambulating and ascertaining the metes and boundaries of his majesty's Forest of Knaresborough, parcel of the possessions of the said Duchy of Lancaster, in the County of York; and for other the purposes in the said Commission mentioned:—We, Joseph Tullie, Receiver General of the revenues of his majesty's said duchy; Robert Roper, auditor for the north parts of the said duchy; William Henry Ashurst, auditor for the south parts of the said duchy; William Masterman, Clerk of the Council of the said duchy; William Marsden, surveyor of the lands for the north parts of the said duchy; and Francis Russell, Deputy Surveyor of the woods of the north parts of the said duchy; being six of the Commissioners named in the said Commission, do hereby humbly certify that on the 3rd day of September, now last past, We, the said Commissioners, did repair to his majesty's said Forest of Knaresborough, at a certain place within the said forest, where the water of Crimple runs into the river Nidd, being the place where our perambulation of the forest was proposed and appointed to be begun. Having previously given fourteen days' public notice that we should, at that time and place, begin our perambulation; and from thence proceed in executing the powers and authorities to us given by the said commission, in the several towns of Knaresborough, Ripon, Boroughbridge, Wetherby, Shipley, Harwood, Otley, Pateley-. Bridge, Leeds, Skipton in Craven, Grassington, Settle, Bradford, and Ripley; by causing to be affixed printed notices, signed with the proper names of four of us, the said acting commissioners, in the public market-places, or upon the church doors, or some other notorious place or places within the said several towns, as by the commission we were directed.

And we do further humbly certify, that we did, on the same third day of September, at the place aforesaid, cause his majesty's said commission to be proclaimed and read in an open public manner, in the presence of the Deputy Constable, Deputy Steward, and Bailiff of his majesty's Castle, Honor, and Forest of Knaresborough, and divers other officers of the said forest, and a great concourse of his majesty's copyhold tenants of the said honor and forest, and other persons, then and there met and assembled:—And thereupon, we did proceed from thence forward in perambulating and ascertaining the metes and boundaries of the said forest, and in due execution of all other, the powers and authorities to us given by the said commission, and continued therein from day to day, until the 27th day of the same month of September, when we completed the same; having called to our aid and assistance, and been attended in such service by divers of the officers and tenants of his majesty's said honor and forest, and other ancient persons conversant therein, and residing in the neighbourhood of the said forest.

And we do find, as well by divers ancient Inquisitions,
Decrees, and other evidence remaining on record, in the office
of the Clerk of the Council of the said Duchy, and in the
said Castle of Knaresborough, as by the information of divers
ancient credible persons, and by general reputation, that the
metes and boundaries of his majesty's said Forest of Knaresborough begin at the stream of the river Nidd, where the
rivulet called Crimple runs into the said river; at which place
the said Crimple is bounded, on or towards the south, by
a parcel of enclosed land, in the manor of North Deighton,
belonging to Sir John Ingilby, Bart., called Tomling-Ing; and
on or towards the north, by part of the enclosed land belonging
to Henry Pullein, called Blackstones, lying in the township
of Little Ribston, (which said little Ribston, is within the
boundary of the said forest); and from thence ascending up
the stream of Crimple to Blackstone-Wath, over which the
road from Ribston to Ingmanthorp leadeth; and so along the
stream of Crimple to the south-east corner of Ribston moor,
commonly called Ribston-Green; and from thence, up the
stream of Crimple, to a piece or parcel of ground, formerly an
Island, in the Lordship of North Deighton, called Mill-Green
and Mill-paddock, being the place where the North Deighton
mill formerly stood; and so along the north side of the said
Mill-Green and Mill-paddock, being the ancient course of
Crimple, to the south-west corner of the same; and from
thence along the stream of Crimple, to a bridge, called Crimple
bridge, over which the road from Ribston to Wetherby leadeth;
and from thence along the stream of Crimple, which still
divides the lordship of North Deighton, on or towards the
south, from the said Ribston-Green, lying within the boundary
of the said forest, on or towards the north, to the south-west
corner of the said Ribston Green; thence along the stream
of Crimple, where it divides the said lordship of North Deigh-

ton, on or towards the south, from the enclosed lands, within
the township of Ribston aforesaid, on or towards the north,
to Stock-bridge, otherwise, Newsam-bridge, over which the
road from Spofforth to North Deighton leadeth; and from
thence, along the stream of Crimple, where it leads by the
east, south, and west sides of a certain parcel of enclosed
land, called Newsam, belonging to the said Sir John Ingilby,
and lying within the boundary of the said forest, to Point-
bridge, over which the turnpike road from Wetherby, through
Spofforth, to Knaresborough, leadeth; and from thence along
the stream of Crimple, to Oxen-bridge, near Spofforth mill;
and thence along the stream of Crimple to Guildhouse-bridge,
over which a road from Plumpton to Follifoot leads; and from
thence along the stream of Crimple to Follyfoot wath, óver
which the carriage road from Plumpton to Follyfoot leadeth;
when the open forest begins; and from thence proceeding up
the stream of Crimple to a bridge called Collin-bridge, formerly
a horse bridge, but lately made a carriage bridge; and from
thence along the stream of Crimple, the said open forest lying
on or towards the north, and the township of Follyfoot on
or towards the south, to a certain hill or island, whereon
a mill for smelting iron ore formerly stood, and now called
Mill Hill;* and from thence along the stream of Crimple, by
Fulwith mill to Almsford wath, where a bridge is now built,
over which the turnpike road from Leeds to Ripley leadeth;
and from thence still along the stream of Crimple, by Pannal-
mill, to the foot of a certain syke which runs into Crimple,

*Mill Hill consists of many hundred loads of scoria, slag, or refuse of
iron smelting works. It lies between the brook Crimple and the railway,
near the lower viaduct; it is now planted with larches. It is not mentioned in a perambulation made in 1577; hence we would infer that the
smelting works here were carried on after that period.

called Buttersyke;* and from thence turning southward and
following the said syke, where it divides the township of Rigton,
lying within the boundary of the said forest, on or towards
the west, from the lands of Walton Head,† on or towards the
east, to a small bridge or drain, through which the water in
the same syke runneth; and along the said syke to the north-
east corner of Buttersyke Intake, belonging to Daniel Lascelles,
Esquire; and from thence to the head of Buttersyke, where
the four stones mentioned in the ancient boundary formerly
stood;‡ and thence again cross the said turnpike road leading
from Leeds to Ripley, southwards to Dry-dyke, dividing the
lands of Swindon, belonging to — Bethel, Esq., on or towards
the west, from the open common of Walton Head, on or towards
the east; and from thence to a syke, sometimes called Double
Dike, coming from Walton Head; and so up the same syke
to a place in Walton Head Lane, being the church way from
Rigton to Kirkby Overblow; at which place two stones, mentioned in the ancient boundary, formerly stood;§ and from
thence directly through a close, called Wareholes, to a well
called Wareholes well, out of which Swindon syke springeth;
and so down Swindon syke to Bowhill yate, standing in the
high road which leads out of the West country to Wetherby,
which Swindon syke divides the lordship of Swindon on the

*At the junction of this watercourse with the Crimple, the three town-
ships of Pannal, Rigton, and Follifoot meet each other, and that of Kirkby
Overblow comes to within four hundred yards of the same point.

†Walton Head is that mass of high land on the right of the turnpike
road from Harewood bridge to Harrogate, near Buttersyke toll-bar; the
highest point is 400 feet above the sea level. Though there is only one
dwelling there at present, it is styled a manor in Domesday survey, and
belonged to William Percy.

‡"So upp Butter-sike to fower stones, standing in the head of Buttersike."—*Perambulation of* 1577.

§"And up the same sike to two stones standing in Walton Head layne."
—1577. This place is now marked by one stone, bearing the letters K. F.,
1767.

west, being within the boundary of the said forest, and the
lordship of Kirkby Overblow, on or towards the east; and
from the said Bowhill-yate, following the same syke to the
middle stream of the river Wharfe, dividing the lands on or
towards the west, in the township of Dun-Keswick, being within
the boundary of the said forest, from lands on or towards the
east, in the township of Keerby-cum-Netherby; and from
thence turning westward, and ascending up the middle stream
of Wharfe to Harwood Bridge, over which the said turnpike
road, from Leeds to Ripley, leadeth; the lands in the township
of the said Dun-Keswick adjoining upon the north side of the
said river; and from thence still ascending up the middle
stream of Wharfe, where the lands in the townships of Dun-
Keswick, Weeton, and Casly, likewise adjoin on the north side
of the said river, to the west side of Casly Ings; and so along
the lane, across which a small rill of water, called Dead-water,
runneth; and out of the said lane, into and over the westward
side of Dead-water close, and several other closes, which form
the west side of Casly township, and join upon a part of
Leathly lordship to Riffoe-wood, and so by the eastward side
of the said Riffoe-wood to Riffoe-yate; and from thence, into
and over a close in Stainburn lordship, called Buck-roods,* to
Riffoe-beck, which is the boundary between Stainburn and
Leathley moor; and from thence along the said beck, to a
breach in the ground called Crammock Hole;† and from thence
up the said beck, there called Thrispen-syke, otherwise called
Thrisfen-syke, which said syke divides Stainburn field and
Leathley moor, to the south-west corner of the same field,
(now enclosed and divided,) by which corner the turnpike road
from Bradford to Ripley leads, and near which, on Leathley
moor (now enclosed), is a boggy place called Thrispen, other-

* "Buckrodds," in 1577. This is now the name of a detached farm.
† "Cramock," in 1577.

wise Thrisfen Head,* out of which the syke, there called
Thrisfen syke, and afterwards Riffoe beck, springeth; and from
thence to Swankin well,† otherwise Swanrood Keld, which
springeth a little south from a great stone with three holes
in it; and from thence by the syke coming from the said
well (where was formerly a road, but changed at the enclosing
of the said Stainburn field), to Holbeck, and so down Holbeck
to the stream of Washburn,‡ and so up Washburn to Lipley-
wath,§ otherwise Lipersey-wath. The township of Lindley,
within the boundary of the said forest, being on or towards
the north, and the township of Farnley on or towards the
south; and from thence up Washburn to Dog Park Bridge;
and from thence to the foot of Rigeman Beck;‖ and so up
the same beck to the foot of Timble Gill beck, and so ascending
up a branch of the said beck, to the south end of Sewerbarge
lane, and following the said branch, there called a syke, to
the south-west corner of Sewerbarge field, which field is in
the township of Timble; and from thence turning southward
by an old syke (upon which syke part of a cottage standeth,
and some encroachments have been made by the owners of
a township called Askwith), to a parcel of rocks upon the open
common called Millstones: and so by the same syke to a place

* Now called " Trispin Head."

† " Swankell-well," in 1577. *Rood* is the old term for cross; *keld* is the
spring or well head.

‡ Holbeck falls into Washburn a short distance below Lindley mill.

§ " Lethley wath " in 1577; now " Lippers wath."

‖ This boundary includes the whole of Little Timble, which is not within
the Forest. The perambulation of 1770 gives this part of the boundary
much fuller and clearer than this, as below—" thence following Washburn
by Dobb Park Bridge (the lordship of Weston lying on or towards the
south), to the foot of Ridgeman beck; and so following Washburn to
Wroughten Wath, over which the road from Knaresboro' to Timble
leadeth; and still following Washburn by Fewston mill and Fewston
bridge, to a place where the old mill stood; where leaving Washburn, and
proceeding southward by Mill Syke House, and following the boundary
between Little and Great Timble to Timble Gill beck."

called Standing Stone, upon the Crossridge; and so up the
same ridge to Dannock-bower,* sometimes called Elleker-dike,
(the said forest being on or towards the north, and the open
commons of Askwith and Denton on or towards the south),
and so to Lipersley Pike;† and from thence to Gaukhall Ridge,
and so up Gaukhall Ridge to the rock called Gauk-Hall, where
the open commons of Denton and Middleton, on the south
divide; and where those parts of the forest called Timble moor
and Blubber-house moor, on or towards the north also divide;
and up Middlegill-head,‡ and by the upper end of Lostshaw
gill to Fewber Pike,§ being a pile of stones upon a high hill
above Beamsley; and from thence turning northwards to a scar
above Ingengill,|| *alias* Inkhorngill∗ house, on the west part of
the Queen's Fold, and so to Pacehouse beck; and so following
Pacehouse beck eastwards to the Black syke, and following the
Black syke to a hill called Carlhow; and so from thence
directly to another hill called Harden-Head; and so to th
south side of the Dry Tarn; and so to the rocks called Lord's
Seat; and so by the south side of a hollow place called Gowland
Maw, to Esp gill; and so by the same gill unto the lower end
of Middletongue, towards Appletreewick; and then up Armshaw
gill to Lyard Yate; and so following the said gill, now called
Lyard gill, to the head thereof; and from thence to the top
of a hill called Rear Clouts, and so over Munga gill to a place
where Craven Cross formerly stood,† which is over against the
end of Munga gill; and so from thence to Craven Keld, by the

---

* "Dunocksboure," in 1577.   † "Lepsley Pike."   ‡ "Mekellgill."

§ "Fawsber Pike." || "Farkehowgill."

∗ This should be Ickeringill house, the name of a detached farmstead,
near Kexbeck, just outside the boundary of the forest of Knaresborough;
the original home of the Franklands of Thirkleby, near Thirsk, and yet
belonging to that family.

† The words are the same in the perambulation of 1577; hence it is
evident that Craven Cross had been removed before that time.

highway which leadeth from Hebden to Pateley Bridge, now
a turnpike road, to the place where Craven Cross and the
turnpike house now stand; and from thence proceeding along
the said highway to Greenhow Hill,. and turning by the skirt
of the south side of the said hill, by a certain way which
leadeth towards Ripley; and so by the same way to the end
or head of Greenhow sike, between Cawdstones and Redlish;
and so descending down the same syke to Plumpton Gate;*
and so following the same gate to Pallas-Stone,† commonly
called the Abbot's Hand; and thence up to a certain old dike,
dividing that part of Hayshaw Moor called Braithwaite Side,
on or towards the north and north-west, from his majesty's
said forest, on or towards the south and south-east to the
head of the Monk wall, where the aforesaid syke entering the
enclosed lands of Padside, takes the name of Padside beck;‡
and from thence to Harrogate,§ following the said wall, which
stands on the north and north-west sides of the said beck, till
it falls into Darley beck; and still following the said wall,
standing on the north and north-west sides of the said Darley
beck, to the river Nidd, on the south side thereof; and so
directly across the said river, unto the said Monk wall on the
north side of the same; and so as the same Monk wall leadeth,
in some places by the edge of the said river, and in others
at some distance from the same, to Haxby bridge, otherwise

---

*The 1770 perambulation has the following addition here—" where
stands a large stone at which the manors of Dacre-with-Bewerley and the
Forest are said to divide."

† " Pallice stones."

‡The 1770 has this addition—"then down the fence to the close of
Edward Yates, in which are three bounder stones marked F on the south
for Forest, and I. for Ingilby on the north; and then through the house
of the said Edward Yates, and by four encroachments taken from Hayshaw moor to Harrow gap, where the Monk wall begins." Here is a slight
discrepancy between the two accounts as to where the Monk wall commences; the first is probably the correct one.

§A refinement for "Harry-gap," the name it now bears.

New Bridge; and from the said New Bridge, proceeding on the north side of the river, to the now apparent remains of the said Monk wall, to a dwelling-house, commonly called New-bridge house, belonging to Samuel Moorhouse, (part of which house is built upon his majesty's said forest, and the other part upon the lands in the township of Hartwith-with-Winsley,) and thence following the said Monk wall, by the north side of a certain parcel of land, near the said house, called Wreck-holm, to a corner of the said Monk wall, bearing on or towards the south-east, and following the said wall as it there turneth northward, to Burnt Yates, through which the turnpike road from Ripley by Brimham, to Pateley Bridge leadeth: and from thence, still following the said wall, to Cow Yate, standing near a corner of the said Monk wall, which beareth on or towards the north-east; and so to Bishop Thornton beck, which beck divideth Bishop Thornton liberty on the north from the township of Clint, part of his majesty's said forest, on or towards the south; and following the same beck to Askwin Wath, otherwise Scaro Wath, (being the boundary between the said forest, the lands of the Lord Archbishop of York, and the lordship of Ripley), and still descending down the said beck, to Godwin bridge, otherwise called Scaro bridge; where leaving the said beck, and turning westward up a little syke, called Black syke, which runneth on the north, or outside of a hedge or fence, where Ripley Park pale formerly stood; and so ascending up the same syke (in this part thereof now called Godwin syke), to a place where a certain tree called Godwin Oak* formerly stood; and so pursuing the said

* This oak appears to have been standing in 1577, as the words in that perambulation are—"and uppe a lytle syke called Black syke running upon the out syde of Ripley pke payle unto Gawdewane oke." Godwin's name in connection with this place appears now to be forgotten, but it is of very early occurrence, as we find that "William de Goldburgh, the king's servant, with the consent of Avice his wife, and William his heir,

syke up to the head thereof, being at the north-west corner
of a parcel of enclosed land, parcel of the said Ripley Park,
called Dob, otherwise Dob Croft; near which corner is a well,
out of which the said Godwin sike springeth; and from thence
turning southward, by the westward side of the said Dob,
or Dob Croft, to a stone cross called Monk Cross, otherwise
Monkhead Cross, standing in Whipley lane end; and still proceeding southward, down a lane called Dob lane, otherwise
Dog lane, otherwise Ash lane, otherwise Whipley lane, leading
by the west side of an enclosure called High Rails, formerly
parcel of the said park, to a place near Ripley Park gate,
near which a large stone, called Corps Cross, otherwise Cap
Cross, formerly stood; which gate is placed in the bridle way
leading from Ripley to Clint; and so down a syke which runs
by the west side of a wood, formerly called Robter, otherwise
Robert's wood, and now called Holly-bank wood, into the
water of Nidd; and so following the north side of the said
river, into certain enclosed lands, part thereof called Ladylaw
Croft, and another part thereof called Fat Pasture, being within
the lordship of Ripley, and heretofore the inheritance of Sir
William Ingilby, Knight, and now of Sir John Ingilby, Baronet;
where leaving the present course of the said river, and following
the apparent ancient course thereof, commonly called Old Nidd,
which leadeth by the east, north, and westward sides of a
certain parcel of land called Round Fleets, within the boundaries of the said forest, into the said river again, and so to
Killinghall bridge; and from thence descending down the said
river to Knaresborough Low bridge, to Grimbald bridge; and
from thence, still descending down the said river by Little

gave all his land in Godwin-scales, in Ripley, as is described by the
boundaries, to the abbot and convent of Fountains'.—*Burton's Mon. Ebor.*"
The 1770 has—"formerly a park fence, in which are the remains of an
old oak tree known by the name of Godwin oak, where stands the bounder
stone marked 43 K.F. 1767."

Ribston, to a place where Crimple runneth into Nidd, the place before mentioned, and where the said boundary was begun. All which we humbly certify and submit.

In witness whereof, we, the said acting Commissioners, have unto this our return, contained in five skins of parchment, at the foot of each of the first four of the said skins, set and subscribed our respective hands; and have also unto this fifth or last of the said skins, set our several and respective hands and seals; and have also unto the said schedule hereunto annexed, contained on four skins of parchment, to each of the said skins, and also to the said plan, set and subscribed our respective names, the twenty-second day of January, in the eighth year of the reign of his majesty, king George the Third, and in the year of our Lord one thousand seven hundred and sixty eight.

JOSEPH TULLIE,	WILLIAM MASTERMAN,
ROBERT ROPER,	WILLIAM MARSDEN,
WILLIAM H. ASHURST,	FRANCIS RUSSELL.

The following perambulation of what may be called the Copyhold Forest was made by the Enclosure Commissioners in 1770. We only give the boundaries where they are different from those already given.

"Beginning at the river Nidd, at the south-east corner of the said forest, commonly called Thistle Hill, and from thence proceeding along such open parts of the said forest, by St. Ives's, *alias* Iles's corner, as joins upon Plumpton and Rough Farlington, the estate of Daniel Lascelles, Esq., to the water of Crimple; where encompassing an encroachment, occupied by James Collins, Esq., or his assigns, the said boundary extends westward up Crimple aforesaid; the township of Folly-

foot lying on or towards the south side thereof to a certain
hill, commonly called Mill Hill, whereon a mill for smelting
iron ore is said to have stood; and from thence along Crimple
aforesaid to Foulwith mill, (the property of Oliver Coghill, Esq.)
and from thence along Crimple to Almsford Wath, where a
bridge was lately built, over which the turnpike road from
Leeds to Ripley leadeth, (the township of Follyfoot still on
or towards the south thereof); and from thence along Crimple
to Pannal church and Pannal mill, and by the foot of a certain
syke called Buttersyke, to Burnt bridge, over which the ancient
road from Leeds to Newcastle leadeth; and from thence along
Crimple to the lane called Shaw lane, through which is a road
leading from the forest on the north to Rigton on the south,
and from thence following Crimple to a bounder stone, marked
on the south-eastward side E.L. denoting Edward Lascelles,
and with T.F. denoting Thomas Fawkes, on the opposite side;
which stone shows the division of the township of Rigton on
the east, from that of Stainburn on the west; from thence
to Beckwithshaw bridge, over which the turnpike road from
Knaresboro' to Bradford leadeth; and from thence following
Crimple to the head thereof (the township of Stainburn being
on or towards the south); and from thence along a syke called
Mansty syke, to a stone at the head thereof marked F on
the south side; then in a direct line by three bounder stones
marked F on that part of the boundary called Casten dike,
and by the said dike which appears in different places, to
another bounder stone marked F; from thence by five bounder
stones also marked F to an earth-fast stone, lying north-east
of Little Almes Cliff, marked also with F; from thence by
other four bounder stones marked F to Sandwith Wath; from
thence following Sandwith syke by five bounder stones, marked
also with F to Sandwith Brigstone (where the townships of

Stainburn towards the east, and that of Lindley towards the
west, are divided); from thence up White Marsh, by four
bounder stones marked as before, to an earth-fast stone, called
Black stone, marked with F upon it; thence to a large stone
called Hunter stone, marked with a X and W but part of
the W defaced; from thence by another bounder marked F
to Akey Bank Well; thence proceeding southward by an earth-
fast stone with P upon it, to another earth-fast stone marked
with W.P. at Blaw Syke Head; and following the said syke
to Sunderland Beck Head; and so following the said beck
through a wood belonging to Francis Fawkes, Esq., to Lippers-
worth bridge, and from thence to the foot of the said beck,
where it formerly discharged itself into Washburn; then by
four stones marked F standing in the ancient course of Washburn, to the present course thereof." The old boundary of
the forest is then followed up Washburn and Great Timble
until the boundary of Timble moor and Blubberhouse moor
is reached. "Then turning northward to Gauk Hall Gill, and
so following the said gill eastward by Blay Scar to Stainforth
Gill; and from thence by Beck-meetings, the top of Blubberhouse enclosure, down Gill beck and Thackwray beck, to
Washburn; then turning westward up Washburn to Blubberhouse bridge; from thence following Washburn to the foot
of Redshaw beck; thence following Redshaw beck, Redshaw
gill and Ramsgill, by Willow bog to Black syke—(all of which
last mentioned places, from Gauk Hall Gill aforesaid, are said
to be the boundaries between Blubberhouses and the Forest)."
From this point the old boundary is followed to the starting
point on the Nidd at Thistle hill.

GEOLOGY.

The geological formation of the Forest of Knaresborough is, generally speaking, that of the millstone grit; at the same time it includes small portions of the carboniferous or mountain limestone, as well as the Permian or magnesian limestone. A person travelling from Craven Cross, its most north-westerly extremity, to the junction of the brook Crimple with the river Nidd, its most easterly point, will pass from the middle of the great mass of mountain limestone on Greenhow, across regions of shale and gritstone, alternating with thin beds of coal, ironstone, and a kind of impure or transition limestone, until at Bilton and Rudfarlington he would come upon the magnesian limestone, which would accompany him during the remainder of his journey, especially if he kept close to the right bank of the Nidd; if he kept near the Crimple he would probably miss the magnesian limestone altogether, and pass entirely along the millstone grit formation, which last named rock is prominently developed at Plumpton and near Brame hall.

The thickness of this mass of matter, without counting either of the limestones, is probably 800 or 1000 feet. The rocks are all sedimentary, or owe their origin to the deposition of matter under water. In order of deposition they range from west to east, the oldest rocks being those on the highest ground, the most recent coming on the last; so that they might be arranged in something like the following order—

Mountain limestone	Greenhow Hill.
Millstone grit (similar to Brimham)	Plumpton and Brame.
Coal	Thornthwaite, Birstwith, Bilton.
Gritstone (lower bed)	Fox Crag, Pozstones, Little Almes Cliff, Haverah Park, Birk Crag, Hookstones, Sandy Bank, Great Almes Cliff.
Impure limestone (containing fossils)	Thornthwaite, Saltergate-hill, Clint, The Bank, Beckwithshaw.—A deeper bed at Harrogate.
Ironstone	Rowden Lane, Darley Bank.
Grits, shale, and Plates	Harrogate, Bilton, Birstwith.—Common nearly all over the forest.
Magnesian limestone	Bilton, Rudfarlington, Grimbald Crag; along the river side to Little Ribstone.

The great mass of mountain limestone is of unknown depth. It has never yet been pierced through by any of the mining operations carried on within it. Its culminating point in our district is at Greenhow Hill, where it attains an elevation of 1400 feet above the sea level. It forms, when burnt, an excellent lime for agricultural purposes. It is rich in veins of lead ore; and mines have been worked in it from very early times.

Next to the mountain limestone, the gritstones are the most prominent series of our district. These are seen to best advantage in Great Almes Cliff, and at Plumpton, which apparently all belong to one formation. The Birk Crag, Knox, Hookstones, Haverah Park, Little Almes Cliff, and Fox Crag, quarries and cliffs, are parts of a lower bed. The fine edge of gritstone in Thornthwaite probably belongs to the same formation. These beds yield durable building stone, and some of them have been extensively quarried for that purpose.

The coal is generally found in a seam about a foot in thickness. It comes near the surface, or has been worked at West End, in Thornthwaite, (where it crops out on both sides of an anticlinal), in Birstwith, near Wreaks, where many partially successful attempts have been made to win it, but none of them finally proved profitable; at Bilton the rapid dip of the seam soon drowned out the miners. It is probably the same bed of coal which is reached at all these places, thrown down or up by the undulations of the rock beneath it. At Thornthwaite and Birstwith it rests upon a hard, compact bed of stone, of a gritty texture certainly, but the particles are so small as to be almost confluent. The rounded pebbles of the surface soil appear to be formed from the destruction of this rock.

The Ironstone occurs in nodules in thin beds in the shales. At Rowden lane, above Hampsthwaite, it has been cut through by a deep gully called Hell-hole; at some period it has been worked along the edge of the hill on the eastern side of Cockhill beck; and also in Darley bank, on the road to Otley. On widening the road there a few years ago the old galleries of the workmen were found in the side of the hill.

The first mention we have seen of iron mines in this forest is during the reign of Edward I. That the iron ore has been extensively smelted in this district is evident from the masses of scoria yet remaining. In the valley of the Crimple, at Mill Hill, is an immense mound of refuse, containing several hundred cart loads; and in the same valley, above Burn-bridge, heaps of refuse may be seen in two or three places. Cinder-hills, between Birstwith and Darley, has been the site of another bloomery; another heap of refuse was at Whitewall Nook, in Felliscliffe. This smelting of iron is said to have been the

cause of the destruction of the timber on the forest.*   Thoresby,
the Leeds antiquary, observed the refuse of the smelting works,
and thus mentions it in his diary,† in the year 1708—"This
forest was once so woody, that I have heard of an old writing,
said to be reserved in the chest at Knaresborough church,
which obliged them to cut down so much yearly, as to make
a convenient passage for the wool carriers from Newcastle to
Leeds, &c.   Now, it is so naked, that there is not so much
as one left for a way-mark, such a consumption did the blasts
make ; of which I have seen great heaps of slag or cinders,
overgrown with moss, &c., now often dug into for mending
the highways."

The impure, or transition limestone, appears in many places ;
whether it is one bed that comes to the surface in different
places, or different beds which intersect the forest in bands,
running across it in irregular lines, we will not undertake to
say.   It appears in Clint, Thornthwaite, Norwood, at Saltergate hill, and lower down near the brook called Cow-dike, and
at Beckwithshaw on the right of the road leading to Rigton, and also below Beckwith House, where in the quarry
belonging to the Harrogate Improvement Commissioners it is
seen in a most singular form,—the bed has been lifted up on
both sides from its original stratification, and doubled up upon
itself, so that the fragment remaining presents the appearance
of the letter U exhibiting in the most unmistakeable manner
the violent convulsions which have broken up the surface of

---

* Dr. Michael Stanhope, writing on the Harrogate waters, in 1632, says
—" The whole soil where the water rises is full of ironstone, and the
former ironworks here have occasioned the total consumption of wood
on the forest.   Within a mile of the Spaw are still to be seen the ruins
of a great ironwork ; and by digging a little you may still find plenty
of ironstone in most places, even exposed to the day in broken banks on
the earth's surface."

† Vol. I., p. 424.

this district. The most remarkable appearance of it is at Harrogate, but that is evidently part of a deeper, thicker, and more compact bed than the other. The breakage of the strata here, and upheaval of the lower rock is one of the most singular phenomena we have to record in the physical history of our district, as it has given egress to the saline and sulphur springs of Harrogate, which have done so much for the health and consequently for the happiness of mankind. Judging from appearances, the upheaval of this rock has been caused by the eruption of a body of steam or gas from a great depth below the surface, which has found vent where the Harrogate Bogs now are; forcing its way violently upwards through thick beds of rock, leaving them partly standing on edge, and partly splintered into fragments round the point of dislocation, bringing to the surface rocks whose proper place is deep below it, and cleaving a way for the fountains of sulphur and saline water to rise to daylight. This bed of rock is about 40 feet in thickness, regularly stratified, with three thin bands of black matter, like impure coal, at irregular intervals in its substance. It crops out in a singular manner, forming two sides of a triangle, the apex of which is on the spot where the Royal Pump Room covers the old sulphur wells; one of the sides is formed by the quarry behind Coldbath road, the other ascends the hill to behind Cornwall house. The rock on the base or western side of the triangle, near the Bath hospital, does not appear to have been forced upwards in the same violent manner, as the dislocation is nowhere visible.

Within the orifice formed by this breakage and upheaval, are the Bogs, a triangular piece of marshy ground, on a part of which, about an acre in extent, are sixteen springs of mineral water, walled round and protected by doors on the top. Near as they are to each other, these springs are all different in their mineral impregnation. The real cause of their difference is the beds of shale in which they come to the surface, here standing in an almost perpendicular position, and each spring rises independently of the others, charged with its own proper load of saline matter, or gaseous impregnation.

Being hard and well adapted for the making of roads, this stone has been extensively quarried, so much so as to be almost exhausted, the rapid dip of the beds rendering the cost of removing the superincumbent matter too great to be profitable. Lead ore is occasionally found in this rock, not in regular veins, but in lumps, composed of about an equal bulk of crystals of ore and sandy fragments of the rock. On the 23rd of June, 1866, whilst engaged quarrying the stone, the workmen came upon an old level or drift way, from four to five feet in height, and about three feet six inches wide, roughly hewn through the rock, leading from the level of the Bogs, and entering this bed of stone immediately in the rear of Binns' Hotel. This opening was explored for some short distance, and several pieces of candle were found, which had evidently been left by the miners when the drift way was formed. This had doubtless been the work of some bold adventurer, searching for lead ore, in a place where he would obtain little beyond his labour for his pains.

A mineral peculiarity, to which, we believe, the decomposition of this stone contributes, is small pieces of lucent stone, hard enough to scratch glass, and locally known as *Harrogate diamonds*. The field in which they are most commonly found has been under cultivation, and when recently ploughed, or after a shower of rain, the diamonds were found twinkling like little stars among the soil.

Dr. Short,* speaking of the petrifactions generated by mineral

* *History of Mineral Waters*, p. 104.

waters, says—"There is yet a fifth kind of petrifactions, which as it is the beautifullest of all, so we are intire strangers to their manner of generation, and that is, these transparent brilliant, solid, hard, hexagonal gems, found like small marcasites, in the middle of limestone in Cornwall, and Broughton near Settle, in Yorkshire, and sometimes near Castleton, in Derbyshire, which are called diamonds—every whit as fine as Bristol stone, and will cut glass. They are found on the earth's surface after a sharp shower of rain near Buxton and Harrogate. . . . Those found in the plowed field near Harrogate are not of one certain figure, neither at the ends nor middle, being sometimes triagonal, tetragonal, pentagonal, and hexagonal, in the last, and each almost differing from another in the first."

Wherever this rock comes to the surface, the soil is of superior fertility to that which immediately adjoins it, the latter having been formed from the decomposition of the shale or millstone grit rocks.

Shale and gritstone, of various degrees of fineness, are the upper rocks until we come within a short distance of Bilton, when we meet with a patch of the magnesian limestone. A detached portion of this rock has been worked for lime and exhausted. It was harder, darker in colour, and more compact in structure than the generality of rocks of this class. On the east of Bilton is a quarry, yet open, though it has not been worked for the last twenty years. This stone (upwards of twenty feet in thickness) shows the magnesian characteristics, being yellow in colour, porous in the mass, almost non-stratified, and full of crystallized cavities.

This patch of rock appears to be almost isolated—at any rate its connection with the main bulk is covered by a thick mass of diluvial matter. It appears again in the wood west

of Bilton hall, and then again to the eastward, above Knaresborough High bridge; thence it ranges all along the right
bank of the Nidd to Little Ribstone, where it sinks beneath
masses of diluvial matter; an outlying portion spreads out as
far as Rougharlington.

Over all this region (except the limestones) in the regular
order of geological formation, the coal measures ought to be
found, as they are at some distance both on the north and
south—but they are not. Instead of the coal-bearing strata,
we have nothing but the millstone grit and its attendant shales.
Why is it so? Have the coal-bearing beds of rock never
existed? Or, have they been upheaved after their deposition
above the surrounding district, and swept away by the action
of water? The whole country round about bears marks of
violent disruption and breakage; the dislocation of the strata
near the Harrogate Bogs has been already mentioned; the
grand fracture forming the valley of the Nidd is owing to a
similar cause; besides these, a grand anticlinal axis extends
from the Nidd, near Bilton hall westward, crosses the railway
a short distance north of Starbeck, passes to the south of
Harrogate, thence by way of Harlow Car, Little Almes Cliff,
and Fox Crag, to the Washburn. The central ridge being
elevated like the roof of a house, the strata dipping north and
south on each side of it; the thick bed of gritstone has been
broken, and the edges thrown at least two miles apart, where
they are left standing half on edge. This broken and rugged
surface has been scoured or planed down by immense floods
of water—at first in rapid motion, and afterwards a mass
of clayey shale has been deposited in still water. After this
period of repose, violent currents have rushed across the latter
deposits, cutting through them in many places, and leaving
their traces in gulleys and shallow valleys. Did this elevation

of land take place before the formation of the coal measures?
Or was this district a mountain ridge, or region of high land,
and were the coal measures deposited in basins on each side
of it? If the latter was the case, we need not expect to find
any fragments of them on the central or highest part, but
they ought to approach regularly on each side. If they were
deposited all over our district on an equal plane, and subsequently elevated into a lofty ridge, exposed to the rushing
waves of a tempestuous sea, and finally washed away by its
waters,—then we might hope to find some traces of their
existence on our highest hills, or at the points where, under
ordinary circumstances, the coal measures dip beneath the magnesian limestone formation. This is not the case; as the
coarse millstone grit is the stone which underlies the limestone,
as may be easily seen in the Castle cliff at Knaresborough,
and further down the course of the Nidd as far as Golds-
borough mill, where the limestone is cut through by the river
and the coarse gritstone appears. In Follifoot, where the
railway cuts deep into the hill, after passing the Crimple
viaduct, is a rock of gritstone, of firm compact structure, rich
in fossil sigillaria, which has much the appearance of a rock
belonging to the coal measures. Careful research, and attention
to facts can alone determine this question ; a dogmatic decision
either way at present would be worse than useless.

ROADS.

NOTHING can better represent the state of the trade and commerce of a country than its roads; where these are wanting, or of an inferior quality, those can not be of great extent or importance. The roads intersecting our district divide themselves in the order of time into British trackways, Roman roads, Pack-horse roads, Turnpike roads, and Railroads.

Remains of British trackways can only be expected to be found where the country is in its natural uncultivated state, and consequently the progress of agriculture has nearly obliterated them; yet, slight traces may be seen near "the Bank," in Norwood, and at Fox Crag, on the confines of Norwood and Stainburn; and also in a few other places which the plough has spared. The probability is that the main lines of trackway were afterwards occupied by the military roads of the Romans.

Of Roman roads, two at least crossed the forest, one from north to south, the other from north-east to south-west. The first of these passed from Catterick to Adel, two well-known Roman stations, and ran along the western side of the great vale of York, just where the mountain ridges decline to the plain. This road is not mentioned in any of the Itineraries; yet, we have not the least doubt of its existence, as there is sufficient evidence remaining in old entrenchments, and the

names of places, to convince the most sceptical; it is sufficient
for our purpose to trace it in our own district, which it entered
near Ripley, then passed across Killinghall moor, where, near the
Warren house, is a camp of the undoubted Roman type; thence,
passing southward, we have the significant names of Harlow
(the soldier's hill), and Harrogate (the military way). Near
Pannal High Ash is Castle hill, equally significant of a *castra*
or camp; where tradition says Pendragon encamped with his
army. Further south, at Horn bank, on a point of land
which overlooks the valleys of the Wharfe and the Crimple,
are the remains of three camps—two of a square, and one
of a circular form. At Castley, close to the river Wharfe,
was a castra, camp, or fort, to protect the pass across the
river; a short distance beyond was Burgadunum, now Adel.

The other road from the eastward ran between Isurium
(Aldborough) and Olicana (Ilkley), passing by way of Ripley;
in the wood to the west of which the strata can yet be
distinctly seen, about ten feet in breadth, formed of native
boulders. It next entered the township of Clint, across a
corner of which it passed, fording the river Nidd near Hampsthwaite church; thence up that village, not far from the track
of the present road. At Swincliffe Top it entered the township
of Felliscliffe, which it traversed from east to west; and, with
trifling exceptions, along none of the present carriage roads;
passing through the fields to the southward of the present line of
road, keeping along high ground, and nearly in a straight line
to Whitewall Nook, to which place it can yet be used as a
"bridle road." Formerly it was enclosed on both sides, forming
a narrow lane, yet known by the name of "the Long lane;"
but the fences have been removed—sometimes from one side,
sometimes the other, rarely on both, and it now forms part
of the adjoining fields. At Whitewall Nook a small portion

yet remains fenced on both sides; it is only about nine feet wide, and therefore would not be well adapted for wheel carriages. A few yards west of this point, about the year 1812, a weaver undertook to enclose and cultivate a small plot of ground in front of his cottage. On digging into it, about six inches below the surface, he came upon a compact pavement of stones, set in a kind of brown or rusty-coloured cement, as if it had formed the floor of some building for the accommodation of wayfarers along the road in the old Roman day. The stratum of the road itself was taken up here about the year 1848; it was composed of native boulders, forming a kind of coarse pavement. From this point westward, the line of road is perpetuated by a footpath only, generally distinguishable by a slight ridge in the fields across which it passes. The stratum may also be occasionally detected in the fences; and this state of things continues as far as the Kettlesing tollbar, when it falls into the Knaresborough and Skipton turnpike road, along which its course is parallel, past Dangerous Corner and Spinksburn, to where the modern road bends to the right, a few hundred yards east of the Hopper Lane Hotel. The ancient road then descended the hill on the left, passed Crag Hall, forded the Washburn, and thence ascended the hill on the opposite side, where it is distinctly visible, and so across the moors to Ilkley.

These roads have generally been formed of a pavement of rounded pebbles, gathered from the land in the immediate neighbourhood, the sides being formed of larger stones. Where entire they are generally five or six inches below the surface.

The Pack-horse roads are next in the order of time; but between the Roman roads and them a long period of time elapsed—ages of anarchy, war, and bloodshed rolled away; some of the ancient roads were swallowed up by swamp and

D

morass; others were overgrown by heath and brushwood, and
their very courses forgotten. These roads are narrower than
the Roman ones, seldom exceeding four feet in breadth, sometimes formed of pebbles, sometimes formed of large flagstones,
sometimes merely tracks along the natural ground. Of this
kind of roads many traces can yet be found in the Forest
of Knaresborough; the principal ones were those leading from
the north to Leeds, and from Knaresborough to Skipton. The
first of these entered our district at Harewood bridge, passed
along the present line of turnpike to Buttersike, thence across
the Crimple brook at Burn-bridge, and ascended the slope to
Pannal High Ash (the old trackway is yet visible), thence it
passed along the eastern skirt of Harlow Hill to Irongate Bridge,
by which it crossed Oakbeck, thence across Killinghall Moor,
through the village of the same name, thence crossed the river
Nidd by a bridge, which Leland says was " one greate arche of
stone."

A road of much importance entered the forest from the northern side, and then passed through it to Bolton bridge. This
road was surveyed by Ogilby some time previous to 1674. We
give his survey from Knaresborough to Bolton bridge, published
in the above year, with corrections from the editions of 1711
and 1786.

M. F. from York.		M. F.
17 6	Knaresburgh *vulgo* Knasburgh.	
	Nyd flo: near left, for 8 miles.	
	Beeton Hall on left, (Bilton Hall).	
	By Skooten. (Scotton)...................................	1 7
	Also Nyd Ch: and Hall, 4 f. right. (a church)...............	1 6
	Some lime pits on both sides.............................	0 5
	Killinghall br: and brook, left.	
22 6	Ripley (a church)..	0 6
	Dark Hall* at the end, right.	

* Dark Hall does not exist at present, but has been removed within
living memory. Something like a moat yet remains in the wood, about
a quarter of a mile west of Ripley Castle.

By Clynet (Clint) a village, 2 f. right. (a church).[*]

25	0	Hamsworth br: on Nyd flo:	0 3
		Hempsthwaite or Hamsworth, a long village (a church).	0 2
26	0	By Grafes—Plain moor,[+] left.	
		And several houses on both sides.	
		Over Keskin moor.[‡]	3 3
		East End Houses village and Straling village,[§] left.	
29	0	& two large posts :[‖] near right	0 5
		Cross a rivulet (a)	0 7
		Descent and ascent.	
31	0	By Foyston, 2 f. left, and Swinsty Hall, 3 f. left. } (a church)	1 3
		Cross Washburn flo:	0 6
32	2	By Blew-borrow-houses, near left.	
34	0	Way still, over Keskin moor (b).	
		By a pool near left	3 2
		A rivulet and cottage, right..........................	0 2
		Somer-scales	0 7
		Cross a brook	0 4
		Hessal (c)	0 3
		By Derriston,(d) 2 f. left	0 1
		Sturry,(e) 3 f. right	0 2
		and some Almes-houses,(f) near right	0 2
39	0	Boulton	0 5
		Pass Wharf flo:	

The road from Knaresborough to Otley ran to the south-ward of the present line of road, by way of Rigton *(g)* and

[*] There is no church or chapel at Clint, nor any evidence to show that one ever existed. Clint Hall, the residence of the Beckwith family, probably contained a chapel, as hardly any of the old manor houses were without.

[+] Now Greystone-plain.

[‡] Kettlesing moor.

[§] East End Houses yet exist in the township of Norwood, but Straling appears to be forgotten. It seems to have been somewhere near the ruined hostelry called Penny-pot house.

[‖] These posts appear to have given name to Long Stoup farm.

(a) Whidrah beck. (b) Now Kexgill, an unenclosed moor. (c) Hazelwood.

(d) Deerstones. (e) Storriths. (f) Founded by Margaret, countess of Cumberland, in 1592.

(g) The following extract from an old civil war tract of 1645 has reference to this road.—" The Earl of Newcastle's army do now range all over the south-west parts of this country, pillaging and cruelly using the well-affected party; and the last week there is a garrison of horse and foot layd at Knaresbro, where they began to fortify the town, and pillage and utterly ruin all the religious people in those parts and round about them. On Friday seven-night last, three troops and some other forces, of which

Stainburn. Westward of the latter place, a deep, old, narrow road yet exists, winding between high hedges down the slope to Stainburn beck, which it now crosses by a bridge, and then in a similar deep-worn track ascends the hill towards Lindley. It would be along this road that the beaten royalist garrison of York marched on their way to Otley and Skipton in July, 1644. " Upon Knasborough Forest we made a handsome show with those Troops of our guard, for we march'd with their Colours, but not with above 6 or 7 score men . . but they soon left their colours, and would take ye nearest way to go to ye prince. Our guards we discharg'd at Otley and so march'd on to Skipton."*

On a gate-post in the top of a field a little below the northwest corner of Rudding park is yet legible—"Roade to Spofforth 2 miles,"—"Roade to Leeds, 9 miles,"—"Road to Harrogat, 1 mile,"—"Roade to Knaresbrough, 2 miles." This stone was evidently a guide-post before the enclosure of the forest.†

Another road passed over Knaresborough High bridge, by way of Bilton, which must be the road mentioned in the Stuteville charter, about the year 1200, as "magnum viam

many were French, came from that garrison and pillaged Otley, and there barbarously used some honest women of that town ; and in their retreat to Knaresbro', upon the open forest (Rigton), they took a man and a woman—the man they wounded and beat cruelly, and before his eyes ravished the woman."

* Diary of Sir Henry Slingsby, p. 123.

† Many other singular stone guide-posts are yet to be seen in different parts of the forest. They are generally defaced, but where readable they give miles of great length. One of these yet stands unmutilated, just within the northern boundary of Haverah park, about 2½ miles west of Harrogate. It is a dressed stone, about 10 inches square, and about 6 feet in height above the surface. On the north side is cut the figure of a hand pointing easterly, on the palm of which is inscribed M:IIIr. Knaresbrovgh : —implying that the distance to Knaresborough is 3½ miles, whereas it is at least 6 of our present miles. Below is another hand, pointing westward, similarly inscribed, M:XIr. Skipton. Below is I:W. W:B. Svrvaors. On the west side, fairly cut, is—" Here endith the Constabilre of Killinghall: T:B. Conl 1738."

usque ad Biltonam." The same road is also mentioned in
the foundation charter of the house of St. Robert of Knaresborough, granted by Richard, earl of Cornwall, in 1256, as
"the road which turns from Knaresborough towards Hey-
wray." It was the stratum of this road which "Blind Jack of
Knaresborough" plundered in 1754, when he made the present
turnpike road between Harrogate and Knaresborough. From
the High bridge this road ascended the hill, on the track
of the present one; then it deviated to the right towards
Bilton Hall, from which an ancient paved road is yet visible,
and can be traced as far as Bilton village, when it turned
into the fields to the right, by way of Harrogate Hall and
Bachelor Gardens school, crossed Oakbeck at Knox bridge,
the narrow arch of which yet remains; after which it fell into
the main road from Ripon to Leeds, though there cannot be
any doubt but a continuation of it led by way of Lund lane
to Hampsthwaite.

The northern side of the forest was intersected by another
road, which as the popular voice phrases it, went "up Swincliffe, down Swarcliffe, an' ower th' New brig into Hartwith."
It was towards the repair of this road, on the northern side
of the Nidd, that Francis Ellis and his "concubine" Elizabeth
Thruscrosse, in 1594, were enjoined, after penances done in
the churches of Kirkby Malzeard and Masham, "to repair the
king's highway, called Newbrig lane, in Winsley, and to bestow
20s. thereon."

A road led from Summer-bridge, on the Nidd, in a southerly
direction, by way of Dacre and Darley, to Fewston, where it
bent towards the left into Norwood, by Scough hall, Jack hill,
and Dog Park mill, where it crossed the Washburn,* thence
by way of Clifton to Otley.

* This bridge is maintained at the cost of the parish of Fewston. It
existed in 1560. In 1658 the parishes of Weston and Fewston were pre-

From the same Summer-bridge a road led across Dacre
pasture to Thornthwaite; thence to West End, in Thruscross,
where it crossed the Washburn at Mill bridge,* and then over
the moor to Bolton bridge.

The said "Somerbrige" was a bridge when the monastery
of Fountains was in the zenith of its greatness. It is highly
probable that it was built at the cost of that house. In 1586
it needed repair, when "Robert Beckwith, of Dacre, in Nyder-
dall," being of "hoole mind and good memorie," made his
will, and gave two shillings towards the mending of the same.

Of the bridges which carried these narrow roads across the

sented at the Quarter Sessions, held at Wetherby by the grand jury, for
the non-repair of Dog Park bridge. They are ordered to repair the same
before Pontefract Sessions, upon pain of £20. At Skipton, July 12th,
1659, there was an indictment against the inhabitants of Weston and
Fewston for not repairing Dog Park bridge, and upon the *travish* jury
Fewston was found guilty to the indictment. It was therefore ordered
that Fewston repair the same between and Michaelmas, upon pain of £20.
It was accordingly repaired by the township of Clifton-with-Norwood,
when several parties in the other townships refused to pay their proportion, until compelled to do so by an Order of Session, held at Knaresborough, Oct. 5th, 1665. In 1758 this bridge was ruinous and irreparable,
when it was rebuilt by the parish at a cost of £50, towards which the
Justices in Quarter Sessions, at Pontefract, on April 11th, in the same
year, granted £16 13s. 4d., as a gratuity. In 1822 the sides of the bridge
were thrown off, and it was again repaired at a cost of £20.

   * This bridge is kept in repair by the inhabitants of the township of
Thruscross, and has been a frequent source of litigation. On July 8th,
1658, the Constable of Thruscross was ordered to levy 46s. 8d. upon the
inhabitants, equally, for repairing this bridge. In January, 1659, an order
of the Justices in Quarter Sessions was given to repair the same bridge
before the Easter Sessions, upon pain of £10. In July, 1680, the inhabitants of Thruscross were again indicted for non-repair of this bridge. In
1682, the inhabitants presented a petition to the Justices in Quarter
Sessions at Knaresborough, stating that the Mill bridge was in ruin and
they were not able to repair it. On July 26th, 1684, a fine of 80s. was
ordered to be levied upon the inhabitants for not repairing this bridge.
In the same year, Thomas Gill and George Taylor undertook to repair
the said bridge; and it was referred to Henry, Lord Fairfax, and Sir
Jonathan Jennings, to order and direct who ought to be at the charge of
the said repairs, and in what manner. At the Skipton Sessions, July 13th,
1686, Twelve pounds were ordered to be estreated upon the inhabitants
of Thruscross, for repairing of Mill bridge; 40s. thereof Thomas Gill and
George Taylor are to have for their charges and pains about the said bridge.

brooks only three remain: one, called Irongate bridge, over Oakbeck, near Harrogate, a high, narrow arch, without battlements; now entirely disused—not even a footpath passing over it. Another across the same stream, lower down, at Knox, which has been modernised by the addition of battlements, and is yet used as a foot and horse bridge; the last is the New bridge, in Birstwith, across the Nidd, which has been rebuilt, but of its original size. All the others have either been rebuilt or widened.

During this period the trade of the country was carried on by means of pack-horses, and nearly all travelling was performed on horseback.

The Turnpike roads intersecting our district are from east to west, and north and south. The first of these starting from Knaresborough runs to Harrogate, where it divides into two branches. One, diverging slightly to the right, proceeds through the heart of the forest, by way of Saltergate hill, Kettlesing Head, Blubber houses, Kexgill moor, Hazelwood-with-Storriths, and Beamsley, to Bolton bridge, where it crosses the Wharfe and proceeds to Skipton. The greatest part of this road was laid out and made on the enclosure of the forest, in 1776; and though it is, comparatively speaking, a level and useful road, it passes through the most barren and uninteresting part of the forest, and is also distant from the seats of population. The other branch proceeds westward, until it reaches Beckwithshaw, when it bends towards the left over Burscough Rig, Stainburn moor, and Lindley, to Otley. Great part of this road also passes through a high and sterile country, avoiding the villages, which the old crooked roads appeared to take a pleasure in visiting. Easier access to Otley has since been given, by the formation of a new line of road from Buttersike toll-bar to Pool.

The most important and busy line of turnpike road passed
from south to north, entering our district at Harewood bridge,
passing by way of Spacey houses and Harrogate, to Killinghall
bridge, thence to Ripley. Along this road rumbled the stage
waggons and rattled the stage coaches,* producing a state of
things such as made Byron exclaim—

> "What a delightful thing's a turnpike road !
> So smooth, so level, such a mode of shaving
> The earth, as scarce the eagle in the broad
>   Air can accomplish, with his wide wings waving.
> Had such been cut in Phæton's time, the god
>   Had told his son to satisfy his craving
> With the York mail."

In the summer of 1848, the Royal Mail and fourteen other
coaches, either passed through, or to and from Harrogate daily;
but the steam revolution was at hand, which was destined to
drive them from the roads, and supply their places with
ponderous giants of iron and brass, and whose food is fire
and water.

The next great step in locomotion was from Turnpike roads
to Railroads; level lines were indispensible, and we at once

---

* Hargrove, in his History of Knaresborough, 2nd Ed., 1775, says—
"The fly from Carlisle to London goes and returns through Harrogate
twice a week, takes in passengers at the White Hart, in Low Harrogate.
A waggon from London to Newcastle goes through Knaresborough on
Tuesdays, and a waggon from Newcastle to London goes through Knares-
borough on Thursdays; takes in goods at the Blue Bell, in High street.

A waggon comes from Leeds to Harrogate and Knaresborough, and
returns the same day.

The Fish Machines from Stockton to Leeds, pass through Knaresbro'
and Harrogate every Wednesday, and return on Fridays."

In 1822, writes Edward Baines, in his Directory of the county of York
of that date—"Besides a great number of post carriages, three stage
coaches pass through the place daily; the Telegraph, between Leeds and
Newcastle; the Union and the Tally-ho, between Leeds and Ripon. A
coach also comes from York on Monday, Wednesday, and Friday, and
returns the same days."

At the present time (1868) upwards of seventy trains arrive at and
depart from the Harrogate station daily.

behold a series of tunnels and deep cuttings diving through the hills, and lofty viaducts bestriding the valleys with their multitudinous arches. The first iron railway which invaded our district was the Harrogate and Church Fenton, a branch of the North Midland Company, which was completed and opened in 1848. After passing through a short tunnel under Follifoot Rigg, it enters the Forest of Knaresborough by a stupendous viaduct of thirty arches, each of fifty-two feet span; the centre being one hundred and thirty feet above the waters of the brook Crimple. The piers are of rustic stone, in large blocks; the arches are turned in brickwork, faced with hewn stone. The length of this magnificent piece of work is 1,850 feet. Although apparently slender, when viewed at a distance, it is really a massive and substantial work. This railway terminated in a station near the Bruns- wick hotel (now the Prince of Wales), Harrogate, and gave access to London and the south of England.

The Leeds and Thirsk railway was the next line finished; indeed it was in progress during the formation of the last mentioned. It enters our district at Castley; crossing the valley of the Wharfe by a lofty embankment and viaduct, the latter consisting of twenty-one arches, each sixty feet in span and ninety feet high in the middle, containing upwards of 50,000 tons of stone. A short tunnel and deep cutting carries the line through Wescoe hill, a mass of clay and shale; thence it curves onward by way of Pannal, passes through one of the arches of the Crimple viaduct, and then crosses the brook Crimple by a viaduct of ten arches, each of fifty feet span and fifty feet high; thence to Starbeck, about midway between Knaresborough and Harrogate; thence, by way of Bilton, to the river Nidd, which it crosses by a viaduct of seven arches, each of 50 feet span and 104 feet in height; thence proceeds to Ripon and Thirsk. It was finished and opened in 1849. The stations in our district are Weeton, Pannal, and Starbeck.

In connection with the last named line was formed the East and West Yorkshire Junction railway, which extended between Starbeck and York. It was begun in 1847, and is carried under part of the town of Knaresborough by a tunnel, and then over the river Nidd by a viaduct of four arches, three hundred feet in length, and ninety feet in height. The foundation stone was laid in April, 1847, and the work was rapidly approaching completion, when, on the 11th of March, 1848, about noon, the whole mass of stonework and scaffolding fell down with a tremendous crash into the river below. This accident was caused by some deficiency in the construction of the piers. The damage was estimated at £10,000. It was afterwards built in a more substantial manner, and is now one of the most interesting objects in the town of Knaresborough. On whatever side the railways enter the Forest of Knaresborough they have to do it by means of lofty viaducts.

The above mentioned railways, though projected and made by distinct companies, became amalgamated, along with many others into a great system or union, called the North Eastern Railway Company. This Company having obtained the requisite powers, formed a branch railway to Pateley Bridge up the valley of the Nidd. This is but a single line, 11¼ miles in length from its junction with the main line near the Nidd viaduct to Pateley Bridge. The cost was about £8000 a mile. It was finished and opened May 1st, 1862. The stations upon the Forest are Hampsthwaite, Birstwith, and Darley.

The next piece of railway made in our district was for the accommodation of Harrogate. The nearest station from which the inhabitants and visitors of that town could obtain access to the populous districts of Yorkshire and Lancashire was at Starbeck, two miles from the centre of the town. To remedy this inconvenience the Company obtained powers for connecting the Leeds and Thirsk line with the Church Fenton, near the southern end of the Crimple viaduct, thence crossing the Stray, and passing through the centre of the town, forming a junction with the old line near Bilton Gate, and with the York line at Starbeck; thus making Harrogate a central station, and the terminus of the Church Fenton, York and Harrogate, and Nidd Valley Railways. The works in connection with this extension were opened August 2nd, 1862.*

* This line is only about 4½ miles in length, yet it cost upwards of £100,000. The cost of the land was a considerable item in this amount; 5a. 1r. 7p., out of one estate, cost £4,850. Being generally on elevated ground, a great part of the line is a cutting. Over and under it there are fifteen bridges. W. Mc.Cormack, Esq., M.P., was the contractor.

KNARESBOROUGH FOREST.

"It was a salvage wood of ancient growth,
With dreary paths, and caves, and thick-set trees,
And darkened miles of land from north to south.
                              —*Spenser.*

What a train of associations is awakened by the word Forest!
We pass at once in thought to the remote days when our British
ancestors dwelt in the wild oak woods, and their priests cut the
mistletoe with their golden knives, and taught the doctrine of the
immortality of the soul beneath the solemn shades. We also
picture to ourselves groves of lofty oaks where the axe of the
woodman has never been heard, and groups of wild deer sweeping down the glades, or cropping the herbage at their ease.
Then again we see them peopled by the stalwart forms of outlaws, desperate men, at war with all the world, but yet we do
not fear them—they are the followers of some Robin Hood, terrible only to the proud and tyrannical, kind and courteous to
the poor and humble. Such associations are pleasing to the
mental vision, and the forests of our native land are full of
them.

"Dreams that the soul of youth engage,
  Ere fancy has been quelled;
Old legends of the monkish page,
Traditions of the saint and sage,
Tales that have the rime of age,
  And chronicles of eld."

There can be little doubt but that at an early period the whole of our island, from sea to sea, was covered with forests and marshes, and that up to the time of the first Roman invasion. Julius Cæsar found by experience what British trees and forests were, and he has described them with forcible truth. A town, he says, among the Britons, is nothing more than a thick wood, fortified with a ditch and rampart, to serve as a place of retreat against the incursions of their enemies.

The forests were not only useful as affording means of subsistence and a secure retreat from an enemy to our British ancestors, they were also devoted to religious purposes—"The groves were God's first temples," and within their gloomy recesses the Druids practised the rites of their mysterious faith. During this early period it is probable that what is now called the forest of Knaresborough was one wide hunting ground. Yet traces remain of British occupation: at Almes-Cliffe we can point to the monogram of the Celtic Jupiter engraved upon a rock in the shape of a large oak tree, near which are three large rocks fluted with rays from their apex downward, symbolical of Baal or the sun, a deity worshipped by the Druids: two of these rocks yet stand upright, and one has been thrown down. Close to these, and in front of the first named rock, is a gigantic Tolmen —so that this place may be regarded as a Druidical temple nearly complete. Druidical rocks and idols also exist at Little Almes-Cliffe, Plumpton, and in other places. "Pippin Castle,"

in Haverah Park, are large tumuli belonging to the same age.
At "The Bank" in Norwood, and also at Fox Crag, in the same
township, are the remains of pit-dwellings. Circles and earthern
mounds belonging to the same people can also be pointed
out; but on the whole, this district is not nearly so rich in
British antiquities as the Yorkshire Wolds and Eastern Moorlands.

The power of the British Brigantes passed away before the
stern pressure of the Roman arms; and these last were not
"mighty hunters;" they appear to have used the forests only
for purposes of utility; they certainly contributed largely to
their destruction, both by the axe and fire, as is evident from
the marks of both yet remaining on trunks and roots of trees
buried beneath masses of peat; indeed, their destruction of
forest trees appears to have been a great cause of the formation of peat, by interrupting the flow of the waters by the
trunks and branches of fallen trees: thus destroying the strong-
holds of their British enemies, and rendering their conquest
of the country more certain. But no forest boundaries were
marked by them; no enclosures were made; and the woodland parts of the country remained free for all, as they
were under the Britons.

Of Roman occupation our district yields proof in roads
crossing it from north and south, and east and west, and in
traces of at least two camps—one on Horn Bank, the other
on Killinghall Moor.

When the Saxons came the previous state of things was
entirely altered. That hardy race were hunters from their
childhood; they loved to chase the wild boar and the deer
through primeval forests; and they boasted of their exploits

in hunting with as much pride as of their daring deeds
in war. The same spirit animated their near relations, the
Danes.

The first body of forest laws were those made by Canute,
one of the Danish kings of England, about the year 1016.
These laws were cruel in the extreme. In each forest there
were usually *verderers* appointed to its charge; and so sacred
were their persons held, that if any man offered force to one
of them, he was, if a freeman, to lose his freedom and all
his property, and if a *villein*, his right hand was to be struck
off, and for the second offence the penalty was loss of life.
It was death also to kill a deer in the royal forest; sometimes
the offender had his eyes put out: and even if any one,
through sport or malice, should chase a deer until it *panted*,
the lowest penalty was a fine of ten shillings—an enormous
sum in those days.

A code of laws of this character could not fail to be highly
gratifying to William the Conqueror, and he accordingly confirmed them without any hesitation, and used the power thus
bestowed upon him in the most arbitrary manner. All have
heard how he cleared a large district in Hampshire of all
traces of industry to form the New Forest; but we have no
evidence that a process of a similar kind was employed in
the formation of Knaresborough Forest, nor are we even sure
that it was formed during his reign—indeed, the little evidence
there is on the subject seems to indicate that it was not.
Though a great portion of this district consisted of

"Wild heath and shaggy wood,"

it was not a royal forest when the Domesday survey was made,
about A.D. 1086. So far as we can glean from that invalu-

able document, the following were the manors, towns or places within it at that time.

Modern name.	Ancient name.	Owner in time of Edward the Confessor.	Value in Edward's reign.	Owner when Survey was made.	Val. when Survey was made.	Quantity.
Little Ribston	Ripesten ...	Turber ..	20s.	William de Percy	10s.	1½ car.
Plumpton	Pluntone ..	Gamelbar	20s.	William de Percy	20s.	2 car.
,,	,,	Gamelbar	20s.	Giselbert Tyson	5s.	2 car.
Rougharlington	Rofellington	Gamelbar	20s.	William de Percy	20s.	2 c. 2 ox.
,,	,,	Gamelbar	8s.	Giselbert Tyson	5s.	14 oxgs.
Brame ,, ...	Micklebram	Gamelbar	40s.	William de Percy	30s.	4 car.
,,	,,	Gamelbar	20s.	Giselbert Tyson	Waste	4 car.
,,	Littlebram	Gospatric	20s.	Ernegis d'Burun	20s.	4 car.
Bilton........	Biletone ...	Gamelbar	,,	Giselbert Tyson	3s.	3¼ car.
,,	,,	Archil ...	10s.	Archil	Waste	3¼ car.
Rosset	Roserte	Ulf	10s.	The King......	10s.	1½ car.
,,	,,	Gamelbar and Ulf	,,	Giselbert Tyson	Waste	2 car.
Beckwith.....	Becvi	Gamelbar	,,	Giselbert Tyson	,,	3 car.
Killingball....	Chenihalle	,,	,,	The King......	,,	1 c. soke
,,	Kilingala ..	,,	,,	Abp. of York ..	,,	1 car.
Whipley (Clint)	Wipelaie ...	Archil ...	2s.8d	Archil	Waste	½ car.
,,	,,	,,	,,	The King......	,,	1 c. soke
,,	,,	Gospatric	,,	Ernegis d'Burun	Waste	1 car.
Birstwith.....	Beristade ..	Gospatric	,,	Gospatric......	,,	1 car.
,,	,,	Gamelbar	,,	The King......	5s.	1 car.
Fellischiffe	Felgescliff..	,,	,,	The King......	,,	3 car.
Rowden	Rodon	,,	,,	The King......	,,	2 car.
Fewston	Foston	,,	,,	The King......	,,	3 car.
,,	Besthaim ..	,,	,,	The King......	,,	4 car.
,,	Elseworde] Clifton .. } Timble...]	,,	,,	The King......	,,	3½ car.
Rigton	Ristone....	Gamelbar	,,	Giselbert Tyson	Waste	2 car.
,,	Ritone	Ligulf ...	16s.	Ligulf	10s.	3 car.
Stainburn	Stanburne	4 Thanes	40s.	The King......	40s.	5 car.
Weeton	Widetune..	Chetel ...	,,	The King......	16d.	3 car.
,,	,,	Gospatric Elwin,	,,	Gospatric......	7s.	2½ car.
Castley	Castelai ...	Berne & } Elflet .. }	,,	The King......	16d.	2 car.
Dunkeswick..	Chesvic....	Ulchil ...	8s.	The King......	5s.	4 car.

This survey is imperfect. What are now the parish towns of Pannal and Hampsthwaite are not mentioned, and only a part of Killinghall is given; Clint is not mentioned, but is

probably included in Whipley. Fewston is only partially surveyed, while the north-west portion of the district, including
Blubberhouses, Thruscross, Padside, Thornthwaite, Menwith,
and Darley is not mentioned at all.

From a glance at the above table, it is evident that Gamelbar
before the conquest, was owner of the best part of what was
afterwards known as Knaresborough Forest, and, as the places
there enumerated, were not the whole of his possessions, we
may infer that he was a person of considerable wealth, that he
was disposessed of his lands at the conquest was also evident,
but of the events of his after life we know nothing.

Giselbert, or Gilbert Tyson, was one of the Norman followers
of William, a member of a powerful house of that name, who
ruled the tract of country in the department of Calvedos, known
as *Le Cinglais*. In his charters he is styled "the great standard
bearer of England," so that he was certainly a warrior of importance, for William was not the man to give the bearing of his
standard to a feeble hand. As a small portion of his reward, he
received from his master a large portion of the forfeited estates
of Gamelbar. Over his subsequent career there is much mystery
and uncertainty. The probability is, that during the reign of
William Rufus, by the powerful influence of Robert Mowbray,
Earl of Northumberland, he was drawn into the rebellion against
that king, and as it was unsuccessful, its adherents were punished
with merciless severity. Tyson might be one of those who
suffered on that occasion, as about this time he underwent a
great reverse of fortune, and his lands were seized by the king.
King Henry I. is said to have restored him some of his lands,
but not those in the neighbourhood of Knaresborough. He left
a son and heir named Adam, who, in 31st of Henry I. (1136),
rendered account to the Exchequer of the debts of his father,
and of a fine not to plead for his lands till the son of Nigel de

E

Albini (Roger de Mowbray) was a knight. The grand-daughters
and heirs of Adam married into the families of Constable and
Beauvoir.

It has been frequently asserted that the Forest of Knaresborough was formed by the Conqueror himself, and that he
devastated the district in order to make it waste and fitting for
his purpose. Of this, we believe there is no evidence. The
Domesday survey shows that the country was not more devastated, nor even so much so, as the more fertile and level districts
to the east of it. If a considerable portion of it was not surveyed,
it was doubtless owing more to its wildness and remote situation,
than to its fitness for a royal chase, or its being prepared for such.

By the forfeiture of the fee of Tyson, the king would become
the principal landowner in the district, and might form it into a
royal chase without doing much violence to the rights of private
property, but there is no proof that he did so. The probability
is that the forest* was not formed till the reign of Henry I.,
when the castle was built; and that the formation of the first,
was the main cause of the building of the latter.

* Manwood, in his work on forest laws, thus defines a forest—"A forest
is a certen territorie of wooddy grounds and fruitful pastures, privileged
for wild beasts and foules of forrest, chase, and warren, to rest and abide
in, in the safe protection of the king for his princely delight and pleasure;
which territorie of ground so privileged is meered and bounded with ine-
movable markes, meeres, and boundaries, either known by matter of record
or els by prescription. And also replenished with wilde beastes of venarie
or chase, and great coverts of vert for the succour of the said wilde beastes
to have their abode in; for the preservacion and continnance of which
said place, together with the vert and venison, there are certain particular
laws, privileges, and officers, belonging to the same, meete for that purpose, that are only proper unto a forest, and not to any other place."
The way of making a forest is thus: "Certain commissioners are appointed
under the great seal of England, who view the ground intended for a
forest, and fence it round with metes and bounds; which being returned
into the chancery, the king causeth it to be proclaimed throughout the
county where the land lieth that it is a forest, and to be governed by the
laws of the forest, and prohibits all persons from hunting there without
his leave; and then he appointeth officers fit for the preservation of the
vert and venison, and so it becomes a forest by matter of record."

The first authentic fact relative to the building of the Castle is in the 31st of Henry I., A.D. 1130, when Eustace Fitz John held the *ferme* of *Burc* and *Chenaresburgh* at the rent of twenty-two pounds per annum, of which sum in that year he paid eleven pounds into the treasury, and the remainder was expended on the works of the king at Knaresborough. This we learn from the pipe roll of that year, and the inference follows that he did not succeed to the barony as next heir to his uncle Serlo de Burgh, but merely as *custos* for the king, and from the extensive works carried on at that time, it is equally clear that the castle was in building.

Eustace Fitz John was amongst the most considerable persons of his time. His contemporary, Ailred of Rievaulx, as we learn from Dugdale, " saith of him that he was one of the chiefest peers of England, and of intimate familiarity with Henry I., as also a person of great wisdom, and singular judgment in counsel, He had to wife two of the richest heiresses of his time, namely, Beatrix, the daughter and heir of Ivo de Vesci, by Alda, the daughter and heir of *William* son of Gilbert Tyson, and Agnes, the daughter and heir of William Fitz Nigel, baron of Halton, and constable of Chester. He had sons by both—by the first, William, who appears with the addition of de Vesci ; and by the second Richard, commonly called Fitz Eustace, who married Albreda de Lizours, whose issue were eventually heirs to the two great houses of Laci and Lizours."*

While residing at Knaresborough Castle, in 1133, Eustace Fitz John relieved the monks of Fountains, when on the point of starvation, with a cart load of bread. He lived till the 3rd of Henry II., 1157, when he was slain in the wars in Wales; with this honourable distinction, " that he was a great and

* " Hunter's Deanery of Doncaster," vol. ii., p. 3.

aged man, and one of the chiefest English peers, most eminent for his wealth and wisdom."*

During the early part of the reign of Henry II. the *ferme* of Burc and Knaresburgh was accounted for annually by the sheriff of Yorkshire. In the second year of that king's reign the assized value was sixty pounds, as is proved by the pipe roll of that date.

In 1159 the value was £64; but of this sum £19 were abated at the exchequer, by reason of the king's grant of lands and soke during that year, to Hugh de Morville, who at that time had custody of the castle, to which he fled, along with his associates in crime, after the murder of Thomas-a-Beckett, archbishop of Canterbury, in 1171.

---

* Though the posterity of Eustace Fitz John were not the custodians of the castle of Knaresborough, they did not lose all connection with the place, or were deprived of their lands there, as in the year 1219 the following mandate was issued by the king, relative thereto—" The King to Robert Lupus, greeting. We have commanded you to cause our beloved uncle W. Earl of Salisbury, or his certain messenger bringing these letters, to have seizin, without delay, of the lands and fees, with the appurtenances which were of Eustace de Vescy, in the confines of the castle of Knaresborough. The custody of such lands and heir we have committed to him, retaining in our hands the lands and fees which to the custody of the castle aforesaid pertains; and only act therein so that there may be no necessity for us to take the matter in hand."

The probability is that this fee of Vescy were the lands of Gilbert Tyson inherited by that family. William de Vesʌy, son of Eustace Fitz John, by Beatrix, daughter and heiress of Ivo de Vescy, by Alda, daughter and heiress of William, son of Gilbert Tyson, died in 1185, leaving the second Eustace, who was one of the most active of the barons who opposed king John. When the barons, towards the close of that reign, invited the kings of Scotland and France to their assistance, Eustace de Vescy, attending the king of Scotland, making an attack on Barnard castle, then held by Hugh de Balliol, was there slain by an arrow. He left William, his son and heir, who had John and William de Vescy, in whom the direct line of this noble house became extinct in the reign of Edward I.

That some of the lands of the Vescys were in Plumpton is proved by an Inquisition, held early in the reign of Henry III., on the death of Nigel de Plumpton, when it was found that he held in Plumpton, of the fee of William de Vescy, in demesnes, rents, villenages, and other issues from land, without the dowers of three *Dominæ*, the value of ten marks two shillings and threepence.

In 1177, king Henry II. granted to William de Stutevill, and his heirs, the *wardship* of the castle of Knaresburgh, with the manors of Knaresburgh and Burgh, for the slender service of three knights' fees, as a reward for services done the king during the civil wars raised by prince Henry against his father.

King Richard I., in the second year of his reign, exacted a fine of two thousand pounds from William de Stutevill, for permission to retain unmolested possession of Knaresborough and its dependencies.*

From king John, William de Stutevill also sought a confirmation of his title, and readily obtained a ratification of his father's charter, dated at Guildford, April 22nd, 1199.

Stutevill granted, in the first year of king John (1199), to Nigel de Plumpton and his heirs, for the usual services, and one horse of the value of one hundred shillings, all that portion or the forest within the bounds of Plumpton and Rudfarlington—that is to say, along the Crimple so far to the west as Osberne-stahe-bec (Starbeck), along that beck to Puddingstain Cross,† thence to Harelow, thence by the great road to Bilton, thence to Stokke-brigg, thence to Holebeck, thence to the Nidd, and along the Nidd to Crimple; with permission for the said Nigel and his heirs to enclose and cultivate the lands within the aforesaid bounds; and also license to hunt the fox and hare throughout the whole Forest of Knaresborough, saving to the lord the royal beasts of chase, the stag, the hart, and the roebuck.

These limits would include the whole of the district now

* "Pipe Roll," 2 Ric. I.

† These boundaries are difficult of identification: that along Starbeck is sufficiently obvious; Puddingstone Cross has disappeared. Herclaw means Harrogate, and not the present hill called Harlow, to the west of Harrogate. Stokke-brig has been exchanged for Stone, wherever it was. Holbeck is a small brook, flowing from near Belmont farm, and falling into the Nidd on the north side of Thistle hill.

known as the townships of Little Ribston and Plumpton;
though much difficulty would be found in identifying the limits,
when not formed by the streams of Starbeck, Crimple, and
Nidd.

He also alienated Blubberhouses to Robert le Forester and
his heirs.

William de Stutevill died in 1203, and was buried in Fountains Abbey, to which, for the right of sepulture, he had
given all his lands in the vill. of Kirkby Ouseburn.

Robert de Stutevill, son and heir of William, at the time
of his father's death had not attained his majority; therefore,
on the 11th of July, 1203, Hubert, archbishop of Canterbury,
fined in the sum of 4,000 marks to have the wardship and
marriage; when Robert assented to his keeping the inheritance in his hands four years, until he got his money again,
or was indemnified his reasonable expenses.

Neither the archbishop nor his ward lived over the term,
and on the 7th of king John, August 5th, 1205, Nicholas de
Stutevill fined in the enormous sum of 10,000 marks, to have
livery of the land of which his brother William had died
seized, as his inheritance; except the Castle of Knaresborough,
and Boroughbridge, which were to be retained in the king's
hands until the whole sum was paid.

On the 21st of December, 1204, the king issued a precept
to the sheriff of Yorkshire, to cause the forest of "Cnarre-
burgh" to be restored to the state it was in when king
Henry granted it to William de Stutevill, and to deliver the
same entire to the archbishop.* Among the sufferers by this

* The kings of the Norman race were extremely addicted to hunting;
and in order to enlarge their forests were continually making encroachments on the property of their subjects, that at length it is believed they
had one-eighth of the country in their possession as royal forests. This
state of things could not continue for ever; the nobles were injured, as
well as the peasants and farmers, and their combination wrung the *Carta*

proceeding was Nigel de Plumpton. who in February, 1205-6, had to give a palfrey for leave to hold his land of Rudfarlington and Ribstone, and the appurtenances, with the chattels in the said vill., until the king should come to York, they having been seized into the king's hands *pro wasto forestæ*. There the matter was investigated; and the result was a fine of twenty marks for restitution of the land, which fine was paid into the king's privy purse, at Nottingham, March 9th, 1205-6, by Brian de l'Isle, the constable of the Castle of Knaresborough, and the other officers in charge of the honour.

King John disafforested all the Forest of Wherndale.* This we believe to be that portion of the Forest of Knaresborough which occupied the northern slope of the valley of the Wharfe, and included the townships, or places, of Rigton, Stainburn, Castley, Weeton, Dunkeswick, and Swinden; of a great part of which Brian de l'Isle, or Insula, obtained possession, and which is yet held by his successors, the earls of Harewood.

de Foresta from King Henry III., in the 41st year of his reign. By this charta restitution was to be made of all lands which the kings had improperly taken. It is there stated—"All forests which king Henry, our grandfather, afforested and made, shall be viewed by good and lawful men, and if he have made forests of any other wood more than of his own property, whereby the owner of the wood hath sustained injury, it must forthwith be disafforested. . . . All woods which have been made forests by king Richard, our uncle, or by king John, our father, unto our first coronation, shall be forthwith disafforested, unless it be our own property." Another enactment softens the rigour of the forest laws—"No man from henceforth shall lose either life or limb for killing of our deer; but if any man be taken therewith, and convicted for taking our venison, he shall make a grievous fine, if he have anything on which to levy a fine, and if he have not, he shall be imprisoned a year and a day; and after the year and day have expired, he shall be liberated, if he can find sureties, and if not, he shall abjure the realm."

* In a Commission issued 7th Henry VII., to the Sheriff of Yorkshire, to collect arrears of rents and services in the Honour of Knaresborough, we find the following names of places—Warsdale Forest, Swynden Forest, Okeden Forest, and Fullwyth Forest. These are all in our district. The first is merely a misprint for Warndale, or Wharfdale; the next is Swinden, in the parish of Kirkby Overblow, closely adjoining the last; Fullwith is now a mill and farm, on the Crimple, in the parish of Pannal; and Okeden is the district now known as Okedale, about a mile west of Harrogate.

Brian de l'Isle was a great man, and a faithful officer of the king. In 1205 he was appointed constable of the castle of Knaresborough. In 1207, and the following year, he was carrying on extensive works for the king there, one of which was making the ditch or moat of the castle. In the first year of Henry III. (1217), he had a grant of the castle and all its appurtenances at the old *ferme* of £50, until the king should have completed the fourteenth year of his age. In the 7th of Henry III., there was a further grant to him of the same honour* during the king's pleasure, at the above rent.

In 1229, the castle and honour of Knaresborough, with Aldburgh and Boroughbridge, with the knights' fees, soke, and appurtenances, and also an assignment of the debt of 10,000 marks, which the heirs of Stutevill owed to redeem the same, were granted by the king to Hubert de Burgh, and Margaret his wife.

This lord of the Forest of Knaresborough was for a while one of the greatest men in England—a learned lawyer, a brave soldier, and a loyal patriot, his career forms a bright spot in the otherwise dark reigns of John and Henry III.;† and yet Henry, without cause, threw off this faithful minister, and left him exposed to the violent persecutions of his enemies. He fell from the height of his greatness; but even his enemies in his downfall respected his virtues; and when opportunity again offered of attaining power, he refused it.

* Honour is especially used for a more noble seignory or lordship, on which other inferior lordships and manors do depend, by performance of customs and services. Originally no lordships were honours but such as belonged to the king, though afterwards they were given in fee to noblemen.

† On the death of John, Hubert de Burgh, constable of Dover, with a body of English sailors, and William de Collingham, with the archers of Sussex, drove the French prince out of the kingdom, put down the barons, and obtained the confirmation of the great charter from Henry III., with a new charter, "the charter of the forests."—*Cassell's History of England.*

In 1233, the king resumed his grant of Knaresborough and its appurtenances; and in the following year conferred them on his brother Richard, earl of Cornwall, elected, and commonly called king of the Romans.

The most important action of Richard's life in connection with Knaresborough, was the foundation of a priory there for brethren of the Holy Trinity, in 1256, which he endowed with the chapel of St. Robert, the church of Hampsthwaite, and other lands and privileges, principally in the Forest of Knaresborough.* During this earl's time Henry de Perpunt was steward, and William Irreby bailiff of the honour of Knaresborough; and these men wielded their delegated authority with great severity, and many acts of extortion and unjust dealing were charged against them; one of which was, that Henry de Perpunt received from Henry Locken, a known thief, seven marks per annum for his protection. The inhabitants of Aldburgh complained of the heavy tolls levied on the crossing of the river there; and the citizens of York, and the men of the wapontakes of Birdforth and Bulmer, complained of the increased tolls on the river Ouse, between Boroughbridge and York.

Richard died in 1272, and was succeeded in the Honour of Knaresborough by his son Edmund, also earl of Cornwall. Edmund was a distinguished character, equally a statesman and a soldier; and during the whole of his lifetime was much employed and trusted by king Edward I., than whom none knew better how to distinguish merit. He took a principal part in all the wars waged in Edward's reign, both in Wales and Scotland.

Edmund granted to the monks of Fountains Abbey the

* In the 85th Edward I., the minister and brethren of St. Robert's of Knaresborough had the liberty given to them, and their servants, of taking turves and peats (turbas et bletas), in the Forest of Knaresborough.

privilege of taking "housbote" and "haybote" in his woods,
within the Forest of Knaresborough. He likewise gave them the
bees and honey found in his woods, and also liberty to enclose
the wood of Brimham, but in such a manner that the beasts
of the forest might pass in and out thereof. This was probably
the origin of the fence called "the Monk wall," which runs
along the northern side, and forms the boundary of the Forest
of Knaresborough from Padside-head to Thornton beck, at
Shaw Mills; the lands of the said abbey adjoining the same
on the north, the whole length of its course. He also gave
to the said monks, and their servants, a free passage along
the river Ouse, from Boroughbridge to York.

In the year 1285, on Saturday next after the Annunciation
of St. Mary, it was agreed at Knaresborough, between Edmund,
earl of Cornwall, and Sir Robert Plumpton, that the latter,
and his heirs, should have by way of fee, half the americaments from attachments for transgressions committed in the
green and the dry *(de viride et sicco)*, in the demesne woods
of the said Sir Robert, within the Forest of Knaresborough,
whether the acts of strangers or their own tenants, leviable in
the court of the said earl and his heirs, at Knaresborough,
to be received at the hands of the seneschal or bailiff for the
time being; but not those from attachments for transgressions
in cutting down timber, or for waste. Sir Robert and his
heirs were also to have the pannage of the swine agisted in
their own woods; and to be allowed to assart the demesne
woods of Bircom, Loxley, and Hadlaugh, near Grimbald-brigg;
and the hays growing in the cultures of Plumpton, on the
east side of the ditch and hedge extending from Plumpton to
the bank-side of Nidd, opposite the gateway of the house of
St. Robert of Knaresborough, called Braistergarth; with the
exception of the woods and covers of Grimbald-staines and

Hybank; so, nevertheless, that the assarts and cultures remained within the bounds and Forest of Knaresborough. Haybote and housebote were to be allowed of all other woods; and they and their tenants were to be quit of "Castell-boone" and of drink money to the foresters, upon payment of a rent of four shillings a-year. The agreement concludes with a saving of the right of common in all places without the enclosure of the parks of the said earl, in their then state; and is attested by Sir Richard de Cornwall, Richard de Goldsburgh, Peter Becard, William de Hertlington, Richard de Stokeld, knights, and other witnesses of lesser note.*

Edmund died without issue, in 1299, and consequently his vast possessions escheated to the crown. From the *Inquisition post mortem*, made in the above year, we find that he was seized of the following places in our district—Roudon, Stocton, Rosthurst, Bekwith, Panhalle, Clifton-Elsworth, Foston-Best-aine, Timble-Brian, Timble-Percy, Thorescrosse, Pateside, Thornthwaite, Derlemonwith, Felisclive, Birscale, Sprokesby, Hampsthwaite, Clint, Kellingholme, and Bilton.

During the remainder of the reign of the first Edward the Honour of Knaresborough remained attached to the crown; and Miles Stapleton and John de Insula were appointed constables of the same.

Like Sherwood and other English forests, that of Knaresborough was occasionally the resort of outlaws and deer stealers. In 1302, king Edward I. issued a precept to John de Insula and Sir Miles Stapleton, commanding them to enquire concerning malefactors and disturbers of the peace within the chase of Knaresborough; and also of those who fly there, and those who without license sport in the same, and all trans-

* "Plumpton Correspondence," p. xix.

gressors; and hear and determine according to law concerning
the same; and if convicted, commit the said offenders to prison
within the castle of Knaresborough, until the fines assigned
for their redemption be fully paid.*

In the same year the king issued a mandate to Miles Stapleton, commanding him to cause to be cut down within the
chase of Knaresborough, and in places belonging to the same,
timber to the value of forty pounds, and make sale of the
same, on view and testimony of Henry de Scriven† and Thomas
Rossell, foresters of the said fee.

From what remains, we can easily imagine what the forest
was at this early period. In the summer season, when the
trees were in full verdure, and the sunshine streaming over
its many-coloured scenery, it would be a wild, but not unlovely
region. Near the steep sides of the brooks, and on the richer
soils, grew oaks, old and hoary, twisted and knotted together,
their limbs dark with the moss of centuries, shading the ground
so as to make the noonday beneath them seem dark. More
scattered, and in less numbers, grew the ash; not unfrequently

---

* Pat. Rolls, 31st Edward I.

† The office of chief forester was claimed as hereditary by the family
of Scriven, of Scriven, of whom Gamellus, surnamed Auceps, or the fowler,
had confirmation of his lands from king Henry I. He was probably the
first who held that office, as the forest was only formed about that time.
He was succeeded in his office by his son, Baldwin, who in his turn was
succeeded by his son, Henry de Scriven, who was forester in the reign
of Henry III., and was succeeded by his son, Thomas, who was succeeded
by Henry de Scriven, who was forester when Edward II. gave the Honour
of Knaresborough to Peter de Gaveston, when William de Vaus, seneschal
of the said Gaveston, attempted to oust him from his office; when the
above facts were proved at a court held at Knaresborough, in the second
year of Edward II., on the oaths of Robert de Staveley and other jurors.
The family of Scriven became extinct in the above Henry, who had two
daughters, of whom Johanna was married to William de Slingsby, of
Studley, whose second son, Richard, in right of his mother, became capital
forester of the forest and parks of Knaresborough; which office is held
to be hereditary in his descendants.

arose a thickly-matted copse of underwood, the black thorn
and the white, the bramble and the hazel, twisted together
into an almost impervious mass. In watery places, the alder
and the willow formed close clumps or long thickets; the craggy
slopes were clothed with heath and fern, above which rose,
scattered at intervals, the graceful birch, dark-green holly, and
beautiful mountain ash; broad patches of gorse or whin, tall
as the tallest forester who trod their intricate paths to rouse
the deer, were not unfrequent. Many a bleak heathy ridge,
extending from Harlow, miles to the westward, was covered
with ling, broken at intervals by grey crags, swamps, and
pools of miry water; the dawny cotton grass, and a host of
aquatic plants growing in profusion around them. Here and
there amid this wilderness, were pieces of cultivated land,
meadow, or pasture, where the foresters had built their humble
cottages—some singly, some in clusters. Three parish churches
arose amid this wilderness, Pannal, Hampsthwaite, and Fewston, which constituted them centres of social life and inter-
course. The inhabitants of the wilder part of this region were
the royal beasts of chase, the red deer and the roe-buck, the
wolf, the wild boar, the badger, the fox, the pine-martin, the
hare, and all the smaller "rascale" tribe. Of birds—the grouse,
the partridge, the hawk, the heron, the curlew, the bittern,
the buzzard, the shoveller, the plover, the wild goose, the
duck, the widgeon, the raven, rook, and crow, with all the
smaller songsters, then as now, making wild music. Many
a gay scene these hills have witnessed in the old days of
chivalry, when

    " To drive the deer with hound and horn,"

the proud baron took his way, attended by a numerous train

of friends and retainers, each gallant young forester burning to distinguish himself.

> "All in a woodman's jacket was he clad,
> Of Lincoln green, belayed with silver lace,
> And on his head a hood with aglets sprad,
> And by his side his hunter's horn he hanging had.
>
> Buskins he wore, of costliest cordawain,
> Pinked upon gold, and paled part per part,
> As then the guise was for each gentle swain;
> In his right hand he held a trembling dart,
> And in his left he held a sharp boar-speare."—*Spenser.*

We can also imagine other scenes—the cruel game laws, cruelly enforced; the faction fight; the march to distant wars—for the foresters were a warlike race, and frequently called away to fight.

This is no mere fancy sketch: the trees and vegetation, yet growing on uncultivated parts, are sufficiently indicative of what the scenery of the forest was when nature reigned supreme.

In the first year of his reign (A.D. 1807) king Edward II. granted to Peter de Gaveston, and his heirs, the Honour of Knaresborough, with the manors of Roecliffe and Aldburgh. In the following year Gaveston was driven from the kingdom by a combination of the barons against him; by which event the Honour of Knaresborough again reverted to the crown, with which it continued until the recall of Gaveston, in 1811, when the Honour of Knaresborough, with the parks La Haye, Bilton, and Haywray, were re-granted to him and his heirs, with free chase in all lands belonging to the said Honour, the privilege of judging malefactors taken either within or without the said manor, and one gibbet and one gallows for the execution of such offenders, and all their cattle and goods, together with all those animals called waives, and the return of all writs; also two coroners, whose jurisdiction should extend over all the county of York; the inhabitants of the said honour to be free of all fines, and americaments for toll, pontage, murage,

&c., throughout the kingdom. These were great and important privileges, both to the lord and his tenants.

Gaveston's tenure of greatness and life was but a short one: a combination of the nobles was again formed against him; he was captured in the castle of Scarborough, and beheaded at Deddington, July 1st, 1812.

Immediately after the downfall of Gaveston, the king committed the keeping of the castle of Knaresborough to William de Vallibus, or de Vaus, who held the office till 1814, when the king gave the custody thereof to Roger Dammory, for the annual rent of 200 marks.

During the unfortunate and disgraceful reign of the second Edward, this district suffered severely. In the year 1317, John de Lilbourne, an officer of the earl of Lancaster, surprised, or rather stole into the castle of Knaresborough, with a few followers, for the purpose of holding it against the royal power. The king immediately issued orders to Nicholas de Grey, sheriff of Yorkshire, to take possession of the said castle, together with the goods, armour, and victuals, and keep the same for the king's use. The castle was quickly invested by the sheriff, and Lilbourne, seeing no prospect of relief, surrendered; having first destroyed all the records and written memorials of the liberties, customs, and privileges of the honour. These were again in some measure recorded, so far as they could be collected from the memories of men then living, and enrolled at a court held at Knaresborough, May 10th, 1867.

The defeat of the English army at Bannockburn, the discontent of the nobles, and the misgovernment of the king, began to be felt with disastrous effect by the kingdom. In 1818, the Scots entered England under the command of Lord Randolf and Sir James Douglass, and wasted the northern

counties with fire and sword, almost without opposition. They
poured like a torrent of fire across the wapontake of Claro;
murdering, plundering, and burning all before them. The
Forest of Knaresborough suffered greatly from their ravages.
They abode some time at Pannal, making the church their
head-quarters, which they wantonly burnt on their departure.
Petitions for a remission of taxation, from nearly every place
in the forest, were sent to the king; to which his majesty
returned the following most gracious answer—" The king to
his beloved and faithful John de Wysham, his keeper of the
Castle and Honour of Knaresborough, all health. Since we
have received information by the inquisition, which through
our beloved and faithful Robert de Lapey, and Gilbert de
Wiggeton, we have caused to be made; that several men and
tenants of our Castle and Honour of Knaresburgh aforesaid,
in the townships of Knaresburgh, Skrevyn, Burbrigg, Minskip,
Tymble, Clifton, Fuston, Thruscross, Menwyth, Clynte, Fellescliff, Birstall (Birstwith), Hampthweith, Kyllinghall, Rosehurst,
Bilton, and Nidd, by the burning of their houses, the plundering
of their cattle and goods, by the hostile attacks of the Scots,
our enemies, are in a great measure ruined. And the same
men, our tenants, have applied to us to relax, or spare them
the farms and rents, or at least a part of them, which by
reason of their fealty to the Castle and Honour aforesaid they
are bound to pay.

We, therefore, pitying their desolate and depressed condition,
forgive them the farms and rents which they are bound to pay
to us, at the term of St. Michael last past; which amount to
the sum of sixty and twelve pounds, three shillings, and seven
pence, as by the aforesaid investigation more fully appears.
And, therefore, we command you fully to discharge the said

tenants from their farms and rents due to us, even so far as
the before-mentioned sum."

On the 25th of November, 1819, writs were addressed to
the assessors and collectors of the "Eighteenth," in the West
Riding of Yorkshire, on behalf of Alianora, widow of Henry
de Percy, and her men and tenants of Spofforth, Wetherby,
Linton, Leathley, Kerby, Kirkby, and other places, which had
been burned, spoiled, and plundered by the Scots, that they
were to assess the remains of the goods of the inhabitants,
but to stay the collection until further instructions.

Similar writs were addressed to the abbot of Fountains, and his
men and tenants of the townships of Rigton, Stainburn, Ripley,
and Grafton, who had been plundered in a similar manner.

From which we may infer that no place within the Forest of
Knaresborough had escaped the ravages of the Scottish patriots.

In 1819, the king gave the custody of the castle, with the
profits of the Manor and Honour of Knaresborough, to John
de Wysham, for the term of his life, at an annual rent of
800 marks.   This nobleman was actively engaged for many
years during these troublous times in the service of his country.
In 1822, he was one of the chief supervisors of array in the
West Riding, empowered to proceed from township to township to levy forces.   In 1824, he was one of the justices
empowered to degrade and pass sentence of death upon Andrew
de Harcla, earl of Carlisle.   In the same year he was returned
as knight to parliament, for the county of Gloucester.

King Edward III., in the first year of his reign (1826),
resumed possession of the Castle and Honour of Knaresborough,
granting in exchange to John de Wysham, who had a life
interest in the same, the manors of Fullbruck and Westhall,
in Oxfordshire, which had previously belonged to the king's
late enemy, Hugo de Spenser.

r

In 1329, John de Wanton, or Wauton, was appointed governor of the castle, and custodian of the Honour of Knaresborough.

The Castle and Honour of Knaresborough were settled by king Edward III. on his queen, the heroic Philippa; and she slept a night in the castle, in the year 1333, when on a journey to Durham to meet the king.

In 1356, Thomas de Abington was appointed governor of the castle by Philippa, queen of England, and gave half a mark to the king for the confirmation of the same.

In the fortieth year of his reign, king Edward confirmed the queen's letters patent, by which she appointed John atte Halle atte Barowe keeper of the parks within the lordship of Knaresborough.

In 1369, Philippa, queen of England, died seized of the Castle of Knaresborough, and the manors of Snaith and Cowick, in Yorkshire.

In 1371, the house of St. Robert, with the Castle, Manor, and Honour of Knaresborough, with all belonging thereto, were granted by the king to his dear son John, king of Castile and Leon, and most illustrious duke of Lancaster. From that time to the present the Honour of Knaresborough has remained attached to the duchy of Lancaster.

John of Gaunt, or Ghent, so named from the place of his birth, was the fourth son of Edward III., born in 1340. Having married Constance, the daughter of Peter, king of Castile and Leon, he claimed the throne of those kingdoms on the death of his father-in-law, but never enjoyed anything but the empty title. He was a man of liberal ideas and tolerant disposition, a lover of learning and learned men; at once the patron of Wickliffe, the first great English reformer, and Chaucer, the morning star of English poetry. His name is yet familiar in this district: the ruined lodge on the top of Haverah park yet bears the name of "John o' Gaunt's castle." He married for his third wife Catherine Swinford, sister of the wife of Chaucer, the great English poet. He died in 1399, and the Castles of Knaresborough and Tickhill were assigned to his widow in dower. She survived him four years, dying on the 10th of May, 1403.

Sir Thomas Chaucer, son of the renowned poet, was constable of Knaresborough Castle at this time, on the nomination of his uncle, John of Gaunt.

In 1387, John de la Pole was chief seneschal of the duke of Lancaster, north of Trent; and Sir Robert Plumpton, of Plumpton, was constable of the Castle and master forester of the Forest of Knaresborough.

"Time honoured Lancaster" ought to have been succeeded in his honours and estates by his eldest son, by his first wife, Blanch, daughter of Henry, duke of Lancaster, who is well known in history as Henry Bolingbroke, duke of Hereford; but he had been banished the kingdom from "the lists of Coventry," and on the death of his father was an exile in a foreign land. He, however, claimed his patrimonial estates, which the weak king not only refused to give up, but condemned to death the duke's attorney for faithfully executing the trusts of his master. Henry returned from banishment. On the 22nd of July, 1399, he landed at Ravenspurne, on the Yorkshire coast, having with him the archbishop of Canterbury, Sir Thomas Arundel, and about one hundred men-at-arms. They directed their course northward, passing peaceably across the East Riding, and reached the castle of Pickering in three days. This castle Richard had placed in the custody of the earl of Wiltshire, who entrusted Sir William le Scrope with the command of it. On the first appearance of Henry he was admitted into it. He stayed at Pickering two days, and .then

marched to Knaresborough. Some opposition was here made
to him; but at length he gained possession of the castle and
placed a garrison in it. Pontefract was the next point. During
this time there was a continual influx of gentlemen, knights,
and squires, with their dependants, from the counties of Lancaster and York; among whom were the earl of Northumberland and his son, the valiant Hotspur, the earl of Westmorland,
the lord Willoughby, and many others of great influence; so
that when Richard returned from Ireland he found his kingdom
in possession of another. He surrendered himself to Northumberland, and was conveyed a prisoner to Flint castle. He was
afterwards removed a prisoner from one castle of Lancaster's
to another, first to Leeds, then to Pickering, next to Knaresborough, and lastly to Pontefract—where, either the axe of
the assassin, or the more lingering pangs of hunger ended his
unhappy life, sometime during the year 1400.

Sir Robert Plumpton appears to have retained the office of
constable of the castle and chief forester of the Forest of
Knaresborough, until his death in 1406; when he was succeeded in his offices by his grandson,

Sir Robert Plumpton, who held the above offices until his
death, in 1421; when his eldest son,

Sir William Plumpton, being a minor, was sometime a ward
of the earl of Northumberland. He was appointed to his
father's offices in the Forest of Knaresborough in 1439, which
he held till the end of the reign of king Henry VI.

At this time a quarrel, ending in bloodshed, took place
between the king's tenants of the Forest of Knaresborough
and the men of John Kemp, cardinal and archbishop of York.
The origin of this feud was the refusal of the tenants of the
Forest of Knaresborough to pay the tolls demanded by the
archbishop's bailiffs in the market towns of Otley and Ripon,

and which the other were determined to enforce. Much ill-
feeling in consequence existed between them for the space of
three years at least, and many were the acts of violence committed, especially by the foresters. On the 22nd of July,
1439, the men of the forest, to the number of 700, "by the
covyne and assent of Sir William Plumpton, knight, arrayed
in manner of war, and in riotouse-wise entered the town of
Otley, under the leadership of Thomas of Beckwith, John
Fawks, William Wakefield, and John Beckwith of Killinghall,
not to buy, nor make fruit of merchandise there, in the fair
at that time held," but rather disposed to create a disturbance
with the officers and men of the archbishop. Their entering
the town put Robert Mauleverer, steward, John Thoresby,
bailiff, and others of the cardinal's servants, in great fear and
doubt as to the safety of their persons. For the foresters told
them "that they should not take, ask, nor receive any toll
of any men of the said forest." Not satisfied with this, "they
letted the steward, bailiff, and other officers, that they might
not freely, nor surely occupy, nor use the rule and governaile
of the said fair, nor gather in the name and right of the said
cardinal and archbishop, the toll due and accustomed; and
caused much people, that coming to the said fair to have
bought and sold, to depart from the said fair without their
buying and selling; and also letted other to come thither, to
the great prejudice, hurt, and harm of the said cardinal and
archbishop, and great affray of the king's people." This was
certainly a lawless action of the foresters; but we must bear
in mind that by royal charter they were free of "all toll,
pontage, murage, &c., throughout the kingdom." Not satisfied
with this, in the month of August following, the foresters,
amongst whom were Thomas Beckwith, John Fawks and Ralph
Pulleine, committed "divers outrages on the person and property

of John Walworth, bailiff of the cardinal, dwelling in Thornton
wood." What these outrages were we are not informed. And
then to aggravate the wrong, Sir William Plumpton, Thomas
Beckwith, and others, refused "to treat with Master John
Marshall, an officer of the said cardinal, and Richard Redmayne,
Esq., for the recognition of the king's peace."

The archbishop finding complaints useless, determined to
enforce his claims by force of arms; and accordingly at the
fair held at Ripon, in the month of May, 1441, he mustered
a little army to collect the toll from the men of the forest.
Two hundred men-at-arms, from Tynedale and Hexhamshire,
and other parts near Scotland, came into Ripon, "like men
of war, with breast-plate, vambrace, and rearbrace, greves and
quishers, gorgets and sallets, long spears and lancegays, and the
simplest arrayed of them all had either a gestiment or a hawbur-
geon, or a thick jack upon him, and either a pricknaghate or a
sallet upon their heads." This force was increased by the addition of one hundred men from Beverley, Cawood, and York, which
were arrayed in a similar manner to the others, save the spears,
lancegays, and breastplates, and also further strengthened by
men from Otley and Ripon—so that it might be considered
superior to any force which the foresters could bring against
it. "They went robling up the said town and down," and said
openly during the said days of the fair, "Would God these
knaves and lads of the forest would come hider, that we might
have a fair day upon them! and other words of great scorn,
rebuke and provoking." None of the lads of the forest appeared
at the fair to receive the beating prepared for them; which
was a great disappointment to the archbishop's men, as they
were fully prepared to settle all old scores with them, and wipe
out all disgraces previously received at their hands. Seeing
they did not come, a consultation or council of war was held,

to consider what was best to be done. The marchmen were
ashamed to go away without having had a fight, as it was
one of the pleasures of their lives, and they had also come
a great distance for that especial purpose. It was determined
that they should ride to York with the men of that town, and
those of Cawood and Beverley; and, that in so doing, by way
of bravado, they would pass through Boroughbridge, a town
belonging to the Honour of Knaresborough; and it was believed
that passing through this town would either provoke the foresters
to fight, or be an acknowledgement of their weakness or cowar-
dice. Certain friends of the foresters in Ripon sent word to
Boroughbridge of the purposed ride through that town. Intelligence from thence passed to Sir William Plumpton, who sent
word to the bailiff of Boroughbridge to hold the town that
night, and he would be with him in the morning. On this
occasion the foresters appear to have laid their plans with
considerable skill for enclosing their dangerous enemy, and
compelling him to fight at a disadvantage. On the night before
the intended march, besides occupying the passage of the river
Ure, at Boroughbridge, they took the further precaution of
sending a party to occupy Skip-bridge, across the Nidd, about
nine miles further on the road to York, where that river was
deep and narrow, and not fordable, and which the northern
men would be obliged to cross, had they either forced the
passage at Boroughbridge, or got over at any other point.
During the night they also occupied Thornton-bridge, across
the river Swale, with a detachment of forty men, should their
enemies attempt to pass that way, which was possible, but by
which route they would not touch upon any part of the Honour
of Knaresborough. Not satisfied with this, and knowing there
was a ford across the Swale at Brafferton, they left it apparently
unguarded, but laid an ambuscade in the village of Helperby,

which close adjoins that of Brafferton, under the command of
Thomas and Ralph Beckwith, which employed itself in fastening
a "ledyate in the highway, at the town end of Helperby,
towards York, with stoks, thorns and otherwise." In order to
get to York with anything like directness, the archbishop's men
would have to pass some of these fords or bridges, which
could not be done without fighting and winning a battle. The
force of the foresters was so stationed that one part of it could
assist another, if necessary, except the detachment at Skip-
bridge. Though we have no account of the number of foresters
engaged on this occasion, it must have been considerable, otherwise they would not have been able to have guarded so many
points at one time, without weakening their main force at
Boroughbridge, which a skilful leader like Sir William Plumpton
would not be likely to do. Before sunrise on the morning of
Monday, May 5th, Sir William Plumpton himself arrived at
Boroughbridge, with only twenty-four men with him, according
to his own account; but his men were all at their posts before
that time. And on that morning the archbishop's men started
on their journey from Ripon to York. Having learned that
Boroughbridge was occupied by the foresters in force, and knowing they would not be able to force the passage of the long narrow
bridge in the face of a body of skilful archers, they turned
aside, thinking to pass the Swale at Thornton-bridge, and so
reach York by that route. Here the foresters were beforehand
with them again; the bridge was occupied by a force strong
enough to keep them at bay for some time. The main body
from Boroughbridge was already advancing upon them from
that side, threatening, in military phrase, their right flank and
rear. Seeing this, they hurried to the apparently unguarded
ford at Brafferton; by which time the force from Boroughbridge came "pricking altogether, with all diligence that they

could, making a great and horrible shout." The party from
Thornton-bridge was also dangerously near; so that having
crossed the river and entered the village of Helperby, the
archbishop's men fell into the ambuscade, and found themselves
completely out-generalled and surrounded by the "knaves and
lads of the forest." These latter, now that they had their
enemies within reach, were not backward in giving them a
taste of their quality; showers of arrows from the long bow
were only the preliminaries to a closer combat with swords,
knives, and battle-axes. The archbishop's men, finding the
road stopped in front, and being rudely assaulted by the ambuscade, as well as by those who had crossed the river after
them, fell into disorder, and made but a feeble resistance.
Considering that many of them were borderers, "bred to war,"
their conduct in the fight was most cowardly, and not at all
accordant with their former boastful language. One thing may
be said in excuse of the flight of the Tynedale men—there was
little chance of plunder had they stood and fought; besides
they were opposed to an enemy well trained in the use of the
long bow, that most dangerous weapon of mediæval warfare,
and animated on the present occasion by a long-standing personal quarrel. The archbishop's men were driven down a
narrow lane, some over the hedge into a field, many of them
into a mire, half a mile from the village; their enemies shouting
—"Slay the archbishop's carles!" and—"Would God we had
the archbishop here!" Very significant words—which the archbishop afterwards grievously resented. His force was completely beaten, scattered over the country, killed, or wounded
on the field, or prisoners in the hands of their enemies. The
archbishop himself furnishes the list of killed, wounded, and
missing. Of these—Thomas Hunter, gentleman, and Thomas
Roper, yeoman, slain outright. Christopher Bee, wounded in

such manner in the mouth, and so through the mouth into the throat, by which he lost his cheek bone and three of his fore teeth, and his speech was so much blemished and hurt that it was not easy to understand what he said, nor could he use the remnant of his teeth and jaws in eating, as he could before. William Humberstone was wounded in such wise that the calf of his leg was near hand departed from his shin bone. John Creven was grievously beaten and wounded on divers parts of his body, in especial in his right leg, which was near hand hewn in two, with many other wounds, so that he was left for dead, and lay on the field after all other folks had departed, and was found about four o'clock in the afternoon of the same day, by some of the dwellers in the town of Helperby, who finding him not fully dead, brought him into the said town, and there refreshed and relieved him in such wise that he was turned to life; howbeit he was perpetually letted off occupying of his craft of tailor, that he used before, in so much that he could not endure to lay his leg under him in such wise as his craft would ask. John Burton, Henry Fox, William Playne, and others, to the number of sixteen, were grievously beat, wounded, and hurt; and the remnant were greatly afraid, and doubted of their lives. And no marvel that they were so, says the complaining archbishop, consider- ing that there were shot at them a thousand arrows and more, by which many of the said cardinal's officers', servants', and tenants' horses were slain and grievously wounded. Peres of Cawood, and Thomas Mayne, squires, and Henry Fox, yeoman, were taken prisoners by the misdoers, and some of them laboured and treated by them to make them "fynance," as they had been the king's enemies. And many and divers were dispoiled of their horses, harness, and also gold and silver.

Such was the contemptible ending of so much assurance and

boasting on the part of the archbishop's men. Though the foresters were certainly acting in an illegal manner, we cannot but admire the courage and conduct they employed in bringing their haughty enemies to shame.

To the complaints of the archbishop before the king and council, Sir William Plumpton made answer in denial or explanation; but as no further proceedings appear to have been taken, it may be presumed that a compromise was effected. Sir William Plumpton must have been a daring man thus to set the spiritual and temporal sword at defiance.

In 1446, Sir William Plumpton, with the men of the Honour of Knaresborough, joined the forces of the earl of Northumberland, and rode northward for the purpose of making an incursion on the Scottish borders.

The "Wars of the Roses" now commenced, and swept over the country with desolating fury for many years. Though the Forest of Knaresborough was in some measure exempt from their immediate effect, the men of the forest and honour took a prominent part in them on the side of king Henry VI., and in consequence suffered severely. When Edward IV. had assumed the crown, and was on his march northward to vindicate his title by the sword, two mandates in rapid succession reached Sir William Plumpton: the first tested at York, March 12th, 1460, contained an order for Sir Richard Tunstall, knight, Sir Richard Tresham, knight, and Sir William Plumpton, knight, "to summon all the men of the forest or demesne of Knaresborough to set out with them to meet the enemy." The second on the following day, straitly charging "our well beloved knight, Sir William Plumpton, to repair to the royal presence with his array in all haste possible." The king's need was great and the occasion urgent. Sir William accordingly led his foresters to the field; and on the 29th of the same month, being Palm Sunday, the terrible battle of Towton was fought.

"Where the red rose and the white rose
    In furious battle reel'd;
And yeomen fought like barons,
    And barons died ere yield.

Where mingling with the snow storm,
    The storm of arrows flew;
And York against proud Lancaster
    His ranks of spearmen threw.

Where thunder like the uproar
    Outshook from either side,
As hand to hand they battled,
    From morn till eventide.

Where the river ran all gory,
    And in hillocks lay the dead,
And seven and thirty thousand
    Fell for the white and red."

The men of the forest suffered severely; the earl of Northumberland, their general, was slain on the field, and also their more immediate leader, Robert Plumpton, eldest son of Sir William Plumpton; and Sir William himself was either taken prisoner or otherwise compelled to throw himself on the mercy of his enemies, which was accorded to him, as on the 18th of May following he received a letter of protection from king Edward IV., and a general pardon shortly afterwards. Being now reputed a loyal subject, in the year 1468, he was restored to his offices of constable of the castle and master forester of the Forest of Knaresborough.

Such were the rapid changes of those times, that in 1471 the king made the earl of Northumberland steward and master forester of the Castle, Lordship, and Forest of Knaresborough; who appointed his brother-in-law, William Gascoigne, of Gokethorpe, his deputy.

The royal officers at Knaresborough were often changed at this time; for in 1472, Richard, duke of Gloucester, was chief seneschal of the king's duchy of Lancaster, and as such, leased to Sir William Plumpton the farm of the corn mills, and office of bailiff of the Burgh of Knaresborough, for the space of twelve years.

In 1480, Sir Robert Plumpton, son of the above named Sir William Plumpton, was appointed constable of the castle and master forester of the Forest of Knaresborough, under the earl of Northumberland; with whom, he and the forces of his district served in the expedition into Scotland, when Berwick was taken, in 1482.

On April 24th, 1489, the earl of Northumberland wrote a pressing note to Sir Robert Plumpton, entreating him to march with his nephew, Sir William Gascoigne, with such armed followers as he could trust, to the town of Thirsk, on the Monday following the date thereof. Sir Robert obeyed the summons, and led the foresters to the assistance of his superior lord, but not in time to prevent the massacre of the earl by an enraged populace, at his manor of Topcliffe, four days after the letter was written. Henceforward Sir Robert was actively employed with the men of Knaresborough in suppressing the insurrection of the Commons, which commenced with the murder of the earl, and was not finally subdued until the battle of Ackworth, in May, 1492. During these troubles Sir Robert demeaned himself in such a manner as to receive a special letter of thanks from the king, "for his great and agreeable services."

King Henry VI. granted to the prior of Bolton a right of common on the Forest of Knaresborough, which was to extend from Washburn head and Timble to the fyle of the said water. The abbot of Fountains had also a grant of common on the forest; the limits and value of which were thus described at the dissolution of that house—"Common of pastore upon Grene hoo morez, from Craven Cross to Craven Keld, and to Washe

burne hed, Plompton Gate to Pawlez Stanez, and to Bartlett's
stile to Padsydebek, and by the Monk wall to Derlay bek and
to the water of Nyde, without stynt; by yere lxxs."*

The prior and abbot each opened mines for lead ore in their
respective grounds, which gave great offence to the foresters in
general, and occasioned numerous complaints. The foresters
not being able to prevent the monks from getting lead ore,
endeavoured to possess themselves of the same privilege, and
obtained a grant to open mines at Middle Tonge, Monga-gill,
Craven Cross, and Greenhow, and worked many of them with
good success. The prior of Bolton, enraged at this, and eager
to make reprisals for former injuries done to his lead works,
employed a number of riotous persons, who made forcible entry
into the premises and took away the ore, cast in the mines,
and did other damage, on the 6th of March, 1529. The
sufferers complained against the prior and his adherents, and
obtained a commission of inquiry, directed to Sir William
Mauleverer and others, who, repairing to the forest for the
purpose of executing the commission, were met by a number
of the prior's party, who threatened the commissioners, and
behaved in so outrageous a manner that they could not proceed with the business at that time.† The dispute is said to

* Memorials of Fountains, vol. i., p. 353.

† "About this time there was a suit in the court of the Duchy of Lancaster, in which Thomas Pulleyn and William Deconson, farmers of the
king's waste, in Knaresburgh Forest, were plaintiffs, against the prior
of Bolton, for trespass on the lead mine and lead ore within the waste
ground called Monghagill, and breach of decree."—*Knaresburghe Forest.*

In the 25th Henry VIII. (A.D. 1533), there was another suit in the same
court; in which William Deconson and Thomas Pulleyne were plaintiffs;
the abbot of Fountains, the prior of Bolton, and others, defendants. The
matter was a disputed claim to lead mines in Knaresburge Forest, Nether-
dale Forest, Craven Keld, Craven Cross, and Brimham.

Disputes respecting boundaries were not uncommon between the foresters
and the monks of Fountains on this part of their domains. A royal commission was issued July 17th, 1502, to ascertain the boundaries between
the Forest of Knaresborough and the free chace of Nidderdale. Sir
Richard Gresham obtained an exemplification of the same, in 1544.

have ended in favour of the prior and abbot; but their triumph was only a short-lived one, as the days of monkery were numbered in England, and in a few years the claims of both parties passed into the king's hands.

During the time of the Norman kings and their successors, down to the reign of James I., the English forests belonging to the crown were kept up and managed without any regard to gain or profit. The object was not to grow good timber, but to rear good deer; not to bring revenue, but to bring majesty amusement and pleasure. Charles I. was always in want of money, and cared little for hunting; and as the crown held the forests uncontrolled, many a good round sum in ready cash did the king derive from the sale of their produce. During the civil wars the forests almost ceased to have any management; nor was that of Knaresborough any exception to the rule.

During the reign of Elizabeth, the timber on the forest suffered severely, from the dishonesty of a person who obtained a grant from government for using all *leafless* trees for the purpose of smelting iron ore. Taking advantage of the ambiguous expression, during the winter season when nearly all trees are leafless, he made fearful havoc amongst the woods, so much so that the forest never afterwards resumed its former sylvan appearance.

In 1616, king James I. granted the castle and lordship of Knaresborough to his son Charles, prince of Wales; who, on his marriage, settled the same in trustees for the use of his queen, Henrietta Maria. On the 10th of January, 1638, only two of the trustees being surviving, they assigned the remainder of a term of 99 years to the earl of Holland, earl of Dorset, lord Savage, Sir Robert Ayton, Sir Richard Wynne, Sir Thomas Hatton, and Sir John Finch. After the decease of Holland, Dorset, Savage, Ayton, and Wynne—Finch, one of the sur-

vivors, released his trust to Hatton, who, in his will, made
dame Mary Hatton, his wife, John Fountain, Henry Winn,
and John Coell his executors, and died possessed of the
premises. The executors proved the will; and on October
20th, 1660, assigned the same to the hon. earl of St. Albans,
Sir Kenelm Digby, Sir John Wintour, Sir Charles Harbord,
Sir Robert Long, Sir Peter Ball, and Sir Henry Wood, in
trust for the said queen mother for life, and after her decease
in trust for king Charles II., his heirs and successors. Queen
Henrietta Maria departed this life August 10th, 1669. On
the 31st of July, 1671, the earl of St. Albans, Sir Robert
Long, Sir John Wintour, Sir Charles Harbord, and Sir Peter
Ball, being the surviving trustees, by command of Charles II.
transferred the premises to Denzill, lord Hollis, William, lord
viscount Broncken, hon. viscount Cornbury, Sir Richard Bell-
ings, John Hervey, William Montague, and John Hall, esquires,
their executors and assigns, for the residue of the term of
99 years, as jointure for queen Catherine, with power to
make leases.

On April 19th, 1697, a lease of the Honour of Knaresborough, under the great seal of the duchy of Lancaster, was
granted to Sir Robert Howard, knight.

On the 25th of March, 1752, king George II. did demise
for the consideration therein mentioned, to Richard, earl of
Burlington, divers cottages and encroachments theretofore made
upon the Forest of Knaresborough; and by another lease, dated
July 2nd, 1757, the same king did demise to William, duke
of Devonshire (who had married, March 28th, 1748, Charlotte,
daughter and sole heir of the said Richard, earl of Burlington),
divers offices, lands, tenements, mines, rents, fines, americaments, heriots, reliefs, waifs, estrays, and divers other profits,
emoluments, privileges, commodities, and advantages, within

the said Honour or Forest of Knaresborough, from the death
of the then Duke of Devonshire, for the term of 99 years, if
lord Richard Cavendish and lord George Cavendish, the second
and third sons of the said duke, or either of them, should so
long live. This lease has since been renewed.

Though the duke of Devonshire, as lessee, exercises and
possesses all manorial powers and rights, yet Her Majesty the
Queen, in right of her duchy of Lancaster, is in reality Lady
of the Manor, Castle, and Honour of Knaresborough.

On Knaresborough Forest was found a capital medal, in-
scribed **JO. KENDALL. RHODI. TVRCVPEL-
ARIVS** round his head in bold relief; reverse, round his arms,
**TEMPORE. OBSIDIONIS. TVRHCORVM.
M,CCCC,LXXX.** The post of Turcopolier, or colonel
of the cavalry, belonged particularly to the English nation.
This family were of note in these parts at that time. This
medal was in Mr. Thoresby's museum, and engraved in his
Ducatus, and bought at his sale by the Duke of Devonshire.*

---

* This medal is engraved in Pinkerton's Medallic History of England,
4to., 1790. Brother John Kendal, Turcopolier of Rhodes, was the com-
missary and deputy of Pope Sextus IV., throughout the globe, in aid of the
expedition against the Turks, in 1480. He was prior of the Hospital of
St. John of Jerusalem, at Clerkenwell, and died in November, 1501.

ENCLOSURE OF THE FOREST OF KNARESBOROUGH.

MANY projects were started at different times for the enclosure of the forest before it was finally accomplished. One of these was in 1618, when a survey was made of all the lands, of which the following is a copy—

"Percelle of the Forrist of Knaresbroughe, measured by Salomond Swale, Anno. Dom. 1618.

	Acres.
All the Forrist betweene Pannall, west, Plumpton and Nidd water, east, Harrigat and Bilton Park, north, conteineth	2901
Harley and Harley Plaine	996
Harrigat Knocks	201
Killinghall Moore	722
Ockden	1062
Shaw Moore besides Sir Guy Palmes' clame conteines	1529
Sir Guy clames there	877
Sir Guy clames in Sandwith	98
Sandwith and Norwood conteines besides	1606
Brame Hill	86
West from Shutt' Nook to a powle	1123
Between that powle and Knocks Cross	568
Between Knowles and Spincke-borne	493
Ingleshaw Banck	16
Between Spinck-borne and Mr. Tho. Graver's woold	159
Cocke-hille	4
Beeston Leaz, with a peece between Wattling streete and it, conteineth	69
Timble Moor, east from Gott' House	283
Sir Tho: Fairfax clame there	65
From thence to Liperley Pik, south from Ragill beck	527
From Liperley Pik west, from a Goot to Gawkhall	69
Bloberhouse, between Kexgill beck and Green sike	886
S——— Marsh	894
Between Kexgill Gill and Ridshaw Gill to Black Sike	1043
Betweene Ridshaw and Corppshaw beck, with the blanck 'neath Ridshaw and Cockbore	990

	Acres.
Mr. Middleton's clame in Tymble Moore	181
Mr. Clapham's clame there	162
The Totall of all the perticulars above-named is	17110
Whereof the clames conteines	3706
So being deducted there remains	13404

Measured by Robert Wray.

The Waste called Poxtonnes, begininge at Walter Waite's barne, and bounded according to the ancient perambulation on the north with Fall Sike, and Greenay Sike, to Greenay Hill, and south to Craven Crosse, Rearecloutes, and Midle-tonge; north-east to Gouldin and May, south to Earle-Seat and by the boundaries of Ramsgill, and north to a longe stone and Oxenbeck to Breakes Sheephouse; and west, north, and east bounded with the copies-hould of Throscross—conteining	6640
From the aforesaid Waite's Barn extendinge east to the Copie-houldes to Red Sike, which bounds Menwith Hilles, and south by William Dayes copie-holde to Meagill, and from Meagill bounded with the copie-houldes to Mr. John Franckland's, and from thence to Ratton Rowe, and so to Mawkin Crosse, from the crosse to Throscrosse, conteining	1719
From the aforesaid Meagill south to Watlin Street at Bloberhouse Lane, and east from thence to Knowles Crosse, by Watlin Street, and so to George Holmes', from thence to the Staupes, and so bounded on the east and north parts to William Dayes, con-teininge	2180
Menwith-hill, Dayrley, and the Holme	230
Swarclif and Low Moore	630
Tonge and Kettlesinge	99
Swinclif and Graystones	211
Yearwith Hollinges	66
Whipley More	314
The totalle of these perticuleres is	12089

In 1651, the principal inhabitants of the forest entered into an agreement for the purchase of the manor and lordship thereof; of which agreement the following is a copy.*

"Knarsbrough.—Note of Agreement betwixt the Trustees and Foresters. Whereas the Manno* and Lordshipp of Knares-burgh, lying within the disforested Forest of Knaresburgh is exposed to be sold by Act of Parliament, and the Coppiholders and Customary tenants having for the most part agreed together to purchase the said Mannour or Lordship, with all the waists,

* Furnished by Mr. R. H. Skaife, of the Mount, York.

comons, rights, royalties, proffits, and advantages whatsoever
thereunto apperteyning to the use and behoofe of all such of
the said Coppiholders theire heires and assignes, and such
other persons as (in default of the said Coppiholders that shall
refuse to purchase theire owne proporciones) doe, and shall
furnish their proportionable share of moneys for defraying the
purchase thereof, and other charges incident thereunto; intending nevertheless to have our Court, and all other advantageous
customes continued amongst us, in such manner as by Councell
learned in the Law shallbe advised, and by us in the behalfe
of the rest of the purchasers consented unto. And in order
thereunto the said Coppiholders and Customary tennants having
elected us—Thomas Stocdale, Esquire, Robert Atkinson, John
Burton, and William Hardestie to be their trustees, to take
the freehold of the said Lordship and Mannour in our names.
And us George Waide, John Mathew, Henry Clint, Thomas
Wescoe, Arthure Burton, William Burton, John Reinolds,
Thomas Simson, Arthure Hardestie, George Spence, Marmaduke Bramley, Leonard Atkinson, Samuel Midgeley, Thomas
Scaife, Francis Day, John Benson, Henry Robinson, Stephen
Gill, Richard Roundell, William Mann, Robert Atkinson, and
Anthony Pullen, to be their Feoffees to article and contract
betwene the said Feoffees and Trustees in all things whatsoever
tending to the securing of the estate soe to be graunted as
aforesaid. To be settled for the only use, behoofe, and advantage of the said purchasers, theire heires and assignes for
ever, without any proffit or advantage to arise or accrew unto
the said Trustees or Feoffees or theire heires. But that all
rents, dutyes, and proffits, certain and casuall, should be disposed of in such manner as the coppiholders, customary tenants,
and purchasers aforesaid shall at their generall meeting which
shallbe from tyme to tyme hereafter appointed. And all the

courts to be held for the said Mannour shall be by them, or
the major part then present, ordered and approved of. And
that it should be in the power of the Coppiholders and Customary tennants to elect, make, and approve of such customs,
orders and Bye-laws for themselves to be governed by, as
heretofore they, with the consent of the kyngs of England and
dukes of Lancaster, former Lords of the said Lordshipp and
Mannour, had power to make, setle, and establish. And likewise to ellect, constitute and make such officers for ordering
of the courts and such other affairs therein as shall be requisite.
Now, we the said Trustees and Feoffees doe hereby declare
that the trust reposed in us is merely for the good of the
said Coppiholders and Customary Tennants: and that we doe
promis faithfully to performe and execute the said trust in all
things: And we the said Trustees doe promis for us and our
heires by Indentures by us on the one parte, and the two-and-
twenty Feoffees before-named of the other parte, To make
declaration of the trust imposed in us, and to give assurance
that from tyme to tyme as there shallbe occasion, we will
seale and perfect such deeds, graunts, and other conveyances
and declarations as shallbe requisite for perfecting of the said
intended worke. The charges incident thereunto defrayed by
the parties concerned. In Witness whereof we have hereunto
subscribed our names the sixteenth day of October, one thousand
six hundred and fifty one.

THO: STOCDALE,

ROBERT ATKINSON.

WI: HARDESTIE.

JOHN BURTON.

RICHARD ROUNDELL.	ARTHURE BURTON.	WILLM: MANN.
THO: WESCOE.	WILLM: BURTON.	FRANCIS DAY.
HEN. CLINT.	ROBERT ATKINSON.	LEONARD ATKINSON

HENRY ROBINSON.   SAMUEL MIDGLEY.   GEORGE SPENCE.
THOMAS SKAYFE.   GEORGE WAID.   ANTHONY PULLEYN.
MARMADUKE BRAMLEY. JOHN MATTHEWS.   THOMAS SIMPSON.
    His × mark.   his ○ mark.
STEPHEN GILL.   JOHN RAYNOWDES.
                                        ARTHUR HARDISTIE

All projects for the purchase of the manor or enclosure of
the forest proved abortive until 1770, in which year an Act
of Parliament was obtained "for dividing and inclosing such
of the open parts of the district called the Forest of Knaresborough, in the County of York, as lie within the eleven
constableries thereof, and for other purposes therein mentioned."
The quantity of waste land is stated to be upwards of 20,000
acres, of which the king in right of his duchy of Lancaster
was seized; and to whom one-tenth part of the commonable
land was to be allotted, in right of the said duchy of Lancaster,
free and exempt from all manner of tithe.   To the king, or
his lessees or grantees were reserved all mines, minerals, and
quarries (except stone quarries), and all rents, services, courts,
perquisites and profits of courts, goods and chattels of felons,
&c.   The custom of seizing heriots was abolished, and a money
payment substituted in its place.   Lands were to be allotted
in lieu of tithes to rectors, vicars, and impropriators.

The stone quarries, woods, and underwoods were vested in
the respective owners of the soil; and all foresterial rights and
privileges belonging to his majesty were abolished.

The boundaries known for the previous forty years were to
be deemed the true and permanent boundaries.

Commonage enjoyed for the previous forty years to establish
a right.

Stone quarries and watering places were to be provided; and
the public roads were to be sixty feet in breadth at least, "in
the clear between the fences."

Land was to be set out and sold by auction for the purpose of paying all expenses of obtaining the Act of Parliament, making the ring fences of the allotments, and the public roads and highways.

The commissioners appointed were William Hill, of Tadcaster, gentleman, Joseph Butler, of Bowthorp, surveyor, William Chippendale, of Ripley, surveyor, John Flintoff, of Boroughbridge, surveyor, and Thomas Furniss, of Otley, gentleman.

The surveyors were Richard Richardson, of Darlington, William Chippendale, of Ripley, and John Flintoff, of Boroughbridge. By another act, obtained in 1774, Richard Richardson was appointed a commissioner.

Their Award was completed and signed by William Hill, Joseph Butler, William Chippendale, John Flintoff, and Thomas Furness, August 19th, 1778.*

In 1789, another act was obtained for the purpose of reviving certain powers granted in the first act, and to make the two

---

* The Award is a ponderous affair, consisting of 53 closely written skins of parchment. The stone quarries are first named, next the watercourses, then the carriage roads—public and private, and afterwards the footroads. At No. 8 the Award of allotments begins: the first entries relate to exchanges between the king and Robert Stockdale. Alexander Wedderburne, Esq., receives an allotment of 271a., 2r., 38p., in Harrogate, in lieu of tithes; James Beckwith is the only one of that name mentioned in the Award, and he receives only three small allotments, about 25 acres. Six of the name of Bilton have lands awarded to them. The Blue Coat Boys' Charity, at York, has three allotments, about 83 acres: Clint school, 3a., 2r., 19p. The family of Day have 12 allotments at, and near Day Ash. Robert Dyneley, Esq., has two allotments in Pannal, near Beckwithshaw. Francis Fawkes, Esq., has 30 allotments, chiefly in Norwood and Timble. Lady Frankland, 84a., 1r., 4p., in Thruscross, at Willow Bog freehold. Mary Fairfax, 6a., 0r., 10p., in Pannal, at Beckwith Head. Joshua Hardisty had 21 allotments, chiefly in Norwood. The Devisees of Sir John Ingilby, Bart., deceased, 23 allotments. William Lawrence, Esq., had 10a., 2r., 18p. in Clint. Five of the name of Pullan receive allotments. Robert Stockdale had five allotments, near Starbeck. John Watson, Esq., had six allotments adjoining Bilton Park. Andrew Wilkinson, Esq., five allotments, in Killinghall, near Grain Well. William Williamson, five allotments, in Bilton-with Harrogate, on Jenny Plain, and one at Hampsthwaite, near the Hollings. Henry and Richard Wright receive four allotments, one of them of 101 acres, at Birch Crag Beck. Sir Cecil Wray, Bart., receives an allotment of 2,751 acres, at Hanging, in Thruscross.

first acts more effectual, from which it appears that four of the commissioners, Butler, Chippendale, Flintoff, and Furness were dead; and this act gave power to appoint another, two being required to render any of their actions valid. John Bainbridge, of Pannal, surveyor, was appointed. By this means certain exchanges of land which had taken place were ratified.

The Enclosure and its effects are thus described by a contemporary writer.*

The Forest of Knaresborough till the year 1775, consisted of a great extent of ancient enclosed land, comprised within eleven constableries, or hamlets; to which belonged a tract of upwards of thirty thousand acres of common, between the river Nidd on the north and the river Wharf on the south, whereon Knaresbrough and several other towns, not within the eleven constableries, claimed and had exercised a right of common and turbary equally with the owners of property within these eleven constableries. This waste in its open state yielded the inhabitants fuel, and pasturage for their sheep, horses, and stock of young cattle; and some opulent yeomanry profited exceedingly thereby; but to the necessitous cottager and indigent farmer, it was productive of more inconvenience than advantage—if not to themselves at least to the public at large, who were by that means deprived in a great measure of the exertions of the farmer, and the labour of the cottager and their families; for it afforded their families a little milk, yet they would attempt to keep a horse and a flock of sheep. The first enabled them to stroll about the country in idleness, and the second, in the course of every three or four years, were so reduced by the rot, and other disasters, that upon the whole they yielded no profit.

* General View of the Agriculture of the West Riding, 1794.

In 1770, an act was obtained to divide and inclose this
extensive waste, and the powers thereof committed to no less
than five commissioners, and three surveyors, all, or most of
them unequal to the undertaking, from whom both great delay
and expense were incurred. After four years had elapsed, an
amendment of this act became necessary, which was obtained
in 1774. Thereby a sixth commissioner was named, who had
been appointed a surveyor by the first act, and who had thought
proper to execute his duty by a deputy. In 1775, the commissioners made out a description of their intended allotments,
and in or about the year 1778, they executed their award,
which unfortunately was extremely defective : but with all these
inconveniences, the generality of proprietors to whom allotments
were made, and particularly the small ones, set about a spirited
line of improvement. The poor cottager and his family exchanged their indolence for active industry, and obtained extrava-
gant wages; and hundreds were induced to offer their labour
from distant quarters; labourers of every denomination, joiners,
carpenters, smiths, and masons, poured in and met with constant
employment. And though before the allotments were set out,
several riots had happened, the scene was quite changed; for
with all the foreign assistance, labour kept extravagantly high,
and the work was executed defectively, and in a few years
many inclosures almost prostrate, and of course required making
a second time. All these circumstances taken together were
a heavy burthen upon the allotments, and in general rendered
them very dear purchases. The forest, however, got in a great
measure cultivated, and the public soon derived a great increase
of product, though at the expense of individuals. A turnpike
road was opened through the centre of the forest, by which an
easy communication was attained between Knaresborough and
Skipton in Craven, and the manufacturing towns in the north-

east of Lancashire. In consequence the product has increased beyond conception, the rents are more than trebled, and the population has augmented to an astonishing degree; for the old inclosed lands, as well as the common, being exonerated from tithes, a full scope was given to spirited cultivation.

COURTS AND COURT ROLLS.

THE Honour of Knaresborough is parcel of the duchy of Lan.
caster, and includes the Forest, the Forest Liberty, the Manor
or Soke, and the Borough of Knaresborough. The Forest
Liberty is situate on the north-eastern side of the river Nidd,
and comprises Great Ouseburn, Farnham, Staveley, Burton-
Leonard, Stainley-with-Cayton, Brearton, Scotton, Scriven-with-
Tentergate, and Arkendale. The limits of the Forest have
varied at different times, as grants of portions of the same
were made to different individuals. Thus Ribston, Plumpton,
Swinden, Dunkeswick, Weeton, Castley, Rigton, Stainburn,
Lindley, and Blubberhouses, were in early times separated
from the forest, though they were all included within the
boundary in the perambulation of 1767. In the last year of
Philip and Mary (1558), we find the names of the detached
places thus entered on the Court Roll—

Lyndley.

Castley.

Rygton, Brackenbarght-cum-
Blayberrycroft.

Lyndley-et-Stainburn.

Weeton, Wescowhill-with-
Hoby.

Dunckeswyke-cum-Hill-
thwaite Hill.

Plompton-et-Rybbeston Parva.

Swindone.

Brayme-cum-Newsome.

The Forest proper, in early times was divided into three
constabularies—those of

THRUSCROSS, with seven hamlets, viz.: Hill, Bramley, Padside, Thornthwaite, Menwith, Holme, and Darley.

CLINT, with five hamlets—Birstwith, Felliscliffe, Fearnhill, Hampsthwaite, and Rowden.

KILLINGHALL, with four hamlets—Beckwith, Rossett, Bilton, and Heywraygate.

These were afterwards divided into the following eleven constabularies—Bilton-with-Harrogate, Beckith-with-Rossett, Killinghall, Clint, Hampsthwaite, Birstwith, Felliscliffe, Thruscross, Menwith-with-Darley, Timble, and Clifton.

The Court for the Forest is styled the Sheriff Torne, or Great Court Leet, and is held in the castle of Knaresborough twice a year, within a month after Easter and at Michaelmas. The adjourned Court, called "The Grand Inquest," is held in different parts of the Forest, as fixed at the Sheriff Torne. Constables for the district were formerly appointed at this Court, but this part of its power was taken away by an Act of Parliament, passed in 1842. This was also a Court for the recovery of debts, and carrying on of civil actions, and was held every Wednesday three weeks for the Forest and Forest Liberty: the county courts have entirely absorbed this part of the business. Though shorn of much of its former greatness this Court cannot cease to exist, as the greatest part of the land in the Forest is held by copy of Court Roll; and the principal business now is receiving surrenders, admitting copyhold tenants, presenting nuisances, receiving rents, and fines for encroachments, &c. The officers are—a high steward, a learned steward, an under steward, and a bailiff; a grave and bedel are chosen annually by the jury.

The Records of the Honour extend from the 16th Edward III. to the present time; those previous to that time were destroyed by John Lilburne, a partisan of the earl of Lancaster, who

stole into the castle with a few followers, about the year 1815,
but being besieged therein, and seeing no prospect of relief,
surrendered the same to Nicholas de Gray, sheriff of Yorkshire,
after having destroyed all the records and written memorials
of the liberties, customs, and privileges of the Honour. These
were however again in some measure restored, so far as they
could be collected from the memories of men then living, and
enrolled at a Court held at Knaresborough, May 10th, 1867.*

The earliest roll we have seen bears date 16th Edward III.
(1342), and from that time down to the year 1708, the rolls
are yet in existence, and generally in a good state of preservation.   These are preserved, along with a quantity of books
and papers belonging to the Record or Debt Court, in a room
in the ruins of the castle.   From 1708 to the present time
the transactions of the Courts are entered in large books, which
are kept in the office of the under steward.   The rolls are
written on slips of parchment, nine or ten inches wide, and
about two feet in length; some of them contain seven or eight
membranes, which are stitched together at one end, rolled up,
and tied with a string.   First comes the heading of the roll,†
then the names of the Jurors—first of the Forest, next of the
Liberty; in the year 1668 the names of the forest towns are
entered in the following order—

* See "Ancient Customs, &c."

† The following heading is copied from the first page of the first volume
in the steward's office—
"Turnus sive Curia Magna Leta dominæ reginæ communiter vocata Le
Sherriffe Torne, tenta pro dicta domina regina, pro Honore sua de Knares-
brough, infra castrum suum ibidem, die Jovis, scilicet, vicesimo, secundo
die Aprilis, anno regni dictæ dominæ reginæ, Anno Dei gratia Magnæ
Brittanniæ, Franciæ et Hiberniæ, septimo, annoque Domini, 1708, coram
Ricardo, comite Burlington, capitale Senescallo Honoris prædictæ."
In Vol I., p. 5, occurs the following variation—
"Curiæ dominæ nostriæ, Annæ, Dei gratia Magnæ Brittaniæ, etc. Re-
ginæ, tenta pro foresta et libertate suis de Knaresbrough prædicta infra
castrum suum ibidem."—16 June, 1708.

Killinghall, Vill.	Thruscross, Vills.
Bilton-cum-Harrogate, hamlet.	Menwith-cum-Darley, hamlet.
Clint, Vills.	Timble-cum-Fewston, Vills.
Hampsthwaite, hamlet.	Clifton-cum-Norwood, hamlet.
Birstwith, hamlet.	Pannall.

Next are entered the Inquisitions made, and the "pains" laid upon the transgressors. In the above year these were only seven in number, of which the following is a specimen—

The jury present Richard Broune de Staveley p. p. *mittend equos suos depasturare in le corn feild. Ida est in mca, cura pro sit,* &c. Fine vij.d.

Then follows an Inquisition with a long muster roll of names attached, the crime of whose owners had been "*p. fodien d sespites sup. Foresta,*" and for which they are in mercy, and ammerced in sums varying from 2d. to 7d. each. William Hardestie de Killinghall was ammerced at the same time 6d., "*pro mitend filices super comai.*"

Then follow the records of the Court for the recovery of debts, &c., held every three weeks.

At the Court held "Pasche, Anno. Eliz. 16th (1576)," the following "pains" were laid—

"FORESTA DE KNARESBURGHE."

"Paynes sett by the greate Inquest of the Forest of Knaresburgh, at the Sherif Tourne holden their.

A paine laid that no person or persons dwellinge or inhabitinge within the said Forrest, nor any person dwellinge without the same, (the quenes majesties copyholders and freeholders ther exceptid,) shall within the boundes and lymyttes of the said Forest, cocke,—that is, go abrode in wynter season, in, and thoroughe the woodes and other places within the precyncte of the said Forest with his bowe, his boltes or arrowes, pretendynge to kill the woodcock, oneles he or they have a speciall lycense by writinge under the hand of the quenes majesties head steward

ther, or under the handes of the deputie stewardes and learned
steward jointlie, upon pane to forfeit to the quenes majestie xxˢ·
And the same partie so lycensed not to take, kill, or distroie
anie haire, conye, ffesaunt, or partridge, or anie beaste or fowle
of warraunt, upon paine likewise to forfeit xˢ· And the same
partie so lycensed beinge disposed to sell suche woodcockes
or other foule as he dothe take or kill within the said forest,
to send or carie and sell them to the heade steward, deputie
stewards or learned stewarde aforesaid, or to gentlemen or
other inhabytantes within the said forest, for ther money before
any other straungers, upon paine to forfeit likewise xxˢ·

A paine laide that no person or persons inhabitinge within
the said forest nor any person dwellinge without the same,
not beinge the quenes majesties copyholder or freholder ther,
shall take or kill anie partridge within the said forest withe
settinge spanyell or nett, or by dryvinge the same withe horse
or paynted clothe, or by anie other policie, practise, or devise,
except he or they be speciallie licensed by writinge under thande
of the heade stewarde, or under the handes of the deputie
stewardes or learned steward, or under the handes of two of
them, upon paine to forfeit (to) the quenes majestie xxˢ· And
the partie so licensed, if he be disposed to sell, to sell them
to the stewardes, gentlemen and inhabitants of the said forest
before anie other, upon paine to forfeit xiijˢ· iiijᵈ·

A paine sett that no straunger or forener dwellinge without
the said forest, nor any person inhabitinge within the same,
shall follow the trace of any haire in the snowe, havenge with
him any dogge or bytche, or carienge with him or about him
any bowe, bolte, or arrowe, or any other engyne, or devise
to kill the same hayre, upon paine to forfeit to the quenes
majestie xˢ· And if any straunger or inhabytant, as is before-
said, by such tracynge, do, with dogge or bytche, or by any

other meane or devise, take or kill any haire in the snare within the said forest, to forfeit to the quenes majestie for everie offence xiij[s.] iiij[d.]

A paine sett that no person or persons dwellinge within the said forest shall kepe or have in his house, or otherwise any fyrrett, cony, haire, or other nett or netts, except he or they have a lawfull graunt, warraunt, or lycense to have and kepe conyes within the said forrest, or that he or they have conies within his or ther freehold ther, or that he or they be warrenner or conykeper to suche person as haithe suche lawfull graunt, warraunte or license, upon payne to forfeyt to the quenes majestie xx[s.]"

To this Honour was also attached a peculiar jurisdiction, or Court of Probate, extending over the whole of the forest, and partially over the Forest Liberty, in which probate of wills and administrations were granted by the steward, and which Court continued to exercise its functions until the year 1858, when all the wills preserved at Knaresborough, from the year 1640 until that period, were removed to Wakefield, where they are at present deposited.

For the purposes of tracing the descent of property, or the pedigree of families within the district to which they belong, the Court Rolls are invaluable documents, as they contain the admittance of every tenant to every copyhold estate, whether by purchase or inheritance, and a copy of the will of every person dying possessed of any copyhold estate; with other matters, such as fines for offences committed within the jurisdiction, and give, as it were, a moral and social history of the district from the age of the third Edward to the present time. To form even a brief abstract of the matter contained in these rolls would be a labour of great length and some difficulty, yet we are convinced that until that be done, the history of the Forest of Knaresborough will never be completely written.

THE ANCIENT CUSTOMS OF THE FOREST

OF KNARESBOROUGH.

THIS code of ancient laws and customs, some of them peculiar to the Forest of Knaresborough, extant from the time of Edward III., was further settled, ordered and decreed, by a commission, in the fifth year of the reign of Elizabeth, directed to the right honourable Henry, earl of Cumberland, Sir William Ingilby, knight, and others, to inquire by the oaths of twelve honest and indifferent persons, dwelling within the said Forest of Knaresborough, of the said ancient customs and things, which of old time had been used within the same. The enquiry was held, and a final order made therein, May 24th, 1563.

That is to say—that after the death of every customary tenant, dying seized of any messuage, parcel of the said lordship or manor, whether there be any lands lying to it or not, that the officer there for the time being shall seize, to the use of the queen's majesty, her heirs and successors, his best beast,—that is to say, horse, ox, or cow, or any beast of the like kind for his heriot,* that is or shall be, either pastured

---

* Jacob, in his *Law Dictionary*, quoting Spellman, says this word is from the Saxon *here*, an army, and *gate*, a beast: and signified originally a tribute given to the lord of a manor for his better preparation for war. Sir Edward Coke makes "heriot" the lord's beast, from *here*, lord. The custom of seizing heriots was abolished on the enclosure of the forest, and a money payment substituted in lieu thereof.

H

within the said Forest of Knaresborough or elsewhere, wheresoever the same shall be found.

And also, that every customary tenant dying seized of any manner of building, and of six acres of customary lands there, shall give such his best beast for his heriot, as before is rehearsed, in such manner and form as before is expressed; albeit the buildings upon the same be no messuage.

Also, that every customary tenant dying seized of six acres of lands there, or above, shall pay for his heriot his best beast as aforesaid.

And also, that every customary tenant dying seized of less lands there than six acres, whether he have any building upon the same or not, so that the building be no messuage, shall pay for every acre two shillings, for and in the name of his heriot, and none other heriot.

Also, that every customary tenant dying seized of more messuages than one, or of more acres of land than seven, shall pay but one heriot, how many messuages soever he have, or how many acres soever he have.

Also, if any customary tenant die seized of any customary lands there, in fee simple, if the next heir, by himself or by his friends, come not at the next court, or before the year and day expired, after the death of his or their ancestors, to make his relief, that then the said lands shall be seized into the hands of the lord of the said manor, and the next heir not to have them until he pay three years' rent, for and in the name of a fine, unto the lord of the same manor, over and besides his relief.

Also, that no customary tenant may let his customary lands to another person, by word, indenture, or other writing; but only by surrender in the court there, for thirty-one years or under, and not above, at any one time; whereupon the accustomed fine, which is threepence for every acre thereof, shall be from time to time answered unto the lord, upon the grant of every such lease.

Also, that if any customary tenant do suffer any person or persons to dwell and inhabit in any builded house or cottage, by the space of one quarter of a year, not being any messuage-stead or ancient building decayed, that then the said new building shall be forfeit to the lord, after the lawful term of the said person or persons, the same new building shall be expired, forfeited, or surrendered.

Also, if any tenant, seized of any customary land whereupon any great trees of the age of twenty-four years or above, be, or shall be growing, shall cut them down and sell them, or any of them, he shall grievously be amerced;* but yet nevertheless, it shall be lawful to and for the said customary tenants to take fire-wood meet for fuel, growing upon his or their customary lands, to burn in their houses, upon the same lands and holds, and to take trees growing upon the same, meet for repair, or to build his or their messuages or ancient buildings there.

Also, if it chance any customary tenant there at any time hereafter, to do or commit any felony, or any other act, for which by the laws of this realm of England, he or they should lose their lives, if the heir of the said customary tenant, after a year and a day expired after the death of his said ancestor, come into this court before the chancellor and council for the time being, and offer to make his fine there, or in the court at Knaresborough; that then, upon petition made to the said chancellor and council of this court, he shall be admitted tenant thereof, paying to the queen's majesty, her heirs or successors, for his fine, six years' rent for the said lands, besides relief.

* This custom was abolished by the act for the enclosure of the forest, by which all trees, woods, and underwoods, were declared to belong to the persons holding the lands on which they were growing.

Also, if any customary tenant seized of any customary lands, and take a wife, and die seized of the same, having issue by her, that is heir to the same lands, that then the said wife may come after the death of her said husband, into the court of the lord there, and there make a fine; and at her prayer shall be admitted tenant of the whole or third part, at her liberty. If she pray the whole, then she to have the whole lands for her dower, during her life, if she keep herself sole and unmarried; and, if she marry, then she to have but the third part of the said customary lands, paying for every messuage twopence, and for every acre threepence, and so after the quantity of the land by her prayed. And if she make fine for the whole lands, then the wife to have no part of her husband's goods, but at his will and pleasure.

And also, it is further ordered, that the lords, owners and occupiers of all and singular manors and lordships, that do adjoin upon the said Forest of Knaresborough, and have used to have enter common there, and which have enclosed their common and waste, belonging to the said manor or lordship, from the said forest, shall be secluded from having or using any common within the said forest, except they have special charter grants for the same.

Also, that the customary tenants, seized of any lands within the said Forest of Knaresborough, and no other, ought, and may choose the grave * and bedel † of the said manor of Knaresborough, at the next Court Baron, holden within the said manor of Knaresborough yearly, after the feast of St. Michael the archangel, and at no other time.

---

* *Grave* is the same as *greve*, and is from the Saxon *gerefa*, signifying power and authority; almost synonymous with sheriff.

† *Bedel* is the Saxon *bydal*, a cryer or messenger of court, who cites men to appear and answer.

And the said grave and bedel to gather the estreats accustomed, make impanels for the lord, and between party and party, to arrest or seize all felons' goods within the said forest, and to do all other things to their office belonging.

Also, that every customary tenant within the said Forest of Knaresborough may surrender his customary lands into the hands of the lord, by the head steward, learned steward, clerk of the court, grave, or bedel of the said Forest of Knaresborough, being nominated, known, and appointed; and in peril of death to two tenants of the same tenure, without the grave or bedel, or any other the officers aforesaid, to the use of any person or persons, for term of years, for term of life, or in fee simple, and not in fee tail.

Also, that every customary tenant dying seized of any customary lands, within the said Forest of Knaresborough, in fee simple, shall pay for his relief, for every messuage eightpence, and for every acre of land twelvepence, and so after the rate.

Also, that he to whom any surrender is made of any messuage in fee simple, shall pay for his fine fourpence, and for every acre sixpence, and for every pennyworth a penny, and for every halfpennyworth one halfpenny, and so after the rate; and shall do suit to the Lord's Court, and do fealty, pay heriot, take upon him the office of grave and bedel, when he shall be chosen; and to do other customs, as hath been used.

Also, that he to whom any surrender is made of any messuage for term of life, for term of years, or of any reversion, shall pay for every messuage twopence, and for every acre threepence, and so after the rate.

And also, that every customary tenant may make a surrender to any person or persons, of his customary lands, after his death and his wife's death, or either of them, by force whereof he and she shall hold the land for term of his and her life;

and he to whom the surrender is made shall have but one reversion, after their deaths, and shall pay for his fine, as for one reversion, and the wife to pay one fine, as tenant for term of life, and one heriot to be paid of the goods of him that maketh the surrender.

Also, that every customary tenant may surrender to the grave or bedel of the said Forest of Knaresborough, his customary lands, by bill indented, to the use of his wife, children, servants, or debtors; and that the same customary tenant may command the same grave or bedel to keep the same surrender or surrenders in his hand, unto the next Court Baron, or court called the Sheriff's-turn, to be holden next after the feast of St. Michael, next after the surrender made, and not to present the same, unless the said customary tenant die before the said court; and if the customary tenant be living at the said court, then the surrender to be void.

Also, every customary tenant may surrender his customary lands to the grave or bedel of the said Forest of Knaresborough, to the use of any person or persons, declaring by bill indented any condition to be performed by him that maketh the surrender before the next Court Baron and Sheriff's-turn, to be holden next after the feast of St. Michael, next after the said surrender made, if the same intent, condition, or meaning, be performed before the said Court Baron; that, then the said surrender to be void; and if it be not performed, then the grave or bedel to present the same surrender simply, without any intent or condition.

Also, that if any customary tenant make a surrender, upon any consideration, to the grave, bedel, or two tenants of the same tenure, by bill indented, not restraining the said grave, bedel, or tenants, to make the surrender at the next court, if they present not the same surrender at the next court after the surrender made; then the grave, bedel, or tenants to pay to the lord for a fine twenty shillings, and for not presenting at the second court other twenty shillings, and for not presenting at the third court forty shillings; and that then the said grave, bedel, or tenants to forfeit to the lord all his, or their, lands.

Also, that every customary tenant may implead one another, in the Court of Knaresborough, for debt, if the debt or damage amount not over or above the sum of one hundred shillings; and that the party defendant may be arrested by his body, to answer the said debt or damage.

And that all customary tenants within the said forest shall prove their testaments in the court of the lord, and shall take letters of administration there of the goods of the dead.*

And also, that if any customary tenant suffer his messuage or ancient building to decay, and suffer the same house to lie waste by the space of one year, and by three Court Barons, holden then next ensuing, the customary tenant shall forfeit the same house to the lord.

Also, that if any tenant die seized of any customary lands, and have issue divers daughters, they being not married at the time of the death of their ancestor, the eldest daughter shall have the lands.

And if the eldest daughter be married in the life of her ancestor, then the land shall descend to all the other daughters unmarried, and not to the eldest; and if all the same other daughters be married in the life of their ancestor, but one, then that one, so unmarried in the life of her ancestor, shall have the land to her and her heirs for ever.

And if all the daughters be married in the life of their

* This custom was abolished by Act 20 and 21 Vic., cap. 77, intitled, "An act to amend the law relating to probates and letters of administration in England."

ancestor, then the eldest daughter shall have all the lands, as she heir to her ancestor.

And also, that the next friend of the party of the mother, to whom the heritage may not descend, shall have the custody of the heir, and shall find surety in the court of the lord, to give the profits of the land to the heir, at his full age.

Also, that if any man hath title to demand any customary lands, he shall make his relief; and immediately upon that, he shall make fine to the lord, for to have certain lawful men of the same hold to try his right; and shall pay for every poll a penny, to the clerk of the court of Knaresborough.

Also, that all the customary tenants inhabiting within the same forest, ought to make suit to one of the king's mills, within the said Forest of Knaresborough, of all the grains growing within the said forest.

And also, that the customary tenants, within the said forest, shall have common of pasture for all kind of cattle, except swine, without number, in, and upon, through, and by, all the said forest, belonging to their messuages, ancient buildings and lands there, as they have used time out of mind of man, and shall pay yearly a certain rent, called gelde,* in consideration of the same.

Also, that all forfeitures, by order of the common laws, that is to say, alienation by deed and livery of seizin, escheats, refusing to take the office of the grave or bedel, or refusing to make the mill-dam, being required by the lord's officers, or by the farmers of the said mills, to be forfeits of the said customary lands.

* This payment, under the same name, is yet received by the tax-gatherer of the township of Clint, from certain houses in Scaro, Birthwaite, and Ripley, at the rate of 2d. per homestead; hence it is evident that these householders, though situated outside the forest, had yet a common right within it.

Also, that all person and persons, having any lands or tenements bounding upon the said forest, ought to make their fences between their said lands and the said forest.

Also, that the constable of the Castle of Knaresborough, or his deputy, shall from henceforth ride once in three years, to and about the metes and bounds of the said forest, accompanied with the ancient persons inhabiting within the said forest, and they to take, every one of them, a child or boy behind every of them, of the age of ten years, or thereabouts.

Also, that after the death of every customary tenant, his next heir ought to have for his heir-looms—the best wain, the best cowpe, the best plough head yoke bolt and shackle, and one team, the best cupboard, the best table, and best standing bed, best cawderne, the best pot, the best arke, the best charger of pewter, and the best bason and ewer, if any be.

And also, that the customary tenants within the said forest may, at all time and times, as need shall require, after the grave or bedel have made their drifts* within the said forest, drive again the cattle pasturing of the said common, within the said forest, and them impound; taking of every beast there pasturing, and have no right of common, twelve-pence—whereof one half to the lord, the other to those that taketh pains to drive as is aforesaid.

And also, that no customary tenant, or other which holdeth any lands or tenements, within the said Forest of Knaresborough, shall let any part or parcel of his said customary lands to any stranger or foreigner, inhabiting within the said Forest of Knaresborough, to the intent to have common of pasture within the said forest, or to take any manner of cattle to gist.†

* "Drift of the forest" is a view or examination of what cattle are in the forest, that it may be known whether it be surcharged or not, and whose the beasts are, and whether they are commonable.

† Gist, or agist, signifies to take in and feed the cattle of strangers in the king's forests, and to gather up the money due for the same.

And also, that the head steward, learned steward, clerk of the court of Knaresborough, for the time being, may examine a woman married, being in the presence of the grave or bedel, or two of the queen's majesty's customary tenants, and of her take surrender accordingly.

And where also the queen's majesty's tenants are bounden by the tenure of their lands, having wood delivered for piles and windings, to repair, maintain, and uphold certain mill dams, within the said Forest of Knaresborough—that is to say, the mill dams of Killinghall, Hampsthwaite, Thruscross, and Fewston; that the same tenants so bounden, shall have wood delivered to them, by the queen's majesty's officers there, for the time being, for piles and windings, as is aforesaid, for the repairing and maintaining of the same mills, when and so often as the same mill-dams shall need to be repaired and upholden, according to the ancient custom always used within the same Forest of Knaresborough.

And finally, that all laudable customs between party and party within the said Forest of Knaresborough, beforetime used and not in this decree declared or expressed, being in no case prejudicial or hurtful to the queen's majesty, her heirs or successors, may lawfully, at all times hereafter, for ever, be used, and be in as full strength and force as though they had and were here within this decree been named, expressed, or declared.

HARROGATE.

THE district included under this term is the most populous and important in the Forest of Knaresborough, containing the medicinal springs and the fashionable town of Harrogate.

The proper name of the township is Bilton-with-Harrogate. It is bounded towards the north and north-east by Oakbeck and the river Nidd, on the west by the parish of Pannal, on the south and east by the brook Crimple, the township of Plumpton, and out-lying portions of Knaresborough and Scriven. It was formerly a township in the parish of Knaresborough, but since the great increase of its population it has been detached, and divided into district parishes.

Bilton was in early times the more important place, as is evident from it being first in the name of the township; recently it has been cast into the shade by its more important and populous neighbour. At the time of the Domesday survey it was held by Giselbert Tyson, and a king's thane, whose respective portions are thus recorded—

LAND OF GISELBERT TYSON.

"Manor. In Biletone, Gamelbar had three carucates and a half to be taxed. Land to two ploughs. Giselbert Tyson has these lands, but they are all waste, only Bilton pays three shillings."[*]

LAND OF THE KING'S THANES.

"Manor. In Billeton, Archil had three carucates of land and

* Bawdwen's Dom. Bac., p. 194.

a half to be taxed, Land to two ploughs. The same now
has it, and it is waste. Value in King Edward's time, ten
shillings."*

Soon afterwards the fee of Tyson came into the king's hands,
and a royal park was formed at Bilton.

At the time of the above survey Harrogate appears to have
been too insignificant to be mentioned. The first time we find
it in any document is in the Stuteville charter, about the year
1200, where it is designated "Harelow."† It is now one of
the most noted inland watering places in England, situate on
the western verge of the great plain of York, about 3 miles
from Knaresborough, 15 from Leeds, and 21 and 11 respectively
from the cities of York and Ripon; about midway between the
east and west seas; and at nearly an equal distance of 200
miles each from London, Edinburgh, and Dublin.

The town is scattered over a piece of lofty table land, along
the bottom and up the corresponding slope of a small valley,
without much order or regularity of design; yet presenting from
all points of view an open, airy, elegant, and substantial appearance. The buildings are of stone, which gives them an air of
massiveness and durability; while the peculiarity of their situation will prevent them from ever becoming crowded, as the

* Bawdwen's Dom. Boc., p. 229.
† As recently as 1558, in the Knaresborough Court Rolls, we find the
name written "Harloo-cum-Bylton Banks." The name appears to be
capable of many derivations. Hargrove says it is from *Haywra*, the park
of that name in the forest above, and *gate*, a road leading to it.—*Hay-
wragate*, by contraction *Harrogate*. Thoresby derives it from the Saxon
Hearthg, an uncut grove or thicket of trees, and *gate*, as above—the road
through the thick wood. More probably its etymon is the same as that
of *Harlow*, the soldier's hill, and *gate*, the road to it—simply, the military
way from the Roman road (probably on a British trackway) which passed
through, or close to it, from Adel to Catterick. In the reign of Edward II.
we find it written *Harlowgate*, which strengthens the last etymology. In
1461, *Harrogat* and *Harrygate*. In the 28th of Henry VIII., *Harrogate*,
as at present. In the 13th Elizabeth, *Harrowgait*, which orthography
was prevalent less than a century ago, and with the exception of the last
syllable, yet occasionally occurs.

parks, or Stray, comprising two hundred acres of land, are, by act of the legislature, for ever devoted to the exercise and recreation of the residents and visitors of this place; so that, whatever may be its ultimate growth, it will always possess the features of a village. The situation is lofty and pleasant, commanding extensive views of the surrounding country, and within easy distance of some of the finest scenery and most interesting places in Yorkshire. From its height, and unsheltered situation, the climate is cold in winter; yet the air is always pure and bracing, and probably has a large share in the restoration of invalids to health. It is remarkably free from epidemics, and the inhabitants are generally long-lived and healthy.*

Originally a small scattered hamlet, this place has outgrown all its neighbours in size and importance, owing principally to the springs of medicinal water with which providence has stored its not otherwise fruitful soil.

Very rarely do we find the name of this place mentioned before the discovery of its first spring of mineral water, by Sir William Slingsby, in the latter part of the sixteenth century. The exact date of this discovery has not been clearly ascertained. "Edmund Dean, doctor in physick," in his *Spandarine Anglica*, published in 1626, says—"It was discovered first about fifty years ago, by one Mr. William Slingsby, who had travelled in

* The salubrity of the air of Harrogate is too self-evident to need proof. The following list of aged people, long resident in the town, was made in 1868; it included 46 females and 45 males; of the females—one was 89, one 88, one 87, one 86, two 85, three 83, five 82, two 81, six 80, six 79, two 78, one 77, three 76, five 75, two 74, one 73, one 71, and one 70; their united ages being 3634 years, or an average of 79 years each. The males were—one 94, one 91, one 88, three 86, one 84, two 83, two 82, one 80, one 79, one 78, six 75, one 73, six 72, one 71, and seven 70; making a total of 2698 years, or an average of 77 years each.

April 23rd, 1868.—Died at Park Parade, Harrogate, Hannah Blackburn, aged 95 years.

July 9th, 1868.—Died at the Star Inn, Harrogate, George Dodsworth, aged 94 years.

Germany in his younger years, seen, and been acquainted with
theirs; and as he was of an ancient family near the place, so
he had fine parts and was a capable judge." This gives the
year 1576 as the time of discovery, which is 20 years too early.

Sir William Slingsby was the seventh son of Francis Slingsby,
Esq., and Mary, only sister of Thomas and Henry Percy, successively earls of Northumberland, and born at Scriven, January
20th, 1562. Of his youthful years we have very little information. He studied the law at Grey's Inn, and afterwards made
the tour of the continent. When travelling in Italy, in 1594,
he was imprisoned for a time in the castle of Como, but soon
contrived to make his escape. In 1596, he took part in the
great expedition which sailed from England to revenge upon
the king of Spain the injuries he would have done to England,
had his invincible armada been successful. The rich and
important town of Cadiz was taken by storm and given up
to plunder. The damage inflicted on the Spaniards by this
enterprise was calculated at nine millions sterling; besides the
indignity which that proud and ambitious people suffered from
the sacking of one of their chief towns, and the destroying in
their harbour of a fleet of great force and value.

In 1597, through the influence of his father, captain Slingsby
was elected burgess to represent his native borough of Knaresborough in parliament.

On the accession of James I. to the throne of England,
captain Slingsby appears to have exchanged his active life of
a naval officer for that of a courtier; and in 1603 was appointed
honorary carver to Anne of Denmark, queen consort.

In 1617, he was appointed lieutenant of the county of Middlesex; and in the same year the family pedigree, a work of great
labour and research, was compiled under his superintendence.
This year also he was married to Elizabeth, daughter of Sir

Stephen Board, of Board Hill, in the county of Sussex, by whom he had three sons and one daughter. He was knighted by king James, in 1608, and died in August, 1634. He was buried amongst his ancestors in the Slingsby chapel, in Knaresborough church, where an elegant monument yet remains to his memory.

The discovery of the medicinal spring at Harrogate proves that he was a man of extensive knowledge, as well as close observation; hundreds of men, during the lapse of ages, had seen the water stealing along the marsh, leaving its ferruginous deposit along the sides of its uncertain course, yet none of them had the knowledge before he came to perceive its uncommon virtues; his station also in society gave him opportunities of making known these virtues in quarters where they were likely to be understood and properly appreciated. He ordered the spring to be walled about, to protect it from pollution. Hence originated the celebrity of Harrogate as a watering place; and Sir William Slingsby may, with propriety, be styled its founder.

The spring thus discovered was that known as the Tewhit Well; but so insignificant was Harrogate at that time, that it was never mentioned in connection with its famous waters, which were known to the world under the designation of "The Knaresborough Spaw," for in that town the water drinkers were obliged to make abode.

In 1641, the number of nobility that came to drink the water was considerable. "The lord Fauconbergh, and much company, both of the gentry of the county, and of the commanders reformados, are now at the Spas."* These were the leaders of that army which behaved so disgracefully before the Scots at Newburn-upon-Tyne, and which was afterwards quartered in the

* Fairfax Correspondence, Vol. ii., p. 214.

towns and villages of this part of Yorkshire, where they were allowed to plunder the inhabitants with impunity. Captain Langley's company of that disorderly force was quartered at Harrogate, previous to its removal to Fewston, on Christmas Eve, 1640.

In 1661, John Ray, the celebrated naturalist, notes in one of his diaries—"We went to the Spaw at Harrigate and drunk of the water. It is not unpleasant to the taste, somewhat acid and vitriolick. Then we visited the sulphur well, whose water, though it be pellucid enough, yet stinks noisomely, like rotten eggs, or *sulphur auratum diaphoreticum*."

In 1663, the great Presbyterian conspiracy, which exploded in the Farnley Wood plot, was organized at Knaresborough and Harrogate. A Dr. Richardson, then residing at the Spaw, was one of the principal plotters in this rash undertaking, the ramifications of which extended through all the northern counties. Liberty of conscience was the chief watchword of the insurgents. But although there was much energy and determination evinced, they had neither system nor plan. There was no leader of any name to give his authority to the movement; for men like Fairfax and Wharton held themselves cautiously aloof. There were too many masters, with no presiding genius to direct them. The house, therefore, while it was in the builder's hands, crumbled to the ground. The night of the 12th of October witnessed the beginning and end of the Westmorland plot. The Bishopric men rose at the same time, with a similar result. In Yorkshire, however, some large preparations had been made. Farnley Wood, near Leeds, was the rendezvous of the insurgents, who assembled there on the night of the 12th in some force, and actually threw up intrenchments, which were abandoned at the approach of day. Concealment was impossible; and the cavaliers were at once upon them. Numerous arrests were made

throughout the north of England; and in the winter a special
assize was held, at which the offenders were brought to the
bar.* Twenty-two were executed in Yorkshire, and four at
Appleby. Many others were kept in prison a long time; and
so severe an example was made that the flame of treason was
thoroughly stamped out.†

The following notice of the spaws occurs in the life of Marmaduke Rawdon, of York, 1664.‡ "Wednesday, July 20th, they
went to the spaw at Knaresborow; thir are tow wells, which
they call the Sulphurus Spaw, of a most unpleasant smell and
taste, and stinks like the smell of a sinke or rotten eggs, but
is very medicinable for many deseases; also halfe a mile from
thence is a nother well, which they call the Sweet Spaw, in
tast much like the waters of Epsome and Tunbridge; of the virtue
of thesse waters, one Dr. Deane haith write a smalltreatice."

In "Blome's Britannia, 1673," is a brief notice of these
Spaws, under the head of Knaresborough.—"Nigh unto this
place, in a moorish, boggy ground, ariseth a spring of vitrioline
taste and odour; and not far off is a sulphur well, which is
good for several deseases."§

* Amongst the prisoners taken and tried for high treason, belonging to
our neighbourhood, were—John Sergeant, of Harrogate, yeoman, William
Stockdale, of Bilton Park, Esq., and Thomas Pickells, of Beckwithshaw.
They were sentenced "to remain in gaol, without bail, till the delivery of
the gaol.
† Raine's preface to "Depositions from the Castle of York."—Surtees
Soc., 1861.
‡ Edited for the Camden Society by R. Davies, Esq., F.S.A., 1863. The
editor appends the following note.—"Dr. Deane's small treatice was not
the earliest work in which Knaresbrough Spaw was mentioned. The
medical writer by whom the mineral springs upon Knaresbrough Forest
were first noticed, and who gave them the name of the English Spaw, was
Timothy Bright, Doctor of Physicke, the author of 'A Treatise on Melan-
cholie.' His therapeutical essays were published between the years 1583
and 1589. Edmund Deane, M.D., practised for many years as a physician
in York. He died there in 1640, and was buried in the church of St.
Crux."
§ F. 259.

I

In 1687, a public house was built on the verge of the waste, for the accommodation of those who came to drink the waters. It received the name of the "Queen's Head," and though it has since expanded into a gigantic establishment, it is yet known as "the Queen."

The following extracts from the diary of Ralph Thoresby, the Leeds antiquary, are interesting, as they show the manner of taking the waters, and the class of society frequenting the Spaws at an early period.

"1679—June 17th. Went to the Spaws and stayed till Saturday. I went to Knaresborough to see St. Robert's chapel in the rock, and the admirable petrifying well.

"1680—Aug. 20. Evening. Took horse and rid with cousin Ruth to Pannal, whither, though late enough, and in the dark, we got very well.

"21. Went early to the Spaws; drank of both waters freely, and hope for benefit by them.

"23. Drank the waters before noon, after rid to Knaresborough church, and took the inscriptions of the monuments of the Slingsby's, and much pleased with the serious humour done, where, above all, stood an angel with a trumpet, calling *Venite ad Judicum.* Under the name and titles of the knight in his winding sheet, *Omnia vanitas.*

"1681—June 18. Morning. Drank the waters, and afterwards rode to St. Mungo's Well, at Cotgrave, the coldest of all waters I ever knew.

July 8—9. Both days spent at the Spaws in drinking the waters at the usual times; and in company, wherewith better furnished than ordinary, with Sir Ralph Jennyson, of Newcastle, and his lady (my dear father and uncle's friends); and that accomplished gentleman, Charles Scrimshaw, Esq., of Staffordshire, from whom I received the pleasing account of some protestant benefactions in those parts. Mr. Chetwynd, yet living, who built and endowed a church, and Mr. Taylor, his father-in-law, who built some alms houses at Chesterfield.

"11 and 12. Spent both days in drinking the waters, and the usual recreations, walking, &c. Went to Knaresborough, writ the heads of St. Robert's life from an old manuscript, gathered some remarkably petrified moss: viewed the castle, &c., with the ingenious Mr. Scrimshaw (since Sir Charles).

"1682—July 18. After the morning's drinking, had the additional felicity of Mr. Henry Fairfax's company, which was still the more acceptible, because most of the guests at this house are papists.

"1692—Jan. 12. Rode with Mr. Ibbetson to Knaresborough, found the way not so ill as dreaded; was preserved from danger, though many others were for several hours lost in the terrible mist upon the forest.

"1698—July 8. Morning, rose pretty early, drank of the Sulphur Spa; afternoon, rode with Mr. Ibbetson to St. Mungo's well, at Copgrave; and he with me two miles further to see Sir Edmund Blackett's stately house, which is indeed a most noble fabric; to which are adjoined very curious gardens, with delicate statues and pleasant walks, &c."

In 1781, the author of the "Memoirs of John Buncle, Esq.," gave the following account of Harrogate. "Of all the watering places I know, Harrogate is, in my opinion, the most charming. The waters are incomparable; no air can be better; and with the greatest civility, cheerfulness, and good humour, there is a certain rural plainness and freedom mixed, which are vastly pleasing. The lady of pleasure, the well-drest tailor, and the gamester, are not to be found there. Gentlemen of the country, and women of birth and fortune, their wives, sisters, and daughters, are for the most part the company. There were

at least fourscore ladies in the country dances every evening
while I was there ; and amongst them many fine women."

In 1768, Dr. Alexander Carlyle,* a Scotch presbyterian
minister of some eminence, paid a visit to Harrogate, of which
he made notes, which have since been published in his "Auto-
biography." Eating, drinking, and fashionable society, appear
to be the only subjects worthy of his notice. He arrived in
July of the above year, and made his abode at "the Dragon."
He writes—"Harrogate at this time was very pleasant, for
there was a constant succession of good company, and the best
entertainment of any watering-place in Britain at the least
expense. The house we were at was not only frequented by
the Scotch at this time, but was the favourite house of the
English nobility and gentry. Breakfast cost gentlemen only
2d. apiece for their muffins ; as it was the fashion for ladies
to furnish tea and sugar ; dinner 1s. ; supper 6d. ; chambers
nothing ; wine and other extras at the usual price, and as little
as you please ; horses and servants at a reasonable rate. We
had two haunches of venison twice a week during the season.
The ladies gave afterwards tea and coffee in their turns, which
coming but once in four or five weeks, amounted to a trifle."

The celebrated general lord Clive was at Harrogate at that
time : he stayed at "the Granby," and is thus described by
the Scottish divine—"Clive was an ill-looking man, with the
two sides of his face much unlike, one of them seemingly dis-
torted as if with palsy. He seemed to converse with nobody
during dinner, and left the table immediately after."

In the Act of Parliament obtained for the enclosure of the

* He was commonly called late in life *Jupiter Carlyle*, from having sat
more than once for " the king of gods and men " to Gavin Hamilton.   He
is styled by Sir Walter Scott—"the grandest demi-god I ever saw ; a
shrewd, clever old carle was he, no doubt, but no more a poet than his
precentor."

forest, in 1770, the following clauses were inserted for the
preservation of the mineral springs of Harrogate—"There are
within the said constableries of Bilton-with-Harrogate and Beckwith-with Rossett, or one of them, certain wells or springs of
medicinal waters, commonly called Harrogate Spaws, to which
during the summer season great numbers of persons constantly
resort, to receive the benefit of the said waters, to the great advantage and emolument of tradesmen, farmers and other persons
in the neighbourhood; and the persons resorting to the said
waters now have the benefit of taking the air upon the open
parts of the said constableries; to the end therefore, that such
privileges may be continued and enjoyed, be it further enacted
for the purposes aforesaid, two hundred acres of land adjoining
or near to the said springs of water, and to be ascertained and
set out by the said commissioners, or any three or more of
them, shall be left open for the purposes hereinafter mentioned
and declared concerning the same."

"And it is enacted that the said two hundred acres of land
herein before directed to be set out and ascertained near unto
the said springs of water, shall be, and they are hereby directed
to be converted into a stinted pasture."

"And the said two hundred acres of land shall for ever
hereafter remain open and unenclosed, and all persons whomsoever shall and may have free access at all times to the said
springs, and be at liberty to use and drink the waters there
arising, and take the benefit thereof, and shall and may have,
use, and enjoy, full and free ingress, egress, and regress in,
upon, and over the said two hundred acres of land, and every,
and any part thereof, without being subject to the payment
of any acknowledgment whatsoever for the same, or liable to
any action of trespass, or other suit, molestation, or disturbance
whatsoever in respect thereof."

"And to the intent the said springs of medicinal waters may be preserved for the benefit of all persons having occasion to make use of them, and to prevent any damage being done thereto, be it further enacted, that it shall not be lawful for any person or persons whatsoever, at any time after passing of this act, to dig or sink any pit or pits, or work any quarry or mine whatsoever, or do any other act whereby the said medicinal springs or waters may be damaged, polluted, or affected ; and that all and every person or persons so offending may be prosecuted, convicted, and punished as for a public nuisance."

These clauses are conceived in a spirit of liberality which looked far into the future, providing for the health and recreation of unborn generations on the fine breezy lawns which surround the town.

In 1777, Thomas Pennant, the antiquary, paid a visit to Harrogate. His description is brief and meagre. He says— "The places of entertainment consist of several excellent inns, scattered along the edge of a dreary moor. The company eat together. Each house is furnished with a large parlour and breakfast room." Speaking of the wells, he says—"That which occasions the great resort of company is the *Sulphur Well*, in a bottom, at what is called Lower Harrogate; and near which are considerable buildings for the reception of patients, amidst a vapour most fetidly salutory. This spring is remarkably efficacious in scorbutic complaints, and has effected such cures as have brought it into very great and deserved reputation. The bathing is in tubs in the distant houses, or in baths in those near the springs."*

In 1786, lord Loughborough began to form plantations on his estate about Wedderburne House and Woodlands, on the

* Tour from Alston moor to Harrogate, p. 113.

south side of the Stray. Previous to this Harrogate almost deserved Smollett's description—"a wild common, bare and bleak, without any signs of cultivation." Since then numerous plantations have been formed, and the trees, now grown up, add much to the beauty and variety of the scenery.

In 1788, when the amusements of the sock and buskin were in higher estimation than at present, a theatre was built here by Mr. Samuel Butler. Previous to that time "theatricals were enacted" in a barn belonging to the Granby hotel. Among Mr. Butler's company, who here played mimic parts, were some who were afterwards destined to be distinguished on the world's wider stage,—as Mrs. Jordan, whose charms captivated the duke of Clarence, afterwards king William IV. of England; Miss Mellon, afterwards duchess of St. Albans; Miss Wallis, of Covent Garden theatre, who was patronised by and domi- ciliated with lord and lady Loughborough; Mrs. Entwistle, mother of Miss Mellon; Mr. and Mrs. Jones; Miss Hilliar, afterwards wife of Thomas Dibdin, and Thomas Dibdin himself— a truly splendid array of dramatic talent. Mr. Butler was manager until his death in 1812, when his son, also named Samuel, succeeded in the direction of the dramatic corps.

The theatrical season was during the months of July, August, and September; and the evenings of performance were Tuesday, Thursday, and Saturday in each week.

> " The public to please, they laboured and play'd,
> They laboured in vain and they failed in their trade."

The company became bankrupt; the theatre and all the decora- tions were sold; and the place where "the poor player fretted his hour upon the stage" was converted into a lodging house, now known as Mansfield House, situate in Church-square, nearly opposite the Granby hotel.

The Race Course on the Stray was first laid out in 1793,
under the superintendence of colonel Clement Wolsley. It is
a mile and a half in circumference, and sixteen yards wide.
Though few places are better adapted for such purposes, races
are held here only at rare intervals.

The following lively sketch of society at Harrogate in 1825,
is from a letter written by a gentleman at that time.

"Oct. 1. The season is drawing to a close and the visitors,
like migratory birds, are taking flight in various directions, some
to their own firesides, and others to Bath and Cheltenham.
Here two guineas and a half a-week is the charge for bed
and board, without wine, of which little is drank, for, with
a disinterested regard to the health of their guests, the landlords
furnish that beverage of such a quality, containing such an
undue proportion of alcohol, the sherry tasting like cognac,
and as for the port—

> "Sloe juice and hot Geneva they combine,
> Then call the fatal composition wine!"

that few take a glass unless mixed with water.

· The three principal houses, the Granby, Dragon, and Crown,
are frequented by well-bred people (the two former especially, for
the latter is said to have a plebeian mixture), who all dine at
the same table, and take tea and pass the evening together.
Each house gives a ball once a week, to which the inmates
of the other two houses are invited; and cards, chess, and
social chit-chat serve to occupy the other evenings. The *season*
here, however, is a short one, lasting only from the beginning
of July to the end of September, and so rapid has been the
migration within these few days, that at the Granby, where
a fortnight ago eighty sat down to dinner, the number is now
reduced to fourteen, and at the Dragon to a still smaller number.
At the Crown, however, which is situate close to the nauseous

well, where invalids continue late in the autumn, some forty
or fifty persons remain for the benefit of their health. Nearly
one half of the visitors this year have been Irish. . . .
Several legislators have been here, and Sir John Beresford, with
Lord Clifton and his beautiful bride (a daughter of Sir Henry
Parnell), still remain drinking the waters. Sir John means to
relinquish Berwick I hear, and take his seat for Northallerton,
a more quiet borough. Sir James Mackintosh left this on
Wednesday with his daughter, on a visit to Mr. Brougham
and the lakes. . . . One of the clergymen here (Mr.
Kenyon), without being remarkable for eloquence or learning,
is admired and followed for the soundness of his doctrines,
and the exemplary virtue of his private life. His history is
rather curious: a few years ago he was a stock broker, and
having realised, it seems, a moderate fortune on the Stock
Exchange, he withdrew from that bustling scene to devote himself to the care of souls.

"Besides, we have at Knaresborough, two miles from hence,
a female prodigy, Mrs. Stevens, the sister of the rector of that
place, who preaches four times a week *extempore*, with a fluency
of language and compass of thought very surprising, and very
attractive to the gay and fashionable, as well as religious visitors,
so that what was said at Bath may apply here—

> 'Whoe'er has a notion
> For cards or devotion
> Make this their delightful retreat.'"

In 1835, Mr. Joseph Thackwray, proprietor of the Crown
hotel, having sunk a well on his premises, only 82 feet distant
from the Old Sulphur Well, which it was believed to injure,
was indicted under the provisions of the Knaresborough Enclosure Act. The plaintiffs were Messrs. Jonathan Shutt, John
Dearlove, and Jonathan Benn. The case came on for hearing

at the York Assizes, March 14th, 1887, before Mr. Baron
Alderson, and a special jury. The court was filled by a most
respectable auditory, and a great treat was expected from the
number of scientific men* who had been summoned to give
evidence. They were, however, disappointed, as Mr. Thackwray consented to give up the well to the use of the public,
and a verdict of "not guilty" was recorded,—subject to the
following rule of court; " It is ordered by, and with the consent
of the parties, their counsel and attorneys, that there be entered
a verdict of "not guilty," and that the defendant shall appropriate the well in Mr. Husband's shop to the public, by putting
a pump into it, and that the room be converted into a public
pump room; but that it shall not be maintained at the expense
of the defendant, unless he thinks fit; and the room to be open
to the public from six o'clock in the morning until six o'clock in
the evening of each day ; and the defendant shall only use the
pump and water in common with the rest of the public. And
it is further ordered that there be two locks affixed to the
pump room door, and that the key of one be kept by the
defendant, and that of the other by the prosecutors, who hereby
bind themselves to open their lock at six o'clock in the morning,
and not to close it before six o'clock in the evening. The
defendant hereby also undertaking not to deepen any other
wells on his premises. And it is further ordered that this order
be made a rule of his majesty's court of king's bench, if the
said court shall so please."

The plaintiffs who gained the cause had to disburse £1,852

* These were—for the prosecution, Professor Daniel, King's college,
London; Dr. Dalton, Manchester; Dr. Smith, Scarborough; and Professor
Phillips, York : for the defence, John Buddle, H. Mc.Gregor, and Thomas
Sopwith, civil engineers, Newcastle; Dr. Clanny, Sunderland; Dr. Murray,
Scarborough; Professor Johnstone, Durham University; Mr. W. C. Willi-
amson, Manchester; George Knowles, Esq., Scarborough; and Nicholas
Brown, civil engineer, Wakefield.

7s. 8d. for their victory; towards which sum the visitors contributed £14 2s.; and the defendant, who secured the nominal
ownership of the well, died a few weeks after the assizes. This
well and pump are now seldom used.

In 1841, an act of parliament was obtained *—"For improving
certain parts of the townships of Bilton-with-Harrogate and
Pannal, commonly called High and Low Harrogate; for pro-
tecting the mineral springs, and regulating the stinted pasture
in the said townships." By this act the government of the
town within certain limits was placed under the control of
twenty-one commissioners, who are elected for three years,
seven of whom retire annually, but are eligible to re-election.
The qualification required is a rating to the relief of the poor
in the sum of £35 annually. or the possession of lands, &c.,
of the yearly value of £20. All persons, owners or occupiers,
rated at £8 and upwards, can vote for any number of commissioners then to be chosen. This body has power to appoint
a clerk and treasurer, enter into contracts, borrow money (not
to exceed £3,000),† make bye-laws for the management of the
mineral springs, grant licenses, and regulate the fares of hackney
carriages, make and repair footpaths, construct common sewers,
remove nuisances, regulate the building of houses, cleanse the
streets, provide markets, &c., &c.

During the year 1842, the commissioners erected the Royal
Pump Room, over the Old Sulphur Well; removed the dome
which had previously occupied its place, and erected it over
the Tewhit Well; and also built the pump room over the Sweet
Spaw, or John's Well.

* The total cost of obtaining this act was £1,207 4s. 7d.

† This act has since been supplemented by the adoption of "The Local
Government Act," by which the borrowing powers of the commissioners
have been largely increased.

The town was first lighted with gas in 1846, by means of a joint stock company. The works are situate in the Oakbeck valley, on the left of the Ripon road, on a piece of land awarded at the enclosure of the forest for a public stone quarry. The works have since been considerably enlarged.

In 1848, an act of parliament was obtained for supplying the town with water. The first reservoirs were constructed on the northern slope of Harlow hill, the springs on which yielded the water supply. This being found inadequate, the company obtained permission to bring water from Haverah Park, a district about three miles to the west of the town; and in 1866 a reservoir was constructed there, capable of containing upwards of twenty millions of gallons. A reservoir is now being constructed on the eastern slope of Harlow hill, for the purpose of supplying the new district known as the West End Park. The water is remarkably pure and soft.*

The formation of the Victoria Park was commenced in 1860, by a company† buying a large plot of ground lying between High and Low Harrogate, and laying the same out in building lots, after making drains and roads; the main avenue from east

---

* The following analyses of the Haverah Park water was made by Mr. R. Holden, of York, in August, 1863.

Solid contents in the gallon.

	grains.
Chloride of sodium, with strong traces of carbonate of potash	1.80
Carbonate of lime and magnesia, with traces of alumina, and (very slight) of iron	2.00
Sulphate of lime (gypsum)	.20
	4.00

Gaseous contents the same as common air—*i.e.*, oxygen, nitrogen, and carbonic acid.

† The capital of the company consisted of £28,000, divided into 56 shares, of the nominal value of £500 each. Of these 20 were held by Richard Carter, 20 by Richard Ellis, and 16 by John Richardson. On the death of the last-named partner, in 1861, his shares were purchased by Nicholas Carter. The partnership was finally dissolved in 1868, when Richard Ellis became owner of the residue of the unsold estate.

to west was opened in the same year. This was the first great systematic plan formed for the improvement of the town, to which it has contributed in an eminent degree, added much to its population, and also to its beauty, by the introduction of a superior style of architecture to any which had previously existed here.

The avenues of ornamental trees along the sides of the roads leading across the Stray were planted in 1860.

The railway was brought through the town and the new station built in 1860-2; thus placing Harrogate directly on the main line, with easy access to all quarters. This gave a great impetus to the enlargement of the town, by bringing many merchants and manufacturers to reside here, whose places of business were in Leeds, Bradford, and other large manufacturing towns of the West Riding.

In 1864, Harrogate was made a polling place for knights of the shire for the West Riding, for the townships or places of Bilton-with-Harrogate, Birstwith, Clint, Felliscliffe, Hampsthwaite, Haverah Park, Killinghall, Pannal, Rigton and Weeton; which district contained in 1867—427 voters, and in 1868, after the passing of the last Reform Bill—846.

In 1867, the "West End Park" land company was formed, who purchased nearly seventy acres of land from the North Eastern Railway Company, abutting on the east on the Leeds road, and towards the north on the Otley road, and fronting the open Stray on both these sides. This plot of ground they laid out in building lots, upon a most comprehensive and elegant plan; buildings of the most substantial and beautiful kind are already rising up along the front sides, and when completed it will form a little town of itself.

In 1868, after some previous failures, the thorough sewerage of the town was completed, and the whole of the matter conveyed

to one outlet, on the western side of the Ripon road, where
by means of proper cuttings it is spread over a plot of land,
and heavy crops of rich grass obtained from what had previously
been a polluting nuisance.

THE WATERS OF HARROGATE.

"Water, great principle whence nature springs,
The prime of elements, and first of things."

THE origin, progress, and present state of Harrogate are
entirely owing to the presence of the extraordinary waters,
which a kind Providence has bestowed upon it. Were these
fountains dried up, the town would become a ruin—a Palmyra
of the forest. As already shown, the first of these springs used
for medicinal purposes was the chalybeate, now known as

THE TEWHIT WELL.

This is situate in the South Park, between the Leeds road
and the railway, nearly in front of the Prince of Wales hotel.
Nearly three hundred years have passed away since Sir William
Slingsby made its virtues known to the world, and during that
period its reputation has not materially declined.

In 1626, Dr. Dean* wrote a treatise on its use, in which
he says—"It dries the too moist brain, and helps rheums,
catarrhs, palsies, cramps, &c. It's good against inveterate head-

---

* "*Spandarine Anglica*, or the English Spaw Fountain ; being a brief
treatise of the acid tart fountain in the Forest of Knaresburgh, in the West
Riding of Yorkshire : also a relation of other medicinal waters in the said
forest. By Edm. Dean, Doctor in Physick, Oxon., dwelling in York.
London, printed by John Grismond, 1626."

aches, megrims, vertigo, epilepsy, convulsions, and the like cold
and moist diseases of the head. It cheers the spirits, strengthens the stomach, causes a good and quick appetite, and
promotes digestion. It's good in the black and yellow jaundice
and hippo, as also in a cachexy, and beginning dropsy, seeing
it opens obstructions and expels redundant seriosities." This
is perhaps enough; though there is a further list of equally
formidable diseases which the worthy doctor says this water
will either relieve or cure.

The next writer on this water was Michael Stanhope,* in
1682, who gives "a true relation of certain cures done by the

* "Cures without care; or a summons to all such as find little or no
keep by the use of physick, to repair to the Northern Spaw, &c., &c. 1632."
Besides the above, these waters have furnished a subject to a whole host
of writers; and it would be a task of some difficulty to enumerate all the
treatises and articles in scientific and medical journals which have been
produced on this subject. We give the following list of treatises, without
being certain that it is a complete one.
"The Yorkshire Spaw; or a treatise on four famous medicinal wells,
&c., near Knaresburgh, Yorkshire; by John French, M.D., 1654."
"Hydrologiæ Chymic, by Dr. Simpson, 1671."
"The natural, experimental, and medicinal history of the mineral waters
of Derbyshire, Lincolnshire, and Yorkshire, by Thomas Short, M.D., of
Sheffield. 1734."
"Plain and easy directions for the use of the Harrogate waters, by
William Alexander, M.D., 1773."
"An Essay on the waters of Harrogate and Thorp Arch, by Joshua
Walker, M.D., 1784."
"Observations on the Sulphur Wells at Harrogate; by the Right Rev.
Richard, bishop of Landaff,"—appeared in the Philosophical Transactions,
1786.
"A Treatise on the mineral waters of Harrogate, by T. Garnett, M.D.,
1791."
"An Essay on the mineral springs recently discovered at Harrogate,
and on the springs of Thorp Arch and Ilkley, by A. Hunter, M.D., 1819."
"A Treatise on the mineral waters of Harrogate and its vicinity, by
Adam Hunter, M.D.; 1830."
"The Spas of England, by Dr. Granville, 1840."
"The Harrogate Medical Guide, by Alfred Smith, M.R.C.S., 1842."
"A few practical hints for invalids, interspersed with cases on the use
and efficacy of the mineral waters of Harrogate by Joseph Frobisher,
1842."
"Observations on the Sulphureous Springs of Harrogate, by William
Bennett, M.D., 1843."

mineral waters near Knaresburgh,"—from which we select the
following.—"In 1626 Mrs. Rolf, of Hadley, in Suffolk, fell
into the gravel, got the best advice she could, but found no
relief, till she was brought to the Tewhit Well; in a fortnight's
time she voided an hundred stones of several sizes; her pain
went off, she recovered and continued well. Henry Curra,
of Whardale, in the west of Yorkshire, aged about fifty years,
servant to Sir Peter Middleton, was a great sufferer many
years, could neither ride, walk, nor move; he came here, and
in a month's time, by the use of the same spaw, he voided
many stones, several of them as big as peas; he also recovered
a firm state of health. Henry Rowley, of Linton, near Wetherby, aged sixty years, was long tormented with a stoppage of
water, till this spaw opened the flood-gates, and let off great
quantities of mucus and gravel, whereby he was restored to
health. . . The Countess of Buckingham (all other means
failing) repaired hither for the cure of a severe asthma, and
went back cured. Mrs. Fairweather, of York, having long
been troubled with a swimming in her head, finding no relief
from the best advice and means, till she came hither and
met with a very acceptable cure. The lady Hoyh, of York,
after she had borne four children, in her fifth was taken with
a swelling, redness and knobs in her face, about the eleventh
week after conception, the pain whereof was so great, that
she miscarried of this and two other conceptions successively.

"Harrogate and its resources. Chemical Analysis of its medicinal
waters, by A. W. Hofmann, F.R.S., 1854."
"Observations on the medicinal springs of Harrogate, by G. Kennion,
M.D., 1857."
"Harrogate Spas, with introductory essay, by G. G. W. Pigott, M.D.,
1858."
"Practical Observations on the Harrogate mineral waters, with cases, by
Andrew Scott Myrtle, M.D., 1867."
"Hydrotherapeutics: the resources of Harrogate specially considered;
by A. S. Myrtle, M.D., 1870."

After some years spent in this languishing condition, physic availing nothing, she came to the Spaw, was cured, and had several children after. Mrs. Sadler, the daughter of that famous lawyer, Sir Edward Coke, came hither for a long and violent pain in her head, and found relief."

Dr. Short, in his "History of mineral waters," speaking of these cures, says, "Some whereof are perhaps the greatest and most remarkable, filed up in the authentic records of physic, down from Hippocrates to this day."*

The above cases are sufficient to show that the report of the medicinal virtues of the water had spread far and wide; and that many high and noble came to drink and found relief.

Notwithstanding all its virtues, and the praises lavished upon it, the ground, and the well itself remained for upwards of two centuries much in the same state as when left by Sir William Slingsby. Dr. Short, in 1734, says—"It rises up into a round stone bason, which contains about twenty pints of water, rising up through a hole in its bottom. On the south, west, and north sides of it is a wall of a foot height, open above, being most probably the very bason Mr. Slingsby made for it."†

In the year 1842, the pillared dome which had stood over the Old Sulphur Well was removed and placed over this spring, by order of the Improvement Commissioners.‡ The ground around has also been drained and the approaches greatly improved.

JOHN'S WELL, OR THE SWEET SPA.

This well is situate on the Stray, on the left of the road leading to Wetherby, a short distance south-east of High Harro-

* P. 243.
† Ibid, p. 250.
‡ In the accounts of the Improvement Commissioners, for 1842, we find £96 2s. 2d., paid to John Stead, for work done at the Tewhit Well; and in 1846 further improvements were made, for which Charles Winterburn received £29 9s. 6d.

gate church. It was discovered in 1631,* by Dr. Michael Stanhope, of York, who thus describes it,—"Dr. Dean, of York, having wrote upon and recommended the *Tuewhet Spaw*, about six years ago, in several distempers, we are now to give an account of several surprising cures done by it. But give me leave to advertize you, that last year, 1631, I discover'd a new spring, a quarter of a mile nearer, which exceeds the former on this account. 1.—It's situate on the descent of a great hill, has firm ground, and dry walks round about it: the other lies in a flat, the ground about it is boggy, other waters sink in, and there is little room for exercise. 2.—This changes sooner and deeper with galls than the other. 3.—It's lighter, less nauseous, and goes sooner off than the other. 4.—It will carry further, and keep better and longer, being put in clean, new, close bottles. 5.—Besides the iron and vitriol, this has also a little sulphur, which makes it more balsamic and healing."†

Great pains appear to have been taken to establish a reputation for this well immediately after its discovery, and also to make the place attractive to the drinkers. It is thus described by Dr. Short, in 1734. "It springs up into a stone bason, containing about eighteen pints, surrounded by a stone wall four-square, covered with a pyramidal roof, supported by four pillars, each a foot and a half high, set on the corners of the wall, which is about two foot high. On the top of this small

* The "Sweet Spa" was the name by which it was first known, and which continued in use down to a recent period. In 1830, Dr. Hunter calls it "the Old Spa, or Sweet Spaw." The name of John's Well was derived from John Hardestie, who was many years the attendant here, and who died only a few years ago, at the age of 96. A predecessor of his in the same office was William Westmorland, who died in 1798, aged 99 years. He enjoyed such an uninterrupted state of good health, as to be able to attend constantly at the Spa, until within a fortnight of his decease.

† "Cures without care, &c."

pyramid is a knob or ball. The situation is in a rushy moist ground. It is ditch'd round, both to drain the earth, and prevent other springs getting in. The enclosure within this square ditch is fifty-two yards every way. At its east and lower end is a necessary house for the drinkers to retire to. In the upper west corner have formerly been seats of earth for the weak or weary to rest upon. It's a large half mile south-east of the Sulphur Wells, and a quarter of a mile from the village. This well was not known till sixty years after the other was discovered. It's oker is less, of a lighter colour, and not so styptic as that of the other. The bason and house over it were built in 1656."*

To prevent any one from claiming the land thus set apart, a stone was placed on the western side of the well, inscribed—

All This Ground within these Walkes Belongs to the Forist of Knaresbrobgh: 1656. John Stebenson.

In 1786, Alexander, Lord Loughborough, owner of the adjoining estate of Woodlands, erected a dome of stone over it, which continued until 1842, when the Improvement Commissioners erected the present pump room.†

THE SULPHUR SPRINGS.

These waters were not used medicinally until some time after the Chalybeates, though we cannot believe that they were unknown; their appearance, taste, and smell would betray them to the most careless observer.

Three of them are mentioned by Dr. Dean, as known in

* History of Mineral Waters, p. 251.
† In the Commissioners' accounts for that year are £93 4s., paid to Messrs. Wilson and Benson for work done at the Chalybeate Well.

1626. He says—"They are called by the populace *stinking wells*, because they have a fetid smell, consisting most of *sulphur vive*. One of them that has the greatest stream of water is in Bilton Park; the other two are in the Forest; one is near the town, the third is two miles beyond Harrigate Head, in a bottom, on the right hand, and almost at the side of a little brook. These are sulphureous fountains, and cast forth a stinking smell afar off, in the winter season, and coldest weather especially. They are very cold, and have no manifest heat, because their mines and veins of brimstone are not kindled under the earth, being hindered from the mixture of salt therewith. Such as drink the water verily believe there is gunpowder in it, and they vomit it up again. They leave upon grass, leaves, and sticks in their currents, a grey slimy substance, which being set on fire has smell of common sulphur." . . . The common people drink them, and they expel reef and fellon. They soon help and cure by washing and bathing, itch, morphew, tettars, ringworm, and the like."

The last mentioned spring is the now celebrated Old Sulphur Well, in Low Harrogate.

In 1632, a number of cures by drinking sulphur water are recorded by Michael Stanhope, in his "Cures without Care." " Mr. Fowles, an advocate in Edinburgh, aged fifty-one years, from a weakness and relaxation of the solids, had lost the use of both hands, and all his limbs; after a month's drinking of the spaw, and bathing in the sulphur water, was perfectly cured. The like cure in the palsie they performed on Sir Thomas Vavasor's lady. Maud Bogg, of York, had a prodigious swell'd leg for many years, which made her perfectly lame; she was cured in three days, by drinking plentifully and washing in this water. Another poor man, of a long and very hard swelling on his knee, which was cover'd over with thick, long,

and strong hair, and had given the defiance to all other appli-
cations; he came hither, bath'd the part often, and drank
freely of this sulphur water, the tumour broke and discharg'd
incredible quantities of worms, and he soon after return'd home
perfectly cured. Another poor woman it cur'd of a large swelling in her breast. One Smith, a shoemaker in York, was so
over-run with the scurvy, that his life was in danger, medicines
being of no service, was prevailed upon to drink the sulphur
water at home, in the middle of winter, which cured him in
a month. There is nothing more common than for people to
frequent this sulphur well and get cured of their ulcers and
sores, by washing in it. What are its inward uses we know
not yet."

In 1656, here were three wells, as is related by Dr. Neal,
who thus describes an experiment he made upon one of them,*
"Here are, and were, about twenty years ago, three springs
close together, very low, and scarce of water, that all of them
did not afford sufficient water for drinking and bathing. Wherefore, for the greater convenience of the drinkers, I thought it
convenient to take up the uppermost spring, which is weakest
and slowest of them, and made a large bason to contain several
hogsheads of water, and covered it with a large stone to preserve
it from the sun and rain water, and for a week together we
rammed its sides with clay, to prevent other springs from
getting in. The event answered expectation; for we had a fresh
spring of much better and stronger water, which afforded as
much in one hour now as it did in twenty-four before, more
loaded with the minerals than ever, and so of greater efficacy
for either bathing or drinking."†

* Spandacrene Eboracensis.
† Abraham de la Pryme, the Yorkshire antiquary, gives the following
remarkable cure performed by the water of the Sulphur Well, in his *Diary*,
Oct. 2nd, 1695. " I was yesterday with Mr. Anderson, of this town, a fine

Dr. Short, in 1734, thus describes the Sulphur Wells,—
"Near five hundred yards east of the Bogg, over a small dry
hill, lies the first of the three Sulphur Wells, on the north
side of the village. A yard east of this is the second; and
five yards and a half east of this rises up the third. These
three being the only springs of this kind in use here; they
have very pretty little stone basons laid for the water to rise
up into, and are each enclosed in a small neat building of
stone and lime, about a yard square on the insides, and nearly
two yards high, covered over with two thick smooth flag stones
laid shelving."*

To these wells another was added in 1746, "by a person
who, by lease from the earl of Burlington, had acquired a right
of searching for minerals in the Forest of Knaresborough, made
a show as if he had a real intention of digging for coal, on the
very spot where the sulphur wells were situated. This attempt
alarmed the innkeepers and others at Harrogate, who were
interested in the preservation of the wells: they gave him what
legal opposition they could, and all the illegal that they durst.
At length for the sum of £100, which they raised amongst
themselves, the dispute was compromised, and the design, real
or pretended, of digging for coal was abandoned. Sulphur
water, however, had risen up where he had begun to dig.
They enclosed the place with a little stone edifice, and putting
down a bason made a fourth well."†

gentleman, and of a great estate. Talking of the spaw waters of Knaresbrough, but especially the Sulphur Well, and of the great virtue it has.
Amongst other things he told me that he was there this year, and had
a waiting boy with him, that for about a month before had been subject
betimes to have something to rise up in his throat, and then to vomit
blood. He carried the boy to the Sulphur Well, and having made him
drink heartily of the water, he vomited up a skin, somewhat like a bladder,
full of clotted blood. It came up, he says, by pieces, at three or four
vomits. This is very strange, and well worth taking notice of."—p. 70.

* History of Mineral Waters, p. 235.
† Observations on the Sulphur Wells at Harrogate, by the Rt. Rev. R.
Bishop of Llandaff, 1786.

The next improvement was made in 1804, when an improved stone basin was made as a receptacle of the waters, covered by a dome supported by eleven stone pillars, surrounded with a stone table, on which the water was served by female attendants.* This arrangement continued until 1842, when the present pump room was erected. The water is now raised from the spring, by means of an air pump, into the room, along porcelain pipes, into vases of marble, from which it is drawn by taps, and served to the drinkers on a long semi-circular mahogany table.

THE CRESCENT WATERS.

These springs were discovered in 1788; and that event is thus described by Dr. Walker,† "The master of the Half Moon Inn, at Low Harrogate, had occasion this year, 1788, to dig for fresh water in the field behind his house, but, contrary to his expectations, the water he met with was so far from being pure, that it very nearly resembled the water of the Sulphur

---

* The arrangements at this time are thus described in a tract published in 1841, entitled, "Sketches of Harrogate; by a citizen of the world." "Most of the visitors are early risers. At seven o'clock, or soon after, they flock down to the Old Sulphur Well, the waters of which are distributed by some eight or ten nymphs, whose personal attractions are not calculated to make one insensible to the nauseous flavour of the draught which they bestow. The lady paramount of the fount is an old dame, styled indifferently 'Old Betty,' and 'The queen of Harrogate,' over whose head some eighty summers have passed, without diminishing her activity or garrulity. She is a privileged person, and dispenses the waters and quips and quodlibets with equal liberality. It is curious to observe the various effects which these draughts produce upon the countenances of those who partake of them. Disgust is expressed in a thousand ludicrous ways, and those who have accomplished the task may generally be observed consoling themselves with the somewhat uncharitable contemplation of the ludicrous distress of others. The scene is not unfrequently heightened by the very unsophisticated exclamations of some burly novice from the wilds of Yorkshire, or the classic districts of Bolton, Oldham, &c., who imbibes the waters for the first time."

† Essay on the waters of Harrogate and Thorp Arch, p. 97.

Wells both in taste and smell." This spring was first analysed
by Dr. Garnett, in 1790, who wrote a treatise on its virtues.
It is now principally used for bathing purposes. In the same
year another spring was found in the cellar of the same inn,
which is yet occasionally used, and is said to resemble the
Leamington water in its composition as well as in its effects.

Dr. Granville speaking of it, says,* "As it neither contains
sulphur nor a single trace of iron, with the largest proportion
of carbonated soda of any of the springs of Harrogate, the
water is in my opinion a most valuable one, and might be
rendered useful in a variety of complaints in which no other
of the Harrogate waters is suitable."

As this water was not analysed by Professor Hofmann, we
append that of Mr. William West, of Leeds, as the most recent.

	grains.
Chloride of sodium	610
Chloride of calcium	44·5
Chloride of magnesium	14·5
Carbonate of soda	53·0
	722·0

THE ROYAL CHALYBEATE SPA.

This Spa, which consists of a saline chalybeate, or chloride
of iron spring, and a pure chalybeate, was added from the
great laboratory of nature, in 1818. Dr. Adam Hunter, the
first writer on their virtues, thus describes the event,—"These
two springs were discovered by boring in search of sulphur

* "Spas of England," vol. i., p. 59.

water to supply the increasing demand for the baths. The alluvial earth having been removed, a stratum of clay presented itself, beneath which lay a bed of sand, and this was found to cover a dark bluish aluminous earth, from under which the water issued. Three borings were made, each to the depth of eight yards; the first and third in the lowest part of the valley, and a few yards distant from the fence adjoining the road. In the first the water was found impregnated with salt. This was subsequently abandoned upon the discovery of the third, or 'Saline Chalybeate Spring,' which supplies the well now in use. The second boring, on the rising ground, in a line at right angles with the first and third, and at a distance of sixteen yards from the latter, is the 'Chalybeate Spring,' the water of which is conveyed in proper pipes down the declivity, and issues through a parapet wall into a basin placed for its reception.*

These waters are now served in an elegant building of iron and glass, attached to the concert room.

The Saline Chalybeate Spring has been frequently subjected to analysis, and with varying results. Dr. Adam Hunter, in his treatise on the mineral waters of Harrogate, gives the following as the solid contents per imperial gallon.

	grains.
Oxide of iron	5·3
Chloride of sodium	576·5
Chloride of calcium	43·5
Chloride of magnesium	9·65

The analysis of Professor Hofmann will be found among that of the other Harrogate waters, made in 1854.

* "Essay on two mineral springs recently discovered at Harrogate."— p. 9-10.

The following is the analysis made by Professors Muspratt and Miller, in 1865.

	Chloride of Iron spring	Carb'nt of Iron spring
Sulphate of lime......................	—	7·625
Carbonate of lime	—	·341
Oxide of manganese	Trace	—
Chloride of calcium	138·43	2·311
Chloride of magnesium	84·39	13·148
Chloride of sodium	205·92	11·650
Chloride of potassium	3·84	·150
Chloride of barium...................	6·78	—
Chloride of lithium	Bare trcs	—
Protochloride of iron	14·49	—
Protocarbonate of iron	11·62	6·042
Silica	Trace	·2 4
Total........	465·47	41.471
Cubic inches of gases in the gallon of water.		
Carbonic acid	26·28	
Nitrogen	8·08	
Total........	34·36	

THE MONTPELLIER SPRINGS.

These springs are situate in a most delightful piece of pleasure ground called the Montpellier gardens, which is one of the spots most highly favoured by nature, as it contains all the kinds of water most in request—strong sulphur, mild sulphur, saline chalybeate, and pure chalybeate; the three first kinds are brought by means of glass tubes into a neat little pump room, built in the Chinese style (soon to be exchanged for a more lofty and elegant building), where they are served to the drinkers. Dr. Hunter, writing on this spring in 1830, says,—" Thackwray's Garden Spring, or Crown Spa, is situated about two hundred yards distant from the Old Sulphur Well, nearly on a line with it, and in the lowest part of the valley,

in the garden at the east end of the Crown hotel. It was
discovered about twenty years ago, and used for water to supply
the baths, until analysed in 1823, by my friend Mr. West.
The result of that analysis, corroborated by the present, proves
that it is greatly superior in strength to any other of this class,
except the Old Well. Both contain the same ingredients—solid
and gaseous; the New Well has the greatest impregnation of
the gases, the Old Well contains rather more salt. Over this
valuable spring Mr. Thackwray, the proprietor, has erected
a small but handsome building, in the style of a Chinese
temple, and changed the garden and some surrounding land
into pleasure grounds."*

The discovery of the Kissengen, or Saline Chalybeate, is thus
described by Thomas Coates, the person employed in sinking the
wells—"I was employed in digging the foundations of the public
baths, when built by Mr. Thackwray, in 1838-4, when several
mineral springs were met with, which had to be drained away,
except one of Cheltenham water, for which a well was sunk
about three yards deep, and then covered with a flag. About
eighteen months after that well was sunk, I sunk another
well, about three yards distant from it, about eight yards
deep, which contains a spring of sulphur water, and is in no
manner or way connected with the first. In a line with the
last-named spring, there are three sulphur springs in the same
grounds, each about four yards deep; between two of them
is a fresh water spring, the well of which is about eight yards
deep. There are two other sulphur springs in the same grounds,
whereof one is used for drinking, the other is a blackish water."†

The well first mentioned is the Saline Chalybeate, sometimes
called the Kissengen Well. A pure Chalybeate is situate to

* "Treatise on the mineral waters of Harrogate."—p. 43.
† Note in "Geology of Harrogate."—p. 12.

the east of the baths. These waters have been frequently analysed, and are deservedly held in high estimation.

About the middle of the last century, this piece of land belonged to William Layton, of Knaresborough, who by his will, dated January 28th, 1758, gave and devised the same, along with other premises, to his two nephews, James Brown, carpenter, and Charles Brown, merchant; and who were admitted to the same October 29th, 1761. On the 4th December, 1765, they surrendered the same to Joseph Thackerey, of the Sulphur Well; from whom it was purchased by his nephew, William Thackwray, who, by his will dated March 4th, 1813, devised the same to his son Joseph Thackwray, who was admitted to the same July 31st, 1816, who held it until his decease, April 10th, 1837. Afterwards it came into possession of T. Collins, Esq., M.P., of Knaresborough, who in 1870 sold the same, along with the Crown Hotel estate, to Mr. George Dawson, a speculating builder.

THE BOG SPRINGS.

These springs present the most singular phenomena observable either at Harrogate, or elsewhere in England, being sixteen in number, all of mineral water, rising in an acre of ground, and most singular of all, no two of them exactly alike in their composition, though rising within three or four yards of each other. They have been long known, and form an object of wonder and surprise to all beholders. The place in which they rise has evidently been the crater of some grand eruption of the volcanic kind, which has burst through the strata, tearing up the beds of rock, and leaving them standing half on edge on each side.

Dr. Short thus describes the Bog and its springs, in 1734,— "The first is the allum-well in the Bogg, which has a stone bason for its receptacle. . . . About this allum-well is

first black peat moss, about half a yard or two foot deep.
Under this, mixt with it, are heaps of concretions of green
vitriol, both mature and immature, prodigious quantities of
sulphur, and much earth, which calcin'd answers the loadstone.
Under these is a bed of clay, two foot and a half deep, without
any sensible marly of sulphur, except where the sulphur waters
rise.   There is a good descent from this bog, to carry off the
water from it into the brook. . . . The north-east end of
the morass or bogg, lying naked from all grass, is candied over
in the summer time with salt, a part of which is daily picked up
by great flocks of pigeons, which resort thither from all parts."*

   The learned doctor classes this alum well, as he calls it,
among the chalybeates ; though it must have been essentially
different.   It has either entirely disappeared, or it is what is
now called the Magnesia Well.   This view is partially confirmed
by his stating that " twenty-two yards south-west of the alum
well is a chalybeate spring :" and about that distance from
the Magnesia Well is a strong chalybeate spring, in what is
now the Hospital garden.†

   The same author, speaking of the sulphur waters, says,—" In
the bog above the village we find several more of these springs."

   An idea prevailed among all the early writers on the Harrogate waters that this bog was the mother of all the sulphur

   * " History of mineral waters."—p, 240.
   † Dr. Garnett, writing in 1794, after mentioning Dr. Short, says,—
" This writer mentions an alum well, in the bog above Low Harrogate,
which I cannot find at present : some old people in the neighbourhood
remember the situation, and we have often attempted to find it, by
digging in different parts of the bog, but have hitherto been disappointed.
From his experiments it seems to have been a chalybeate water, in which
the iron was held in solution by the sulphuric acid.   I have found two or
three springs of this kind in the bog, very near some sulphur wells, though
not in the least mixed with them : so astonishing is the variety and vicinity
of the mineral waters of this place."—*Treatise on the mineral waters of
Harrogate*," p. 28.
   This alum well was rediscovered in 1870, but was again closed, as being
of no use for medical purposes.

springs. This notion is found in Dr. Short's "History of
mineral waters;" in Dr. Walker's "Essay on the waters of
Harrogate, &c.;" but is perhaps most clearly expressed by Dr.
Garnett, who says,*—"The four sulphur springs at the village
evidently take their rise from the bog, which is three or four
hundred yards above them; from thence the water seems to
be filtered under ground, between strata of shale, and springs
up perfectly transparent, forming the four sulphur wells now
generally resorted to. This bog has been formed by the rotting
of wood; and the earth of the rotten wood, which is everywhere
distinguishable on digging, is, in many places, four or five feet in
thickness, having a stratum of clay and gravel everywhere under it.

Dr. Hunter, in 1830, dissipated this illusion, by declaring
"that if the moss was every particle swept away, or if it was
cut and used for turf fuel, its absence would not in any way
affect these waters."

Only two of these wells are used for drinking—the "Hospital
strong Sulphur Well," over which is a stone dome, and the
"Hospital mild Sulphur Well," or Magnesia Spring, over which
a neat little pump room was built by the Improvement Commissioners, in 1858, at a cost of £100. There is a pump at
the Chalybeate Spring, in the Hospital garden. The other
wells are only walled around up to the level of the surface, and
covered by flap doors.† The water is chiefly used for bathing
purposes.

* "Treatise on the mineral waters of Harrogate."—p. 90.
† These wells were walled round or put into repair in the years 1844 and
1845. The following payments appear in the Commissioners' accounts for
those years.

1844.—July 6th.—Ben. Winterburn repairing wells at the Bogs	6	2	11
Aug. 5th.	do.	do.	14	4	0
Sep. 2nd.	do.	do.	1	16	0
1845.—March 3.	do.	do.	22	12	6
May 5th.	do.	do.	9	6	0
			£54	1	5

In 1870, twelve other wells were opened by the Commissioners. Of these three are pure chalybeates, and according to the analysis of Mr. R. H. Davis, contain 1.527 grains of carbonate of iron per gallon; one is a saline chalybeate, containing 7.545 grains of carbonate of iron, and 194.850 grains of saline constituents to the gallon. Two are strong sulphur waters, similar to the Hospital strong Sulphur Well; and two are mild sulphur, similar to the Magnesia Well. The saline chalybeate, and two of the others, have been conveyed in glass tubes to the Royal Pump Room and the Victoria Baths.

In 1854, Professor Hofmann made the most complete analysis of the waters of Harrogate which had ever been made, including all the principal springs—both sulphurious and chalybeate—the result of which is given in the following tabulated synopsis, which shows the number of grains of saline constituents in the gallon of water.

	I. Old Sulphur Well.	II. Montpell'r strong Sulphur Well.	III. Montpell'r mild Sulphur Well.	IV. Hospital strong Sulphur Well.	V. Hospital mild Sulphur Well.	VI. Starbeck Sulphur Spa.
Sulphate of lime	·182	·594	12·104	51·660	1·215	·870
Carbont. of lime	12·365	24·182	20·457	25·560	19·794	6·960
Fluoride of calc.	trace	trace	trace	trace	—	fnt. trace
Chloride of calc.	81·735	61·910	—	—	—	—
Chl. of magnsm.	55·693	54·667	17·140	11·595	·336	—
Carb. of magnsa.	—	—	3·251	5·797	10·810	5·890
Chl. of potassm.	64·701	5·750	3·975	10·751	24·970	—
Carb. of potassa	—	—	—	—	—	12·207
Chl. of sodium	866·180	803·098	232·413	369·014	220·630	121·798
Brom. of sodium	trace	—	trace	trace	trace	trace
Iodide of sodium	trace	—	trace	trace	trace	trace
Sulph. of sodium	15·479	14·414	3·398	7·155	·801	1·711
Carbnt. of soda	—	—	—	—	—	5·183
Ammonia	trace	trace	trace	trace	trace	trace
Carbnt. of iron	trace	trace	trace	trace	trace	trace
Carb. of mangan.	trace	trace	trace	trace	trace	trace
Silica	·246	1·840	·165	·535	1·49	1·758
Organic matter	trace	trace	trace	trace	trace	1·740
Total..	1096·580	966·456	292·903	437·966	279·046	157·562

Cubic inches of the gases in the gallon of water.

	I. Old Sulphur Well.	II. Montpell'r strong Sulphur Well.	III. Montpell'r mild Sulphur Well.	IV. Hospital strong Sulphur Well.	V. Hospital mild Sulphur Well.	VI. Starbeck Sulphur Spa.
Carbonic acid..	23·03	14·01	14·28	9·54	10·20	9·26
Carbnet'd hydr.	5·84	·53	·90	·15	5·28	5·15
Sulphrt'd hydr.	5·31	—	—	·54	—	trace
Oxygen	—	·48	—	—	1·81	—
Nitrogen......	2·91	4·82	7·67	19·78	5·87	4·21
Total..	·36·09	19·84	22·85	30·01	23·16	18·62

* The water of the Old Sulphur Well was analysed, in 1868, by Dr. Sheridan Muspratt, with the following result—

	Grains in Imp. gal.
Carbonate of lime	10·545
Carbonate of magnesia	2·864
Chloride of sodium	862·412
Chloride of potassium..............	69·897
Chloride of magnesium	61·769
Chloride of calcium................	79·878
Chloride of barium	4·998
Chloride of strontium	} mere trcs.
Chloride of lithium	
Sulphide of sodium	16·418
Iodides, bromides, ammonia, &c.	mere trcs.
	1108·781

Cubic inches of carbonic acid in the gallon   25·55

CHALYBEATE WATERS.

Grains of saline constituents in the gallon of water.

	I. Montpell'r Saline Chalybeate	II. Cheltnh'm Saline Chalybeate	III. Tewhit Well.	IV. John's Well.
Sulphate of lime.........	—	—	·697	·307
Carbonate of lime	—	7·604	1·435	2·264
Fluoride of calcium	—	trace	—	—
Chloride of calcium	159·278	51·629	—	—
Chloride of magnesium	35·635	34·027	—	—
Carbonate of magnesia	41·796	—	2·667	3·039
Chloride of potassium	11·383	27·410	1·323	—
Carbonate of potassa	—	—	1·057	·991
Chloride of sodium	656·838	158·840	·280	1·548
Bromide of sodium	trace	trace	trace	—
Iodide of sodium	trace	trace	trace	—
Carbonate of soda	—	—	—	1·338
Ammonia	trace	trace	trace	trace
Carbonate of iron	2·790	4·627	1·358	·609
Carbonate of manganese ..	trace	trace	trace	—
Silica	·947	1·450	1·041	trace
Organic matter	trace	·282	·663	trace
Total....	908·667	285·869	11·021	10·091

Cubic inches of the gases in the gallon of water.

Carbonic acid	24·17	19·50	11·85	14·95
Carbonetted hydrogen	2·40	5·00	—	·15
Oxygen	·51	1·02	·40	·67
Nitrogen	6·48		5·53	6·35
Total....	33·56	25·52	17·98	22·12

The following analysis, made by Dr. Higgins, in 1780, styled by Dr. Garnett "the nearest the truth of any that has yet appeared," is curious, as showing the state of chemical science and nomenclature at that time.

oz. d. grs.

"A Winchester gallon of Harrogate water contains, of calcareous earth, saturated with acidulous gas.... 0 1 12¼
Marine salt of magnesia 0 4 28¼
Sea salt 1 7 12¼

1 14 0

It moreover contains four measures of acidulous gas, beyond the quantity retained by the calcareous earth in the heat of boiling water; and thirty five ounce measures of fœtid inflammable gas, such as may be extricated from calcareous liver of sulphur by vitriolic acid."

The waters have been thus classified by the medical profession—

I. The strong sulphur waters of the Old Well, and the Montpellier strong sulphur well, are stimulant, aperient, diuretic, sedative, and specific.

II. The mild sulphur waters, of which there are seventeen springs, are diuretic, alterative, resolvent, diaphoretic, sedative, and specific.

III. The saline chalybeates, of which there are two springs, are stimulant, tonic, aperient, diuretic, and deobstruent.

IV. The pure chalybeates, are excitant, tonic, and diuretic.

THE BATHS.

NEXT in importance to drinking the waters is their application by means of the bath. The first method of applying this at Harrogate was of a rude and primitive kind, being by means of long narrow tubs, in shape like coffins,* at the different inns and lodging houses.   In 1832, Mr. John Williams erected a suite of commodious baths, now belonging to a joint stock company, and known as

THE VICTORIA BATHS.

These are situate in Low Harrogate, near the Town Hall, in a low building with an Ionic front, placed within the ground rather than upon it.   The entrance is by two flights of steps to

---

* This manner of bathing has been satirically described by many writers ; among others by Mrs. Hofland, in " A Season in Harrogate," 1811.

Astonished I saw when I came to my doffing,
A tub of hot water made just like a coffin,
In which the good woman who attended the bath,
Declar'd I must lie down as straight as a lath,
Just keeping my face above water, that so
I might better inhale the fine fumes from below.
" But mistress, quoth I, in a trembling condition,
I hope you'll allow me one small requisition,
Since scrophula, leporasy, herpes and scurvy,
Have all in this coffin been roll'd topsy turvy ;
In a physical sense I presume it is meet,
Each guest should be wrapped in a clean winding sheet ?"
" Oh no ! my good sir ; for whatever's your case,
You never can catch any thing bad in this place ;
And that being settled on solid foundation,
We Harrogate bath-women spurn innovation !"
So cavelier like I submitted to power,
And was coddled in troth for the third of an hour.

the sides intended respectively for Ladies and Gentlemen. The bath rooms are thirteen in number, supplied with all things requisite for convenience and comfort. The strong and mild sulphur waters are administered in all the variety of vapour, fume, shower and douche baths. These baths and estate were purchased by the Harrogate Improvement Commissioners in 1870, for the sum of £6,600.

THE MONTPELLIER BATHS.

This suite of baths, situate in the garden of that name, were erected by Mr. Thackwray, of the Crown Hotel, in 1835. They are elegant in appearance and commodious in arrangement. The water is drawn from ten different springs, by pumps worked by a small steam engine, into a reservoir, where it is heated by steam from the boiler. There are sixteen bath rooms, eight on each side, with dressing rooms attached. One side of the building is set apart for ladies, the other for gentlemen. There are two baths especially adapted for old people, or invalids. The strong or mild sulphur water is supplied in any manner the case may require.

THE COLD BATH.

This is, or rather was, situate at the top of Cold Bath Road, to which it has given its name. In point of antiquity, this is far the oldest bath in Harrogate; the spring which supplied it has borne the name of St. Mungo, or St. Magnus Well from the most remote ages. Pennant, who visited Harrogate in 1777, thus speaks of it,—"It appears that St. Mungo, a Scottish saint, who, about the year 543, driven by persecution from his see at Glasgow, to the protection of his friend St. David, in Wales, visited this place, and left his name to a Well which it still retains. It is probable he bathed and bestowed his

benediction on the waters.   They are the annual resort of
numbers of North Britons, who with laudable nationality
bathe with double faith in springs sanctified by their saintly
countryman."*

Dr. Dean, in 1626, says,—" Of Springs, we have plenty,
and of such reputation, that two of them are sainted, viz.,
St. Mungo's and St. Robert's well; to which have flocked
for bathing, innumerable herds of people these last two years,
though they contain no mineral, and are of no credit at
present."

Dr. French, writing in 1656, has a more favourable opinion
of the virtues of this cold bath :—" For if a man bathe or
wash in it a quarter of an hour, when he comes out he will
presently be very hot, and continue so a long time, even in a
cold air, and without his cloaths.   Nay, upon tender women,
who dare not go into water, they sweat towards morning if
they lie in their wet linen all night, whereby they are often
cured of old aches in any part of their body, and of swellings,
hard tumours and agues, and of many other outward distempers,
whether from cold or hot humours.   Such as have tender
heads, and cannot do without many cloaths upon them, or
are liable to frequent severe colds, three or four mornings'
washing their head in this water cures them.   However, I
would have none to use it rashly, without the advice of a
physician.   The well is built four-square, and has a house by
it, to dress and undress in.   The spring rises higher in May,
and falls about September."

Neither its sainted name, its reputed, almost miraculous
virtues, nor its real usefulness have been able to save it from
almost entire neglect, for now it is but rarely used.

* Tour from Alston Moor to Harrogate, p. 114.

· PUBLIC BUILDINGS. ·

THE ROYAL CHALYBEATE SPA AND CONCERT ROOM.

This is the largest and most elegant public room in the town. The entrance is by a flight of steps,* through a lofty portico of six massive fluted Doric columns, supporting a projecting pediment in the same style of architecture. The saloon is one hundred feet in length by thirty-three in breadth, and lofty in proportion, with an elegantly decorated ceiling; it is lighted by fifteen windows. On the right of the entrance is the library, on the left the pump room, where the saline and chalybeate waters are obtainable. It was built at the cost of Mr. John Williams, from a design by Mr. Clarke, of Leeds, and was opened by a grand dress ball, and magnificent display of fireworks, in August 1835. This room is occasionally used for balls and lectures. During the *season* concerts are given every evening by first rate performers, vocal and instrumental. Attached is a piece of ground about six acres in extent, laid out in walks, and adorned with a fountain, statues, beds of flowers,

---

* Near the entrance, on a brass plate is engraved—

	d	'	"
Latitude	53	59	27 N.
Longitude	1	31	53 } West of
Longitude in Time..............	0	6	7·5 } Greenwich.

Elevation above the mean level of the Sea, 829 feet.
Placed in 1847.

shrubs, and ornamented plants; relieved at intervals by easy seats and alcoves. In 1862, this room and grounds were purchased by a joint stock company, for the sum of £5,100, from the representatives of the late Mr. Williams. In 1865, a new terrace was formed, and the grounds much improved.

In 1870, the original pump room was removed and an elegant wing of iron and glass erected on that side. This building stands upon a basement of masonry 71 feet in length by 19 feet in breadth; above which rises the superstructure to a height of 13 feet, where it terminates in an ornamental cornice; above this is the roof swelling upwards in the shape of three domes; the central one being the largest, which is surmounted with an octagonal tower and spire, rising to the height of 55 feet above the basement. This contains pump room, ample and elegant, promenade and retiring rooms,—and is in fact a miniature crystal palace.

THE ROYAL PUMP ROOM.

This building which covers the Old Sulphur Wells, was erected in 1842, from a design by Mr. Isaac Thomas Shutt, at a cost of about £2,000.*   The plan is an octagon, four

* From the Accounts of the Improvement Commissioners we gather the following particulars of the cost of this building:—

	£	s.	d.
Messrs. Simpson, Mason's work	951	0	0
James Holdsworth, Joiner's work	427	7	7
J. H. Place, Plumbing and Glazing	201	13	10
James Nelson, Palisading	90	0	0
Joseph Fortune, Plasterer's work	82	19	8
William Lawson, Painter's work	9	18	6
Architect's Commission	109	0	0
John Uttley, for Ornamental Tablet in Room, with Commissioners' names	10	10	0
Cooke & Co., for Pump	324	16	0
,, Air Pump	42	0	0
	£2249	0	7

of the sides projecting beyond the others, the angles are adorned with moulded pilasters, rising from a moulded plinth, and surmounted by an entablature. The four projecting sides are finished with triangular pediments ; above which swells a dome terminated by eight dolphins supporting a crown and blaze terminal. The diameter of the room is 85 feet, and the height from the floor to the stained glass light 46 feet. The stained glass windows in the interior have been added recently—that on the north bearing the armorial shield of Harrogate, in 1869, that on the south representing an angel " troubling the water " in the centre compartment, and the arms of Sir William Slingsby, Knight, discoverer of the first mineral spring at Harrogate, in the left hand compartment ; and those of Sir Charles Slingsby, Bart., who was accidentally drowned in the river Ure, at Newby Ferry, February 4th, 1869, in the right—in 1870.

This is the Temple of Hygeia, to which the many thousand visitors of Harrogate resort to drink the strong health-restoring waters of the *Old Sulphur Well*,—" the *Magnum Dei Donum*, nature's great endowment—the strength—the glory of Harrogate—which has raised it from an obscure village to its present eminence, and will chiefly contribute to establish it as the Queen of British Watering Places."[†]

The following table extracted from the Subscription Books preserved in the Royal Pump Room, shows the number of

The total cost of building, furnishing, and maintaining the three pump rooms,—the Royal, Tewhit, and John's Well for the first seven years, from 1842 to 1849, was £2,905 12s. 2d.

Amongst the " proffessional work," we find the following items.—" 1842, Jan. 29th, Professor Phillips, for journey and report as to the danger of sinking wells in the neighbourhood of the springs, £6 15s. 0d."

" 1844, June 14th, William West for analyzing Waters, and his expenses, £17 13s. 11½d."

[†] Smith's Harrogate Medical Guide, p. 27.

water drinkers at this well, from the 22nd July, 1842, to the end of the year 1867.

Year	Jan.	Feb.	Mar.	Apr.	May.	June.	July.	Aug.	Sep.	Oct.	Nov.	Dec.	Total.
1842	..	..	..	..	..	..	478	1224	1090	877	89	20	8778
1843	10	1	34	156	561	970	2235	1794	2395	637	63	25	8881
1844	14	10	28	284	602	1041	1909	2630	3579	865	90	18	11070
1845	3	14	36	185	647	1190	1525	2480	2545	771	180	20	9596
1846	21	31	80	160	420	1120	1460	2040	2280	560	120	10	8302
1847	5	12	44	158	560	1120	1320	2006	1800	440	120	11	7596
1848	7	11	37	188	760	960	1240	1818	1884	562	80	26	7573
1849	13	25	74	162	606	1442	1760	2326	2160	960	158	32	9711
1850	31	16	156	310	720	1540	1876	2482	2518	800	160	30	10639
1851	26	48	88	282	716	1122	1380	1766	2081	720	124	26	8379
1852	36	27	113	224	560	1200	1680	2368	2406	766	162	35	9577
1853	44	40	93	326	1000	1321	1440	2240	2086	686	160	17	9453
1854	7	31	125	360	648	1440	1460	2048	2044	840	120	13	·9136
1855	9	8	31	265	640	1052	1484	1930	2014	608	104	6	8151
1856	8	26	99	242	560	1048	1451	1966	2044	642	162	24	8272
1857	24	32	61	248	582	1241	1242	1646	1840	686	80	6	7688
1858	18	33	44	320	500	1010	1086	1606	1848	560	94	22	7141
1859	18	31	76	222	560	1004	1280	1800	1566	606	55	17	7237
1860	15	16	59	212	680	806	1160	1360	1600	546	76	26	6556
1861	9	33	109	282	560	926	1183	1360	1646	568	67	16	6709
1862	27	25	86	286	721	1120	1366	2080	2122	820	118	31	8802
1863	30	60	175	520	960	1480	2008	2160	2304	810	150	55	10712
1864	39	62	196	522	1240	1608	1886	2544	2408	966	133	40	11644
1865	38	24	118	640	910	1909	1813	2405	2450	980	185	53	11525
1866	36	46	198	506	1110	1591	1998	2238	2275	1147	240	60	11445
1867	28	69	148	555	999	1887	1834	2701	2268	892	205	40	11626

THE TOWN HALL, OR OLD PROMENADE ROOM,

Situate near the Victoria Baths, and belonging to the same company, was built in 1806, at the suggestion of G. Cayley,

Esq., M.D., as a promenade for visitors, where they might find amusement in weather not suitable for out-door exercises. It is 75 feet long by 80 wide, and has been generally used for public meetings, and other purposes connected with the business of the town. Here is a Reading Room well supplied during the season with newspapers and periodicals. On the same premises is a public Billiard Room.

THE VICTORIA HALL

Is situate in James Street, near the Prospect House Hotel. This building has a somewhat singular history; in 1749, the materials of which it is composed were built into St. John's Chapel, situate close to where Christ's Church now stands, and was the first building erected for religious purposes in Harrogate, it continued in that state until 1831, when on the present church being built it was sold with all its fittings to the Independents for the sum of £100, who removed it to its present site, and erected it as it was before, with the addition of a new front, and it continued to be the place of worship of that denomination until the erection of their present church, in 1862; when it was sold, and used for no particular purpose, until 1866, when it was purchased by Captain Thomas Holt, who fitted it up as a drill room and armoury, for the corps of Harrogate Rifle Volunteers, a purpose for which it is well adapted. It is also used occasionally for public meetings, concerts and other purposes.

THE BATH HOSPITAL.

This truly charitable institution, built, and entirely supported by voluntary contributions, is situated immediately above the bogs. It is open to the sick poor of the kingdom (with the exception of three miles around Harrogate) afflicted with disorders in which the waters of Harrogate are beneficial

It owes its origin to the exertions of many benevolent persons,
principally visitors, who having themselves derived benefit
from the waters were wishful to extend the same benefit to
others. Amongst these was the Hon. Montague Burgoyne,
of East Sheen, in Surrey, whose humane and persevering
exertions were beyond all praise. Dr. Adam Hunter, of Leeds,
aided the good cause by his pen, and Mr. Richardson, surgeon,
Harrogate, rendered very efficient service as treasurer to the
infant institution. At a public meeting October 2nd, 1848,
the Earl of Harewood in the chair,—it was resolved to build
baths and hospital wards for the poor requiring the use of
the waters. The noble chairman, not only contributed a
liberal sum of money, but also presented the site for the
buildings. "I have on my part done my best," said his
lordship, "next to alienating altogether the land, which I cannot do, to make it a permanent possession to the poor; and
I hope I may answer for the benevolence of my descendants."
The land on which the buildings stand, an acre and a half
in extent, was by the noble earl's descendants, in 1853,
conveyed to trustees, for the use of Harrogate Bath Hospital
for ever. The list of subscribers to the foundation was a
noble one, worthy of the cause, including even royalty itself.*

* King George IV. contributed fifty guineas, the earls Fitzwilliam and
Harewood £50 each; R. F. Wilson, Esq., £50; the Misses Ford £25;
the duke of Devonshire, Montague Burgoyne, Esq., Miss Currer, Rev.
Thomas Collins, Lord Grantham, Sir W. A. Ingilby, Bart., Sir Thomas
Slingsby, Bart., and Mr. Richardson, each twenty guineas; John Watson,
Esq., £15; R. Bethell, Esq., John Blaydes, Esq., James Brown, Esq.,
Colonel Cholmley, E. S. Cooper, Esq., W. Danby, Esq., R. O. Gascoigne,
Benjamin Gott, Esq., the Bishop of Landaff, the earl of Scarborough, W.
Sheepshanks, Esq., the Archbishop of York, B. Thompson, Esq., Sir F. L.
Wood, Bart., and several others, £10 each.

	£	s.	d.
The amount expended in building Hospital and Baths..	1147	19	8
In furnishing the same............................	185	7	8½
In Advertisements, Printing, Stationery and Postages..	19	10	1

£1352 17 0½

Many benevolent individuals have bequeathed legacies to its use.† "And it is a satisfaction to know," writes Dr. Hunter, "that the utility of this charity has more than equalled the most sanguine expectations of its founders. Several hundreds of the worst descriptions of cases, for which these waters are found beneficial, have either been completely restored to health, or very much relieved. Few medical charities have effected more with the same relative means, and no charity can be deserving of more steady and liberal support."

The first buildings were erected in 1823-4, and opened for the reception of patients in the spring of 1825. At first only twenty-five beds were provided. In 1829, it was found that the income was sufficient to support a larger establishment, and it was enlarged. This has been repeatedly done, and at considerable cost; yet the funds of the institution have always been found sufficient to meet all claims. A glance at the buildings will show that no money has been spent in useless ornamentation, at the same time all is plain and substantial, neat and clean. Over the entrance is inscribed—

BATH HOSPITAL.
ERECTED A.D. 1824.
SUPPORTED BY VOLUNTARY
SUBSCRIPTIONS.

During the first twelve years, from 1826 to 1837, inclusive, 2,181 patients were admitted to the benefits of this establishment, at a cost of £3,984 14s.

† Amongst these may be reckoned a legacy by R. Clarke, Esq., of £450, received in 1825; that of Mrs. Lawrence, of Studley Park, £1,000, in 1846; T. Clapham, Esq., £3,600; L. Brande, Esq., £270; R. Richardson, Esq., £100; Misses E. and S. Cawood, £121 18s. 1d., received in 1858; Mrs. Mason, £200; H. Brown, Esq., £50, received in 1861; B. J. Wilson, Esq., £100; W. Pearson, Esq., £18; Miss Beckett £1,000, received in 1866; T. Durham, Esq., £100, received in 1867; Thomas Clayton, Esq., Wakefield, £100, in 1868; Mr. William Sinclair, of Sowerby, near Thirsk, £200, in 1869; Mr. George Rogers, of Harrogate, £250, in 1870.

CHRIST CHURCH.

In early times the township of Bilton-with-Harrogate formed part of the Parish of Knaresborough, and all rites of baptism, marriage, and sepulture were performed at the Church there. Early in the eighteenth century, the increased population began to feel the want of Church accommodation at home, and in the year 1748, a public subscription was commenced for the erection of a Chapel of Ease; the pious and benevolent lady, Elizabeth Hastings, aiding the effort by a donation of £50.* The project was interrupted by the break- ing out of the rebellion in Scotland, in 1745; but was afterwards resumed, and a small Chapel dedicated to St. John, was built and consecrated in 1749. It stood on the north side of the present Church, near the tall elm trees in the burial ground.

In order to form an endowment for their new Chapel, the inhabitants, taking advantage of an Act of Parliament passed in 1718, "for making enclosures of some part of the common grounds in the West Riding of the County York, for the endowing poor vicarages and chapelries for the better support of their ministers." By a general agreement between the lord of the manor and copyholders, a quantity of land was enclosed upon the forest, afterwards known as the "king's chapel land," situate on the east of the Stray, between the Knaresborough road and the Wetherby road. The rent of this land was applied to the maintenance of the minister, which he continued to receive until the general enclosure, when the land was resumed by the crown, and £30 per

* The Subscription list is dated August 2nd, 1748; Lady Hastings gave £50; Richard Arundell, £10 10s. 0d. The whole sum subscribed was £171 1s. 6d., and the number of subscribers 86.

annum assigned to the minister, out of the revenues of the duchy of Lancaster, in lieu thereof.

In the year 1829, this Chapel was found inadequate to the wants of the place, and its entire removal was decided on, and a subscription was at once begun towards the erection of a new Church. The architect was Mr. John Oates, of Huddersfield, and the work was commenced early in the summer of 1830, and the completed building, styled Christ Church, was consecrated and opened for divine service October 1st, 1831. The cost, including catacombs, which extend under the whole building, was £4,500, of which only about £1,800 was assured to the committee when the works were commenced. £800 were raised by voluntary subscriptions,* £700 granted by the Church Building Society, and a donation of £800 was received from the Duchy court of Lancaster. The clock in the tower was the gift of William Sheepshanks, Esq., of Leeds and Harrogate.

The plan consisted originally of a nave with tower. at the west end, in the early pointed style of architecture. It contained at first 1,250 sittings, of which 800 were free; in 1862, it was enlarged by the addition of transepts on the north and south, and a chancel on the east, which with some minor alterations were effected at a cost of £1.500; by this means 240 additional seats were obtained. The reredos added at the same time is a piece of beautifully carved work. In January, 1858, the Church was lighted with gas, at the cost of £100, raised by subscription amongst the inhabitants.

* Among the contributors was the Archbishop of York £50; the Bishop of Chester £50; the Bishop of Durham £50; John Greenwood, Esq., £20; the Rev. Thomas Collins, of Knaresborough, £10; John Baldwin, Esq., £10; the Rev. John Charge, Copgrove, £5. The remainder of the money was received from the inhabitants, visitors, and others residing at a distance from Harrogate.

The interior does not present any thing particularly remarkable, except the number of tablets placed against the
walls, most of them to the memory of strangers, from nearly
all parts of the united kingdom, who have come to Harrogate
in search of health, and found death and a grave. We give
the inscriptions to the two deceased incumbents of the church,
in full, and make a selection, or condensation of some of
the others. At the south-west corner, on a marble tablet is
inscribed :—

"Sacred to the memory of Jane, wife of the Rev. Robert
Mitton. Born, A.D. 1756, Obt. 11th Dec., 1808. Also,
Jane, daughter of the above Robert and Jane Mitton, Obt.
17th January, 1791. Also, of the Rev, Robert Mitton, 56
years incumbent of this Church, Obt. 9th February, 1825.
An. Æt. 86. Also, of Robert, eldest son of the above Robert
and Jane Mitton, Paymaster of His Mty's, 47 Regt., Obt. 6
May, 1826, at Calcutta, An. Æt. 46,"

"Sacred to the memory of the Rev. Thomas Kennion, M.A.,
of Christ's College, Cambridge, for nearly 20 years Incumbent
minister of High Harrogate. He died at Cheltenham, on the
27th of January, 1846, in the 58th year of his age. His
remains are in a vault in the churchyard of Leckhampton.
        'He being dead yet speaketh.' "

One of the most active of the founders of the Harrogate Bath
Hospital* is thus commemorated—

"Sacred to the memory of Robert Richardson, Esq., who·
was for the space of fifty years an eminent surgeon in this
place, and founder of the Harrogate Bath Hospital. He died

* The following inscription on a headstone in the churchyard, is to the
memory of the first matron,—"Isabella Winterburn, who for upwards of
twenty years was the highly respected matron of the Harrogate Bath
Hospital, died Oct. 25th, 1845, aged 65 years. Erected at the expense of
the charity, by order of the committee."

at Cheltenham, 20th May, 1853, in his 81st year. Buried in a vault beneath this Church.

Also, Jane, wife of the above, who died 22nd June, 1828, in the 73rd year of her age."

Here is yet another inscription to what may be styled a public benefactor,—

"John Shearwood Mathewman, of Thorp-arch, born at Leeds, December 5th, 1798, died at Harrogate, August 29th, 1819. Richard Mathewman, his father, died at Harrogate, October 24th, 1843, aged 80 years. Jane Mathewman, his widow, died at Harrogate, June 1st, 1848, aged 83 years. She left to the Borough of Leeds, her native place, the sum of £31,000, for the promotion of divine worship according to the liturgy and usages of the Church of England."

This last is on a large and elegant marble tablet, with a cross and bible carved in relief above, and the motto *In hoc spes est;* above which is a dove bearing an olive branch.

The following are selected and condensed :—

Catherine Parry, of Strawberry-dale Cottage, died March 8th, 1844, resided there 22 years,—a native of Birmingham.

William James Fraser, Esq., of Ladhope, Roxburghshire, died at Harrogate, the 8th of August, 1838, aged 44 years. "A kind master, a warm friend, a most devoted husband; in life beloved, in death lamented."

Thomas James Haskoll, Esq., of Newport, in the Isle of Wight, died at Harrogate, November 11th, 1811, aged 57 years.

The Honourable Mrs. Massy Dawson, of Ireland, died May 26th, 1805, aged 69 years.

William Camac, Esq., of Mansfield Street, London, and Hastings, Sussex; of the Company's Bengal Civil Service; died at Harrogate, August 11th, 1837, aged 67 years.

Hannah Dove, wife of Richard Warner, Esq., of Mortimer Cottage, Berks., died 30th October, 1832, in the 45th year of her age. She was sixth daughter of the Rev. Robert Hoadley Ash, D.D.

Alexander Strachan, Esq., of Tarrie, in the county of Forfar, Scotland, died 21st July, 1808, aged 62 years.

John Todd, Esq., died July 19th, 1804, aged 87 years.

Henrietta Lally, by Ann Lally.

John Hunter, Esq., of Lisburn, in the county of Antrim, Ireland, died at Bilton Park, October 12th, 1823, in the 59th year of his age.

Eliza Outram, daughter of the late Benjamin Outram, of Butterley Hall, Derbyshire, died at Harrogate, 7th July, 1824, aged 19 years.

"This humble tablet, which is placed only to mark the grave of ONE, who was the ornament, the instructress, and the example of her sex, is dedicated to the memory of Elizabeth Hamilton, as a testimony of grief and affection, by her sister and her friend Katherine Blake. She was born at Belfast, July 25th, 1756, and died at Harrogate, July 23rd, 1816."

Ann, wife of William Bingley, of Harrogate, died June 23rd, 1832, aged 52 years. William Bingley, Esq., died January 24th, 1847, aged 78 years. Charlotte, daughter of William Bingley, Esq., died June 8th, 1843. Susanna, daughter of William Bingley, died September 23rd, 1847.

Eleanor Primrose Dundas, third daughter of Major General Thomas Dundas, of Carron Hall, in the county of Sterling, N.B., died 14th March, 1815, aged 26 years.

An elegant decorated tablet commemorates the family of Carter, of Harrogate.

Thomas Whincup, eldest son of Nicholas and Mary Carter, of this place, born 28th March, 1807; died at Gonzales,

Texas, 17th August, 1887. Ellen Darnborough, second daughter, born 26th May, 1810; died at Panther's Hall, near Pitsburgh, U.S., 6th April, 1898. Mary Ellen, eldest daughter, born 17th July, 1808; died at Ilkley, 3rd August, 1850.

Hannah, wife of John Hunter, of Milburne and Hallowell, in the county of Northumberland, died at Leamington, July 18th, 1840, aged 77 years.

The Rev. Arthur Guinness, Incumbent of Seaton Carew, Coy. Durham, died 14th October, 1885, aged 89 years.

Charlotte - Cawthorn, second daughter of Jonathan Shutt, the elder of this place, died October 27th, 1850, aged 58 years.

Ann Powell, relict of the Rev. Francis Meeke, and niece of William Meeke, Esq., of Kirk Hammerton, in this county, died 30th September, 1842.

Sacred to the memory of Thomas Frith, Esq., of Harrogate, who died in London, January 31st, 1887, and was interred at Kensall Green. Also of Jane, widow of the above Thomas Frith, who died at York, November 19th, 1851; and whose remains lie in a vault near this place. Also, of their sons, George, who died June 10th, 1831, aged 15 years; and Charles Frith, Esq., Barrister-at-Law, who died at Dover, October 9th, 1851, aged 80 years, and was interred at Kensall Green.*

James Charles Bladwell Ogilvie, Esq., of Swannington Hall, Norfolk, died at Harrogate, 31st August, 1848, aged 77 years.

* These were the father, mother, and brothers of William Powell Frith, R.A., the celebrated artist. In the church-yard, north of the church, are the following inscriptions, also belonging to the same family.—" Sacred to the memory of Elizabeth Frith, who died December 19th, 1828, in the 74th year of her age." The above is on an upright stone. On a slab on the ground close adjoining is,—" Beneath are deposited the mortal remains of George, the eldest son of Thomas and Jane Frith, who departed this life June 10th, 1831, in the 15th year of his age. His life and death were a bright example of early grace."

Edward Dearlove, Assistant Surgeon in the Bombay division of the army of the Punjaub, died at Sukker, June 20th, 1849, aged 32 years.

Anne Browne, wife of Henry Browne, Esq., of Bilton House, Harrogate, died 15th February, 1857, aged 57 years. Henry Browne, Esq., died 22nd April, 1859, aged 59 years.

Elizabeth Susannah, daughter of John Martin, Esq., of Roundhay, near Leeds, died at Harrogate, March 7th, 1861, in the 19th year of her age.

Rachael Benn, wife of Jonathan Benn, of Harrogate, died March 3rd, 1851, aged 70 years. Jonathan Benn, died November 22nd, 1858, aged 69 years.

In memory of Fountain Brown, Esq., of Harrogate, who died March 15th, 1851, aged 80 years. Henry, son of the above, captain in her majesty's 54th regiment, died at Dominica, West Indies, September 19th, 1849, aged 41 years. Frances, relict of the above Fountain Brown, died March 21st, 1861, aged 82 years.

Thomas Holt, of Wedderburn House, Harrogate, died March 9th, 1855, aged 74 years. Also, Elizabeth, his wife, who died at Headingley, November 28rd, 1860, aged 72 years.

Sarah Reed, wife of George Reed, of Harrogate, died May 19th, 1845, in her 59th year.

Charles Charlesworth, Esq., of Harrogate, died December 2nd, 1836, aged 57 years. Also, Mary, his wife, who died March 13th, 1833, aged 58 years.

Thomas Maude, Esq., formerly of Saville Place, Newcastle-on-Tyne, for several years resident at Woodlands, near Harrogate, died January 28th, 1831, in his 61st year. Also, Jane, widow of the above, who died December 11th, 1833, in her 60th year.

On a board at the west end is inscribed,—"This Church was rebuilt and enlarged in the year 1831. It contains sittings for 1,250 persons, and, in consequence of a grant from the Incorporated Society for promoting the enlargement, building, and repairing of Churches and Chapels, 800 of that number are hereby declared to be free and unappropriated for ever.

THOMAS KENNION, A.M., Incumbent Minister.
THOMAS FIRTH, Churchwarden."

The stained glass windows in the transepts are all memorials. That in the south was erected by public subscription in memory of the late Prince Consort. Here are four different subjects, all suggestive of the virtues of the departed prince, as well as the armorial bearings of the prince and her majesty Queen Victoria. That in the north transept to the memory of the Rev. Robert Mitton, 56 years incumbent of this church, who died February 9th, 1825, aged 86 years. This window also contains representations of six events in which water acts a prominent part, and which consequently may be said to be typical of Harrogate—these are "Moses striking the rock in Horeb, and the water flowing therefrom." "Naaman the Syrian, dipping in Jordan." "The Baptism of Christ in the River Jordan." "The Pool of Bethsaida." "The Samaritan Woman at the Well of Sychar;" and "The Pool of Siloam."

The chancel window of three lights is filled with stained glass; that on the northern side represents "Christ bearing the Cross," and the "Raising of Lazarus." At the bottom is inscribed,—"In memory of Mary, wife of Henry Forbes, Esq., of Harrogate. She died October 9, 1866, aged 68 years."

The central one is inscribed "To the glory of God, and to the memory of John Green Paley, of Oatlands, who died

October 9th, 1860, aged 86 years;" and bears representations
of, " The Nativity," " The Crucifixion," and " The Ascension."

The other is inscribed, " In memory of Fountain and
Frances Browne, of Harrogate. The former died March 15th,
1841, aged 80 years; and the latter, March 21st, 1861,
aged 82 years ;" and contains representations of the "Raising
of the widow of Nain's Son," and "*Noli me tangere*."

The Church-yard is of a square form, fenced from the
Stray by lofty palisades of iron; trees have been planted around
the sides, which add much to the beauty of its appearance;
the lofty elms on the north, which sheltered the chapel of
St. John, have quite a venerable aspect.* The whole of
the ground is full of memorials of the dead, and mingled
with the natives are many strangers. The oldest we have
observed is to the memory of James Cope, who died in 1764.

An upright headstone on the south side of the church
bears the following singular inscription :—

" Dear wife ! the trumpet shall sound and the dead shall
arise."

Near the south-west corner of the ground is the following :—
" Sacred to the memory of James Brougham, Esq., of
Stobars, near Kirkby Stephen, in the county of Westmorland,
who departed this life, at Low Harrogate, on the 9th day of
September, 1845, in his 71st year.

His hope was altogether founded on the promises of a
covenant God in Christ Jesus. His life was an illustration
of the gracious effects of gospel principles, and his end was
peace. `He lived generally beloved, and died sincerely and
deeply lamented."

* The site of the altar of the old chapel of St. John is marked by a low
gravestone, on which is a brass plate, formerly inside the chapel, on which
is inscribed,—" Sacred to the memory of Phœbe Benson, who departed
this life the 20th day of August, 1793, in the 22nd year of her age."
" Blessed are the dead which die in the Lord."

"Other foundation can no man lay than that is laid, which is Jesus Christ."—I. Cor., iii. c., 2. v.

"Blessed are the dead which die in the Lord."—Rev. xiv. c., 13 v.

On a slab of red granite, inserted in a square tomb, is inscribed,—"Sacred to the memory of Margaret Ewart, widow of the late William Ewart, Esq., of Liverpool, and daughter of Christopher Jaques, Esq., of Bedale, who died at her residence, Spring Bank, Low Harrogate, on the 22nd of January, 1844, in the 71st year of her age."

On an upright headstone south of the church, is—"In memory of the Rev. Edward Fielde, M.A., fourteen years incumbent of Rock and Rennington, in the county of Northumberland, who died at Harrogate, January 25th, 1851, aged 57 years."

At the west end of the church is a monument erected by public subscription, to the memory of Dr. Kennion. It is about 16 feet in height of Carrara marble, in the form of a broken column with drapery, and a bas-relief medallion portrait; beneath which is inscribed—

Sacred to the Memory of

George Kennion, M.D., M.R.C.P.

Born November 18th, 1813,

Died June 30th, 1868.

The Registers for baptisms and burials begin in 1758, that for marriages in 1828.

By the provisions of the Act, 58, George III., cap. 45, and an order in council, dated June 28th, 1828, a district parish was assigned to this church, about eleven miles in circumference.* This has since been reduced in extent by

* The following is the boundary, as defined by the Order in Council.— "To commence at Collins' Bridge, passing westward up the river Crimple to the boundary of Pannal parish, so following the line of the boundary of

the severance from it of the district assigned to St. John's church, Bilton, and also that of St. Peter, in central Harrogate.

The living is a vicarage in the gift of the Bishop of Ripon. After the enclosure of the forest the endowment was only £80 per annum, paid out of the revenues of the duchy of Lancaster. In 1816, it was augmented with a parliamentary grant of £1,200, and in 1831 was returned as worth £96 per annum. In October, 1842, it was further augmented by the Ecclesiastical Commissioners with £54 per annum; and in 1861, it received another augmentation, in a gift of £2,000, by a member of the congregation, to the Incumbent, who paid the same over to the Ecclesiastical Commissioners, who added a £1,000 from the funds at their disposal, so that the living was improved by the interest of £3,000; which, with the parsonage, erected in 1860, may be said to have doubled its former value, although it is now returned as only worth £145 10s. per annum.

There have only been five incumbents of this church,—

The Rev. Robert Mitton, presented 1769, died 1825.

Rev. Thomas Kennion,	,,	1825, died 1846.
Rev. Thos. Sheepshanks,	,,	1846, resigned 1856.
Rev. Horatio James,	,,	1856, resigned 1870.
Rev. Wm. Wynter Gibbon	,,	1870, present incumbent.

the said parish, crossing Hookstone road to Tewit well, then westward over the Leeds and Ripon turnpike road to Gamsgate, from thence in a north-westerly direction to the Otley and Knaresborough turnpike road to the Cold Bath, from thence following the brook north-east to the junction of the two brooks from Cold Bath and the Crescent, Low Harrogate; thence in a westerly direction up the Crescent brook, to the top of the same in the king's allotment and from thence in a northerly direction in a straight line to Ock beck, so following the stream of the said Ock beck until it falls into the river Nidd, and following the river Nidd to the eastern part of the Spring Wood, in Bilton Park, including Spring Wood, Ox Pasture, Savage Wood, Savage Close, Well Close, Little Close, and Moor Close to Harrison Hill road, thence proceeding along Harrison Hill road easterly to the Knaresborough and Harrogate road, at Forest Lane Head, and thence in a southerly direction along the westerly side of Rudding road to Collins' bridge."

THE CHARITIES consist of two rent charges of 20s. each, left by the will of Thomas Boddy, in 1742.

A rent charge of £2, left by the will of William Roundell, in 1729, to be given yearly before the nativity of our Lord Christ, for ever.

A rent charge of £1, given by deed of William Carter, in 1699, and also the interest of £15, given by his will.

The sum of £1 6s. 8d., given by the will of Anthony Acham, in 1638, to be given in wheaten bread, so long as the world shall endure, on the first Sunday in the months of March, May, July, September, November, and January.

The interest of £10, given by the will of William Lupton, in 1788.

A rent charge of £1, given by William Baxter, and the interest of £10, given by a person of the name of Jeffray, are believed to be lost.

And the rent of two pieces of land encroached from the Common, one of 26 perches near Grove House, the other of one rood and eleven perches near Christ's Church.

ST. JOHN'S CHURCH, BILTON.

This Church, which is situate near the northern extremity of the town of Harrogate, was built at the cost of William Sheepshanks, Esq. It is an elegant and substantial specimen of early English architecture, designed by George Gilbert Scott, Esq., A.R.A., London. The plan consists of a chancel, with vestry on the north side, nave, with north and south aisles, porch, and tower at the west end, which is intended to carry a lofty spire.* The aisles are divided from the nave by five acutely pointed arches on each side, supported by four

* The dimensions of the Church are, tower 20 feet by 16 feet, nave 82 feet by 25 feet 6 inches, aisles 11 feet wide, chancel 36 feet by 20 feet.

clustered columns, the capitals adorned with masses of carved
foliage.   The arch opening from the nave into the chancel is
lofty, bold, and elegant, the springers foliated.   The pulpit
(of Caen stone) and the reading desk are placed on opposite
sides, near the chancel arch, the lectern in the shape of a
brazen eagle standing between them.   The roofs are open;
that of the nave arched and trussed, that of the chancel
groined.   The sittings are open stalls throughout, and all free.
The font is a massive arcaded column of Caen stone, near
the western entrance.   The organ, a sweet and powerful
instrument, by Hill and Son, of London, is placed near the
pulpit, at the east end of the north aisle. The chancel is lighted
with seven lancet windows, filled with stained glass, memorials
of different members of the family of the founder.   The first
on the north side, " In memory of Sarah, the beloved wife
of William Sheepshanks, the founder of this church,—born
November 8th, 1787, died July 28th, 1828 ;" bears in panels
representations of different scenes in scripture,—" The blind
receiving their sight." " The dead are raised up." " The
poor have the Gospel preached unto them."   " The lame
walk."   The next, "In memory of Catherine Sarah Eleanor
Sheepshanks, born October 27th, 1853, died September
4th, 1855." Above are depicted scenes inscribed, "Beloved
stand at the door and knock." "He shall gather the lambs
in His arms." "Suffer the little children to come unto
me." "She is not dead, but sleepeth." The eastern window
of three lights is "In memory of Thomas Sheepshanks, born
March 27th, 1788, died December 26th, 1854." "In memory
of Richard Sheepshanks, born July 30th, 1794, died August
4th, 1855." "In memory of Eleanor Nicholson, who died
December 22nd, 1855, aged 77." A vesica light above
represents the descent of the Dove. Above are represented

scenes from Scripture. On the southern side of the chancel, beneath a figure of St. John the Baptist, is inscribed, "In memory of George Nicholson, born January 12th, 1789, died February 10th, 1856." The next window on the same side, beneath a figure of St. John the Evangelist, is inscribed, "In memory of Elizabeth Nicholson, born at Leeds, died January 29th, 1832, aged 46." A window at the east end of the south aisle bears representations of scenes in the career of the Prodigal Son, inscribed, "I will arise and go to my Father." "And he arose and came." The western window of two lights, opening into the basement of the tower, contains representations of the symbols of the four Evangelists. The lower windows of the nave are single lancet lights; those of the clerestory double, with trefoil heads, and a quatrefoil in the sweep of the arch.

The tower is divided into three stories: the first open to the nave, through which is an entrance, each side externally adorned with an ornamental niche; the second is the ringers' chamber, which is arcaded externally; the belfrey is lighted by four double lancets, above which are two bold quatrefoils; the whole is surmounted by a massive entablature. The spire is yet wanting. The tower contains only one bell. A moulding runs round the outside of the chancel at the base of the windows, above which rises an arcade of six arches, two of the central ones, being open, form windows. All the windows are shafted on the outside, the capitals foliated, from which spring the arches.

The whole of the interior is lined with white limestone from the Huddlestone quarries; the angles of the buttresses outside, and tracery and mouldings of the windows, are of the same material; the remainder of the stone of a reddish colour was obtained in the neighbourhood. The whole of the materials were carefully selected, and the fabric constructed in the most substantial manner, and is said to have cost upwards of £17,000. The ceremony of consecration was performed by the bishop of Ripon, November 12th, 1857.

The living is a perpetual curacy in the gift of the founder. By deed, dated August 12th, 1857, the Rev. Thomas Sheepshanks granted an annual payment of £100 out of an estate situate at Humberstone Bank, in the townships of Hampsthwaite and Thruscross, to the incumbent for the time being of St. John's, Bilton. One thousand pounds, 8 per cents., were transferred by the Rev. Thomas Sheepshanks to the Ecclesiastical Commissioners, who undertook to pay £154 per annum to the incumbent of Bilton, in two equal portions, on the 1st May and 1st of November in every year.

The parsonage adjoining the church was built in 1868, also at the cost of William Sheepshanks, Esq,

The district assigned to this church by an order in Council, of August 27th, 1858, includes the northern side of the ancient township of Bilton-with-Harrogate. The boundary begins at a point on the river Nidd, in Spring Wood, west of Bilton Hall; passing thence across the country to the top of Walker's Road; thence by the Skipton Road to Oakbeck, following the course of that stream to its junction with the Nidd; then down the latter river to the starting point in Spring Wood.

Though this district is now but thinly inhabited, it was certainly the earliest settled, and at one time the most important part of the township.

Incumbents of St. John's, Bilton.

1858. Rev. Thomas Sheepshanks, ... resigned.
1865. ,, John Bickford Heard, ... resigned.
1868. ,, John Sheepshanks, ... present incumbent.

ST. PETER'S CHURCH.

This church is situate between Chapel Street and James Street, and is intended for the accommodation of the inhabitants of central Harrogate. On the erection of the school here, in 1865, divine service was held within it, either by the incumbent of Christ Church or his curate. On the demise of Mrs. Fielde, in 1867, she gave the land suitable for the site of the church, a liberal donation towards its endowment, and the house in which she resided, as a residence for the minister. A subscription for the erection of the church was commenced soon afterwards, and the foundation stone was laid in April, 1870, but as yet little progress has been made with the superstructure. The church is of the decorated style of architecture, from a design by Mr. Hirst, of Bristol, and is to consist of a nave of five bays, 70 feet in length by 27 feet in breadth, with north and south aisles, each 15 feet 9 inches wide; the last bay at the eastern end of the aisle on each side, projects outwards to double its former breadth, in the form of a transept, which is gabled outwardly; the chancel will be about 35 feet in length by 22 feet in breadth, terminating in a circular apse, the interior of which will be arcaded. A tower, bearing a spire, is situate at the west end of the south aisle.

The district attached to this church comprises that portion of Bilton-with-Harrogate which is bounded on the north-west by the brook Oakbeck, which divides it from Ripley; on the west and south-west by the district parish of Low Harrogate; and on the east by an imaginary line, commencing in the middle of the Leeds and Harrogate turnpike road, near the boundary stone inscribed P. on its southern side, and S.W.T. on its northern side, and following the line of the same road northward to the end of the street called Albert

Place, when it turns eastward, and passes along the above
named street to Station Parade, which it crosses, close to
the house called Scriven Lodge, and extends in the same
direction to the railway, when it turns northward, and passes
down the middle of the same to a point in the centre of
the bridge or culvert, which carries the said railway over
a small brook which flows from High Harrogate, thence past
the southern side of the Strawberrydale Cottage, and thence
along the same stream to its junction with Oakbeck, where the
boundary first commenced.

The living is a curacy or vicarage, the income of which
is £100 a-year, paid by the Ecclesiastical Commissioners.
The first incumbent—the Rev. L. E. W. Foote—appointed
in 1870.

CHAPELS.

THE WESLEYAN METHODIST CHAPEL, situate in Chapel Street,
is a large and commodious building, capable of containing
upwards of a thousand hearers. It was erected in 1862,
from a design of Messrs. Lockwood and Mawson, architects,
of Bradford. It is a plain building, with the exception of
the front, which is in the Italian style. The entrance is by
three doors, between half columns of the Corinthian order.
Within the pediment, on a large shield of stone adorned
with foliage, is carved, "Wesleyan Methodist Chapel, 1862."
The interior is fitted up in a superior style, with galleries
and an organ.

The first chapel of this religious body was built in 1796, in
what at that time was called Paradise Row,* now Park Parade,

* This building is now used as a club room, in the kitchen of which, on
a flag stone about two feet square is engraved, "This chapel was built
Anno Domini 1796. 'Jesus stood and cried, saying, if any man thirst let
him come unto me and drink. And let him that is athirst come, and
whosoever will let him take the water of life freely.' John vii, 37.
Rev. xxii, 17."

nearly opposite Christ Church, which was used until 1824, when it was found too small for the largely increased congregation, and a larger building was erected in Chapel Street, capable of containing about 550 hearers; this was also found inadequate to the wants of the society in 1862, when it was sold, and converted into a lodging house, now known as Beulah House, and the present substantial building was erected.

Previous to 1857, Harrogate formed part of the Knaresborough circuit; in that year, Harrogate was constituted a district circuit, with its own resident minister.

A small Chapel was built by the Wesleyans in Skipton road, in the year 1865, which will accommodate about 150 hearers.

THE INDEPENDENT CHAPEL OF CONGREGATIONAL CHURCH, is situate on the north side of Avenue road, fronting the Victoria and West Parks, and was built in 1861-2, from a design by Messrs. Lockwood and Mawson, architects, of Bradford. It is in the early decorated style; the length is 72 feet, the width 44 feet 2 inches, and the height 88 feet 6 inches, the height of the tower and spire is 180 feet; at the eastern end are attached large school and class rooms. In the chapel are seats for 700 people, in the school accommodation for 200 children. The cost of the building was £4,500.

Some time previously to the year 1810, this religious body worshipped in a large room, near what is now called Gascoigne's hotel, under the ministry of Mr. Howell, of Knaresborough. In 1822, they built the Cross chapel, in Skipton road, opposite to Grove house, now used as a National School, which they occupied until 1831, when they purchased, for the sum of £100, the old episcopal chapel of St. John, which they re-erected, with the addition of a new front, on Prospect hill, which they abandoned on the completion of the present building.

THE UNITED METHODIST FREE CHURCH, situate in the Victoria Park, near the Railway Station, was built in 1865, from a design by Mr. J. H. Hirst, of Bristol. It is in the early English style, with a tower and spire 100 feet high. A spacious school and class-rooms are attached. This church will accommodate 700 hearers, and the school 200 children.

This body of religionists, on its first formation, had a small chapel in James street, built in 1850, which was sold on the completion of their present church, when it was converted into a fine arts repository, called "the Pantheon."

THE PRIMITIVE METHODIST CHAPEL, built in 1856, is situate in Westmorland Entry; it will accommodate about 200 hearers.

THE FRIENDS' MEETING HOUSE, a small neat building in Chapel Street, was erected in 1854. It will accommodate one hundred hearers, and is well attended in the summer season by parties visiting Harrogate, though but few of that society permanently reside in the town.

THE ROMAN CATHOLIC SCHOOL, also used as a chapel, and the house for the officiating priest, are situate in South Station Parade; they are of brick, with white stone quoins, and were built in 1864.

SCHOOLS.

Few places of the same size are so well supplied with schools as Harrogate. Private boarding and day schools, for youth of both sexes, are numerous—some of them of high reputation; and from the purity of the air and abundance of open ground for recreation, a more appropriate place for such establishments could not have been easily selected. Our business is only with the public schools.

HARROGATE NATIONAL SCHOOL, situate in Skipton road, opposite Grove house, was established in 1832. It is under the superintendence of the incumbent of Christ church, open to children of all denominations, and supported by voluntary contributions, principally collections in the church.

THE BRITISH SCHOOL, in Chapel street, was built in 1885, and at first intended only for a Wesleyan Sunday School; in the following year it was thought proper to add a Day School, which is also supported by voluntary subscriptions, chiefly from the various dissenting bodies. The building is secured by deed to trustees, and will accommodate about 140 scholars.

THE INFANT SCHOOL, in Church square, High Harrogate, was founded in 1837, by William Sheepshanks, Esq., at whose cost it was built and is entirely supported, who provides not only education, but also books and all things necessary.

ST. PETER'S INFANT SCHOOL, situate in Chapel street, was built in 1865. It is a neat and substantial building, in the Tudor style of architecture. The school and class rooms are large, lofty, and well adapted for their purpose. The late benevolent Mrs. Fielde, of Belle Vue, was the original projector of this school; she gave the land on which it was built, was a liberal contributor to the building fund, and the principal supporter of it during her lifetime. It is now under the superintendence of the Incumbent of St. Peter's district church; and, until that church shall be finished, divine service is celebrated here.

THE CEMETERY is situate to the north of the town, on a piece of level ground between Baker Lane, Skipton Road, and the Railway. It consists of about four and a half acres of land, enclosed with a high wall. Near the entrance is the keeper's house, and a short distance within are two chapels, of similar design and construction, each consisting of what may be styled a porch, nave, and vestry. Above the entrance, which is towards the north, arises a square tower, which at

M

the height of the roof of the nave terminates in four acute
gables, in each of which is a small window of two lights, and
each apex is adorned with a finial; above this rises a most
elegant octagonal spire, in which is a bell-turret, containing
one steel bell. The nave is lighted on each side by three
windows of two lights each, and on the southern end by one
of three lights, with quatrefoils in the sweep of the arch.
These chapels are in the early English style of architecture,
from designs by Mr. T. C. Sorby, of London. The cost of
the land, chapels, keeper's house, enclosing, draining, and laying
out the ground, was about £5,000. The western portion of the
ground and one of the chapels were consecrated by the Bishop
of Ripon, April 23rd, 1864.

In the year ending February 28th, 1870, the number of
interments was 82, and the total number up to the same
period, 842.

THE STRAY.*

The wide sea-like extent of grass land which surrounds the
town is known as "The Stray," and is protected for the use
of the public by a special clause in the act of Parliament for
the enclosure of Knaresborough Forest. In the *Award*, made
on the completion of the same enclosure, it is thus described,
and its uses defined, "The said two hundred acres of land
shall, for ever, hereafter, remain open and unenclosed; and
all persons whomsoever shall and may have free access at
all times to the said springs, and be at liberty to use and
drink the waters there arising, and take the benefit thereof,
and shall and may have, use, and enjoy full and free ingress,
egress, and regress, in, upon, and over, the said two hundred

* The land grazed, or *strayed* over by cattle. An extensive pasture is
frequently called *a stray* in the north of England.

acres of land, and every and any part thereof, without being subject to the payment of any acknowledgment whatsoever for the same, or liable to any action of trespass, or other suit, molestation, or disturbance whatsoever, in respect thereof." By the third Enclosure Act, a few pieces of waste land, about fifteen acres in extent, which belonged to the king, as lord of the manor, were added to the Stray, "In order that the said plot of waste land may be gradually improved by enclosure, and trees planted thereon, for shelter and ornament, without diminishing the quantity of two hundred acres."

By the Forest Award, the Stray was converted into a stinted pasture, and apportioned into fifty cattle gates, which at that time were held by twenty-six owners, of which number the devisees of Sir John Ingilby, baronet, held twelve.

The stint at the same time was fixed as follows:—

One cow, ox, steer, or heifer, of more than two years old, as one gate; three beasts, of two years old each, as two gates; one calf, one year old, as half a gate; one horse, mare, or gelding, two years old, as one gate; a foal, of one year old, as three quarters of a gate; a mare, with a foal unweaned, and under one year old, as one and a half gates; four sheep, each above one year old, as one gate; one ewe, with her lamb or lambs unweaned, as one fourth of a gate; two weaned lambs, under one year old each, as one fourth of a gate.

No sheep or lambs were to be despastured during the first seven years after the execution of the Award; nor any asses, mules, goats, swine, or geese, at any time.

The present value of a cattle gate is about £155.

By the Harrogate Improvement Act, 1842, the management of the Stray was vested in a committee, consisting of nine of the owners thereof, with power to appoint Stray masters, herdsmen, and other officers; also, to make bye-laws for the

regulation of the said Stray, and to raise money to defray
the cost of draining and improving the same.

Since that time it has been much improved by draining,
levelling, and manuring; so that the old coarse forest vegetation
has been changed into good pasturage. The ornamental
planting has not been so fully carried out as it might have
been: avenues of trees by the sides of the principal roads
were planted in 1861, at the cost of the Stray owners—the
Improvement Commissioners providing iron guards to protect
the trees.

PAROCHIAL AFFAIRS, STATISTICS, &c.

In parochial matters Bilton-with-Harrogate is within the
Knaresborough Poor Law Union, to which it elects four
guardians. Previous to the formation of that Union, in 1854,
the houseless and infirm poor were kept in a workhouse at
Starbeck, which building is now used as a boarding school,
known as Beech Grove Academy.

A few notes from some of the books may be interesting,
as they will show the difference between the past and present
methods of relieving the poor, and the difference of the rateable
value of the township at different periods.

In 1808, this was the cost of a pauper's funeral—

"Dec. 24. Ellen Meldrum's funeral: ale and bread 10s.,   }
cheese, 6¼ lbs., 5s. 5d., sugar, &c., 1s. 7d., coffin 18s. 6d.,   £2 1 10
funeral fee 6s. 4d."................................}

In 1809, the parish authorities purchased for John Poppleton,
March 8, "A shuttle, pair of brushes, six dozen bobbins, and
pair of pinkers," for the sum of 11s. 4d.

1808.   April 30th. Relieved a pauper with a pass..........6d.
  ,,   June 1st. Relieved a pauper with a pass ....4d.
  ,,   October 10th. Relieved a pauper with a pass ....6d.

This year the rents of thirty-six poor people were paid
half-yearly, the rents varying from 13s. to £2 the half-year.
Coals were given by the overseers to forty-three persons, in
quantities varying from two bushels to twelve corves, the prices
were 1s. the bushel, and 2s. 0½d. the corf. The total
expenditure for the year from April 20th, 1808, to April 20th,
1809, was £750 14s. 10¾d.

The largest proprietor on the rate-book is John Watson,
Esq., of Bilton Hall, who is personally the largest rate-payer,
and has twenty-nine tenants beside; Lord Harewood, ten
tenants; Ely Hargrove, self and six tenants; Sir John Ingilby,
Bart., eight tenants; James Brown, fourteen tenants; Dr.
Jaques, self and six tenants. Between 1808 and 1835 the
proprietory appears to have completely changed, and John
Greenwood and William Sheepshanks have come conspicuously
forward as landowners.

In 1835, the number of rate-payers was 546, and the rateable value £8,300.
In 1856,   ,,   846,   ,,   £20,254.
In 1862,   ,,   994,   ,,   £23,646.
In 1866,   ,,   1262,   ,,   £30,158.
In 1869,   ,,   ,,   £35,564.

As the hotels are the most conspicuous objects in Harrogate,
and as their increase in value may be considered an index to the
progress of the town, we will give the value of a few of them,
at different periods, from the overseers' books:—

	1864. £ s.	1856. £ s.	1862. £ s.	1866. £ s.
George	15 15	70 0	95 0	112 0
Dragon (56 acres of land)*....	254 14	374 0	412 0	87 15
Prospect....................	86 0	....	279 0	303 0
Queen (26 acres of land)+	110 19	300 0	480 0	525 0
Granby (14 acres of land)‡....	177 2	330 14	387 0	356 10
Swan (33 acres of land)§......	112 15	335 13	400 0	450 0
Gascoigne's (82 acres of land)‖	106 0	236 14	236 15	274 10

* Only 3½ acres of land now.
+ Only 3 acres and 19 perches of land now.
‡ Only 7 acres and 1 rood of land now.
§ Only 5 acres and 18 perches of land now.
‖ Only 69 acres of land now.

In 1856, a new kind of rate-payers have come into existence which were not to be found in 1834; these are the Waterworks Company, £20, the Gas Company—works and piping—£125, Leeds Northern Railway Company, £458 9s. 8d., Montpellier Baths, £245. The Earl of Rosslyn is entered as owner of the tithes of Bilton Park, £33, and the Vicar of Knaresborough as owner of the small tithes of the same park, 12s.

In this year, thirty-five are rated at £100 and upwards, and 456 at £10 and upwards. In 1866, 686 were rated at £15 and upwards.

In 1866, we find amongst the land owners Baron de Ferrars, owner of one and a half cattle gates on the Stray, and Baroness de Boyce, as owner of a stone quarry in Barker lane. Scotton Flax Mill, though on the northern side of the river Nidd, is rated to this township, at £32; and the Forest Lane Windmill, with eleven perches of land, is rated at £15.

The Telegraph Companies also come in for a share of attention.

	£	s.	d.
The Electric has 2 wires, 880 yards each (Harrogate branch) ..	0	7	6
„ 4 „ 2,970 „ (H.B., north side)	2	10	6
„ 4 · „ 1,180 „ (Knaresbro' branch)	1	0	0
The Magnetic has 8 wires, 3,774 yards (main line)	6	8	6
„ 8 „ 2,970 „ (Harrogate branch, N. side	2	10	6

The following is a statement of the valuation and extent of the North Eastern Railway Company's property in this township:—

	Rental.				Rateable.		
	£	s.	d.		£	s.	d.
Station and offices	160	0	0	..	120	0	0
Refreshment rooms	60	0	0	..	45	0	0
Rails, south side, 40 chains ⎱	546	0	0	..	546	0	0
„ north side, 135 chains ⎰							
„ Knaresbro', 54 chains	101	0	0	..	101	0	0
Northern Reduction, 2 m. 1 f. 34 yds.	508	0	0	..	508	0	0
Station master's house....................	20	0	0	..	15	0	0
Four cottages, at £8 each	32	0	0	..	24	0	0
Signal house	2	0	0	..	1	10	0
„ Knaresbro' branch	2	0	0	..	1	10	0

	Rental.				Rateable.		
	£	s.	d.		£	s.	d.
Signal house, Bilton Junction..............	2	0	0	..	1	10	0
Two gate houses, Bilton	12	0	0	..	9	0	0
Two do. Harrogate Junction	12	0	0	..	9	0	0
Signal house..........................	2	0	0	..	1	10	0
Land	3	3	0	..	3	0	0
Knaresbro' new branch, 180 yards..........	15	6	9	..	15	6	9
Land (late Barker), 2 a. 1 r.................	3	7	6	..	3	4	0

£1480 17 3   £1404 10 9

The ratability of the Gas Company has increased from £125, in 1856, to £482 15s., in 1866.

The valuation of Bilton-with-Harrogate, as assessed to the county rate, in 1849, was £18,057; in 1859, £23,904; and in 1866, £31,779.

The population at the different decennial periods has been as follows:—In 1801, 1195; 1811, 1583; 1821, 1934; 1831, 2812; 1841, 3372; 1851, 4262; 1861, 5567. The number of houses at the last mentioned period was 1132.

The following is a statement of the rainfall at Harrogate during the eight years from 1861 to 1868, inclusive. The gauge was fixed at six feet from the ground, and 420 feet above the sea level. Communicated by Frederick Bainbridge, Esq., surgeon, Harrogate.

	1861.	1862.	1863.	1864.	1865.	1866.	1867.	1868.
	Inches.	Inches.	Inches.	Inches.	Inches.	Inches.	Inches.	Inches.
January ..	—	2·09	6·32	1·23	1·60	3·86	2·92	3·28
February ..	3·57	1·04	·98	1·93	2·04	4·41	2·40	1·49
March ..	4·83	4·86	1·89	2·91	1·63	1·76	2·54	2·79
April ..	1·22	2·53	·88	1·75	1·25	1·57	3·84	2·18
May ..	·71	3·25	1·93	2·63	2·22	1·95	2·24	1·93
June .	2·43	2·51	3·56	2·36	·90	4·89	1·79	·86
July ..	3·18	2·31	1·65	·70	1·91	3·94	3·28	·62
August ..	1·70	3·82	4·01	·89	4·44	3·25	3·80	3·11
September ..	3·50	2·50	3·10	2·10	·30	6·11	1·85	3·89
October ..	1·98	4·95	4·55	4·75	5·79	2·52	2·31	3·31
November ..	3·43	·89	3·35	2·35	3·43	1·70	1·29	2·59
December ..	1·59	1·83	2·54	2·88	1·21	2·83	2·47	7·78
Total ..		32·58	34·76	26·48	27·74	39·44	30·33	32·83

During the year 1862, rain, more or less, fell on 204 days; in 1863, on 188 days; in 1864, on 162 days; in 1865, on 145 days; in 1866, on 210 days; in 1867, on 172 days; and in 1868, on 160 days.

The greatest quantity recorded as having fallen in one day was on October 11th, 1865, when 2·16 inches fell.

Thunderstorms are recorded as having occurred six times in 1862, eight times in 1863, six times in 1864, thirteen times in 1865, three times in 1866, and three times in 1867.

The prevailing winds are the N.E., S.E., S.W., W., and N.W. The strongest winds, or gales, are from the S.W. and S.S.W.

TOPOGRAPHICAL SURVEY.

A walk round the town of Harrogate and its immediate neighbourhood will enable the reader better to comprehend the different localities, and also give an opportunity for the introduction of matter not admissable by any other method. Commencing our survey at the northern extremity, the cemetery is the first object deserving of attention. The two small elegant chapels, with their slender spires, are observable at a considerable distance. From its recent formation, this place has not yet become so interesting as it will do in the course of time; for the places where the dead are buried are always regarded with veneration by the living; while the monuments—sometimes by their elegance—sometimes by the inscriptions they bear, recording the talents or virtues of those sleeping below—demand our veneration; while the plain grassy hillocks preach a sermon whose moral is *memento mori*.

A short distance east of the cemetery is the Harrogate National School; opposite is Grove House, a large lofty building, surrounded by a grove of sycamore trees, the property of John Greenwood, Esq., of Swarcliffe Hall, and now occupied by Mrs. Dury, widow of the Rev. Theodore Dury, rector of West Mill, in Hertfordshire. This building has had a somewhat eventful history; it was originally built for an inn, and was known as "The World's End," by which name it is frequently mentioned in the Forest Award; afterwards it was used as a boarding school; about the year 1805, Mrs. Hofland, then Barbara Hoole, a well-known authoress, resided here. and kept a ladies' school. Here she wrote her poem, in imitation of Anstey's Bath Guide, which she styled "A Season in Harrogate," and some others of her works. On her marriage with Mr. Christopher Hofland, the artist, they removed to London. In 1822, it was occupied as a school by the Rev. T. B. Wildsmith; afterwards, for a while, it was unoccupied, and had the reputation of being haunted.*

After crossing the railway, a short distance on the right, we see what was the Dragon hotel, now converted into a school, known as High Harrogate College. It is an old, irregular, weather-stained building, like half-a-dozen small houses thrown into one. In early times it was the most noted place in Harrogate for high class society; the tide of popular favour afterwards ebbed away, and left it somewhat neglected. Could its old walls relate their history, what a chronicle of the past they would give us! One episode in its domestic life is a pleasant one; it was kept by a Mr. and Mrs. Liddle, who on the 25th of June, 1764, took the oath at Dunmow, in Essex, and obtained the flitch of bacon. The gentlemen of the neighbourhood, to celebrate so unusual an instance of conjugal

* This ghost was said to have the appearance of a woman without a head, and which only made its appearance at certain times. It was subsequently found to be the moonlight shining through one window, thrown back by another, upon an opposite wall. Captain Chesney—since distinguished for the part he took in forwarding the East Indian mails by way of the Persian Gulf—lodged for some time here, in 1821.

felicity, sent in each some elegant or plentiful dish, and
all dined together at the house of the happy couple.* Within
these old walls was also reared the celebrated artist, William
Powell Frith, A.R.A.; his birth-place was the village of
Aldfield, near Ripon.

A short distance further south, also on the right hand,
is Westmorland street, principally built in 1842. On the left is
Devonshire House, seat of John James Harrison, Esq. This
house formerly belonged to the family of Thackwray, which at
that time had also considerable estates in the neighbourhood.

The Post Office was situate here for many years, until
removed in 1865. The green area of the Stray here expands
before us, and the lines of buildings diverge on each hand;—
Devonshire Place, at one time called Silver Street, on the left,
and Regent Parade on the right; the last consisting of a range
of substantial lodging houses and well-furnished shops; near
the middle, on the premises now occupied by Mr. Stokes, the
draper, resided for many years Mr. George Wright, the
artist, a Royal Academician, distinguished for his miniature
portraits. He was a native of Littlethorpe, near Ripon, but
settled in Harrogate, where he died, May 9th, 1854, aged
68 years.

Passing along Devonshire Place, we soon reach Gascoigne's
Hotel, a good commercial house. It was formerly known as
the "Salutation Boarding House;" in 1822, it bore the name
of "Hope Tavern." A little further, close to the pathway, is
the "Black Spring," a well of remarkably pure water. The
next object of interest is the Granby Hotel, one of the largest of
its class in the town, containing upwards of one hundred and
fifty bedrooms, and other accommodations in proportion. It
arose in some shape (not its present one) previous to the year

* Annual Register, for 1764.

1700, and was first known as the "Sinking Ship," afterwards it bore the name of the "Royal Oak," and finally assumed its present aristocratic title. It has often been improved and enlarged, and now is of gigantic proportions. It was styled by Dr. Granville, in his "Spas of England," "the truly aristocratic hotel of the Spa, with the best aspect on this wide expanse of ground." In the barn behind, the first plays acted in Harrogate were performed; traces of its fittings up at that time yet remain.

The cluster of houses opposite the Granby, surrounded by the Stray, are known as Church Square. Here stood the theatre, now converted into a lodging house, called Mansfield House. Here is also situate the Harrogate Infant School, built and maintained by William Sheepshanks, Esq. Immediately to the westward is Christ Church, surrounded by its grove of trees and crowded burial ground—

"Fraught with the relics of mortality."

Close to the right of the road leading to Knaresborough, is the parsonage belonging to the incumbency of Christ's Church; a picturesque building in the early English style, erected in 1859. In the same direction, just outside the verge of the Stray, are the villas, "Elmwood House," "Willaston House," (both built since 1861), and "The Hollies," the last on a plot of ground, which projects into the Stray, where formerly stood the "New Cold Bath." Close adjacent is John's Well, or the Sweet Chalybeate Spa, known by its octagonal pump room. Directly south is Wedderburn House, so named from its builder, Alexander Wedderburn, Lord Loughborough, who purchased the estate, built the house, and laid out the plantations, and otherwise greatly improved the domain about the year 1786. The Earl of Rosslyn, his nephew, to whom he bequeathed it by will, in 1805, sold it afterwards to John Jaques, M.D., after whose decease it came into possession of John Jaques Willis, Esq., the present owner.

Returning past Christ Church to the top of Regent Parade, the premises now occupied by the Misses Langdale, booksellers, known as Library House, was once the property of Ely Hargrove, author of a "History of Knaresborough," and many other valuable local tracts. He died in 1818.

The mansion on the right, surrounded by trees, is the seat of William Sheepshanks, Esq., of Leeds and Harrogate, one of the largest landowners in the township, and who has been the most liberal benefactor to Harrogate, that it ever had. The building and maintenance of the Infant School, in Church Square, and the erection and endowment of St. John's Church, Bilton, need only be mentioned to prove the above assertion. His estates in Harrogate have been purchased and this house built since 1834.

The family of Sheepshanks, now of great wealth and importance, originated with Richard Sheepshanks, of Linton, in Craven, yeoman, who was born March 26th, 1711, and died December 22nd, 1779. He married Sushannah Garside, of Stainland, by whom he had issue—

William, born at Linton, March 18th, 1741, M.A., prebendary of Carlisle, rector of Ovington, Norfolk, and curate of St. John's, Leeds.

Whittel, born 14th Nov., 1743, who afterwards assumed the name of York, died August, 1817. His descendants reside at Wighill Park, near Tadcaster.

Richard, born September 14th, 1727, of Leeds and Philadelphia, merchant, died in America, in 1797.

Thomas, born December 21st, 1752, M.A., rector of Hanpole and Aspenden, in Cambridgeshire.

Joseph, born May 8th, 1755, of Leeds, merchant—of whom hereafter.

James, of Leeds, merchant, died *s.p.* 1789.

John, born May 4th, 1765, M.A., Fellow of Trinity College, Cambridge, vicar of Wymeswould, and curate of Trinity Church, Leeds.

Joseph married Ann, daughter of Mr. Richard Wilson, of Kendall, by whom he had issue—Thomas. William, of Leeds and Harrogate—of whom presently. John, born in 1787, died October 5th, 1863. He collected the famous "Sheepshanks' Gallery" of pictures, which on his decease he bequeathed to the nation. Richard, A.B., of Trinity College, Cambridge, and a noted astronomer. Anne and Susanna.

William Sheepshanks married Sarah Nicholson, of Roundhay, near Leeds, by whom he has issue—Thomas, present incumbent of Arthington; and two daughters.

Arms—*Azure*, a chevron, *erminois*, between three roses in chief, and a sheep passant in base *argent*.

Crest—On a wreath of the colours, a mount *vert*, whereon a sheep passant, as in the arms.

A short distance further, in a westerly direction, is "The Queen," the largest as well as the oldest of the Harrogate hotels. It was first built in 1687, and named the "Queen's Head." It has undergone frequent renewals and enlargements; the centre was rebuilt, and the western wing added in 1855; and in 1861 the eastern portion was renovated and enlarged; and the whole has now an elegant modern appearance. The gardens and grounds around are kept in the neatest order, while the tall sycamores in front point it out as a spot which has long been enclosed and inhabited. Queen Street and the range of villas fronting the Stray have all been built since 1855.

On the southern side of the Stray is Oatlands, the seat of
Miss Ann Paley, a comfortable looking house, situate in a grove
of trees. The house, with the farm and lands adjoining, were
purchased by the late John Green Paley, Esq., about the year
1836. On his decease, October 9th, 1860, he bequeathed the
same to his daughter, the present owner, for her life. On
the enclosure of the forest, this plot of land was awarded to
John Coates; afterwards it was possessed by Mr. John Dearlove,
who disposed of the same to Captain Thackwray, who built
the present mansion, and afterwards sold it to Mr. Paley.

Passing westerly, on the right is the long line of houses
known as "York Place"; on the left, the wide level grassy
expanse of the Stray, across which runs the railway, spanned
by three bridges, and enters the town by a deep cutting, on
the east side of which a new street, called Park Road, winds
among the villas in the Victoria Park; on the western side
is another street, called South Station Parade, which runs in
a straight line from the Royal Hotel to the railway station.

The Royal Hotel was built in 1847, and enlarged in 1864.
At a short distance southward, on the same side, is the Roman
Catholic School of St. Robert, with the house for the officiating
priest, erected A.D. 1864. A short distance further are Albert
and Alexandra Terraces, both on the same side; the opposite
side presents a range of detached houses and villas.

Returning to the Royal Hotel, and looking southward to
the angle formed by the railway and the boundary of the Stray,
we see the pillared dome which covers the Tewhit Well, the
first known of all the mineral waters of Harrogate.

At the corner formed by the intersection of the roads from
Leeds to Ripon, and from Knaresborough to Otley, stands the
Prince of Wales Hotel, a large and handsome building fronting
the south and west. It was built by Michael Hattersley, about

the year 1820, and was for some time known as Hattersley's Hotel; it afterwards received the name of "The Brunswick," which it retained until 1866, when it assumed its present title. It was rebuilt in 1860-1, on a much more extensive scale than before.

At the corner on the opposite side of the road stood the Low Harrogate railway station; it was the terminus of the Church Fenton and Harrogate railway, and was used until the opening of the present one, in 1862, when a portion of the railway was abandoned, the station cleared away, and the land on which it had stood thrown to the Stray, as compensation for the ground taken in passing across it by the same company's line lower down. In 1867, about seventy acres of land, situate at this corner, were sold by the Railway Company to a Joint Stock Company, who laid it out in building lots, upon a most comprehensive and elegant scale, which, when realized, will form a new and beautiful suburb, under the name of "The West End Park."*

Turning to the right, and proceeding northward, we next pass the Clarendon Hotel, which was enlarged and adapted to its present use in 1847. The large, rough, upright boulder on the left hand, about nine feet in height and two feet square, has been mistaken by a clever antiquary† for a Druidical stone; it is merely the boundary of two Turnpike Trusts, which meet here. It was erected on the enclosure of the forest, about

---

* On the enclosure of the Forest, in 1778, this plot of ground was awarded to Dorothy Wilks and Ann Bainbridge, who held a fourth part of the appropriate rectory of Pannal, in lieu of tithe; afterwards it came into possession of the Ecclesiastical Commissioners, with whom it continued until 1846, when it was purchased by the North Midland Railway Company, for their Harrogate and Church Fenton line. After the amalgamation, it formed part of the North Eastern system. Such was the commingling of lands produced by the Forest enclosure, that this plot of ground is in the three townships of Pannal, Scriven, and Knaresborough.

† Mr. Thomas Wright, in his "Celt, Roman, and Saxon."

1778, and in the "Award" then made it is styled "the great
stone pillar erected at Harrogate corner." On the east side
is inscribed, "The boundary of Leeds and Ripon Turnpike
Road." In 1870 it was enclosed with an iron paling, to
protect it from desecration. On the opposite side of the Stray
(here called West Park,) is a line of elegant villas, called Beech
Grove, which have all been built since 1848. On the enclosure
this land was awarded to the king, as Duke of Lancaster, and
it yet belongs to that duchy. Considerable plantations of beech
trees have been made upon it—hence its present name.

The Commercial Hotel is next passed, which was rebuilt in
1838, on the site of an earlier place of rest for travellers, which
was known by the sign of "The Obelisk." Tower Street opens
on the right—so named from its direct view of the tower on
Harlow Hill.

At the end of Brunswick Terrace is "The Belvidere," an
elegant mansion in the Tudor style, erected by the late Mr.
John Smith, banker, in 1861; one front faces the Victoria
Avenue, the other the West Park. On the opposite side is the
Congregational Church, with its tall and graceful spire. Passing
along the Avenue, some distance on the right, is the group
of almshouses, built in 1868. These houses are twelve in
number, and form three sides of a square, with a grass plot
in the centre, and a raised terrace on each side. The buildings
are two stories in height, constructed externally of stone, roofed
with Coniston slate, surmounted with ornamental chimney
stacks, and a red ridge. The sitting rooms are 14 feet by
15, and 9 feet 6 inches in height, neatly corniced, and lighted
by a mullioned window of two lights. On the ground floor
there is also a pantry, scullery, and coal place. The bedrooms,
15 feet by 14, are lighted by dormer windows of two lights.
All the windows are made to open, and the comfort and

convenience of the inmates have been attended to throughout. In the centre of the eastern side is a handsome clock tower, 65 feet in height, the angles of which are ornamented with gurgoyles, above which rise gables with gilt finials. The roof is a slated spire, ending in a finial, which serves both as weather-cock and lightning conductor. At the western base of the tower, above a sculptured bee-hive (emblematical of industry) is inscribed, "𝔊eorge 𝔯ogers, 1868." The two western gables present buttresses, and ornamental windows, of five circular lights each. The doorways are protected by sloping stone pediments. At the two corners, on the eastern side, are ash pits and wash houses. The whole block is enclosed on three sides by a wall, and on the other by a neat iron palisade. The style partakes largely of the early English. The architects were Messrs. Andrews and Pepper, of Bradford. The total cost was upwards of £4,000; in addition to which, a much larger sum is invested in trustees, for the purpose of paying £20 a-year to each pensioner, with a margin for incidental expenses. Nine of these almshouses are intended for women, either widows or spinsters, who have moved in a respectable position in life, but who have been reduced to poverty by circumstances over which they had no control, and who have lived within three miles of Bradford Parish Church for three years immediately preceding their application, and have attained the age of sixty years. The other three houses are for similar persons, who have resided for three years within three miles of Christ's Church, Harrogate.

The funds for the support of this trust consist of £2,500, Great Western Railway Six per cent. Stock, and £2,000, Great Western Irredeemable Stock, 1866; producing a present income of £270 per annum.

The affairs of this charity are under the management of a

committee, consisting of the vicar of Bradford, the mayor, the two senior aldermen, the minister of Horton Lane Independent Chapel, and the incumbents of St. Peter's and Christ Churches, Harrogate.

The whole cost was defrayed by Mr. George Rogers, formerly a merchant and manufacturer in Bradford, who, after a career of successful industry, retired to Harrogate, and employed his fortune in doing good to his fellow-creatures—not for his lifetime alone—for this foundation will remain a monument of his charity and munificence long after the head which conceived, and the hand which so freely gave, have departed hence, and will send down his name to future generations as a benefactor of his species.*

The Avenue, opened in 1860, intersects the Victoria Park from west to east, passing from the West Park to Queen Street; the space between, on both sides, is laid out in building lots, and a considerable portion of it already occupied.

Resuming our survey at the Congregational Church, the next opening on the right is Raglan Street, in which is situate the Police Station, a neat brick building, erected in 1866. Passing along Prospect Place—a pleasantly situated range of lodging houses, all of them built since 1814—the next opening is Albert Street. In the house on the left, now used as offices by the Harrogate Improvement Commissioners, died, August

---

* Mr. Rogers died at his residence, Claro Villas, High Harrogate, July 5th, 1870, aged 65. By his will, he bequeathed £250 to the Bradford Infirmary, £250 to the Leeds Infirmary, £250 to the Harrogate Bath Hospital, £250 to the Ilkley Wells Hospital, £250 to the Bradford Mechanics' Institute, £250 to the Bradford Tradesman's Benevolent Institution, £250 to the Bradford Town Mission, £250 to the Church Missionary Society, £250 to the London Missionary Society, £250 to the British and Foreign Bible Society, and £250 to the Religious Tract Society. He also left an additional sum of £2,000 towards the further endowment of the almshouses erected by him at Harrogate, so as to enable the trustees to pay ten shillings a week to each of the inmates.

22nd, 1861, Mr. Richard Oastler, a noted character in his day, generally known as "The Factory King." On the right of this street is the Methodist Free Church. The Albion Hotel at the corner was built in 1840; it has since been enlarged.

At the lower end of Prospect Place stands the Prospect House Hotel, the most trim and ornate of all the Harrogate hotels. It was rebuilt, in 1859, on the site of a smaller hotel of the same name, and enlarged to double its former size in 1870. The delightful little *pleausance*, used as a croquet ground, on the opposite side of the street, belongs to it. Immediately behind the Prospect Hotel is the Victoria Hall, and drill ground of the Harrogate Volunteer Rifle Corps.

Passing along James Street, on the right is the Post Office,* easily distinguishable by the royal arms on the pediment, and the arcade at the entrance. The situation is central, and the building an ornament to the town. It was built, in 1864, by the Victoria Park Company; and forms part of a range of buildings, in a similar style, fronting James Street and Princes street.

At the end of this street is the Railway Station, a long range of buildings of red brick, with a square water-tower at each extremity—between which is the array of refreshment rooms, booking offices, waiting rooms, and all the adjuncts of a first-class station. Turning down North Station Parade, in front of Beulah Terrace and Place, we pass Mr. Hardy's galvanic bath establishment and enter Chapel Street, in which is situate the old Wesleyan Chapel—now Beulah House; on

---

* Hargrove, in 1775, wrote in his History of Knaresborough, "A letter carrier is constantly employed betwixt the inns at Harrogate and the post office at Wetherby, who is paid for every letter he carries there one penny, and for each he brings from thence twopence, over and above the postage." Now there are three deliveries of letters a day; and the staff of the office consists of the postmaster, clerk, and eight letter carriers,—whilst three more are employed in the telegraphic department.

the same side are the British School and St. Peter's Infant School, and Belle Vue, the parsonage belonging to the new district of St. Peter's. This house was built by Captain Thos. Thrush, R.N.,* and occupied by him until his decease, in 1848, and afterwards by his widow. After her decease, in 1848, the house was purchased by the Rev. Edward Fielde, M.A., who had been incumbent of the parish of Rock and Rennington, in Northumberland, which having resigned on account of failing health, he settled here, and occupied this house until his death, in 1851; after which it was occupied by his widow until her death, in 1867, when she gave the same to be used as a parsonage for the district of St. Peter. She also gave the land on which St. Peter's Church and School are built, which immediately adjoin it towards the south.

* He was born at Stockton-on-Tees, in 1761. During his youth and manhood he served in the Royal Navy; and, in 1809, was promoted to the rank of post-captain. His health having become somewhat impaired, he was recommended to invalide, which he did in the same year, and never after engaged in service. In his sixtieth year he applied himself to the study of the Greek language, that he might read the new testament in the original. When searching the scriptures he was struck with the contrast between the precepts of Christ and the practice of Christians, especially as regards war. On studying the subject carefully he came to the conclusion that war was a crime, and that he was not justified in continuing a naval officer. His half-pay formed nearly the half of his limited income; and his naval rank he had always highly prized as the honourable reward of years of painful watching, labour and exertion. Yet, notwithstanding these things, on his sixty-fifth birthday, he resigned his commission, and addressed a letter to the king, stating in a respectful but firm manner the grounds upon which he had adopted so unprecedented a measure. For taking this step, all his friends abandoned him, as a senseless visionary and dangerous schismatic. This was in 1825; and he lived eighteen years afterwards. His body was crippled by rheumatism; but his mind was active and vigorous, and his manners cheerful and amiable. He employed his old age in writing—giving to the world many productions, which he thought calculated to promote the cause of truth. These he latterly printed himself—sitting in his arm-chair—with a press of his own contriving, characterised by its cheapness and simplicity; and which he had made by a joiner and blacksmith of Harrogate, at a cost of less than £2. When eighty years of age, he published "Last Thoughts of a Naval Officer on the Unlawfulness of War."

On the right is the Wesleyan Methodist Chapel; and nearly adjoining it is the Friends' Meeting House. On the hill, on the southern side, stands Prospect Cottage, an old and respectable building, of considerable size. Within living memory, it was the only substantial house between Spring Bank and Harrogate Corner. In early times, with the lands adjoining, it belonged to the family of Burnand; from whom it passed to that of Trappes, of Nidd; afterwards it came into possession of the Ingilbys, of Ripley Castle, by whom it was held until 1810; when Sir John Ingilby, Bart., sold the same to James Franklin, Esq,, who, owing to some litigation with regard to title, did not enter into possession until 1814. After that period he occasionally resided here, until his death, in 1826, when the estate passed to his only child, Elizabeth, married to James Bayley, Esq., of Willaston Hall, Cheshire. She died September 30th, 1867, leaving two daughters only surviving—a son having died during his mother's lifetime, who also left two daughters.

In 1859, this house, and much of the land adjoining, were purchased by the Victoria Park Company; and the increase of buildings around has almost hidden this venerable fabric from view.

Passing along St. Peter's Place, we enter Parliament Street, nearly opposite the Somerset Hotel (recently rebuilt). This is one of the principal streets in the town; near the bottom, on the left, are the Montpellier Gardens, and a little lower the open green called Cheltenham Square. On the right is the Royal Chalybeate Spa, concert room, and pleasure grounds. On the left is the George Hotel, rebuilt in 1850, on the site of an old public house, called "The Chequers;" and on the right, Spring Bank Villa. Further along the Ripon road are the Springfield Villas and Harrogate College; the

latter erected in 1864. About a mile distant along this road
are the Gasworks.

Retracing our steps, we pass in front of the Springfield
Villas to the Swan Hotel; a large establishment, on an old site.
It stands in a pleasant situation, and commands a fine view
of the town and country; attached to it is one of the prettiest
pieces of pleasure ground in Harrogate. Promenade Terrace is
on the right, the Victoria Baths and Town Hall on the left,
and immediately in front of it is the Royal Pump Room.
Turning to the right, and ascending the hill, we reach Pittville,
a dwelling-house built in the hollow of an old quarry; the
stone is the transition mountain limestone, which at this place,
and on the corresponding side of the valley, has been upheaved
from some unknown depth by volcanic action, brought to the
surface, and there left standing half on edge; while the orifice
between these edges of upcast rock gives birth to the saline
and sulphur springs. Behind Cornwall House, which stands
on the hill immediately above, the rock may be seen in *situ*.
A short distance south-west is the Bath Hospital, and that
singular piece of ground called "The Bogs"—one of the greatest
natural curiosities in the kingdom, with its many springs of
mineral water. It is as obvious to the eye of the observer as
any evidence can make a fact, that these springs rise from
the crater of an ancient volcano.

Returning down the footpath we reach the town, close to
the Royal Pump Room. In Crescent Place is the Crescent
Hotel, first known as "The Half Moon," the oldest unchanged
hotel in Harrogate; belonging to it is the Leamington Spring,
which contains the greatest quantity of salt of any of the
Harrogate waters, without being either sulphurious or chalybeate.

Passing from the Royal Pump Room, on the right is Royal

Parade—a range of houses and shops, built since 1846; and
the White Hart Hotel, rebuilt in 1846, in a style at once
elegant and substantial. On the left is the Crown, the oldest
and most noted of the Low Harrogate hotels. Some parts of it
are very old—a type of its younger day; the centre was rebuilt
in 1847, and the eastern portion re-edified in 1870. For
several generations it was kept by the family of Thackwray,
who raised it to high distinction.*

How suggestive of thought and reflection are these old
hotels, with their myriad scenes and associations! The history
of old baronial halls and feudal castles has often been written,
and found interesting. Yet few of them can equal in variety of
scene and interest an old watering place hotel. Collected from
all quarters, the characters are the most diversified that can be
imagined, and their actions correspond. Within these walls the
historian might pass "from grave to gay, from gentle to severe,"
without doing violence to truth. In one room might be
witnessed beings "fairer than feigned of old, or fabled since,"
gaily and gladly threading the mazes of the merry dance; while
beneath the same roof might be seen the heart-sick parent,
seated beside the bed of some favourite child, only to see the
feebly flickering lamp of life expire; and whose remains must be
stolen, as it were, away by night, that the other inmates,

* The first of the family was Joseph Thackerey, who, in his rhyming
epitaph (said to have been his own composition) in Pannal churchyard,
says—

"In the year of our Lord 1740
I came to the Crown;
In 1791 they laid me down."

Death "laid him down," November 26th, 1791; when he was succeeded
by his nephew, William Thackerey, who died March 29th, 1814; when his
son, Joseph Thackwray—who altered the spelling of his name—succeeded
to the Crown, and died April 10th, 1837, in the 49th year of his age.

sleeping less soundly beneath the same roof may not be alarmed
at the sight.*

In the autumn of 1806, Lord Byron, the poet, with his
friend Miss Pigot, and his dogs, Nelson and Boatswain, took
up their abode at the Crown. The shy poet and his companion always dined in the public room, but returned very
soon to their private one. They lived retired, and made few
acquaintance. While here his lordship met with Professor
Hailstone, of Cambridge, called on him one evening, and took
him to the theatre; and sent his carriage for him another time
to the Granby. The dogs of the poet had a mortal antipathy to
each other, and whenever they met a battle was the consequence,
and they were only parted by thrusting poker and tongs into
the mouths of each. One day Nelson escaped out of the room
without his muzzle, and going into the stable yard, fastened
on the throat of a horse, from which he could not be disengaged.
The stable boys ran in alarm to find Frank, the valet, who,
taking one of his lordship's pistols, shot Nelson through the
head, to the great regret of the poet. Byron wrote here his
poem, entitled "To a Beautiful Quaker."

Here the learned Surtees, the historian of Durham, met
the more learned Tate, of Richmond, whom he thus describes
in an epistle to their friend, the learned Dr. Raine—

"Doctus Tatius hic residet,
Ad Coronam prandit, ridet,
Spargit sales cum cachinno,
Lepido ore et concinno,
Ubique carus inter bonos
Rubei Montis præsens honos."

* "Stone walls, they say, have ears.—'Twere scarcely wrong
To wish that these walls likewise had a tongue:
How many gracious words would then be said,—
How many precious counsels uttered!
What terse quotations—fresh applied and fit,—
What gay retorts, and summer-lightning wit!
What sweet and deep affections would find vent,—
What hourly invocations upwards sent!"

Sir Alan Chambre, Knight, one of the judges of the Court of Common Pleas, died here September 20th, 1828.

Adjoining the Crown Hotel, on the east, are the Montpellier Gardens—a most delightful piece of ground, in which are situate the springs and baths of that name. This highly favoured spot forms a complete watering place within itself, containing the strong sulphur, the mild sulphur, and the Kissingen, or saline chalybeate—the three waters most in request—and a suite of baths, where the waters can be applied in any form required. The garden has been laid out with great skill, and is kept in the neatest order. During the season a fountain plays in front of the baths; and a band of musicians play in the grounds during the times for drinking the water in the mornings and afternoons. Amongst the trees in the garden is a large and venerable thorn—a genuine relic of the old forest. To fix its exact age may be impossible; yet, we have no hesitation in saying, that it was a tree when the *Wars of the Roses* were fought. It rises from the ground by one massive stem, and at 18 inches high is 10 feet 8 inches in circumference; it then divides into half-a-dozen main branches, above which rise a mass of close inwoven boughs and foliage, in summer, impervious alike to sunshine and shower. It yet vegetates vigorously, blossoms, and bears fruit in abundance. Such was its state and appearance until a great storm of wind, in February, 1869, "laid half its honours low."

The footpath leading from near the gate of the Montpellier Gardens into Parliament Street, is called "The Ginnill"—a north country word, signifying a narrow passage.

The range of shops and houses forming the lower part of Montpellier Parade, Montpellier Street, and Crescy Lodge, have all been built since 1868, with the exception of one house (now in two) called Ashfield House, and it has been renovated. On the Stray, nearly opposite Crescy Lodge, is St. Ann's Well—a spring of pure water, protected by a stone dome, said to make the best tea of any in Harrogate.

On the opposite side of the green is the Esplanade, behind which are St. Mary's Church, School, and Parsonage, which will be described when treating of the Low Harrogate District Parish.

Passing up Cold Bath Road, on the right are three large hotels, known as the Wellington, Binns', and the Adelphi; further up, on the left, is St. Magnus' Well—sometime used as a cold bath—whence this street derives its name.   On the back of this street, towards the west, is a quarry of the transition limestone, which dips so rapidly that only the upper edge of it can be worked.   On the same side is the field in which the Harrogate diamonds are found.

On the south-eastern side of the township is Stonefall, late the seat of Mrs. Penelope Osborne, who died at York, December 23rd, 1869, aged 93.   This place was the residence, for some years, of Mrs. Maria Stevens, a lady of a most christian spirit, who devoted much of her time and fortune to promote the temporal and spiritual welfare of her neighbours.   She wrote and published "Devotional Comments on the Scriptures," which extended to twenty volumes.   Her style is clear and luminous; often grand and poetical.   She died July 8th, 1840, and was buried in Knaresborough Church.

A plot of land here (158 acres in extent) belongs to the vicarage of Knaresborough, to which it was awarded on the enclosure of the Forest, in lieu of tithes.   Further south is Bilton Court, the residence of Mr. Hanson Freeman.   This mansion was much enlarged and the grounds improved in 1865. The hamlet of Crimple, which comprises the bleach works of Messrs. Walton and Co., a few farm houses, and a number of cottages, is situate near the brook of that name. On the opposite side of the stream in Follifoot, in a piece of marshy ground, is a spring of sulphur water, now neglected and disused. Further up the stream is a fine substantial viaduct of ten arches, which carries the Leeds and Thirsk railway across the valley; near which is Mill Hill, now covered with a clump of larches, the site of an iron smelting furnace; large masses of the slag and refuse yet remain. On the verge of the hill are the Hookstone quarries, where the upper bed of millstone grit has been worked for building purposes. This bed of stone is the southern side of a great anticlinal upheaval, the corresponding side of which is found at Birk Crag. A copious spring of water rising here was, many years ago, enclosed in a small building, for bathing purposes, but is now neglected and disused.

On the north-eastern side of the township is Bachelors' Garden School, which was founded in 1798, by the brothers Richard and Francis Taylor, bachelors—hence its name—who vested in seven trustees upwards of seventeen and a half acres of land, as an endowment, for the education of thirty children, residents of the township of Bilton-with-Harrogate, who were to be taught reading, writing, arithmetic, and the church catechism; previous to admission they must be able to read the new testament. The term of education is for two years, or longer, at the option of the trustees. This school is situate in the most fertile part of the township. The master's house and school is a substantial building of stone. On a slab over the door is inscribed, "THIS SCHOOL WAS ENDOWED BY MR. FRANCIS AND MR. RICHARD TAYLOR, TWO BROTHERS, WHO DWELT HERE, AND BUILT IN THE YEAR 1798."

In a fence near the school is a mulberry tree, the only one we know of growing exposed in the neighbourhood.

HARROGATE HALL, situate near the school, is a farm house, rebuilt about the year 1820, and now, with a considerable estate around, the property of John Greenwood, Esq., of Swarcliffe Hall. At what time the original hall was built we have no direct information. In 1558, John Burnand, of the family of that name located at Knaresborough and Nidd, was owner of an estate here,* which extended to where the town of Harrogate now stands. John Burnand was succeeded by his son, Robert Burnand, whose only daughter, Anne, married Francis Trappes,† of London, Esq., who, in right of his wife, became seized of lands in Knaresborough, Harrogate, and Nidd.

The estate continued in this family until Robert Trappes Byrnand, Esq. (aged 20 years, in December, 1619) being a catholic recusant, in order to avoid forfeiture of this estate, conveyed it upon trust to Sir William Ingilby, Bart., of Ripley Castle, with whose descendants it continued until the year 1809, when it was purchased from Sir John Ingilby, Bart., by John Greenwood, Esq., of Swarcliffe Hall, grandfather of the present owner.

Bilton is a small old-fashioned hamlet, situate on the outside of the park pale, and consists of half-a-dozen farm houses, a few cottages, and a public-house.

At this place the geologist will find a patch of magnesian limestone, the upper part of which was quarried for lime, and exhausted about thirty years ago; the railway passes over it near the Bilton-gate house; the eastern part yet remains in

* In 1558, Thomas Bellingham, Gent., occurs on the Knaresborough Court Rolls, as holding lands, called "Crokesnabbe" and "Jennyfield," in the "hamlet of Harlogait," of John Burnand, senr. Crooksnabb is the land lying between Parliament Street and Strawberry Dale; Jennyfield, now Jenny Plain, is situate on both sides of the turnpike road between Harrogate and the Gasworks.

† The family of Trappes was settled at Theydenboys, in Essex., from the time of Henry V.; previously they were of Juppille, in the province of Luxembourgh.

position, occupying an area of nearly half-a-mile square, and has been quarried to about forty feet in depth. The upper beds are soft, and of a yellowish colour, imperfectly stratified, and full of hard nodules, crystallized in the inside.

A thin seam of coal was also worked here, as is evident from the remains of a dozen old shafts. The coal was only of poor quality, and chiefly used in the burning of lime. A tramway was laid down for its conveyance from the pit to the kilns, which were little more than a quarter of a mile apart. The limestone offers a field for profitable speculation; though probably no advantage could be derived from the coal.

A short distance north of Bilton the railway crosses the river Nidd—which here runs in a deep, narrow valley—by a viaduct of seven lofty arches. From this point to Knaresborough the banks of the river are steep, and generally thickly wooded; the river, from Scotton flax mill, where it is crossed by a dam, for a considerable distance upward, is a fine full stream, like a canal winding between woods; lower down it is frequently shallow and rapid. The Bilton woods being possessed of much variety of soil and situation, present a favourable field to the botanist.

BILTON PARK.

Of the formation of this park we have no direct information. In the 31st year of Edward I., Henry de Scriven, of Scriven, petitioned the king, stating that his ancestors had enjoyed the office of foresters of the Forest of Knaresborough, and had for the same sixpence per day, and common pasture in the said forest, and the parks of Hay and Bilton, before the said parks were enclosed, and after the enclosure of these parks, for all beasts of their own breed, except sheep and goats; that they were now interrupted in the enjoyment of the above privileges by Sir Miles Stapleton, the steward of Knaresborough. In answer to this petition, it was decreed that the petitioner should continue to enjoy, without interruption, all the said privileges; and, also should take from the king's woods there, all reasonable housebote, haybote, &c., for which he may have occasion; so that he do not cut down any oak, ash, hazel, or any tree growing or bearing fruit. It was also granted that he should have pasture in Bilton, for his oxen used in the plough, and for his milk kine.*

Sometime previous to the year 1472, a mill was built at Bilton,† and on the 29th of February in that year it was leased by Richard, Duke of Gloucester, seneschal to the duchy of Lancaster, to Sir William Plumpton, Knight, along with the corn mills of Knaresborough, and the burgh of Knaresborough, for the space of twelve years; he rendering for the first 20 marks, for the second 46s. 8d., and for the office of bailiff 46s. 8d.

In 1502, Peter Ardern, deputy of William de la Poole, Earl of Suffolk, chief steward of the duchy of Lancaster, let to farm to Johanna, widow of Sir William Ingilby, Knight, deceased, the herbage and agistment of the park of Bilton.

So long as it continued a royal park,‡ the timber growing

---

* Sixteenth Edward III.: John de Dacre was fined sixpence for not repairing "hayam suam circa parcum de Bilton."—*Knaresborough Court Rolls.*

† This mill has entirely disappeared. On the right bank of the river Nidd, almost opposite to Gateshill, is yet to be seen a mill-race, conveying water, as if to a mill; and at the place where the water runs again into the river, appears the site of a building, where a mill may have stood. On enquiring what had been the use of this artificial water course, we were gravely told that it was made on purpose to turn a wheel for pumping the water from the coal pits above.

‡ About the year 1548, there were deer both in the parks of Bilton and Hay, as is evident from the following extract from a letter written by John Doddington to William Plompton, Esq.:—"Pleaseth yᵗ you to understand my master hath written his letter to Mr. Goldsbrough, for a *do* for your mastership, in Bilton Park, or the park of Heay, at your pleasur."—*Plumpton Cor., p. 243.*

in a place called Bilton Banks, or Blancks, was reserved for the repairs of the castle mills at Knaresborough, and other necessary works within the manor.*

Dr. Dean, writing in 1626, styles this "a large impaled park of His Majesty's, called Bilton Park, well stocked with fallow deer."

Bilton Hall probably stands on the site of the park-keeper's lodge, in which, about the year 1500, Peter Slingsby, keeper of Knaresborough Castle, resided.

In the beginning of the sixteenth century, Bilton was disparked, and came into possession of the family of Stockdale;† of whom—William Stockdale, of Green Hammerton, was living in 1586, who, by his second wife, Dorothy, daughter of Thomas Mill, had a numerous family, amongst whom was Thomas, of Bilton Hall, born in 1598, who married Margaret, daughter of Sir William Parsons, by whom he had one son and two daughters.

During the troublous times of Charles I., Thomas Stockdale was a magistrate and member of parliament, and took an active part in politics, with a strong leaning towards the patriotic or country party. Many of his letters are yet extant, in which strong and decided opinions are expressed. Writing to Lord Fairfax, with whom he appears to have been in close intimacy, he thus expresses himself, in reference to the trial of Lord Strafford:—"April 10th, 1641. And I assure your lordship, it will be no small encouragement to the subject to see justice done upon that great engine, the Lord Strafford, who hath in a manner battered down their laws and liberties, and levelled

---

* In the forty-first Elizabeth, the Attorney-General prosecuted, in the Duchy Court, Thomas Matthew, Robert Matthew, John Benson, and others, for intrusion thereon, and for the felling and destruction of timber.—*Cal. of Pleadings in Duchy Court.*

† Arms—Ermine, on a bend sable three pheons argent, in the sinister chief an escallop gules; a crescent for difference.

them with the most servile nations. His friends are all hopeful
and almost confident of his deliverance; yet methinks it is
impossible that good language and elocution can wipe off the
guilt off his crimes. Rich apparel makes not beauty—it only
dazzles weak sights. Injustice and corruption have been punished
in this land with death; and certainly oppression and tyranny
in such a high strain as they are charged on him, are offences
of a transcendant nature, and deserve punishment (if any there
were,) greater than death, and confiscation of estate. The
country generally, and especially those well affected in religion,
are sensible that to bring him to trial for his offences hath
already cost them £600,000; and now (your lordship will
conceive), if he should by any artifice escape a deserved censure
of the crimes proved against him, the people will be extremely
discontent, and murmur against it; and besides, it is hoped
that the confiscation of his estate, and others that are delin-
quents, will either pay the Scots, or stop some other gap
made by these turbulent times.*

In 1642, when Sir Henry Slingsby was voted "unfit for
Parliament, because he neglected his duties, and had signed
an offensive petition," Mr. Stockdale was elected in his place, as
burgess for Knaresborough, which town he continued to
represent until his death, in December, 1653. He was buried
in the chancel of Knaresborough Church, where an inscription
upon a marble slab yet remains to his memory. He was
succeeded by his eldest son,

William Stockdale, who was elected representative of
Knaresborough in 1660; he was again returned in 1678;
and sat for that borough until his death, in March, 1692 or
1693, when he was succeeded by his nephew,

* Fairfax Correspondence, vol ii., p. 104.

Christopher Walter, or Watter, son of Robert Watter, of
Cundall, and Lettice Stockdale, who, on his accession to the
estate, assumed the name of Stockdale. He represented Knaresborough in parliament from 1695, until his death, in September,
1713. He was succeeded by

William Stockdale, who resided here until 1742, when, having
suffered great losses in the South Sea scheme, he sold the
estate, in that year, to John Watson, Esq., son of George
Watson, Esq., of Old Malton Abbey.

As no accurate account of this family exists in print, except a
meagre pedigree in one of the older editions of "Burkes' Landed
Gentry;" and, as the family is extinct in the male line, the
following sketch, compiled from original materials, may be
worth perusing.

The family came originally from the East Riding; and had it
not been for the "contumacy" of the head of the house, in
1665, a full and accurate pedigree of the family would have
been handed down to his descendants; for in that year Sir
William Dugdale issued his summons to all the Yorkshire
gentry, to furnish him with copies of their pedigrees and arms.
One-third of them, however, he tells us, treated the summons
with neglect, and amongst the offenders we find—

"WAPENTAKE OF RYDALE, OLD MALTON...MR. WATSON."*

Incidental notices of the family, however, occur in the
"Visitation," so that with the help of the parish registers,
tombstones, and monumental inscriptions, the following account
has been compiled—

I. The first of the name of whom any mention occurs is
William Watson, of Scagglethorpe, in the parish of Rillington,
who, at the age of thirty years, was married, before Sir William

* "Dugdale's Visitation of Yorkshire," Surtees' Soc. Preface, p. 13.

O

Strickland, in his capacity of justice of the peace, to Jane
Watson, of Knapton. This must have been in the times of
the Parliament. From this William descended (probably his
son),

II. George Watson, of Old Malton, born about the
beginning of the seventeenth century. This is probably the
"Mr. Watson" who treated Sir William Dugdale's summons so
"contumaciously," to the great loss of his descendants. He
and his wife, in 1671, gave ten shillings each for the restoration
of Old Malton Church, which had been much injured in the
Parliamentary wars. He died February 2nd, 16—, and is
buried in the chancel of the church; aged 87 years. He was
father of

George, who succeeded; and Ruth, who, about 1650, married
John Barton, of Cawton, from whom the Cawton family
descended.*

III. George was of Old Malton Abbey. This property,
known as the Abbey Grange (the dwelling-house called the
Abbey being built over the crypt of the old Priory; for the
building was really a priory of Gilbertines, not an abbey),
though never held in fee by the Watson family, was yet
held by them, for at least four generations, at a nominal
rent from Hemsworth Hospital. The freehold property of the
family consisted of about 400 acres, in the manors of Scagglethorpe, Rillington, and Thorpebasset, all on the borders of the
North and East Ridings, and the estate of Bilton Park, acquired
as stated above, in 1742.

He married and left several sons and daughters—

Elizabeth, born 26th September, 1686 (registered at Old
Malton); married the Rev. Joseph Kerr; died 10th October,
1791, and is buried in Old Malton churchyard.

* See "Dugdale's Visitation," p. 124.

Mary, born 24th January, 1689.

Pleasance, born 15th September, 1691; succeeded.

Guy, born 1st March, 1693.

John, born ——, 169—; purchased Bilton Park, in 1742.

Jane, born ————; married, in 1706, James Baird, of Chesterhall, in Midlothian; one of whose representatives was the late Rev. Dr. George Smith, of Edinburgh. In the Edinburgh register of births, under date 22nd June, 1718, is an entry of the baptism of George, second son of this James Baird and Jane Watson; one of the witnesses being "George Watson, of Old Malton Abbey."

George Watson, died in 1732.

Before tracing the Bilton Park branch, it may be as well to show how the Malton branch terminated.

IV. Pleasance; succeeded, and married, leaving one son and several daughters. He died 20th March, 1756. The children were—

George, born 1732; succeeded.

Mary, born 15th August, 1735; and two other daughters.

V. George; succeeded to Malton Abbey, and was the last of the family, the succession going to his sister's children. He was a magistrate, and was generally known as "Justice Watson;" and was, moreover, a sportsman of the true English type. He died, unmarried, 9th April, 1803, and is buried in the chancel of Old Malton Church. The following inscription is on a marble tablet—

Hanc tabellam
memoriæ
Georgeii Watson, Armiger,
Sacrum
Pietatis ergo
Posuit

Gulielmus Wood Watson, Armiger,

Nepos ejus ex sorore.
Kal. April, obiit
Octoginta Annos natus
Anno Domini
MDCCCIII.

As he left no issue, the succession to his freehold property went to his sister's children.

The first married —— Wood, Esq., and left William Wood, who succeeded in 1808, and, in 1818, assumed the name of Watson. He also died without issue.

The second married —— Baker Esq., of Ebberston, and left Richard, who succeeded his cousin above, and, by license, dated 15th August, 1817, also assumed the name of Watson. He too died without issue.

The third married —— Newton, Esq,, who had a son, William, who succeeded, and, as both his cousins had done, assumed the name of Watson. He left three daughters, co-heiresses, amongst whom the property was divided.

To return to the Bilton Park branch.

IV. John Watson, who purchased this estate, was a solicitor, and married Hannah Bagwith, of Whitby—said to have been a co-heiress, of a good Yorkshire stock. Her father was a lawyer, and his portrait was, and probably still is, at Bilton Park. He died in 17—, and was buried at Malton, leaving two sons and four daughters—

George, who succeeeded.

John, who died, unmarried, in 1758, and was buried at Knaresborough; in the church there is a monument to his memory.

Elizabeth, born in 1709, died 1798. She married the Rev. W. Ward, M.A., rector of Scanby, and perpetual curate of

Yeddingham, and master of the grammar school of Beverley; author of "Essay on Grammar, as it may be applied to the English Language," "Translations from Terence," and other works; who died in 1772, in the 68rd year of his age, and was buried in St. Mary's Church, Beverley. They left several children, of whom the eldest representative is Charles Ward, Esq., of Chapel Street, London.

Jane, married —— Dixon, Esq., of Beverley.

Hannah, married —— Wingfield, of Hull, and left issue.

Mary, married John Farsyde, of Fylingdale, in Whitby Strand, who died in 1755, leaving a son, John, who succeeded, as heir of provesion, to Bilton Park.

V. George, of Bilton Park, married Clementina Kennedy, daughter of Sir John Kennedy, of Colzean, by his wife, Jean Douglass, of the family of Mains. Her brother ultimately succeeded as ninth Earl of Cassilis.* By her he left no issue, and died in 1755, and is buried at Knaresborough. By his will, he devised his estate to his nephew, John Farsyde.

VI. John Farsyde, son of John Farsyde, of Fylingdale, and Mary Watson above, was born at Whitby, in 1749. By royal license, dated 27th April, 1755, he assumed the name of Watson, and bore the arms of Watson and Farsyde, quarterly. A pedigree of the Farsydes will be found in various histories of the landed gentry. They claim to be cadets of the ancient Scottish family of Fawside, of that Ilk, of which, however, there appears to be no direct evidence. John Farsyde Watson died in 1810, leaving

VII. John Farsyde Watson, eldest son, who succeeded to Bilton Park, and by his wife, Hannah, daughter of the Rev. James Hartley, rector of Staveley, had two sons and one

* "See Douglas's Peerage of Scotland," by Wood, vol. i., p. 887.

daughter—John Farsyde Watson, who succeeded; George James, of Fylingdale; and Mary. He died in 1810.

VIII. John Farsyde Watson, born at Bilton, July 2nd, 1808. He was of Christ Church College, Cambridge. He married, in 1880, Miss Georgiana Watson White, and died in London, April 20th, 1881, leaving an only daughter.

IX. Georgiana Farsyde Watson, born April 18th, 1881; present owner and occupier of Bilton Hall.

The arms of the family are, quarterly, first and fourth, Watson. *Argent*, on a chevron engrailed *azure*, between three martlets *sable*, as many crescents *or*. Second and third, Farsyde. *Gules* a feu between three bezants *or*. This latter being the arms of the Fawside, of that Ilk.

Bilton Hall is a brick-built house, in the Tudor style of architecture, partly rebuilt and much enlarged in 1853. It stands, most pleasantly, on a hill, and commands a prospect of great extent and beauty. The woods on the north side slope grandly down to the river Nidd, in all the wildness and majesty of nature; whilst the ancient camp of Gateshill, marked by a few solitary firs, crowns the opposite height; and immediately in front rises the town of Knaresborough—singular and various —enclosed on each side by the woods of Scriven and Belmond; the whole forming a picture of exquisite beauty and variety.

> " There along the dale—
> With woods o'erhung, and shagg'd with mossy rocks,
> Whence, on each hand, the gushing waters play
> And down the rough cascade white dashing fall,
> Or gleam in lengthened vista through the trees—
> You silent steal: or sit beneath the shade .
> Of solemn oaks—that tuft the swelling mounts,
> Thrown graceful round by nature's careless hand—
> And pensive listen to the various voice
> Of rural peace: the herds and flocks, the birds,
> The hollow-whispering breeze, the plaint of rills,
> That—purling down amid the twisted roots
> Which creep around—their dewy murmurs shake
> On the sooth'd ear."

Near the hall is a sulphur spring, the water of which rises into a stone basin, and is protected by a dome of masonry, bearing on its front, J. W., 1778. The water is beautifully transparent, and bubbles of gas, every two or three minutes, rise to the surface of the water; and the stream, as it flows down the hill, shows its petrific quality, by turning the leaves, sticks, and mosses, in its track, into stone.

This spring was noticed by Dr. Dean, in 1626; speaking of the sulphur springs, he says, "One of them that has the greatest stream of water is in Bilton Park." He also suggested, at that early date, that *baths* might be most easily constructed here. It is again mentioned, in 1734, by Dr. Short, in his "History of Mineral Waters." The generality of the modern writers on the waters of Harrogate have not even mentioned it, though its situation is the most romantically beautiful of any of them.

PANNAL.

PANNAL is a village and parish adjoining Harrogate on the south-west; and includes within its limits, Pannal, Low-Harrogate, Rosset, Beckwith, and Beckwithshaw. It is bounded, on the east, by Harrogate; on the south, by the brook Crimple, which divides it from the townships of Follifoot and Rigton; westward, it touches Stainburn and Norwood;* while on the north it is bounded by Haverah Park and Killinghall.

The name of Pannal† does not occur in Domesday survey, but Beckwith and Rosset are both mentioned. Among the lands of the king, we find—

"In Roserte, Ulf had one carucate and a half to be taxed. Land to one plough. Waste."‡

Again among the lands of Giselbert Tyson, we find—

"II. Manors. In Rosert, Gamelbar and Ulf had two carucates to be taxed. Land to one plough. Waste."§

Beckwith was also parcel of the lands of Giselbert Tyson.

"Manor. In Becvi, Gamelbar had three carucates to be taxed. Land to two ploughs. Waste."‖

* At Broad-dub—now a running stream, though the name and situation show it to have been the site of a small lake—the townships of Pannal, Stainburn, Norwood, and Haverah Park, almost touch each other.
† This name is probably derived from the Pan, or timber-built hall, of its early owners.
‡ "Bawdwen's Dom. Boc.," p. 37.
§ Ibid, p. 194.
‖ Ibid, p. 194.

These lands were afterwards included in the Forest of Knaresborough, and always passed along with that fee; and subsequently came to be divided among many small proprietors.

In the inquisition, post mortem, held 8th Edward II., on the death of Henry de Percy, it was found that he died seized of four oxgangs of land in *Pathenall*.

The canons of Newburgh were owners of a tenement in Pannal, about the year 1448, the annual rent of which was twenty-four shillings.

In 1539, on the dissolution of their house, the brethren of St. Robert's of Knaresborough held divers tenements and farms in Pannal, of the annual value of £2 16s. 6d.

Some, if not the whole, of these last named possessions are now merged in the Pannal Hall estate,* belonging to the family of Bentley.

The old hall at Pannal was built by the family of Tankred, or Tancred, as was evident from their arms being cut upon a stone above the principal entrance. It was in the shape of the letter L, and in the Tudor style of architecture; but was entirely removed on the erection of the new one, in 1860.

Of the family of Tankred, during their ownership of the hall here, we have very slender information. By inquisition, post mortem, held July 31st, 37th Elizabeth, 1594, we learn that Francis Tankard, gentleman, deceased June 22nd, last past, was seized, at the time of his death, of a grange or capital messuage in Pannal, and divers lands there; and that William, his son and heir, was then of the age of thirty-three years.

---

*In a deed, dated June 9th, 8th James I., from Thomas Hall and Robert Longe, to John Taylor, conveying divers cottages and premises in Pannal, recital is made of a grant from the crown of the same premises, which had late belonged to the brethren of St. Robert's, near Knaresborough. The said premises are said to be of the manor of East Greenwich, by fealty, under the yearly rent of 8s. 4d.

In the 40th of Queen Elizabeth (1597), William Tankerd granted divers long leases of lands in Pannal (subject to small rent charges), to divers persons; one of which was to Richard Allan, of Harrogate, clothier, of the Pasture Close, for the term of 1,000 years, under a yearly reserved rent of 12*d*., if demanded; the others were of a similar kind.

Richard Tankerd, of Pannal, had a son, named Francis, who married Dorothy, daughter of Thomas Slingsby, of Scriven, Esq., and a daughter, named Elizabeth, who married, for her second husband, Christopher, second son of the same Thomas Slingsby, Esq.

The Tankerds were succeeded in this estate by the family of Dougill, who held it for two generations—that of Henry and William Dougill.

On the 2nd of August, 1688, Mr. William Dougill* conveyed to Thomas Herbert, Philip Herbert, Charles Herbert, and James Herbert, the capital messuage or grange called Pannal Hall, with all appurtenances;† and the reversion of a close, called Pasture Close, and the rent of one shilling reserved upon a lease of 1,000 years thereof, made by William Tankerd to one Richard Alline; and also the reversion of a tenement and a close, called Woodcock Hill, and the rent of 2*d*. yearly,

---

* This family does not appear on the parish register before 1608, in which year occurs—"Burials: A child of William Dougill, 6th of June." "1609. Christenings: Martha, the daughter of William Dougill, the 7th of July." "1611. Christenings: Christopher, the son of William Dougill, the 6th of October." They were, however, resident in the township at a much earlier date, as in 5 and 6, Phillip and Mary (1558), the following entry occurs on the Knaresborough Court Rolls—"Robert Bentlaye, of Rosshirste, surrendered one acre of land, in Beckwith and Rosshyrste, to the use of William Dougill, of Rossehurste, his heirs and assigns.

† The parcels are described minutely: some of the names are expressive of their uses—as, the kiln, and kilngarth or orchard, the garden, two barns, one oxhouse, one garth, called Dove Cote Garth, with a dove cote builded thereupon, one stable, sometime used as a messuage, and now standing in a *mease-stead;* Kirke Inge, Kirke Leas, Well Inge, and the Elder Spring thereto adjoining.

reserved upon a lease of 2,000 years thereof, formerly made
by the said William Tankerd to John Poppleton and Elizabeth,
his wife; and the yearly rent of 16d. reserved upon a lease
of 2,000 years, made by Henry Dougill to Thomas Dougill,
of a messuage and divers closes of land; with all tithes, &c.,
common of pasture for all manner of cattle upon the moor
of Follyfait and Follyfait Rigg; and also common of pasture for
all manner of cattle, and common of turbary within the Forest
of Knaresburgh.

The hall is described as "All that capitall messuage or grange
of Pannall aforesaid, commonly called Pannall Hall, wherein the
said William Dougill now dwelleth, and all the doors, windows,
floors, seilinge, wanscot, and glasse in the said house, and
all the courts, courtylays, gardens, and backsydes, to the
same house belonginge."

The new owners of Pannal Hall were descended from the
ancient and noble family of Herbert; the two first named were
sons of Evan Herbert,* of the city of York, who died in 1582,
and was buried in Christ's Church, in that city. Philip, the
second son, was sheriff of York in 1633; he married, first,
Elizabeth, daughter and co-heir of Thomas Thackley, a
merchant in Hull, by whom he had two sons, Philip and
Thomas; secondly, he married Ellen, daughter of Charles
Tankard, of Whixley, Esquire, by whom he had a son, named
Jacob. He died in 1639; and his will was proved on the 28th
of October, in the same year, when administration of his goods
and chattels was granted to his brother, Thomas Herbert,
merchant, of the city of York.

* Probably the whole of them; though their names do not appear in the
pedigree of that family given in "Dugdale's Visitation." (Ed. Surtees'
Soc., p. 148).
Many particulars relative to the family of Herbert were supplied by
Mr. R. H. Skaife. The documents consulted are in possession of Miss
Bentley, of Pannal Hall.

The next dealing with the Pannal Hall estate was on November 19th, 1648; when Thomas Herbert—in consideration of the love to his sister, Elizabeth Pecke, and his nephew, Thomas Herbert—appointed Mark Metcalfe and Thomas Thompson to stand seized of Pannal estate and Pannal Banks, to the use of the said Thomas, for life, and after his decease to Jacob Herbert, son of Philip, and his heirs.

This Jacob Herbert made his will, July 4th, 1661, in which he describes himself as late of Leeds, now of the city of York, cloth dresser; and desires his body to be decently buried in the Church of All Hallows, on the pavement, within the city of York, near the bodies of his late dear father and mother. Having previously given Pannal Hall, or his interest therein, by deed, to his brother Philip Herbert, he now, by his will, ratifies the same. He furthers say, "Whereas Sir Richard Tanckred, Knight, my uncle, was nominated, by my said late dear mother, to be my tutor or guardian, in my minority, by reason whereof he entered to all, or most part of, my said mother's estate, and has not yet accompt rendered of the same, my humble suit and desire is, that the said Sir Richard, my loving uncle, will be pleased to make accompt to my executor, hereinafter named." He gives to his cousin, Mrs. Thornton, five pounds, and a gold ring, with the posie, *Never looks, but remember*. He also gives unto his loving uncle the sum of one hundred pounds, to be paid when he has rendered a true accompt to his executors.

The "loving uncle" did not think proper to comply with the above modest request, without the costs of a chancery suit, in which Philip Herbert was complainant, and Sir Richard Tanckred, Knight, defendant. We do not know the result.

Philip Herbert, brother of the above mentioned Jacob, was born in 1627, and was lord mayor of the city of York, in 1675. He married, in 1654, Mary, daughter of Ralph Bell, of Thirsk, by whom he had three sons, Philip, Thomas, and John, and two daughters, Elizabeth and Mary. The two elder sons died before their father, whose death took place in 1697.

On the 12th of June, 1694, Philip Herbert and his wife mortgaged the Pannal Hall estate to Robert Bell; and on the 4th of November, 1698, for a further consideration, and reciting an annuity of £20 per annum to Philip Herbert and his wife, Dame Mary Herbert, widow, released the premises to Robert Bell, her brother. Robert Bell died in 1707, when the estate came into possesion of his son, Ralph Bell, of Sowerby, Esq., who sold the same to William Pullan, who appears not to have been able to procure the whole of the purchase money, but mortgaged the same to Ralph Bell, at the time of the purchase; and for a further sum on the 1st of November, 1718. Six years afterwards, on November 10th, 1724, Ralph Bell and Samuel Pullan sold the Pannal Hall estate to Mr. George Bentley, by whose descendants it is yet held.

George Bentley, born in 1680, was the son of William Bentley, of Great Rosset, in the parish of Pannal. His wife's name was Mary Godfrey, by whom he had issue—

Mary, born June 6th, 1727.

Anna, born December 20th, 1728.

William, born September 4th, 1730.

George, born May 20th, 1732.

Robert, born August 10th, 1734, died February 15th, 1816.

Thomas, born April 2nd, 1737, died August 15th, 1762.

Penelope, born January 16th, 1739, died January 8th, 1742.

Penelope, born August 23rd, 1744, married to Mr. William Clark, of Ribston; she died May 23rd, 1763.

George Bentley died March 8th, 1765 (his wife died August 1st, 1778), and was succeeded by his eldest son,

William Bentley, who, in August, 1778, married Christiana Bradley, by whom he had—

William, bapt. February 10th, 1779.

Thomas, bapt. May 9th, 1782.

William Bentley died December 23rd, 1813 (Christiana, his wife, died August 31st, 1819), and was succeeded in the Pannal Hall estate by his eldest son,

William Bentley, who, in 1802, married Mary, daughter of Bryan Procter, of Pannal, by whom he had issue—

Thomas, bapt. June 1st, 1802.

Mary Godfrey, bapt. July 8th, 1803, married Mr. William Wright, of Beckwith House; she died July 4th, 1862.

Eliza Penelope, bapt. April 2nd, 1805.

Anabella, bapt. July 16th, 1806, died May 21st, 1855.

William Bentley, died July 13th, 1843 (his wife died October 7th, 1846), and was succeeded by his only son,

Thomas Bentley, who married Mary Ann, eldest daughter of William Wright, of Beckwith House, by whom he had issue—

Ann Elizabeth, bapt. October 15th, 1837, married to Mr. David Wilson, of Pannal.

William George, bapt. November 13th, 1839.

Thomas Bentley died May 6th, 1863, and was succeeded by his only son,

William George Bentley, who married Henrietta, daughter of Henry James Lesley, of Sinnington Lodge, by whom he had one daughter—

Henrietta Maria, bapt. July 10th, 1864, died February 9th, 1866.

William George Bentley died August 2nd, 1866, and, by his will, devised the estate of Pannal Hall to his aunt, Miss Eliza Penelope Bentley, the present owner.

Pannal Hall, rebuilt by the late Thomas Bentley, in 1860, is a modern mansion, situate in a warm sheltered situation, near the brook Crimple, on the western side of the village street. The Pannal Hall estate extends along the valley, down the northern side of the Crimple, from Burn Bridge to Almsford Bridge.

The village of Pannal is situate on the southern verge of the parish, close to the brook Crimple. The houses are scattered irregularly along the sides of a narrow street or road, running north and south. Near the top of the village is Rose-hurst, a delightfully situated mansion, the name of which is beautifully appropriate, for the house is literally situate in "a grove of roses." It was built by the late Mr. James Dickinson, about the year 1833, and is now the property of his son, Mr. Edward Dickinson, of Hill Top Hall.

The school, a spacious and substantial building of stone, which will accommodate upwards of one hundred scholars, with master's house adjacent, situate at the upper end of the village, was erected in 1817, by a public subscription, originated and largely assisted by the late Mr. John Bainbridge, of Crimple Villa; and on his decease the school and premises were vested in trustees for the benefit of the parish. An inscription, painted on a panel at the upper end of the school, thus describes its foundation and object—

PANNAL VILLAGE SCHOOL.

This school, with the cottages and garden adjoining, were devised by the will of the late Captain John Bainbridge, dated the 26th day of June, 1855, and who died on the 19th of August, 1856, unto James Bray, Samuel Bateman, Joseph William Thackwray, Joshua Hardisty Wilkinson, and David Wilson, gentlemen, their heirs and assigns for ever, for the education of the children of the poor of the parish of Pannal, and adjoining townships, with a recommendation to them to collect subscriptions for the maintenance of the school.

Amongst the contributors to the original building fund appeared the names of their majesties Kings George III. and IV., the Archbishop of York, and the Bishop of Durham, Earls Harewood and Rosslyn, Baronets Sir Thomas Slingsby, of Scriven, and Sir William A. Ingilby, of Ripley, Richard F. Wilson, Esq., and many others, men of high station at the time.

The church (dedicated to St. Robert,) is situate on the east side of the village street, and consists of a tower, nave, and chancel; the first and last ancient—probably of coeval date—in the decorated style; the nave was rebuilt in 1772, in the style of that period, with wide, round-headed windows, glazed with large squares, and does not present any feature of interest. The eastern window is of three lights, with quatrefoils in the sweep of the arch.

The principal entrance is through the basement story of the tower. The belfry contains three bells, which are said to have been brought from Fountains Abbey, a tradition of which the bells themselves bear the refutation, unless they have been recast. On the first is inscribed, "*Te Deum Lauda-mus*, 1703;" on the second, "*Gloria Deo in Excelsis*, 1669;" the other bears, "*Honorandus Deus super omnia*, 1669, **B.B., I.C.,** Churchwardens." These two old ones have a very elegant appearance; and on fillets round the upper part is a small shield, bearing **S.S. EBOR.*** frequently repeated amid interlacing foliage.

Opposite the entrance is the font, an elegant oval basin of dark-veined marble, said by the doubtful voice of tradition to have been brought from Fountains Abbey.

* These are the initials of Samuel Smith, bell founder, of York. He lived in Micklegate; and on his decease, in 1710, bequeathed his bell house, on Toft Green, to his sons Samuel and James. Samuel, the younger, was also famous as a bell founder. He was sheriff of York in 1723; and on his death, in 1731, bequeathed his bell house to his brother James.—R. H. S.

In the gallery, which runs across the west end, is a small organ, which was given to the vicar and churchwardens by the will of William Smith Dickinson, Nov. 22nd, 1853.

The whole of the nave is fitted up with pews—some of them cushioned and comfortable. On one side of the chancel arch is the pulpit; on the other, the reading desk and clerk's desk.

On the south side of the nave, on a large slab of white marble, is the following inscription—" Sacred to the memory of Thomas Symeson, of Beckwith, in this parish, gentleman, who died in the year 1558, and was here interred. Thomas Symeson was the second son of Thomas Symeson, of Wipley, gentleman, and of Agnes his wife, daughter of John Atkinson, of Clynte, gentleman; and the sixteenth in lineal descent from Archil, a Saxon Thane, residing at Wipley, in the township of Clint, in the reign of Edward the Confessor, king of England. Also to the memory of Rossamund, the wife and widow of the above-named Thomas Symeson. She died about the year 1559. Also to the memory of William Symeson, of Lund House, in Beckwith, and captain of the West York Militia. He was the second son of William Simpson, Esq., of Felliscliffe, and a lineal descendant of the above-named Thomas and Rossamund Symeson. He died 1786, and was interred in the burial ground of this church."

. The chancel is ancient—yet retaining its piscina and sedilia —and is entirely open, without either pews or stalls. In the first window on the south side, filling the quatrefoil above the double light, is the representation, in stained glass, of an embattled castle, or some ancient building, showing three sides; the entrance arch has a circular head, and apparently a portcullis, *sable*, before it; three towers rise above, *or;* on the sides are oak trees, leaved and acorned, *vert*. This was supposed by Hargrove to be intended for the gateway of St.

P

Robert's priory, Knaresborough, to which house the church was appropriated. Others, with equal probability, suppose it to be intended for the Castle of Knaresborough itself. Below this has been on a shield, *azure*, a cross pateé, *gules* and *azure*—the upright being *gules*, the transom, *azure*; part of the latter is now wanting. Against the walls, on marble tablets, are the following inscriptions,—on the north side—

"In memory of William Bentley, Esq., of Pannal Hall, who departed this life July 18th, 1843, aged 68 years.

Also, Mary, his wife, who departed this life October 7th, 1846, aged 65 years."

"Sacred to the memory of Thomas Bentley, of Pannal Hall, who departed this life May 6th, 1868, aged 60 years.

Also, Ann, wife of the above Thomas Bentley, who died November 7th, 1845, aged 89 years."

"Sacred to the memory of Annabella, youngest daughter of William and Mary Bentley, of Pannal Hall, who died May 21st, 1855, aged 48 years."

On the south side—

"In memory of William Bentley, Esq., of Pannal Hall, who departed this life December 23rd, 1813, aged 88 years.

Also of Christiana, wife of the above William Bentley, who departed this life August 31st, 1819, aged 75 years."

"In memory of William George Bentley, of Pannal Hall, who died August 2nd, 1866, in the 27th year of his age.

Also of Henrietta Maria, the beloved and only child of the above William George Bentley and Henrietta, his wife, who died February 9th, 1866, aged one year and seven months."

Upon the floor, on a narrow slab of gritstone, is inscribed—

"Listerius, filius maximus Annæ et Listerii Simondson, hujus Ecclesiæ minister. Obit Octob. 19. Ætatis 11. An. Salut. 1722."

"Here lies interred the body of George Bentley, of Pannal Hall; he departed this life the 8th day of March, in the year of our Lord 1765, in the 84th year of his age."

"Here lyeth interred the body of Thomas, the son of Mr. George Bentley, of Pannal Hall, who departed this life the 15th day of August, A.D. 1762, and in the 24th year of his age."

"Here lies the body of Mary, the wife of George Bentley, of Pannal Hall; she departed this life the first day of August, in the year of our Lord 1773, aged 74 years."

"In memory of Robert, son of George and Mary Bentley, of Pannal Hall, who departed this life February 15th, 1816, aged 81 years."

"Here lies the body of Penelope Clark, of Great Ribstone; she departed this life August the 3rd, 1783, aged 39 years."

"Here lies interred the body of Anne, the wife of Jeremiah Wright, of Pannal; she departed this life the 14th day of May, 1764, in the 71st year of her age."

"Here lieth the body of Jeremiah Wright, of Pannal, who departed this life yᵉ 22nd day of January, 1776, aged 91."

"In memory of Henry Wright, of Pannal, who departed this life the 24th day of April, in 1799, aged 82 years. May his soul rest in peace!

Also, here lieth interred the body of Mary, the wife of Henry Wright, of Pannal, who departed this life the 9th day of March, in the year of our Lord 1790, aged 71 years."

"In memory of Richard Wright, of Pannal, who departed this life the 30th day of November, in the year 1813, aged 89 years."

"In memory of Henry, son of Richard and Frances Wright, who departed this life the 24th day of June, 1805, aged 30 years."

The first legible registers of baptisms and burials are in 1585; marriages commence in 1607. There are a few deficiencies in the books, at different periods.

During the Commonwealth, when certificates of marriage were signed by the magistrates, Thomas Stockdale, Henry Arthington, and Jo. Bourchier, performed that office for Pannal.

A family of the name of Cheldray appears on the second page of the register, in 1585, and continues down far into the eighteenth century.

At one time there were five families of the name of Bentley, all living, increasing, and multiplying in this parish, as the following extracts will show—

"1655. Baptisms. Francis, son of George Bentley, 4 December."
"1655.   „   Alice, daughter of Thomas Bentley, 8 March."
"1656.   „   Sara, daughter of William Bentley, son of Leonard, 21st April."
"1656.   „   Samuel, son of Henry Bentley, 8th December."
"1656.   „   William, son of William Bentley, of Great Rosset, 1st January."

Next to Bentley, Winterburn is the most frequent name in the early registers; and in the later ones more abundant than any other.

In 1655, the name of Kent first appears; they yet exist, as a wealthy yeoman family, at Tatefield Hall, in Rigton, but are possessed of lands in this parish, in which they resided until about forty years ago. Their tombstones are in the churchyard, south-east of the chancel.

"1607. Weddings. Marmaduke Boulton and Clare Plompton, 28th August."

Was not this the Clare Plompton, of Plompton, whose marriage is not given in the usual pedigrees of that family?

The following most singular name occurs twice—

"Weddings. 1610. Adam Crokebane, *alias* Bickerdike, and Jane Leyming, 22nd of Avrill."

"Christenings. 1610. Thomas, son of Adam Crockbane, 31st May."

"Christenings. 1768. John, a child born at ye Sulphur Well, of parents unknown, August ye 27th."

"Burials. 1848. August 25th, Elizabeth Lupton, *alias* 'Old Betty, Queen of the Wells,' aged 88."

Many instances of more than ordinary longevity have occurred in this parish. The following are either from the register, or from stones in the churchyard—

"Stephen Shann, of Beckwithshaw, buried December 8th, 1806, aged 98."

"Thomasine Shutt, of Harrogate, died March 16th, 1807, aged 94."

"Burials. 1791. April 14th, William Bradley, a pauper from the workhouse, in the 90th year of his age."

"1796. June 16th, Ann Barber, aged 90."

"1846. Matthew Pearson, Knaresbro', aged 112, Nov. 8th."

"1854. Thomas Noble, Jan. 3rd, aged 97."

"Bryan Procter, of Pannal, died January 26th, 1827, aged 98."

"Thomas Grimshaw, of Pannal, died Jan. 12th, 1828, aged 92."

"Mary, wife of Isaac Forrest, died July 8th, 1849, aged 98."

In the churchyard are many tombstones and inscriptions. The oldest is near the south entrance of the church, and is as follows—

"In hope of a glorious resurrection resteth the body of John Bourne, of Pannal, who blessedly expired this life ye 17th day of February, Anno Domini 1688.

> Dum vixi vigne jaceo nunc vermibus esca,
> Munde vale serviis Christe recumbotuus."

The most singular is on a large altar tomb—

"𝔥𝔢𝔯𝔢

𝔍𝔶𝔢𝔱𝔥 𝔱𝔥𝔢 𝔟𝔬𝔡𝔶

OF

JOSEPH THACKRAY by name,
Who, by the help of God,
Brought Sulphur Wells to fame.
In the year of our Lord 1740
I came to the *Crown*,
In 1791 they laid me down.
When I shall rise again
No man can surely tell;
But in the hopes of Heaven
I'm not afraid of Hell.
To friends I bid farewell,
And part without a frown,
In hopes to rise again,
And have a better Crown.

He departed this life the 26th November, in the 79th year of
his age.

Sarah, his wife, died 29th October, 1775, in the 67th year of
her age."

The Sulphur Wells and Crown above mentioned, are the
Wells and Crown Hotel in Low Harrogate.

In 1868, the burial ground was enlarged by the addition
of half an acre on the south side, purchased from Miss Bentley.

The living is a discharged vicarage, at present in the
incumbent's own gift. In 1296, it was returned as worth
£5 per annum. In 1318, the fabric was completely destroyed
by the invading Scots, who spread desolation over this district;
made the church their head-quarters; and, on their departure,
burnt it to the ground, and rendered the living valueless.
Having come into possession of Edmund, Earl of Cornwall,
by exchange for the manor of Rowcliff, it was, by him, given to
the brethren of the house of St. Robert of Knaresborough,
who appropriated the same to their house, and ordained a
vicarage therein, May 19th, 1848. They held possession

of it until the dissolution of their house, in 1589, when it was valued as below—

	£	s.	d.
House, with rectorial glebe	3	0	8
Tithes of corn and hay, per annum	2	6	8
Lambs and wool	2	0	10
Flax and hemp	0	1	8
Oblations	0	8	0
Small and private tithes, as in Easter book ..	2	5	4
	£10	8	2

The Vicarage, at the same time, was returned as—

	£	s.	d.
Money annually paid to vicar	5	0	0
Site of Vicarage house, per annum	0	5	0
	£5	5	0

There was also a chantry in this church, dedicated to St. James, and of which at that time Robert Catton was incumbent; the return of which was—

Rents of lands and tenements belonging to the same ....£3 13s. 4d.

These lands and tenements were situate in Beckwith, Rosset, Rosehurst, and Killinghall.

In 1705, the following curious statement occurs relative to this living*—"Tithes are holden from the church; but whether impropriated is doubted and questioned by ancient men in the parish. They are holden by Richard and John Hill, of Shadwell, near London. The church hath no part of tithe, but is reported to have had a vicarage close and house, which close still goes by the name of 'Vicarage Close,' and the house was sold by the farmers of the tithes in 1654, or thereabouts. Augmented with £3 per annum by Thomas Hill, and 80s. per annum by William Kent. Total value, about £20 per annum. Tithes were paid before the late times of confusion. John Wright, Vic."

* "Notitia Parochialis," No. 892.

In 1711, Mr. John Moon left a close near the Sulphur Well
to the vicar of Pannal for ever, subject to the payment of 5s.
a-year to the poor of the parish.

The following entry is copied from the parish register,—

"The waste land for the vicar of Pannal was set out in
1713-14. Between the Colde Bath and Sulphur Well, 11 acres,
called Nettle Cliff; on the sunside of Hardesty's house, 12 acres;
Lead Hall Inclosure, 7a. 3r.; parcel opposite to Shepherd's
farm, 7a. 2r.; over against Mr. Wescoe's, 8a. 3r.; Birk Crag,
12 acres;—total, 59 acres."

In 1715, the living was augmented with £200, from Queen
Anne's Bounty fund, to meet benefactiods of lands worth £320,
from Mr. John Wescoe and Mr. William Maunby.*

On the enclosure of the forest, in 1778, the impropriators
had awarded to them, in lieu of tithes, the following quantities
of land—

	a.	r.	p.
To Dorothy Wilkes and Ann Bainbridge, who held one-fourth part	58	1	34
To William Bentley—one-fourth	33	3	15
To William Roundell—one-fourth	47	2	8
To Henry and Richard Wright—one-fourth	80	1	8
With money payments for encroachments, amounting in the whole to—	£ 2	s. 10	d. 4

As far as the church is concerned, Miss Bentley, of Pannal
Hall, is now the sole impropriator, who, as a charge attached
thereto, maintains the fabric of the chancel.

In 1831, the vicarage was returned as worth £235 per annum.
The landed estate belonging thereto consists of 76a. 3r. 28p.

The patronage of late years has been in the gift of the
incumbent. It was held by the Rev. Ralph Bates Hunter

* The families of Wescoe and Maunby were both resident in Pannal;
of the former some account will be found hereafter. The Maunbys appear
in the register in 1720, and do not occur after 1785.

until 1835, when he sold it to James Simpson, Esq., of Fox Hill Bank, near Blackburn, Lancashire, for the sum of £2,800, who presented it to his son, the Rev. Thomas Simpson. The latter disposed of his interest therein, in 1862, to the Rev. William S. Vawdrey, present vicar.

The following is the most complete list of the rectors, vicars, and curates, we have been able to obtain.

A CLOSE CATALOGUE OF THE RECTORS OF PANNAL.

(Torre's Archdeaconry of York, p. 201.)

	W. A. Diaconus Roffensis* ....p. resig.
In crast. S. Clemtes, 1271.	Mr. Martyn de Lege, cler., Rex Alemanniæ.
5 Id. Jan., 1311.	Mr. Tho. de Skelelthorp, cler., minr. et fratr. dom. St. Robt.

A CLOSE CATALOGUE OF THE VICARS OF PANNHALE.

5 Nov., 1348.	Fr. Johannes Broun, confr. domus, minr. et fratr. dom. St. Robt. juxta Knaresburgh..pr. mort.	
18 Nov., 1349.	Fr. Will. de Kent, confr. ibidem....iidem....pr. resig.	
12 April, 1364.	Fr. Will. de Pudsey, pbr. confr. ibd. ,, ...pr. resig.	
5 Jan., 1369.	Fr. Ric. de Wakefield, fr. ibidem .... ,, ...p. resig.	
13 Maii, 1370.	Fr. Will. de Berkes, fr. ibidem .... ,, ...p. resig.	
	Fr. Will. Brott .... ,, ...p. resig.	
19 Dec., 1421.	Fr. Joh. Strensall, pbsb. ibidem .... ,, ...p. resig.	
5 Oct., 1454.	Fr. Will. Wyndus, fr. ibidem ...... ,, ..p. mortem.	
20 April, 1459.	Fr. Petr. Patrington, fr. ibidem .... ,, ..p. mortem.	
27 Maii, 1474.	Fr. Laur. Screwton .... ,, ..p. mortem.	
8 Aug., 1475.	Fr. Christoph. Craven .... ,, ..p, mortem.	
8 Jan., 1498.	Fr. Will. Yorke, confr. ibidem .... ,, ..p. mortem.	
19 Sep., 1511.	Fr. Henr. Bell, presb. .... ,, ...p. resig.	
18 Dec., 1515.	Fr. Joh. Godbehere, frat., etc. ..... ,, ..p. mortem.	
6 Oct., 1524.	Fr. Percivall Dibbis, presb.. .... ,, ..p. mortem.	
8 Oct., 1535.	Dom. Will. Lambert.............. ,, ..	

Torre's catalogue ends here. The two following names are from the parish register—

1677.	William Cheldrey, minister.
1683.	William Parsons, ,,

* W. Archdeacon of Rochester, who resigned the rectory of Pannal, Nov. 24, 1271, appears to be identical with William de Sancto Martino, who, according to "Le Neve" (p. 253), was Archdeacon of Rochester in 1267, and died in 1274.

ARCHBISHOP SHARPE'S M.S.S., p. 80.

I find no mention of any vicar instituted here.

6 May, 1694.	Tho. Green, curate.
7 June, 1696.	Christ. Jackson, curate.
1699.	John Wright, curate; died 1707.
6 Sep., 1728.	Lister Simondson, curate.
7 Oct., 1745.	Lister Simondson,* instituted vicar of Pannal on the presentation of the king.
17 Dec., 1750.	William Loup, B.A., pres. Geo. Loup, of Ripon, Gent.
1756.	Robert Midgeley ....p. resig.
29 Dec., 1758.	William Raper, pres. John Raper, Coxwold......p. mort.
2 Oct., 1789.	John Umpleby, pres. John Raper, Easingwold ....resig.
20 Feb., 1816.	Ralph Bates Hunter, pres. John Hunter, Bilton Park, Esq. ....resig.
17 July, 1835.	Thomas Simpson ....resig.
1862.	William S. Vawdrey .. ..present vicar.

The following curates have also officiated at Pannal, under the vicars—

21 Aug., 1730.	Thomas Bolland appointed curate at £18 per ann.
25 Sep., 1743.	John Riley, B.A., „ „ at £15 „
20 Dec., 1747.	Gregory Perkins „ „ at £20 „
18 June, 1758.	John Harker, "a literate person," at £20 „
17 June, 1764.	Beaumont Broadbelt, "a literate person," at £25 per ann.
21 Feb., 1815.	Henry William Powell—at £40 per ann.—to reside at Knaresborough, where he was master of the free school.
18 July, 1824.	Thos. Hellier Madge, at £100 per ann.
5 Sep., 1827.	James Holme—to curacy of Pannal and chapel of Low Harrogate, at £100 per ann.
18 July, 1830.	Joshua Fawcett, B.A., at £80 per ann.
4 Aug., 1833.	James Heyworth, B.A., at £80 per ann., "there being no vicarage house—to be resident near."

The charities consist of—a donation of 5s., left by the will of John Clark, in 1746, to be paid on the 27th of July,

* In the Pannal register he makes the following entry—"Sep. 20th, 1702. I entered on the curacy of Stainburn. The first time I came to officiate at Pannall Church was upon the fifth Sunday after Easter, being May the 18th, 1707, a fortnight, or thereabouts, after the decease of Mr. John Wright.

Witness my hand, Lister Simondson."
He was buried at Kirkby Overblow, where a headstone of white limestone, against the outside wall of the chancel, yet bears the following inscription to his memory—"Here lieth the body of the Rev. Lyster Simondson, vicar of Pannal and curate of Kirkby Overblow, who departed this life the 9th day of November, Anno Domini 1750, aged 72. He was an affectionate husband, an indulgent father, and a sincere friend."

annually, for ever; two small fields on Harlow Hill, set out
by the commissioners on the enclosure of the forest; two small
allotments at Lund's Green—one of 9 perches, the other of
80 perches—on which now stands the building called the
Poorhouse; £8 per annum, payable out of a field near Low
Harrogate; 7s. 6d. a-year out of Benjamin Winterburn's land;
£1 2s. 6d. out of a field near Low Harrogate, belonging to
Joseph Thackrey; and 2s. 6d. out of a piece of land at Beckwithshaw, awarded to Elizabeth Swan.

Mr. Richard Wright, by his will dated June 5th, 1818, left
£8 per annum, payable out of a close at Storey Head, in
Pannal, called Holm Close, to the poor of the parish for ever,
to be laid out in provisions and clothing; and £1 a-year to
the school, for teaching poor children to read the scriptures.

John Moon, who left a close near the Sulphur Well to the
vicar, in 1811, charged it with the payment of 5s. annually
to the poor for ever.

A considerable portion of land at the south-eastern corner
of the parish belongs to the Duchy of Lancaster, now held
on lease by Sir Joseph Radcliffe, Bart., of Rudding Park.
Previously it was held by the respectable family of Bainbridge,
who resided at Crimple House, a mansion pleasantly situate
on an eminence, overlooking the valley of the Crimple, and
the magnificent viaduct of that name, which here spans the
valley. The first who resided here was John Bainbridge, who,
in 1789, was appointed a commissioner for the completion of
the inclosure of the forest. By his wife, Grace, he had a family
of six children, of whom John, his successor, was the eldest.

He took an active part in the foundation of Pannal School,
in 1818; and died August 19th, 1856, aged 75. He was the
last of the family who held lands in this parish. Crimple
House is now occupied by Joseph P. P. Radcliffe, Esq., and
Crimple Villa by Mr. Charles Sowray.

Fullwith Mill, which is situate close to the brook Crimple, from which it derives its motive power, along with eight acres of land in Beckwith-with-Rosset, and twenty-six acres in Pannal, in 1785, belonged to John Coghill, Esq., of Coghill Hall, near Knaresborough, who bequeathed the same to his grand-nephew, Oliver Cramer Coghill, Esq. It is now the property of Mr. William Stables, of Kirkby Overblow.

Pannal House, now used as a boarding school, is a large building, in an open, airy situation, overlooking the valley of the Crimple, and the country beyond. In early times the house situate here bore the name of Wescoe Hall, and was owned and occupied by the old and respectable yeoman family of Wescoe. Their names occur in the parish register from 1599 to about 1735, as resident here, though not in any great number; and, as if to show their consequence, the "Mr." is generally prefixed to the name. Afterwards the estate was held by the family of Crosby, who came from Spofforth. After the decease of the last William Crosby, it was purchased by the late Edwin Casson, Esq., after whose demise, in 1868, it was purchased by Mr. Thomas Watson, the present owner.

Rosset, an important district at the time of the Domesday survey, appears to have lost its ancient importance, as it is now only applied to Rosset House, Rosset Green, and Rosset Moor. It is also used to designate a constabulary, called Beckwith-with-Rosset.

At Burn Bridge, the old road from Leeds to Ripon crosses the Crimple, where is a cluster of cottages—some of them in Rigton—some in Pannal. About five hundred yards north of this bridge, in 1646, King Charles I., when passing along this road in his journey from Newcastle to London, had his high-crowned hat struck from his head, by riding too near the boughs of a large ash tree. The owner, an enthusiastic loyalist, immediately caused it to be felled, to avenge this unintentional insult to royalty. Such is the locality given by Hargrove in his history of Knaresborough; but the voice of popular tradition says that the accident happened at Pannal High Ash, about a mile further northward.

Pannal High Ash is a hamlet, or cluster of houses, near the junction of four roads, on elevated ground, commanding extensive views of the surrounding country. The name is said to be derived from five gigantic ash trees, which grew here until about the year 1810, when they were felled, and sold for common timber, to the great regret of the neighbourhood. They stood between the farm house and the row of cottages on the right of the road. Springfield House (Mr. Joshua Wright) was built in 1828, and Ashville (Mr. Benjamin Wainman) in 1861.

A short distance south of this place is Castle Hill, a name suggestive of the site of some camp, or *castra;* though no traces of any kind of fortification are now visible, yet, from its high and commanding position, it is well adapted for such purposes.

Further south are the Lund House and Lund House Green; names evidently derived from the Laund, or Lund, of the old forest day. Here was formerly a school for the parish of Pannal, which was of considerable note about the beginning of the present century.

As distinguished names confer honour on the places where their owners reside, or with which they are associated, it will afford pleasure to many to know that a descendant of James Torre, the celebrated antiquary, was a land owner here. Previous to coming into possession of the family of Torre, this small estate was held by that of Mann, of Thorpe Underwoods.

On October 18th, 1658, William Mann, the elder, of Thorpe Underwoods, surrendered the reversion of two messuages and

thirteen acres of land, in Beckwith and Rosset, to the use
of Isabella Coghill, for life, and after her death to the heirs
of her body by the said William Mann.

Dec. 2nd, 1662. Isabella Mann, late wife of William Mann,
senr., late of Thorpe Underwoods, deceased, was admitted
to three messuages and twenty-two and a half acres of land,
in Beckwith and Rosset, *pro et nomine dote suæ.*

On August 25th, 1686, Robert Mann was admitted as brother
and next heir of Thomas Mann, late of Thorpe Underwoods,
to two messuages and thirteen acres of land, in Pannal.

On October 17th, 1694, Richard Mann, Gent., surrendered
two messuages and thirteen acres of land, and one other
messuage and fifteen acres of land, in Beckwith and Rosset,
to trustees, for the use of Dinah Kirkby, his intended wife,
and their heirs. Dinah Kirkby was eldest daughter of Mark
Kirkby, a merchant of Hull; and the issue of this marriage was
two daughters—Sarah, married to Jeremiah Horsfield, of Thorpe
Green; and Jane, married, in 1720, to Nicholas Torre, of
Cawood, afterwards of Snydale, son and heir of James Torre,
the antiquary, who became in consequence owner of lands
in Pannal.

On the 22nd of March, 1720, Pethuel Fish, Gent., Dinah
Mann, widow, Sarah Mann, spinster, Nicholas Torre, Esq., and
Jane, his wife, surrendered one messuage and fifteen acres
of land, in Beckwith and Rosset, to the use of the said Dinah
Mann, for life. The same parties, at the same time, surrendered
two messuages and thirteen acres of land, in the same district,
to the use of the said Dinah Mann, for life, and after her death
to the use of Sarah Mann, spinster, her heirs and assigns.

On the decease of Nicholas Torre, Esq., in March, 1749, his
second son, also named Nicholas, succeeded to the Pannal

estate,* who, by his will, proved Oct. 12th, 1796, bequeathed the same to his eldest son, Christopher Mann Torre.

The Wesleyan Methodist Chapel is situate close to the road leading from Daw Cross to Beckwith. Wesleyanism appears to have quickly taken root in Pannal, as the chapel was built in 1784, and John Wesley himself preached within it.

Near the chapel is Hillfoot House, a newly erected comfortable abode, belonging to Mr. Robert Taylor. There was an old house of the same name, which, in the seventeenth century, was occupied by a family named Broadbelt.

Hilltop Hall, as its name implies, stands on the top of a hill, commanding a fine view of the windings of the valley of the Crimple. The building is of considerable age; and modern improvements have not destroyed the peculiarities of the old architecture and arrangements. In houses such as this, wealthy and hospitable yeomen dwelt centuries ago. It formerly belonged, with the lands adjacent, to a family of the name of Coore; afterwards to that of Loup, from whom it was purchased by Mr. James Smith, who gave or bequeathed the same to his nephew, Mr. Edward Dickinson, the present owner.

BECKWITH.

Beckwith† (Becvi) is one of the ancient manors mentioned in the Domesday survey, as having belonged to Gamelbar, and at that time to Gilbert Tyson. More recently it gave name to the old and distinguished family of Beckwith; and

* On the enclosure of the Forest of Knaresborough, in 1778, six allotments were awarded to Nicholas Torre, Esquire, in Pannal, near Lund Green, bounded eastward by the school land, near Pannal Ash and near Harlow Hill; the last, bounded westward by Birch Crag Road, contained 23a. 0r. 36p.

† From *Beck*, a brook, and *with*, a wood; a name indicative of Danish origin.

now forms part of an indefinable district, in the parish of
Pannal, known as Beckwith-with-Rosset. At present it is
a hamlet comprising some half-dozen farm houses and cottages.
From the antique appearance of some of the houses and
buildings around, it is quite evident that this was an early centre
of population. It was for many years in possession of the
family of Beckwith, whose principal residence was at Clint Hall,
near Ripley.

Beckwith House, a seat of the family of Wright, is a modern
house, built in 1821; situate on a hill, in a pleasant spot,
surrounded by fertile fields and fine timber trees, commanding a
prospect varied and beautiful. The home view is delightful—
over the ancient lands of Beckwith and the windings of the
Crimple valley. The old house yet remains converted into
stables and other offices; and over the door, upon a sun dial, is
the date of its erection, 1661.

The first of the family who resided here was Jeremiah Wright,
who, with his son Henry, came from Brackenthwaite, and
purchased this estate.

Jeremiah Wright died Jan. 22nd, 1776, at the advanced
age of 91. Ann, his wife, died May 14th, 1764, aged 71.

Henry Wright, son of the above, succeeded to the estate.
His wife's name was Mary, who died March 9th, 1790, aged
71; and Henry Wright himself departed this life April 24th,
1799, aged 82; leaving a son,

Richard Wright, who married Frances Lawson, of Pannal, by
whom he had issue—

William, born in 1770.

Henry, bapt. March 30th, 1772; buried June 24th, 1805.

Mary, bapt. Oct. 2nd, 1779; married to Mr. Stephen
Parkinson, of Fewston.

Richard Wright died Nov. 80th, 1818 (Frances, his wife, in March, 1828), and was succeeded by his son,

William Wright, who, on June 14th, 1805, married Elizabeth, daughter of Joshua Collett, of Pannal (she died March 6th, 1831), by whom he had issue—

Mary Ann, bapt. April 2nd, 1806; she married Mr. Thomas Bentley, of Pannal Hall, and was buried Nov. 7th, 1845.

Sarah Priscilla, bapt. July 24, 1808; buried March 28, 1809.

Joshua Collett, bapt. March 15th, 1810—of Springfield House, in Pannal—who married Elizabeth Foster, by whom he has issue, two daughters.

Henry, bapt. Oct. 6th, 1811; buried Oct. 21st, 1853.

Priscilla, bapt. March 30th, 1813; buried May 1st, 1838.

William, bapt. March 19th, 1815. *(See below)*.

Ann Elizabeth, bapt. May 20th, 1816; buried July 7th, 1816.

Richard John Mallorie, bapt. April 19th, 1817; buried April 23rd, 1851.

William Wright died Nov. 26th, 1842, and was succeeded, in his estate at Beckwith, by his third son,

William Wright, who married, first, Mary Godfrey, eldest daughter of Mr. William Bentley, of Pannal Hall; she died July 4th, 1862. He married, secondly, Eleanor, daughter of Brian John Procter, Esq., of Gateshead, in the county of Durham, who died Nov. 14th, 1866. William Wright died April 80th, 1868, and, leaving no issue, he bequeathed the estate at Beckwith to his eldest and only surviving brother, Joshua Collett Wright, the present owner.

BECKWITHSHAW.*

This name is given to a district in the parish of Pannal which stretches across it to the west of Beckwith and Harlow

* *Shaw* is from the Anglo-Saxon, and means a little wood or place shaded by trees. It is seldom in popular parlance that we hear a native

Q

Car; from the Crimple, on the south, to Oakbeck, on the north; the western limit appears to be indefinite, and hardly to reach to the parish boundary. From the head of the Crimple to Broaddub, is sometimes called Sandwith; a heathy moorland district—the highest and wildest part of the parish. A large quantity of land in this quarter—upwards of six hundred acres—belongs to the Rev. Sir Henry Ingilby, Bart., of Ripley Castle, who is the largest landowner in the parish. A large area of ground—upwards of eighty acres—on the north of Moor Park, is planted with trees, which have now grown up, and form "a broad contiguity of shade;" amidst which, on a piece of cultivated ground about six acres in extent, stands a game-keeper's cottage, like an oasis in the middle of a wilderness.

William Sheepshanks, Esq., of Leeds and Harrogate, is also an extensive landowner here, by purchase, within the last few years, from the family of Wright, and others. Amongst which is the large section lying between the Otley turnpike road and Oakbeck, and Harlow Car and the Beckwithshaw and Killinghall road; near the middle of which, a few years ago, stood a corn windmill, now demolished. The steep slope descending to Oakbeck, is a large plantation of firs and larches, known as the Great Wood; at the north-west corner of which formerly stood a water mill for grinding corn and rolling lead into sheets; which mill was built by Mr. Heap, of Leeds, and derived its motive power from the Oakbeck stream. A

of the parish give this place its full name; it is spoken of as *Shaw*, or *the Shaw.*

"When shaws beene sheene and shraddes full fayre,
  And leaves both large and longe,
It's merrye walkyng in the fayre forrest
  To heare the small birdes songe."
         —*Robin Hood and Guy of Gisborne.*

In the 16th Edward II. (1322), Henry de Boys held the manor of Usburn Magna, and certain assarts, or cultivated enclosures in the Forest of Knaresborough, called "Beckwithershagh."—*Inquisitiones post mortem.*

dispute with Sir John Ingilby, Bart., the owner of Haverah Park, was the cause of diverting the water, and the mill consequently became useless; when the machinery was taken out, the roof and all the woodwork removed, and the deserted shell put on the appearance of a lonely ruin. About the year 1864, it was pulled down to the foundation, and the materials removed; the site is however yet clearly marked.

This district consists entirely of detached farms, unless a small cluster of houses, at the junction of the roads from Harrogate to Otley, and from Killinghall to Rigton, may assume the name of the village of Beckwithshaw.

Here is the National School, a substantial and neat building of stone, erected at the cost of Mr. James Bray, of Moor Park, in 1865. It consists of schoolroom, classroom, and master's house, all well adapted to their purpose. The land on which it stands was given by Messrs. John and Benjamin Kent, of Tatefield Hall.

A small Wesleyan Methodist Chapel was built here in the year 1845. It will accommodate about one hundred hearers.

Amongst the notabilities of Beckwithshaw must be counted "Old Harry Buck," the wiseman of Knaresborough Forest. In his younger days—about sixty years ago—he resided in a small hut, on the Rigton side of the Crimple; afterwards he was schoolmaster at Lund House Green; next money-taker at the Beckwithshaw toll-bar; during which time he was accounted a learned magician—could tell fortunes by tea leaves at the bottom of a cup, and see as far into the future as an ordinary man can into a millstone. He was remarkably clever in cases

"When brass and pewter hap to stray,
And linen slinks out of the way;
When geese and pullen are seduced,
And sows of sucking pigs are chous'd;

When yeast and outward means do fail,
And have no power to work on ale;
When butter does refuse to come,
And love proves cross and humoursome."

MOOR PARK.

This estate and mansion are situate close to Beckwithshaw,
of which indeed they form a part. The whole domain—upwards
of 227 acres—is surrounded by a lofty stone wall, built by Mr.
James Bray, at a cost of about £2,000. The house was also
rebuilt by the same owner, in 1859, at a cost of upwards
of £8,000. The ground plan is an oblong square, 90 feet
in front by 46 in depth. The entrance is in the centre, above
which rises an elegant square tower, 75 feet high. It is now a
large and commodious mansion. The style is Elizabethan; and
the architects were Messrs. Andrews and De Launay, of
Bradford.

The whole estate is a remarkable instance of what capital
liberally applied can do in improving and adorning a soil and
situation possessing but few natural advantages. It is well
sheltered by plantations, disposed in clumps and masses, and
has become a desirable and picturesque spot.

At the enclosure of the forest, this domain was a tract
of heathy moorland; a large portion of which was set out
in sale lots (that is lots which were to be sold to pay the
cost of enclosure); a number of these were purchased, and
subsequently awarded to "Richard Wilson, Esq., Robert
Stockdale, and Co." This was in 1778, and since that time it
has frequently changed owners;—passing into the hands of Mr.
James Bradbury, then to Mr. William Hirst, of Leeds,
distinguished as a cloth manufacturer, who held it until 1838,
when it was purchased by Mr. Thomas Jemison. In 1846,
it came into possession of Mr. John Bainbridge, of Crimple

(commonly called Captain Bainbridge), from whom it was purchased by Mr. James Bray, in 1848. Mr. Bray was eminent as a railway contractor; and, on obtaining possession, carried out a series of spirited and costly improvements over the whole estate, so much so that it may be said that he created it anew. He retained possession of it until 1869, when it was purchased by Mr. Joseph Nussey, the present owner.

LOW HARROGATE.

Low Harrogate occupies the north-eastern corner of the parish of Pannal, and is included within the Harrogate Improvement Act District. That part of the town known as Cold Bath Road, the Esplanade, Royal Parade, Promenade Square, part of Promenade Terrace, Crescent Place, with the Crown, White Hart, Wellington, Binns's, and Adelphi Hotels; also the Bogs, and Bath Hospital, are all in this district and parish; but as we have previously described them under the head of Harrogate we shall not notice them further.

ST. MARY'S CHURCH.

The great influx of visitors to Low Harrogate, and its distance from the parish church, rendered some place of public worship here absolutely necessary; so the building of this church was determined on. The foundation stone was laid September 4th, 1822, and the finished building consecrated by the Archbishop of York, August 7th, 1825. The design was by Mr. S. Chapman, of Leeds, and partakes of the early English style of architecture. It consists of a nave, chancel (recently added), and a square tower at the west end—through which is the principal entrance. There is accommodation for 800 hearers; and 500 of the sittings are free. The chancel was added in

1865, when upwards of 100 additional sittings were obtained. The whole church was seated anew in 1868, at the cost of Miss Smith, of the Belvidere. The stained glass window was inserted in 1862, as a memorial of the late Prince Consort; the subject is the ascension of our Saviour; and at the base of the window is inscribed, "These three windows were erected by private subscription to the memory of His Royal Highness Francis Albert Augustus Charles Emanuel, Prince Consort, Duke of Saxe Coburg and Gotha, A.D. 1862."

In the summer of 1866, a peal of six bells was placed in the tower, at a cost of about £450, raised by public subscription. They were first rung on September 10th; previously there was only one bell.

The funds for the erection of the building were raised by voluntary subscription, aided by a grant from the Commissioners of the Million Act. The king, as Duke of Lancaster, gave the land for the site and burial ground,* which last is not adapted for its purpose, and has never been used; he also endowed it with £50 per annum, from the revenues of the duchy. The subscriptions fell £1,600 short of the amount required, which sum was supplied by the vicar of Pannal, the patron.

The living is a perpetual curacy, valued, in 1831, at £90 per annum; augmented in 1834 with £200, and £200, to meet benefactions of £400, by subscriptions.

CURATES OF ST. MARY'S.

July 18, 1824.	Rev. Thomas Hilling Madge.	resigned.
Sep. 5, 1827.	Rev. James Holme	resigned.
Aug. 4, 1833.	Rev. James Heyworth	——
	Rev. George Digby	present curate.

This church was constituted the head of a district parish, under the provisions of the act 59, George III., cap. 134;

* The land now occupied by the church, parsonage, and national school, is 2a. 3r. 5p. in extent.

and by an order in council, dated July 19th, 1830, a district
was assigned to it comprising a large portion of the northern
side of the parish of Pannal, the boundary commencing at
the Cold Well, and running along the boundary of the parishes
of Pannal and Harrogate, down Hookstones beck, to the Lime
Road; there turning westward, along the said road and Lead
Hall Lane to Rosset Green; thence north-westerly, up the
centre of the Grass Lane to Pannal High Ash; from thence
south-westerly to Lund's Green; from thence following the road
in a north-westerly direction to the Otley and Knaresborough
turnpike road, and along the said road to Beckwithshaw; there
turning northward, along the road to Pot Bridge; thence down
Oakbeck, past Irongate Bridge, to the boundary of the parishes
of Pannal and Harrogate, along which it passes to the Cold
Well, where it commenced.

The Parsonage is situate in the same valley, a short distance
south of the church.

St. Mary's National School was established in 1837. The
present building was erected in 1851, at a cost of £400,
raised by voluntary subscription. It was altered so as to make
a dwelling for the master in 1866.

HARLOW HILL.

This eminence is about a mile west of Harrogate, yet in
a state of nature, and exhibits the vegetation of the forest
as it existed twenty centuries ago. Though the name is indicative of military occupation,* we have sought in vain for
traces of entrenchment said to exist upon it, and history is
silent as to any battle having ever taken place here; yet
tradition murmurs that the army of Uter Pendragon encamped

* *Here-low*, the soldiers' hill.

upon this hill, about the year 460; and the humble cottage
of a husbandman bore the name of Pendragon's Castle until
quite a recent period.   In the year 1200, *Herslow* is mentioned
as one of the boundaries of William de Stuteville's gift of forest
land to Nigel de Plumpton; but the term at that time applied
strictly to the township of Harrogate.   In 1769, a plot of
about six acres in extent was planted with fir trees,* at which
time many querns, or ancient hand-mills, were dug up.   This
plantation formed a nucleus for a future forest—for within the
last thirty years, from the scattering of the seeds by the winds
and birds, a great deal of the adjoining waste has become
a wood of firs.   The plants may be seen in all stages of
developement—from those of a few inches in height, struggling
for life with the heath, to those of older growth, three or four
yards in height, which have smothered the heath, and are
forming a new soil around them of their own dead leaves.
In some places they stand so close together that they exclude
the sunshine, choke each other's growth, and die.   This continued until 1864, when the present pleasure grounds were
first designed by John Senior, a landscape gardener, in the
middle of the thicket of firs.   On July 10th, 1868, while
sinking a well here to obtain water for household purposes,
at a depth of eleven yards a copious spring of mild sulphur
water was struck, similar in quality to that of Harlow Car.
Like nearly all the sulphur waters, it rises from a bed of black
contorted shale.

The Harlow Hill Tower is a plain square building, without
any pretence to ornament—strong, substantial, and of easy
ascent; 90 feet in height, and 18 feet 4 inches square, within,

---

* This is called the "King's Plantation," and is retained in the hands of
Her Majesty, who also holds other plantations in this parish, to the extent
of 22a. 2. 36p.

at the top. It was built in 1829, by Mr. John Thompson, of Harrogate, at a cost of £500. The ground on which it stands is about 600 feet above the sea level. Inconsiderable as this may appear to the height of many mountains, its situation gives it a prospect excelled by few of them; standing on the verge of the great plain of York, it overlooks the whole of that extensive, fertile, and interesting region, extending from the Tees to the Humber; bounded eastward, at various distances, by the Hambleton, Howardian, and Wold hills; while on the south, west, and north, it commands a magnificent view of mountains, hills, and valleys. Two cities, York and Ripon, with their cathedrals, are distinctly visible; and at times Lincoln is seen, like a small dark cloud on the distant horizon. Seven of the great battle fields of England, and the scenes of at least twenty minor skirmishes, may be seen from hence; twenty market towns, seventeen castles, twenty-three abbeys, and other religious houses, more than seventy gentlemen's seats, and nearly two hundred churches are within the range of vision.

In 1870, a small church, called the All Saints Mission Church, was erected here, with a burial ground attached, for the use of the parishioners of the district of St. Mary's parish, Low Harrogate. The Earl of Harewood gave the land for the site of the church and cemetery; and the ground was fenced and laid out, and the church built, by a rate on the inhabitants of the district, and voluntary subscriptions. The church consists of porch, nave, chancel, transepts, tower, and spire. The whole length is 65 feet, the breadth 24 feet; the transepts project 8 feet 6 inches on each side; and the height of the tower and spire is 62 feet. The foundation stone was laid April 19th, and the finished fabric was opened for public worship in April, 1871. It will accommodate 217 hearers.

Harlow Car is situate in a shallow valley, to the westward of Harlow Hill. It forms within itself a small watering place, possessing four springs of mild sulphur water, a chalybeate, a suite of baths, and a comfortable hotel (now used as a private residence), situate in a piece of ground neatly laid out and adorned with a variety of shrubs and trees, sheltered from the winds, and forming altogether a quiet pleasing retreat.

The springs here are mentioned in 1740 by Dr. Short, in his "History of Mineral Waters";* they were not however cleaned out and protected until 1840. The baths and hotel were built in 1844, at the cost of Mr. Henry Wright, who was then owner of the estate.

Birk Crag, a short distance north of Harlow Car, is a piece of genuine mountain scenery, consisting of a narrow valley or glen, about half a mile in length, through which run the waters of Oakbeck. The southern side is steep, rugged, and, in some places, precipitous; grey crags peer out of its sides the whole length, but it is only for about two hundred yards in the highest part that they assume their proper majesty—grim and lofty, covered with lichens, the growth of centuries, and perched in such a random manner on the edge of the hill, that apparently a slight force would send them crashing to the bottom. The half vertical position of these rocks is another proof of the grand dislocation which has taken place here. The valley is

---

* "About a mile and a quarter west of Harrogate, on the brook side, is a small outbreak of a strong saline, sulphurious spring, which blackens the water of the brook, and makes the earth of a deep ink-black colour. A mile east of this bog, above the village, we find several more of those springs."—*Page* 285.

This is sufficiently explicit to identify the outbreak as at Harlow Car. In 1785, it is again mentioned by the Bishop of Landaff, in the following terms—"On the other side of the hill above the bog, and to the west of it, there is another sulphur well on the side of a brook, and it has been thought that the wells, both at Harrogate and in the bog, are supplied from this well."

clothed with vegetation of the coarsest kind; ferns in abundance, heath, gorse, and whortleberry plants, above which rise the graceful forms of the mountain ash, the thick masses of the white thorn, the sable holly, the ash, and the hazel—while the alder overhangs the brook below. Here we have nature in her primitive form—man has done nothing to mend or mar her originality, except to delve a paltry stone quarry, thereby displaying his lack of judgment and want of taste. This is the grandest piece of scenery in the neighbourhood of Harrogate; and great is the surprise of the stranger looking down from the top of the crag, to see such a scene in such a situation. On a fine day—when the heath is in bloom, with the sunshine streaming over it; thick woods rising darkly on the west; the brook stealing into view from under an arcade of foliage, and winding along the bottom in graceful curves—it forms a picture at once wild, grand, and beautiful. Here the botanist and geologist will find objects to them highly interesting.

About the year 1256, Richard, Earl of Cornwall, granted to the brethren of the house of St. Robert of Knaresborough, pasturage in *Okeden* for three hundred sheep and forty pigs, without paying any acknowledgement. *Okeden*, or Oakdale, at that time must have included the whole of the valley, from the outfall of the brook into the Nidd to the bounds of Haverah Park, as a lesser district would hardly suffice to graze so many sheep and pigs. It is hardly necessary to say that the oaks which gave name to this *den*, or dale, have disappeared, and pigs at present would find but scanty pasturage here.

Irongate Bridge is the name borne by a narrow arch of stone, without battlements, which has only been intended for foot passengers or pack horses. It is now entirely disused, not even a footpath passing over it. The name is probably derived from its being formerly on the *gate*, or road, by which *iron* was carried from the mine to the smelting furnace. Traces of trackways may yet be seen winding up the sides of the valley.

The population of Pannal in 1801 was 789; in 1811, 914; in 1821, 1,814; in 1881, 1,261; in 1841, 1,418; in 1851, 1,870; and in 1861, 1,587.

The annual value of this township as assessed to the county rate in 1849 was £9,570; in 1859, £11,885; in 1866, £18,892; and in 1869, £18,481. The valuation to income tax in 1858 was £18,025.

KNARESBOROUGH AND SCRIVEN.

THESE townships, though the main bulk of them are on the
north-eastern bank of the river Nidd, project a large wedge-
shaped piece of land into the forest,* between the townships of
Bilton-with-Harrogate and Plumpton, on which are some places
of interest, as well as much beautiful scenery. Close to the
right bank of the Nidd is the Long Walk, which was laid out
and some of the trees planted by Sir Henry Slingsby, Bart., in
the year 1739. In summer this is a delightful place; on the
right rises the steep bank, clothed with tall forest trees, with
here and there a rocky precipice, clothed with shrubs, ferns, and
mosses; on the other is the river, full to the brim; lower down
it dashes over a dam, and then runs onward, rippling over
rocks. Beyond the river, on the sides of a steep precipice
of rugged limestone rock, rises the town of Knaresborough—
the houses clinging to the steep sides of the hill in almost every
variety of position, interspersed with rocks and gardens; the
venerable parish church and the ruined castle forming prominent

* Many small detached portions of land on the forest belong to these
townships, which were awarded on the enclosure of the forest. The
limits of these two townships and that of Harrogate, are so intermixed,
that we have not attempted to disentangle them. Some pieces of land,
even in the town of Harrogate, belong to the townships of Knaresborough
and Scriven, while detached portions of Harrogate are to be met with at
Thistle Hill, south of Knaresborough. The windmill, small chapel, and
many of the cottages at Forest Lane Head, belong to Harrogate.

objects in the picture; and then, as if to add to the variety
of the scene, the lofty and massive railway viaduct spans
the valley, far above our heads; the whole forming a picture of
almost unique variety and beauty. In summer the whole of this
plot of ground is full of wild flowers—some of them of the
rarest kinds; and is a choice spot for the botanist and the
lover of natural beauty. Passing along this walk, nearly to the
Low Bridge, we reach

THE DROPPING WELL.

This is one of the strongest and most celebrated petrifying
springs in the kingdom; it is also distinguished as being the
place where the renowned Yorkshire prophetess, Mother Shipton,
was born. Leland, the father of English topography, gives the
following account of this spring—"A little above March Bridge,
but on the farther ripe of Nidde, as I cam, is a well of a
wonderful nature, caullid Droping Welle, for out of the great
rokkes by it distilleth water continually into it. This water is
so could, and of such a nature, that what thing soever faullith
oute of the rokkes ynto this pitte, or ys caste in, or growith
about the rokke and is touched of this water, growith ynto
stone; or else sum sand, or other fine ground that is about the
rokkes cummith doune with the continualle droping of the
springes in the rokkes, and clevith on such thinges as it takith,
and so clevith aboute it, and giveth it by continuance the
shape of a stone. There was ons, as I hard say, a conduct
of stone made to convey water from this Welle, over Nid, to the
priory of Knaresburgh; but this was decayed afore the dissolution of the house."*

Dr. Dean, in his *Spandarine Anglica*, published in 1626,
thus describes this spring—"It is called the *Dropping Well*

* "Itinerary," vol. ii., p. 95.

because it drops, distils, and trickles down from the rock above; the water whereof is of a petrifying nature—turns everything to a stony substance in a short time.   At first it rises up not far from the said rock, and running a little way in one intire current till it comes almost to the brim of the cragg, where being opposed by a dam (as it were artificial) of certain spongy stones, it afterwards is divided into many smaller branches, and falls from on high.   It's said to be very effectual in staying any flux of the body."

A much fuller description is given by Dr. Short, in his "History of Mineral Waters," 1784. He says, "The most noted of the petrifying waters in Yorkshire is the Dropping Well at Knaresborough, which rises up about fourteen yards below the top of a small mountain of marlstone (properly limestone of a very coarse grain) on the west side of the town and river, and about twenty-six yards from the bank of the Nid, where it falls down in the same contracted rapid stream; about a yard, and, at a second fall, at two yards distance it comes two foot lower, then three or four, and so falls upon an easy ascent; divides, and spreads itself upon the top of an isthmus of a petrified rock, generated out of the water, there falls down round it; about four or five yards from the river, the top of this isthmus or rock hangs over its bottom four yards.   This rock is ten yards high, sixteen yards long, and from thirteen to sixteen yards broad, but on the backside it is twelve yards high.   This little island slipt down and started from the common bank about thirty years ago, and leaves a chasm between them from a yard and a half to three yards wide; in this chasm, on the back and lower side of the part that is fallen down, are petrified twigs of trees, shrubs, and grass roots, hanging in most beautiful pillars, all interwoven and forming a great many charming figures.   On

the other, or common bank side of the chasm, are whole banks
or coverings, like stalactites—very hard, and inseparable (without breaking) from the rock, where the water trickles down from
the opposite side. This spring sends out about twenty gallons
in a minute, of the sweetest water I ever tasted. From its rise
till its fall down the common bank are several patrifactions upon
the stones, but none on the grass, &c., till it come within
two yards of the bank top. It springs out of a small hole like
a little sough, in the middle of a thick set of shrubs. This
little isthmus is beautifully cloathed with ash, osier, elm, ivy,
sambucus cervicaria major, geraniums, wood mercury, hart's-
tongue, ladies' mantle, scabious, cowslips, wild angelica,
meadow-sweet, hypericon, &c. This water, both at the spring
and from the rocks, is of equal weight, and each twenty-four
grains in a pint heavier than common water."

Dr. Hunter, in 1830, gave the following analysis of this
water, per imperial gallon—

Carbonate of soda ....   6.
Sulphate of lime .... ``` ....132.
Sulphate of magnesia .... 11.
Carbonate of lime ` .... 23.

Solid contents on evaporation ....172.

"When the water is exposed by slowly trickling over any
surface, the carbonic acid gas flies off, and the carbonate of
lime, which by its means was held in solution in the water,
is deposited in a solid form. The sulphate of lime, a salt
of little solubility, and easily separated from water, also assists
in the effect. The concretions, on analysis, furnish carbonate of
lime, sulphate of lime, carbonate of magnesia, and a trace of the
muriates.*

* "Treatise on the Waters of Harrogate," p. 75.

Michael Drayton, who so sweetly chanted "Polyolbion,"
in song the twenty-eighth thus describes the Dropping Well—

> "And near the stream of Nyde, another spring have I,
> As well as that which may a wonder's place supply,
> Which of the form it bears, men Dropping Well do call,
> Because out of a rock it still in drops doth fall;
> Near to the foot whereof it makes a little pon,
> Which, in as little space, converteth wood to stone."

He also bestows a few lines on the river Nidd and Knaresborough Forest.

> "From Wharnside Hill not far outflows the nimble Nyde,
> Through Nythersdale, along as sweetly she doth glide
> Tow'rds Knaresburgh on her way—
>   Where that brave forest stands
> Entitled by the town, who, with upreared hands,
> Makes signs to her of joy, and doth with garlands crown
> The river passing by."

The greatest seeming anomaly about this rock and spring is
that the water makes the stone over which it flows, which stone
is continually on the increase; and, owing to the dispropor-
tionate weight on the upper part, it has frequently slipped
down, and most certainly will do the like again. The first
known fall was in 1704; it sunk again in 1816, and in 1823.
The scenery around is particularly interesting and beautiful.

Something ought to be said of Mother Shipton, who, according
to the unchanging voice of popular tradition, was born near
this Dropping Well. She is the most distinguished of all the
natives of the Forest of Knaresborough, and her reputation is
one that is not likely to die. This is more due to her extraordinary abilities than to her personal comeliness—for, if we
can believe that the sign of the adjoining public-house is a true
portrait, she was the embodiment of ugliness itself. She is
said to have been born early in the reign of King Henry VII.;
the daughter of Agatha Sonthiel and the *Prince of the air;* to
have delivered her prophecies to the abbot of Beverley; married

R

a man named Shipton; done many most extraordinary acts;—
in short played the part of a prophetess. Finally she died,
and was buried at Clifton, near York, where a stone was erected
to her memory, bearing the following inscription—

"Here lies she who never ly'd,
Whose skill often has been try'd;
Her prophecies shall still survive,
And ever keep her name alive."

As specimens of her talents, we give three of her unfulfilled
prophecies.

I.

"The Fiery Year as soon as o'er,
Peace shall then be as before:
Plenty everywhere is found,
And men with swords shall plow the ground."

II.

"The time shall come when seas of blood
Shall mingle with a greater flood."

III.

"Great noise shall be heard, great shouts and cries,
And seas shall thunder louder than the skies;
Then shall three lions fight with three, and bring
Joy to a people, honour to their king."

On the same side of the river as the Dropping Well, but
lower down, is a piece of ground—now used as a garden and
orchard—open towards the water, but enclosed on the other
three sides by a high wall, which bears the name of "Spittle-
croft"; a name expressive of its former use, and which it has
borne at least six hundred years, as it is mentioned in the
Earl of Cornwall's charter, in 1257, when it was given, along
with other lands, to the brethren of the house of St. Robert
of Knaresborough; the name showing that an hospital had existed here long before that time. The most probable supposition
is that it was an hospital for lepers, founded, in very early times,
by some one whose name is forgotten, and endowed with this
and other lands—some of which were situate at Scotton. From

the Hundred Rolls (1275), we find that the minister and
brethren of the house of St. Robert, held in that village fifteen
oxgangs and two tofts, which had belonged to the lepers.   An
hospital at Knaresborough is mentioned in the Patent Rolls,
13 Edward II. (1319).   From these facts we infer that an
hospital for lepers formerly existed here.

Further westward, on the slope of the hill, are the fields,
wood, and house of Belmond; a piece of finely undulating land,
situate between the river Nidd and Forest Lane Head.   It was
given by the charter of Richard, Earl of Cornwall, in 1256, to
the brethren of the house of St. Robert of Knaresborough, and
is there described as, "all that land which is called Belmond,
between the forest and the little park of Knaresborough."   In
1317, the king, by letters patent, gave the minister and brethren
of the house of St. Robert, license to enclose three acres of land
in the field of Belmond, within the bounds of the forest of
Knaresborough.   It is now the property of Captain Slingsby, of
Scriven Park.

Belmond House was for many years the residence of David
Lewis, who was author of many pieces of poetry—some of them
of considerable merit.   They are chiefly of a comic and descriptive kind.   "The Sweeper and Thieves," in the Yorkshire
dialect, has found its way into many collections.   Another
is entitled "A Week at Harrogate, in a Series of Letters."
"The Landscape," descriptive of the scenery of his native town,
written in 1814, is probably the best; from which we give a few
lines as a specimen of his abilities—

> "Knaresborough! mountain mantling town,
> On field and flood both looking down;
> From its north and eastern brows,
> We see beyond the Vale of Ouse;
> Yellow crops and meadows green,
> Trees, and towns, and woods, between."

Like many others of the poetical race, Lewis, in his old age, was the prey of poverty. He died about the year 1846.

Nearly adjoining Belmond House is the hamlet of Forest Lane Head, consisting of a windmill (now destroyed), a few farm houses, cottages, and a small Wesleyan Methodist Chapel —the last built in 1860.

About midway between Knaresborough and Harrogate is Starbeck, where the railways from York and Harrogate, and Leeds and Ripon, intersect each other. Though Starbeck is mentioned as the name of the brook flowing past this place, as early as the year 1200, until a few years ago it was of comparatively little importance. When the Leeds and Thirsk railway was completed, in 1849, the station for Harrogate and its neighbourhood was made here; and the hitherto quiet, lonely place became a centre of bustle and traffic. The hotel, the large steam corn mill, and brewery, were built by Mr. Charles Faivell, soon after the completion of the railway. Since then many good houses have been built around; and the lonely swamp of the old forest has put on an appearance of respectability and progress.

THE STARBECK SPAW.

Here is situate the Starbeck Spaw, one of the earliest known, and used, of the sulphur waters of this district. It is mentioned by Dr. Dean, in 1626; and it was much resorted to—especially by the country people—until the enclosure of the forest, after which it was entirely neglected; the dome which had covered it was removed, the basin into which it flowed taken away, the current drained into the adjoining rivulet, and the site subjected to the plough; so that it was in danger of being entirely lost. It continued much in this state until the year 1822, when,

chiefly through the praiseworthy exertions of the late Mr.
Michael Calvert,* a public meeting of the inhabitants of
Knaresborough was held, to consider the best means of restoring
to the public this cheap and salutary medicine. A subscription
was entered into for raising the requisite funds; and, on the
23rd of May, in the above mentioned year, the foundation of
the present pump room was laid amid much rejoicing. In 1828,
the baths were erected by a company of proprietors; these comprised a suite of nine rooms, with every requisite for warm,
cold, and shower bathing; they have since been increased to
fourteen, with comfortable waiting rooms attached. These were
the first public sulphur water baths erected in the neighbourhood.

The quantity of water discharged by this spring is about one
gallon in a minute, without any considerable variation, except in
excessively rainy or droughty seasons. The temperature is
about 48 degrees in severe frost, and 53 degrees in summer,
according to Farenheit's thermometer. It never freezes at the
fountain, or in the cold bath; in the latter place the water
assumes a pale blue colour. An analysis of the water of this
spring, by Professor Hofmann, is given among those of the
Harrogate waters.

Many remarkable cures are recorded by the use of this water.
Dr. Hunter says, "It is more suitable to some delicate con-
stitutions, or where there is greater irritability, than the more
powerful waters of the same kind; and is therefore particularly
indicated for tender females, and for children."[†]

Here were formerly three chalybeate springs; but only one of
them remains at present, which is about eighteen yards distant

---

* In his younger days he was a druggist in the town of Knaresborough;
possessed an extensive knowledge of botany; and wrote a history of
Knaresborough, and a tract on Knaresborough Spaw. He died December
3rd, 1862, in the 92nd year of his age.

† "Treatise on the Harrogate Waters," p. 46.

from the sulphur well. "In general properties it coincides with other chalybeates; but the neat state in which it is now kept, and the perfect brightness of its waters, convey an idea of purity and cleanliness to the mind, and make it frequently be preferred to the others, though the weakest of any." *

The neat cottage of the attendant, with the garden and shrubbery, all kept in nice order, two kinds of water, and a suite of baths, render this an attractive and pleasing spot.

The spring of mild sulphur water in the adjoining field, possessed of similar qualities to the original spaw, was discovered in 1868; the suite of baths attached thereto were built in 1869, and first opened to the public in April, 1870. The swimming bath was the first of its kind constructed in this neighbourhood; it is eighteen yards in length, eight yards in breadth, and varies in depth from three to nine feet.

* "Treatise on the Harrogate Waters," p. 71.

PLUMPTON.

PLUMPTON* is a township in the parish of Spofforth; bounded towards the east by Little Ribston, on the north by the river Nidd, on the south by the brook Crimple, and on the west by Bilton-with-Harrogate and part of Scriven.

It is chiefly memorable in ancient times as the residence of a family to which it gave name; and now remarkable for its beautiful pleasure grounds. It includes the ancient manors of Plumpton, Roudferlington, and Brame, or Micklebram; the first of which is thus described in Domesday survey—

"Land of William de Percy, in Borgescire Wapentake. Manor. In Plontone, Gamelbar had two carucates of land to be taxed, and there may be one plough there. Eldred has it of William. There are eight villanes and ten bordars there, with three ploughs, and two acres of meadow. Value in King Edward's time, twenty shillings; the same now."[†]

"Land of Giselbert Tyson. Manor. In Pluntone, Gamelbar had two carucates to be taxed. There is land to one plough. Half-a-mile long, and three quarentens broad. It is now cultivated, and pays five shillings. Value in King Edward's time, twenty shillings."[‡]

* From *Plump*, a woody place—a clump of trees is yet called a *plump* in Yorkshire and the north—and *ton*, a town; that is the town in the plump or grove of trees.
† "Bawdwen's Dom. Boc.," p. 166.
‡ *Ibid*, p. 194.

The Anglo-Saxon Eldred, who held the manor of the Percy
fee in 1086, is supposed by some to have been the ancestor
of the family, for many ages resident here, and highly distinguished under the name of Plumpton; but this cannot be
proved from existing evidence. The first of the name mentioned
is Nigellus de Pluntona, about the year 1168; and from that
time till the year 1760, his descendants held possession of the
estate. To give their history in detail would far exceed our
limits, as they fought on nearly every English battle field,
and took part in every political movement of their times.

In the year 1184, the name of Plumpton acquired a melan-
choly notoriety from an event of a most singular kind. Gilbert
de Plumpton, brother of Nigel, having married the daughter
of Roger de Guilvast, a ward in the gift of the king, without
the proper consent for so doing, was charged by Ralph de
Glanvill with taking her away from her father's house by force,
and stealing thence many articles along with her. Glanvill,
wishing to give the maiden, with her inheritance, to Reiner,
a creature of his own, persuaded those who were to try Gilbert
to adjudge him to death; which was done accordingly. Whilst
he was being led to the place of execution, intelligence of the
case was brought to Baldwin, Bishop of Worcester; whose
attendants exhorted him to rescue the youth from death. The
bishop, moved to compassion, rode to the executioners, who
had already bound a green band before their victim's eyes and
fastened an iron chain about his neck, and were then preparing
to hoist him to the gibbet. The bishop running up to them
exclaimed (it being Sunday), "I forbid you, on the part of
God and blessed Mary Magdalen, and under sentence of excom-
munication, to hang this man on this day; because to-day is
the day of our Lord, and the feast of the blessed Mary
Magdalen." After some altercation, divine authority prevailed,

and the youth was respited for that day, and delivered over
to the keeper of the king's castle for safety. The story coming
to the ears of the king (Henry II.), he enquired further into
it, and the youth was finally set at liberty; and, at the same
time, those who had thus perverted the course of justice were
compelled to pay a fine of a thousand marks to the king.

Sometime previous to the year 1200, William de Stutevill,
lord of Knaresborough, granted to Nigel de Plumpton, and his
heirs, for the usual services, and one horse of the value of
one hundred shillings, all that part of the Forest of Knaresborough which included Little Ribston, Plumpton, and Rudfarlington; along with the right of chasing the fox and hare
throughout the whole forest—reserving to the superior lord the
deer, the hind, and the roebuck.

This Nigel died in the reign of King John, leaving Juliana
de Warewick, his wife, surviving—between whom and Peter de
Plumpton, his son and heir by his first wife, Maria, a fine
was passed of the third parts of the vills of Plumpton, Gersing-
ton, Idell, and Ribstaine, which she claimed as her dower.*

Peter de Plumpton was of the party of the barons against
King John, and had his lands seized; but after the death of that
monarch he did fealty to his son, and was restored to possession.

Robert, brother of the above Peter, was the next owner of
Plumpton; who was succeeded by

Nigel, who died sometime during the reign of Henry III.

Sir Robert de Plumpton, his son and successor, was only
four years and six months old on the decease of his father.†

---

* 14 et 15 Johannis.
† "When Kirkby's Inquest was made (A.D. 1284), Robert de Plumpton
held a mediety of the village of Plumpton, of the heirs of Percy, and
the other mediety of John de Vescy—and the same heirs and John held of
the king, in capite, for the half of one knight's fee."—Ed. Surtees'
Soc., p. 45.

He died about the year 1295, and was succeeded by his eldest son, also named

Sir Robert, who married Lucy, daughter of Sir William de Ros, to whom Sir Robert gave, in frank marriage, land to the value of one hundred shillings, in Middleton and Langbar, with common of turbary and right of stray in the pasture and wood of Nessfield, under a quit rent of a root of ginger to Sir Patrick de Westwick, in lieu of all suit and secular service, save that the tenants were to grind at the mill of Nessfield. Sir Robert died in 1824, and was succeeded by his second son,

Sir William de Plumpton (Robert, the eldest, having died of consumption during his father's lifetime), who married Alice, daughter and heiress of Sir Henry Beaufiz. After her decease he married Christiana, widow of Richard de Emildon, mayor of Newcastle. He was founder of a chantry at the altar of the Holy Trinity, behind the high altar, in the collegiate church of Ripon. He died in 1862, and was succeeded by his eldest son,

Sir Robert Plumpton, who was a deponent in the Scrope and Grosvenor controversy, on the 17th day of September, 1885; being then of the age of forty-five years. From this deposition he appears to have repeatedly served in the wars of his time. He married Isabella, daughter of Henry, first Lord Scrope, of Masham and Upsall. His eldest son, named Robert, was beheaded at York, in 1405, for the part which he took in the insurrection stirred up by his uncle, Richard Scrope, Archbishop of York. Sir Robert himself obtained a pardon for

"In an enumeration of the knights' fees in Yorkshire, made 81st of Edward I., is entered, as of two fees,—of the fee of Percy, two carucates of land; and of the fee of Vescy, two carucates of land;—where fourteen carucates make a knight's fee."—*Ibid*, p. 208.

"To the aid granted to the same king, on the marriage of his daughter, Plumpton contributed 11s. 6d.—that is 5s. 9d. for each portion."—*Ibid*, p. 293.

"In *Nomina Villarum*, 1815, Robert de Plumpton and Henry Beaufix are entered as lords of Plumpton."—*Ibid*, p. 849.

all treasons and felonies; after which he lived two years, and
died on the 19th of April, 1407. He was succeeded by

Robert de Plumpton, his grandson and heir, who was twenty-
four years old at the time of his grandfather's death, and yet
an esquire. By intermarrying with the heiress of Sir Godfrey
Foljambe, he added greatly to the wealth and importance of
his family, by the acquisition of large estates in the counties
of Nottingham and Derby. He was knighted before the year
1410, and chosen representative of the county of York in
1411. In 1414, he was seneschal of the Honour of Knaresborough, and also one of the council of the king of his Duchy
of Lancaster. In 1415, he was retained to serve the Duke of
Bedford for life, in peace and in war—having twenty marks
as his fee in time of peace, and the usual wages suitable to
his degree in time of war; together with *bouche du courte* for
himself and esquire, and his two valets, when at the hostelry
of the prince, or in his company. In 1418, he served in
France, under King Henry V. In 1420, he was again serving
the king in France; and in the following year he died, and
was buried in Spofforth church.

William de Plumpton, his eldest son and heir, was in the
eighteenth year of his age when his father died. As soon as
he attained his majority, he set out for the wars in France,
where he received the honour of knighthood, and did not return
till 1430. In 1435-6, he was a commissioner, along with others,
to array men-at-arms, hoblers, and archers, in the West Riding
of Yorkshire, and send them to the sea coast to repel a
threatened invasion; also to make muster of the said troops,
and to place signals, called *Bekyns*, in accustomed and convenient places, to warn the people of the approach of an enemy.

He was seneschal and master forester of the Honour and
Forest, and constable of the Castle of Knaresborough, from

1489 to the end of the reign of King Henry VI.; during which time the feud and fight with the men of the Archbishop of York, already related, took place.

Sir William was twice married—first to Elizabeth, daughter of Sir Bryan Stapleton, of Carlton; and secondly to Joan, daughter of Thos. Wintringham, of Wintringham Hall, Knaresborough, by whom he had a numerous family. In 1448, he was sheriff of the county of York, and in 1452, of the counties of Nottingham and Derby.

When the *Wars of the Roses* broke out, he espoused the cause of Henry VI., and fought with his foresters at the battle of Towton, in 1461, in which his eldest son, William, was slain; and he was obliged to throw himself on the mercy of his enemies. He, however, received a full pardon in 1462, and was restored to his offices in the following year. He obtained from King Edward IV. a license to embattle his manor house at Plumpton, and to enclose a park there, with liberty of warren and chase. He died May 1st, 1478, and was succeeded by

Sir Robert Plumpton, his eldest son by his second wife, to the prejudice of the heirs of his son William, who had died fighting at Towton Field; the consequence of which was a series of lawsuits, which reduced the head of the family to beggary.

In 1482, Sir Robert Plumpton was serving with the Earl of Northumberland in the Scottish wars, and was knighted by Richard, Duke of Gloucester, in Hoton Field, near Berwick. He attended the coronation of Elizabeth, queen of Henry VII., in 1487. In 1489, he was actively engaged in suppressing the insurrection of the commons, which began with the massacre of the Earl of Northumberland, at Topcliffe, and was finally subdued at the battle of Ackworth. For his services herein he received a letter of thanks from the king.*

The lawsuits above mentioned now came with disastrous weight upon Sir Robert; until at length he was arrested for debt, and committed a prisoner to the Compter. What a fall was here! from the warrior knight receiving the thanks of a king, to a prisoner in jail for debt. This ruin of a noble family was the work of that arch-villain, Sir Richard Empson; and it would probably be some slight consolation to Sir Robert Plumpton to know that his wily and deceitful enemy was beheaded on Tower Hill, while he was a prisoner.†

A final award was made in 1514, by which the manor of Plumpton, and all lands and messuages within the parish of

* Copy of letter from King Henry VII. to Sir Robert Plumpton.— "Trusty and well-beloved, we greet you well. And whereas, we understand, by our squire, Nicholas Kinston, one of the ushers of our chamber, your true mind and faithful liegance towards us, with your diligent acquitall for the reducing of our people there to our subjection and obedience, to our singular pleasure and your great deserts; wee hartily thanke you for the same, praying for your persevering continuance therein. Assuring you, that by this your demeaning, you have ministered unto us cause as gaged to remember you in time to come, in anything that may be to your preferment and advancement; as ever did any of our progenitors to our nobles, in those parties. And as any office of our gift there falls voyd, we shall reserve them unto such time as wee may bee informed of such men as, in the said parties, may be meet and able for the same; praying you that, if there shall happen anie indisposition of our said people, ye will, as ye have begun, endeavour you from time to time for the speedy repression thereof. And furthermore, to give credence to our squire aforesaid, on such things as we have commanded him, at this time, to shew unto you on our behalfe. Given under our signet at our mannor of Sheene, the thirtieth day of October."

† In the year 1499, the plague was sore in England, and carried off some of the domestics of the Plumptons. Robert Leventhorpe writes to Sir Robert Plumpton the following prescription for its removal—"I hard say that a servant of yours was deceesed of the sicknes which had been to your disease, I am right sory therefore. Wherefore I wold advise your mastership, my lady, and all your household many, from henceforth to make promise, and keepe yt, to fast the even of St. Oswald, kyng and marter, yerely; and that promise truly entended to be performed, I trust verely ye shal be no more vexed with that sicknes."—*Plumpton Correspondence*, p. 138.

Spofforth, were to be held and enjoyed by Sir Robert, his son William, and their heirs.

He married Isabel, daughter of Ralph, Lord Neville, by whom he had a numerous family. He died in 1523, and was buried at Spofforth.*

Sir William Plumpton, his eldest son, and heir, married Isabel, daughter of Robert Babthorpe, of Babthorpe, Esq., by whom he acquired considerable wealth.† He died on the 11th of July, 1547.

Robert Plumpton, his eldest son, died during his father's lifetime, at the age of thirty-one, leaving by his wife, Anne, daughter of John Norton, of Norton Conyers, Esq., three daughters, and a son, named

William, who succeeded to his grandfather's estates, on attaining his majority, in 1564. He married, first, Mary, daughter of Sir William Vavasour, of Hazlewood, by whom he had one son, Robert, who died, unmarried, before his father, and two daughters; by his second wife, Anne, daughter of Edward Griffin, of Dingley, he had Edward, who succeeded him, and a large family besides. Firm in their attachment to the Catholic faith, the family of Plumpton suffered severely during the reign of Elizabeth. Sir William died in January, 1601 or 1602, and was buried in Spofforth church.

Sir Edward Plumpton married Frances, daughter of William Arthington, Esq., of Arthington, by whom he had eleven sons and four daughters. The civil wars between King Charles and

* By his will, he gives £10 to be distributed, on the day of his sepulture, unto priests, clerks, and poor persons; to the house of St. Robert 8d. per annum, for ever, out of Blaky Farm, in Knaresburgh; to the church of Spofforth 6s. 8d.; to the house of St. Robert all the right he had in Thorp Garths, in Scotton.

† In the commission of array for the county of York, A.D. 1545, during the war with France and Scotland, William Plumpton was commanded to send thirty men for the king's service.

the Parliament now began, in which the family of Plumpton
espoused the royalist cause. John, eldest son of Sir Edward, a
captain in the king's army, was mortally wounded at the battle
of Marston Moor, July 2nd, 1644; he was conveyed to Knaresborough, where he died, after lingering a few days. Sir Edward
died about the year 1654.

John, eldest son of Sir Edward (slain in battle as above
related), married Anne, daughter of Richard Townley, Esq.,
of Townley, in Lancashire, by whom he had a family of four
sons and six daughters, the eldest of whom,

Robert Plumpton, Esq., succeeded to the estate, on attaining
his majority, after the decease of his grandfather. He married
Anne, daughter of William Middleton, Esq., of Stockeld, by
whom he had two sons and one daughter.

John, the eldest son, died in 1676, without leaving issue, when

Robert, his brother, succeeded to the estate. He was three
times married; first, to Anne, daughter of Nathaniel West,
by whom he had two sons and one daughter; secondly, to
Juliana, daughter of Thomas Appleby, Esq., of Linton-upon-
Ouse, by whom he had three daughters; and thirdly, to Isabel,
daughter of William Anderton, Esq., of Euxton, by whom
he had four daughters.

John Plumpton, Esq., eldest son and heir, succeeded to the
estate. He married Elizabeth, daughter of Sir John Gascoigne,
of Parlington, Bart., by whom he had one son,

Robert, who was born April 23rd, 1721, and who was the
last heir male of the renowned line of Plumpton, of Plumpton.
He forsook the faith of his fathers and conformed to Protest-
anism; but having gone to Cambray, in France, to confer with
his aunt Anne, a Benedictine nun, she recovered him to the
ancient faith; and he died at Cambray, August 8th, 1749,
without leaving issue, and the family became extinct.

After the decease of the last heir, the estate of Plumpton, then reckoned worth about £700 a-year, was sold by Mrs. Anne Plumpton, and her coparceners, to Daniel Lascelles, Esq., for the sum of £28,000. Since that time it has continued in his posterity, and now belongs to the Earl of Harewood.

Of the dwelling of this long-lived family we have no knowledge, as not a vestige of it remains. In some places we find extensive remains of the works of man, of which no scrap of record remains to tell us who their builders were; their very names have perished. Here, on the contrary, we have a long and interesting family history, and no trace of the home in which that family dwelt. Not one stone remains upon another of the embattled mansion erected by Sir William Plumpton, during the reign of Edward IV. Leland, the antiquary, who saw it when complete, styles it "a faire house of stone, with two toures, longging to the same." This is all we know of its external appearance. In the interior was a chapel,* adorned with shields of arms,—Plumpton impaling Clifford; Darell impaling Plumpton; Hamerton impaling Plumpton; and "*Argent,* a fess between three wolves' heads erased, *gules;*" perhaps the arms of office of the master forester of Knaresborough Forest.†
In the hall was a shield, quarterly Plumpton (*azure,* five fusils in fess, *or,* each charged with an escallop, *gules*), and Foljambe impaling Stapleton with the mullet; the armorial bearings of Sir William Plumpton and his first wife, Elizabeth Stapleton.

When the estate was purchased, in 1760, by Daniel Lascelles, Esq., he pulled down the old mansion, intending to build a new

---

* This chapel was dedicated to the Holy Trinity; and in it, in 1468, Joan, daughter of Sir William Plumpton, was married to Thomas Medleton, Esq., of Stockeld; as had previously been, in 1460, her sister Agnes and Richard Aldburgh, Esq. At present their is neither church, nor chapel, nor place of religious worship of any kind within the township of Plumpton.

† "Visitation, Ric. St. George, Norroy."

one, which he actually commenced, and carried up several
stories high; but happening to purchase the Goldsborough
estate, he took up his residence there, and the unfinished
building at Plumpton was taken down to the ground. It stood
to the south-west of the present farm house, and the site is yet
marked by two pillars of limestone, about eighty yards apart.
On the same spot probably stood the Plumpton towers. The
clock now in Harewood Church was carried thither from
Plumpton Hall. All the buildings now existing are modern, and
if the old material was used, it has been redressed.

The pleasure grounds were laid out by Daniel Lascelles, Esq.,
who, taking advantage of a small stream of water, and a piece of
rocky, rugged ground, formed a *pleausance*, almost unique
for its beauty and variety. These grounds comprise about
twenty-three acres, and are disposed with much taste and skill;
the huge grey rocks are pleasingly diversified with shrubs,
flowers, and evergreens. At the foot of the rocks is a lake,
covering about seven acres, which adds greatly to the beauty of
the scenery. The rocks rise around in masses, or in single
blocks, worn and crannied by the restless waters of a shallow
sea, which, at some remote period, has moulded their fantastic
forms, and ebbed and flowed through the openings between
them. They are of the coarse millstone grit, situate on the
verge of the formation, just before it dips beneath the magnesian
limestone. One rock, near the water, is a solid mass, fifty feet
in length, without a joint; from which, conjecture says, the
monoliths, called "the Devil's Arrows," at Boroughbridge, were
taken. Few places combine, within such a narrow compass, so
many natural beauties as are to be found in this highly favoured
spot of ground. The Plumptons, of Plumpton, are gone,

s

but their rocks and woods remain as fresh and beautiful as
when they first looked upon them.

> "Ages on ages slowly pass away,
> And nature marks their progress by decay:
> The plant, which decks the mountain with its bloom,
> Finds in the earth, ere long, a damp, dark tomb;
> And man, earth's monarch, howe'er great and brave,
> Toils on to find at last a silent grave."

ROUGHARLINGTON.

Rougharlington* is a hamlet, or part of the township of
Plumpton—situate on the western side. In early times it was
a distinct manor, and is thus recorded in Domesday survey—

"Land of William de Percy. Manor. In Rofellington, Gamelbar had two carucates and two oxgangs to be taxed, and there
may be one plough there. Eldred now has it of William.
There are three villanes and four bordars with two ploughs.
Wood pasture, one mile long and nine quarentens broad. Value
in King Edward's time, twenty shillings; the same now."[†]

"Land of Giselbert Tyson. Manor. In Rofellington,
Gamelbar had fourteen oxgangs to be taxed. There is land
to one plough. It is at present cultivated, and pays five
shillings. Wood pasture, one mile long and a half, and nine
quarentens broad. The whole two miles long, and eleven
quarentens broad. Value in King Edward's time, eight
shillings."[‡]

This manor became part of the estate of the Plumptons,
of Plumpton, as it is now that of the Earls of Harewood.

---

* Sometimes written *Rudferlington*, *Roudferlington*, &c., evidently a
compound term, and probably derived from some *rood* or cross erected
here in Saxon times; *ing*, a meadow; and *ton*, a town,—that is, the town
in the meadow of the holy cross.
† "Bawdwen's Dom. Boc.," p. 166.
‡ *Ibid*, p. 194.

There was here, in early times, a "capital messuage," or dwelling-house, which is often mentioned in the wills of the Plumptons. It has been rebuilt, as no ancient building now remains, and the whole district is comprised in about three farms.

Near the western side of this district, almost close to the brook, called Starbeck, is St. Hile's, or St. Hilda's Nook, where it is believed the chapel and hermitage of St. Robert stood. From the legendary lives of this saint we must infer that a chapel, dedicated to St. Hilda, stood here in the middle of the twelfth century, and that it was given by the lady of the fee— a Plumpton, or a Percy (more probably the latter)—to St. Robert. A M.S. rhyming life of the saint thus describes the event—

> "Wyst on a time, Robert gan hie
> Unto a widdow that wonned yare by,
> 'Dame,' he said, 'to give me this day
> Of thy almose I thee pray.'
> Then said that wife, mody and mild,
> 'The chapel I grant thee of St. Hylde,
> With all the land that lies partyll
> That thee like, through this my will,
> To thee and thy poormen all ay;
> Against my gift sal no man say.'"

At this place the saint abode with his poormen a whole year; until it befel upon a night foul thieves came with main and might, his bower they broke, and bore away his bread, his cheese, and all his sustenance, when Robert rose, and ran away, and sped him unto Spofforth town. Afterwards he went to reside in a cell of white canons, at Hedley, but, not liking their lax discipline and dissolute life, he returned to his chapel here, deeming it

> "Better to beld with beastes wild,
> Than with merred men, and unmyld.
> When he was comen to his chapelle,
> In deep devotion for to dwell;

Poormen that were penniless,
He sent them food of fish and flesh.
I wis this widow was full fain,
When she wist he had come again.
Men of craft swithe gart she call
To bigg Saint Robert a honest hall,
And mansiones for his men gart make,
And a laith for Robert's sake;
His swine, his cattle, into bring."

This time he had four servants; two to attend to husbandry, one to travel through the country collecting alms for the poor, and one was the personal attendant of the saint. While residing here, his mother, who had been dead some time, appeared to him.

"A time as Saint Robert lay
In a meadow—time of May,
In flowers, slepand in a stede,
Appeared his mother that was dead,
Pale and wan of hide and hue."

She informs her son that she was put to pain

"For metts and measures made unleil,"

but that through the intercession of her son she hoped to be redeemed "from bale." Robert prayed earnestly for the soul of his mother, and at the end of the year she again appeared to him,

"And blissid her bairn that made her blithe:
'Go! and, my son, now shall I swithe;
Wend to wealth that never shall wane!
Farewell! I bless thee, blood and bain!'"

Robert continued here, until one day William de Stuteville,

"Lord of that land, both east and west,
Of frith, and field, and of forest,"

coming past, saw the buildings, and asked to whom they belonged; his servants answered—

"Ane hermit that is full perfyte,
Robert, that is no rebellour,
A servant of our Savioure."

William, in great anger, said Robert was a teacher and

entertainer of thieves, and swore by "God's eyes" that he
should be expelled the forest, and ordered his servants at once
to "ding down his biggins." The servants were loath to do
their master's bidding, and that time to Robert's buildings "did
nea skaithe." A few days after, Stuteville came again, and in
a most furious fit of anger again gave the order of destruction;
the servants were obliged to comply.—

"Then they durst na langer byde,
But unto Robert housying hyed,
And dang them doune, baith less and mair;
Nathing left they standand there." *

On this destruction of his home, St. Robert wandered for awhile
through the forest, and afterwards returned to his "Chapel of
St. Gyle," among the rocks, near Knaresborough.

The proud castle of the lords of Knaresborough became a
ruin—the Plumptons, of Plumpton, passed away from the lands
they held so long—the site of the ruined hermitage remained on
a lonely corner of their domains, bearing the significant name of
"St. Hile's Nook," on, or close adjoining, a piece of uncultivated forest soil—bearing the oak, stunted and old; thickets of
holly, briar, gorse, and thorn, rough with masses of native
rock—called "the Wood." In this state it continued until the
year 1826, when the timber trees were felled, and the greatest
part of the thickets destroyed. In 1848, the catholic chapel at
Knaresborough was built, the stone for which was obtained
at this place; and the foundations of a building, believed to
have been the chapel of St. Hilda, were carefully dug up by Mr.
Swale, tenant of the farm, carried to Knaresborough, and placed
in the foundation of the Chapel of St. Mary there. The land
yet remains uncultivated; rough with crags, or the places

* These extracts, in rhyme, are from a M.S. life of St. Robert, entitled,
De Vita et Confessione Sancti Roberti, juxta Knaresburge; kindly lent by
Mr. Charles Forrest, of Lofthouse, near Wakefield.

whence they have been taken; a few oaks yet stand—memorials
of the past; a few bushes of holly yet survive; the brook still
curves and murmurs along its self-made course; a spring of
water oozes from the foot of a small scarp of rock—which might
supply the hermit with his daily drink; and though little but
the name of the place, the old legend, and the undying tradition
remain to indicate the spot, they are sufficient to make us
believe, that when musing there, we are upon the soil where
once St. Robert dwelt and prayed.

BRAME, OR BRAHAM.

Brame,* or Braham Hall, is situate on the southern side of
the township, adjoining the brook Crimple, and is now merely a
farm-house, with no traces of antiquity about it. At the time
of the Domesday survey, the term appears to have been applied
to a greater quantity of land than at present, divided into
Mickle-brame and Little-brame.

Among the lands of William de Percy we find—

"Manor. In Michelbram, Gamelbar had four carucates of
land to be taxed, where there may be two ploughs. William
has now there one plough and eight villanes, and three bordars
with two ploughs, and one mill of five shillings and fourpence. †
Godefrid holds it. Value in King Edward's time, forty shillings,
now thirty shillings."‡

Again, among the lands of Giselbert Tyson—

"Manor. In Michelbram, Gamelbar had four carucates of
land to be taxed. There is land to two ploughs. It is waste.

---

* From *Brae*, a steep bank, and *ham*, a dwelling—that is the dwelling
on the steep bank—a descriptive epithet. Sometimes called *Braim*,
Breame, *the Brame*. In the summons to the Visitation of 1584, Willus
Paver de le Brame, Gent., is named.
† This mill was probably turned by the water of the brook Crimple, and
no vestige of it now remains. The only mill at present in the township of
Plumpton is on the Nidd, near Grimbald Bridge.
‡ "Bawdwen's Dom. Boc.," p. 166.

Value in King Edward's time, twenty shillings. Wood pasture, five quarentens long and five broad. The whole manor, eleven quarentens long and eleven broad."*

Yet again, among the lands of Ernegis de Burun—

"Manor. In Litelbram, Gospatrick had four carucates of land to be taxed. There is land to two ploughs. Ernegis has there one plough, and three villanes, with one plough. Half a mile long and half broad. Value in King Edward's time, twenty shillings; the same now. Picot holds it of Ernegis. Berewick. One carucate to be taxed, in Michelbram, belongs to this manor. It is waste, but pays sixteen pence."†

In early times this was the residence of a family to whom it gave a surname. Matthew de Bram, living about 1186, was witness to two Plumpton charters.

Nicholas, son of Hugh, son of Hypolitus de Braam, gave to Gilbert, son of Thomas Oysel de Plumpton, one toft in Folyfait, which the said Gilbert gave to the Abbey of Fountains.

In 1310, the heirs of Bram held two carucates of land in Bram.

When Kirkby's Inquest was made (1284), William de Hartlington held Braham of William de Ros, of the fee of Trussbut, and the same William of Robert de Ros, and the same Robert of the king, in capite, for the half of a knight's fee, with a third part of Dunsford-Brampton, and a fourth part of Follifoot.‡

In the enumeration of the knights' fees, 31st Edward I., in Brame, of the fee of Ros, was one carucate of land, where ten carucates make a knight's fee.§

* "Bawdwen's Dom. Boo.," p. 195.
† Ibid, p. 207.
‡ "Kirkby's Inquest, Surtees' Soc.," p. 45.
§ Ibid, p. 205.

Towards the aid for marrying the same king's eldest daughter Brame contributed 4*s.**

In *Nomina Villarum* (1315), Henry de Hertlington was returned as lord of the manor of Braham.

In 1864, King Edward III. appointed Thomas de Spaigne custodian of the manor of Braham, one messuage and forty acres of land in Follyfoot, one oxgang of land in Spofforth, one messuage and two oxgangs of land in Braham, and all other lands and tenements in Brampton-in-Thorns and Parva Dunsford, which had belonged to William de Hertlington.†

The family of Paver were owners and resident here for five generations.

Richard Paver, Esq., of Braham Hall, who had a grant from Henry VIII. of the manor of Collingham Grange, and also possessed lands in fourteen townships, died in 1546. His eldest son, Bernard Paver, Esq., of Branton and Collingham, had two daughters, one of whom married into the family of Beilby, of Micklethwaite, and the other into that of Tancred, of Branton.‡ His third son, Nicholas, was rector of Burnsall. The second son, and heir male,

John Paver, Esq., of Braham Hall, married Catherine, daughter and heiress of John Woodburne, of Glanton, in Northumberland, bailiff of the manor of Spofforth, under the Percys, Earls of Northumberland, by whom he had

William Paver, Esq., of Braham Hall and Lund House, who, for some time, was confined in Durham gaol, on suspicion of being concerned in the rebellion of 1569; and died in 1601.

* " Kirkby's Inquest, Surtees' Soc.," p. 294.
† Rot. Origin, 89 Ed. III.
‡ "Thomas Tankard, of Boroughbridge, Esq., living in 1585, married Jane, daughter of Barnard Paver, of Micklethwaite, and one of his heirs, by whom he had six sons, of whom William was the eldest, from whom descended Sir W. Tankard, of Branton. Aug. 14, 1665."—*Dugdale.*

He married, in 1561, Margery, second daughter of William Hungate, Esq., of Saxton, and had issue—

Richard Paver, Esq., of Braham Hall, who had a lease from James I. of many lands in Yorkshire.* He married Jane, daughter of Robert Oglethorpe, Esq., of Rawden, and was buried at Spofforth, in 1622 or 1624.

From Richard Paver, their second son, descend the brothers Richard and Henry Paver, now both resident in South Africa.

William Paver, Esq., of Braham Hall, the eldest son, married Margaret, daughter of Thomas Denton, Esq., of Warnell-Denton Hall, in Cumberland. (The present representative of the Dentons is the Rev. Charles Jones Denton, M.A., now rector of Askham Richard, near York.)

* In this document the grantee is described as "Ricm. Paver de Braeham, in com. Ebor. Armigum." The consideration given for the lease was £140 3s. 4d. The premises consisted of a messuage and three oxgangs of land in Folefaite, in the occupation of John Luyte, of the annual value of 22s.; another tenement and four oxgangs of land, also in Folefaite, in the occupation of Laurence Danby—annual value 30s.; another messuage and tenement, also in Folefaite, in the occupation of John Galias—annual value 18s.; another tenement and oxgang of land, also in Folefaite, in the occupation of Robert Swayle—annual value 7s.; also a cottage and garden in Folefaite, in the occupation of John Scoles—annual value 3s. 6d.; another cottage and garden in Folefaite, in the occupation of John Allyn—annual value 2s. 8d.; another cottage and garden in Folefaite, in the occupation of Richard Marshall—annual value 2s.; also an acre of meadow, called Cellerer-acre, lying and being in Aykoton, in the occupation of Thomas Midleton—annual value 16d.; also a capital messuage, called Ayketon Hall, in Ayketon aforesaid, in the occupation of Michael Bycardick—annual value 29s. 4d.; also a cottage and oxgang of land in Ayketon, in the occupation of John Dighton; also a cottage and garden in Ayketon, in the occupation of James Tenaunte—annual value 5s.; another cottage and garden in Ayketon, in the occupation of Thomas Baylton—annual value 5s.; also a cottage and garden in Pannal, in the occupation of Miles Sikesworth—annual value 2s. The whole of the above premises formed part of the possessions of the late dissolved monastery of Newburgh. The lands to be held of the manor of East Greenwich, in free socage, and not in capite, or by knight's service, at the annual rent of £4 7s. 6d. for the premises in Folefaite; 55s. 8d. for those in Ayketon; and 2s. for those in Pannal. Tested in Westminster, October 20th, in the second year of King James.

Richard Paver, the eldest son of William, had by Mary Parker, his wife,

John Paver, Esq., of St. Nicholas House, near York, who—by Milliana Woodroffe, his wife, great grand-daughter of Lady Elizabeth, eldest daughter and co-heiress of Thomas Percy, seventh Earl of Northumberland—was lineal ancestor of

William Paver, of York, A.M., &c., and of his only surviving son, Percy Woodroffe Paver, of Wakefield.

A branch of the family of Cholmley afterwards resided here, of which Edward and Thomas Cholmley were living in 1650. Richard Cholmley resided here in 1658, and Henry Cholmley in 1685. It now belongs to the Earl of Harewood.

All around the hill on which the hall stands are many rocks of coarse gritstone projecting from the surface of the soil, in some places forming steep water-worn cliffs.

On the right of the road leading from Plumpton to Spofforth, near a farm-house, called Crosper, is a most singular rock, completely insulated, standing in a low situation, which bears the name of Hell Hole. It rises in an irregular circular mass to the height of 24 feet, while the circumference is upwards of 90 feet; the top is crowned with a mass of mountain heather (*Caluna vulgaris*) growing in peat; through one side is a large perforation, in which is a rock basin, about two feet deep by four feet in diameter; the whole apparently of natural formation, though some antiquaries have supposed that this rock has had some connection with the rites of Druidical worship.

On the southern side of this township, adjoining the river Nidd, are some pieces of remarkable fine scenery; one of these is where a footpath crosses the river, near the dam at Golds-borough Mill; there are steps fixed in the rock in the river's bed; one end of the passage terminates at the mill wheel, the other at the foot of a precipice of rock, up which a road has been cut into steps, which is pleasingly shaded by overhanging foliage.

Along the river from this point, by the Halves Farm, Grimbald Bridge, the lime-kilns, Grimbald Crag, and Birkham Wood, is a choice resort for the botanist, from the many rare and curious plants here found.

The turnpike road from Knaresborough to Wetherby passes through this township. Grimbald Bridge, the point at which it enters, is a substantial fabric of two arches; in Leland's time (about 1586) it was only of one, and he calls it "one very greate bridge for one bowe." It was on this ground, in 1405, that the men of Yorkshire, under Sir Thomas Rokeby, their sheriff, took position against the forces of the Earl of Northumberland, as old Hollingshead relates—"Sir Rafe Rokesby, Sheriff of Yorkshire, assembled the forces of the county to resist the earl and his power, comming to Grimbathbrigs, besides Knaresborough, to stop the passage; but they retourning aside, got to Wetherbie, and so to Tadcaster, and finally came forward to Bramham Moor." The earl shewed prudence in turning aside, for to attempt the passage of the river here, when strongly guarded, would have been akin to madness, and ended in sure destruction.

A short distance above the bridge rises the mass of magnesian limestone rock, called Grimbald Crag; the north and west sides present bold precipices towards the river, which bends round its foot, in a channel of gritstone; the other sides are of easy slope, and covered with grass. From the top a fine view of the valley and windings of the river is obtained, while, if required, it would afford a fine site for a feudal fortress; lofty, and almost impregnable—one half being protected by the river and the rock, while the other might be easily fortified. On the north side is a cavern, which appears to have been inhabited at some period; whether by a hermit of Grimbald, or forest outlaw, is not known.

Birkham Wood, a steep slope, yet "clad in ancient salvage dress," occupies the river's bank for some distance above Grimbald Crag. The voice of the nightingale is said to have been frequently heard in this wood—

> "Past the near meadows, over the hill-stream,
> Up the hill-side; and now 'tis buried deep
> In the next valley's glades:
> Was it a vision or a waking dream?"

Passing upward, among pictures of natural scenery of the most romantic and beautiful kind, we come to Thistle Hill, where the magnesian limestone has been extensively quarried and burnt; so much so that it is exhausted at that particular place. This is chiefly remarkable as being the spot where the skeleton was found, which led to the discovery of the murder of Daniel Clark, by Eugene Aram and others, in 1745. A person who was employed in clearing the earth from the top of the quarry, found a human skeleton, which popular rumour asserted to be that of Clark; when Richard Houseman, happening to take up one of the bones, made the assertion—"This is no more one of Dan Clark's bones than it is mine!" which created a suspicion which led to the discovery of the body in St. Robert's Cave, and the apprehension, trial, and execution of Aram, nearly fourteen years after the crime was committed.

A most singular discovery was also made here in October, 1853; when some quarrymen were at work behind the Union Inn, about 27 feet below the surface of the ground, they came upon a considerable accumulation of water-worn boulders, mixed with fine clay. On removing these, they discovered the skeletons of six or seven human beings, which had been covered by the stones, and embedded in the clay. The skulls were of various sizes, and the teeth in some of them in perfect preservation. One pair of jaws were of rather a diminutive size, the teeth small, white, and regular, seeming as though they had belonged to a young adult female. The right upper jaw of one of the skulls was broken, as if by a blow. No traces of armour were found near the skeletons. Amongst the bones were found the skull of a dog, and the jawbone of an ox. An examination of the place shewed that it was a natural cavern in the limestone rock, about seven feet wide, five feet high, and of considerable length, communicating with the surface above by an irregular fissure, just wide enough to allow a full-grown man to enter. It seems quite clear that this had been the abode, or the refuge, of some family in very lawless times, when the caves and dens of the forest afforded an asylum, and that, most probably, some landslip had happened to block up the entrance, and leave the unfortunate beings within to perish.

On the hill, on the right of the road leading to Plumpton toll-bar, stood the gibbet of Eugene Aram. A conspicuous place, whence it could be seen from the castle yard and many parts of the town of Knaresborough.*

* The gibbet did not stand in the township of Plumpton, but either in Scriven or Harrogate. The body of Aram was the last, though not the first, that was hung in chains in Knaresborough Forest. "On Monday, March 30th, 1594, Richard Craw, aged 28, was executed at the Tyburn, without Micklegate Bar, and the next day hung in chains in Knaresborough Forest, for the wilful murder of Mr. James Giles, of Knaresborough. On Monday, July 27th, 1598, Thomas Henry de Alting, aged 45, a native of Beverley, and Robert Thomas Swedier, aged 33, a native of Sheffield, were executed at the Tyburn, without Micklegate Bar, for housebreaking, and taking twenty-four guineas from Mr. William Boncham, with intent to murder him and his wife, at Knaresborough. After the execution, their bodies were conveyed to Knaresborough Forest, and there hung in chains. On Friday, May 18th, 1668, George Habbishaw, aged 37, and Benjamin Ambrose, aged 29, were executed at the Tyburn, without Micklegate Bar, for the wilful murder of George Lumley, Esq., at Knaresborough, on the 10th day of January, 1666. The body of Habbishaw was hung in chains, early next morning, in Knaresborough Forest, and the body of Ambrose was given to the surgeons of York for dissection."—*Criminal Chronology of York Castle.*

The charities belonging to this township consist of a rent-charge of 8s. 4d. per annum, given by Thomas Bigland, in 1658 (none received since 1768), and a proportion of bread, purchased with the interest of £20, given by Dr. Hutton and Dr. Talbot, for the poor of the parish of Spofforth.

The whole township contains 2,870 acres, of nearly every variety of soil; some of which appears to be particularly well adapted for the growth of the oak and beech, while near the hall the ash attains to a large size. In 1801, the population was 191; in 1831, 221; and in 1861, 219.

The annual value, as assessed to the county rate in 1849, was £2,092; in 1859, £2,385; and in 1866, £2,850. The amount assessed to property tax in 1858 was £2,617.

LITTLE RIBSTON.

LITTLE RIBSTON* is a township in the parish of Spofforth, and is of a triangular form; the south-easterly side being bounded by the brook Crimple; the north-easterly by the river Nidd; thus occupying the land between them to their point of junction; the township of Plumpton forms the boundary towards the west.

At the time of the Domesday survey, this township formed part of the fee of William de Percy, and is thus entered—

"Manor. In Ripesten, Turber had one carucate of land and a half to be taxed, where there may be one plough. Godefrid now has it of William; himself one plough there. Value in King Edward's time, twenty shillings; now ten shillings." †

The Plumptons, of Plumpton, held lands in this township, of the Percy fee, as early as the year 1168; for in, or about that year, Nigel de Plumpton granted to Robert, son of Huckman, his seneschal, along with other lands in Plumpton

---

* Written, at different times, *Ripesten*, *Ribbestain*, *Ribstain*, *Ribstone*, and *Ribston*. The first syllable is from *Ripe*, the bank of a river; *stain* or *stone*—that is the stone on the river's bank, which would be descriptive, as the magnesian limestone appears on both sides of the river Nidd at this place. Or it may, with equal probability, be derived from *Ripa* and *ton*— that is the town on the river's bank;—though we prefer the former. The epithet *Little* is to distinguish this village from Ribston *Great*, which is situate on the opposite side of the river Nidd.

† "Bawdwen's Dom. Boc.," p. 105.

and Scotton, one oxgang and six and a half acres of land, with a toft and an orchard belonging thereto, in Ribstain; where ten carucates of land make one knight's fee; at the same time changing the rent, which had been annually paid for the same, from four shillings, two gilded spurs, and two barbed arrows, to an engagement by the said Robert to serve the said Nigel in foreign parts, or elsewhere.

Amongst the boundaries mentioned in this charter, are places bearing the names of Frodisberi and Godwinsridding; and amongst the inhabitants of Ribston, at that time, were Walter de Ribston,* Richard de Butiller, Ailine, William Straungald, Robert, son of Hulkil, and Richard, son of Bencilum.

By inquisition, *post mortem*, in the year 1314, the lands of Lord Henry de Percy, in Ribston, were returned as one carucate, and in the enumeration of knights' fees, 31st Edward I., as two carucates.

To the aid granted to King Edward I., on the marriage of his daughter, Ribston contributed 6s. 9d.

In *Nomina Villarum* (1315), Henry Beaufiz is returned as lord of Parva Ribston.

Sir William de Plumpton married Alice, daughter and heiress of Sir Henry Beaufiz, in 1322, and Sir Henry died in 1325, whereupon the manor of Brackenthwaite, together with lands in Plumpton, Follifoot, Braham, Kirkby, and Little Ribston, which had been held by the courtesy of England, of the inheritance of his wife, Cecilia, daughter of William de Plumpton (descended from Robert, son of Huckman, seneschal of the manor of Plumpton), was settled—by fine, levied in Hilary term, 19th Edward II., 1325-6—upon Sir William Plumpton and Alice, his wife; with remainder to Thomas, son of Peter de Middleton.

* In 1274, Robert de Ribbestain was one of the witnesses to a charter, by which Henry Prior, of Helaugh Park, released to Sir Robert de Plumpton all claim to the church of Cowthorpe.

At this period the possessions of the Plumptons in Ribston were one messuage, twenty-two tofts, twenty oxgangs, and one hundred and forty-six acres of land, seventeen acres of meadow, and twenty acres of wood.

Sir William Plumpton having no issue by his wife, Alice—who died about the year 1841—the lands in Ribston, and elsewhere, reverted to Thomas de Middleton, and continued with that family until 1468, when, on the marriage of Thomas Middleton, Esq., of Stockeld, with Jane, daughter of Sir William Plumpton, it was agreed that William Middleton, Esq., father of the said Thomas Middleton, should settle an estate, in jointure, of lands and tenements in Ribston.

The Plumptons held lands in this township in 1527, as in that year William Plumpton is warned by the Earl of Northumberland, in a letter, not to fell the wood "of one Spring, liing within the township of Litle Ribston, within my lordship of Spoforth, which, as I perceive, you have bought of Georg Fulbarne, and so entendeth to fell it to your los. I desire, and also chargeth you, that ye sufer the saving of it, unto the time the better we may know to whom the right of the same belongeth."*

The principal landowners now in the township are the Earl of Harewood and Joseph Dent, Esq., of Ribston Hall.

On Ribston Moor, previous to its enclosure, were two small barrows, or *tumuli*, one of them called How Hill, the other Breckon Hill. In 1853, the former of them was opened to the depth of about four feet from its summit, which was its height from the original surface of the ground. In the centre was found a kind of coffin or cist of hardened clay, of a

* "Plumpton Correspondence," p. 227.
The Earl of Egremont, Lord of Spofforth, used to assert his royalty over Ribston, by his agent annually cutting two sods on Ribston Moor.

circular form, about two feet in diameter, which was partly filled with charcoal of oak-wood, and calcined bones. No traces of iron, or other metal were found. All the appearances served to indicate that it had been the burial place of some British hunter, or warrior, in a very remote age—probably before the christian era.

The village of Little Ribston is located on the southern side of the river Nidd; and the turnpike road from Knaresborough to Wetherby passes through it.

The school, a large and substantial building of stone, was erected at the cost of Joseph Dent, Esq., in 1845. Divine service, after the manner of the Church of England, is performed within it every Sunday.

The charities belonging to this township consist of a rent-charge of 3s. 4d. per annum, given by Thomas Bigland, by deed, in 1658, and 20s., being the interest of £20, given by Dr. Hutton and Dr. Talbot, to be expended in bread, to be given to the poor of the parish of Spofforth—a proportion of which is due to the poor of this township.

The Wesleyan Methodists have a small chapel here.

This township contains 855 acres of land; and, in 1858, was assessed to income tax at £1,128. The population, in 1801, was 181; in 1831, 222; and in 1851, 242.

The annual value of this township as assessed to the county rate, in 1849, was £1,062; and in 1859, £1,199.

SWINDEN.

SWINDEN is a township or district belonging to the parish of
Kirkby Overblow, bounded by Dunkeswick on the west, the
townships of Kirkby Overblow and Kearby-cum-Netherby on the
north and east, and the river Wharfe on the south.

In the Domesday survey Swinden is merely mentioned as
a berewick, belonging to William de Percy, and no quantity or
value given.

Swinden is evidently the *dene* or valley of swine; indicating
that it was the place where the oak trees grew, which yielded
the mast for the fattening of swine—hence the significance
of the following grants—

Alice de Romillé, the foundress of Bolton Priory, gave to the
nuns of Arthington the liberty of fattening forty hogs in her
wood of Swinden, during harvest. For this donation, and
the gift of half her lands in Helthwaite, she was permitted
to nominate a nun. These gifts were confirmed and rendered
perpetual by the subsequent confirmations of William de Curcy,
her son, and of Warine Fitzgerald.

During the sixteenth and seventeenth centuries Swinden
belonged to the family of Bethell, who occasionally resided
at the hall. Of this family was Sir Walter Bethell, who married

Mary, daughter of Sir Henry Slingsby, of Scriven, by whom he
had issue—

Sir Hugh Bethell, Knight.*

Sir Slingsby Bethell, sheriff of London, in 1680.†

William Bethell, D.D., rector of Kirkby Overblow.

Walter Bethell, who died November 1st, 1686, aged 73; and
Frances, who married George Marwood, Esq., of Little
Busby, in Cleveland, afterwards Sir George Marwood. While
the last named gentleman resided here, in 1644, the hall was
totally demolished, and the personal property therein plundered
or destroyed, by a marauding party from the royalist garrison
of Knaresborough Castle.

The hall at that time was surrounded by a moat; traces
of which yet remain. Outside of this was an area of about one
hundred yards in length, by eighty yards in breadth, enclosed
by a rampire, consisting of a mound of earth with a trench
outside—similar to that at Rougemont, but not so large.
Enclosures of this kind were probably intended for the protection
of cattle from wolves and robbers, in the old forest day.

* In the parish register of Great Ouseburn are the following entries—
"Lady Mary Bethell, of Alne, died Decem. 18th, and was buried Decem.
20th, 1662." "Sir Hugh Bethell, Knight, her eldest son, was buried Jan.
31st, 1662, aged 50."

† This gentleman wrote—"The Interest of the Princes and States
of Europe," "Observations on a Letter written by the Duke of Buckingham to Sir Thomas Osborne;" and "The World's Mistake in Oliver
Cromwell," which were published with a general title page, in 1694. He
was an Independent in religion, and a republican in principle, and was one
of the most active and zealous of the party which strove to exclude
the Duke of York from the throne. He was of parsimonious habits, and
was censured for being too frugal in his entertainments, when sheriff
of London.

> "Chaste were his cellars, and his shrieval board
> The grossness of a city feast abhorred;
> His cooks with long disuse their trade forgot;
> Cool was his kitchen—though his brains were hot."
> —*Dryden.*

The hall was afterwards rebuilt, but in an inferior style to its predecessor. This building subsequently acquired some slight military reputation, from a troop of cavalry being quartered here during the Scottish rebellion. The room in which their commander slept was afterwards called the captain's chamber.*

After the lapse of hardly two hundred years the second hall had become ruinous, when it was pulled down, and the present good substantial farm-house, yet bearing the name of Swinden Hall, was built about the year 1830.

The hall is surrounded by groves of fine timber, and seated in a fair and fertile spot; and now, with the whole of the district, belongs to the Earl of Harewood.

At Low Sneap House, a farm adjoining the road over Walton Head to Kirkby Overblow, are the remains of another forest peel, or fortress, consisting of moated enclosures. The smaller area, where, we suppose, some building has stood, is about forty-five yards in length, by thirty in breadth; the moat may have been twelve feet wide, within which is a mound formed of the earth thrown out of it. The outer enclosure is about one hundred yards by eighty yards, surrounded also by a trench and mound, similar to the other, which it encloses. At the time of its formation it [has evidently been intended for defensive purposes. The situation is a commanding one, immediately on the verge of the forest, and overlooking the country to a considerable distance north, west, and south. We can easily imagine a time

"When 'neath the peel's rude battlement
The trembling flocks and herds were pent,
And maids and matrons dropped the tear—
While ready warriors seized the spear."

* "Jones' Harewood."

DUNKESWICK.

THIS township for a long time has formed part of the great manor or fee of Harewood; until recently it also formed a part of that parish; now it belongs to the district church of Weeton. The river Wharfe forms its southern boundary; on the east and north it adjoins the parish of Kirkby Overblow, and the township of Weeton on the west, comprising an area of 1,467 acres, the whole of which belongs to the Earl of Harewood.

In the Domesday survey (A.D. 1086), this township is entered as two manors, among the lands of the king's thanes.

"In Chesvic, Ulchel had four carucates of land to be taxed. Land to two ploughs. The same and his wife have now there one plough and one villane, and two acres of meadow. Value in King Edward's time, eight shillings; now five shillings."*

This township is chiefly memorable as the place of residence of the family of De l'Isle, or Insula, a family of great importance and distinction, in very early times; owners of the manor of Harewood, and of great influence in the country around. Of their first settlement at Rougemont† we have no direct informa-

* "Bawdwen's Dom. Boc.," p. 228.
† In the Latin *Rubeo Monte*, in French *Rougemont;* both meaning the *Red Hill*, and derived, we suppose, from its situation upon a cliff or hill of reddish clay. The present name is *Ridgeman Scar*.

tion. The following brief sketch will give some idea of their antiquity and importance—

About the year 1180, Prior John of Hexham witnessed a grant of the manor of Gosforth, from Walter Fitzwilliam to Robert de Insula.

In or about the year 1189, Thomas Insula was witness to a charter of Kirkstall Abbey.

In 1205, Brian de l'Isle, or Insula, was appointed by King John constable of the Castle of Knaresborough, which office he held in 1211, when he victualled and manned that fortress by an order from the king. In 1222, he paid to the king £50, as the rent of the lordships of Knaresborough and Boroughbridge.

The commonly received pedigrees of the family state that Robert, Lord Lisle of Rougemont, inherited the manor of Harewood on the demise of William de Fortibus, in 1260,* and that he married Alicia Fitzgerald, grand-daughter of Warine Fitzgerald, by whom he had issue—

Robert, Lord Lisle of Rougemont, who married Albreda, Lady of Settringham, in the county of York, and had issue—

Warine, eldest son and heir.

Baldwin de Lisle, who had lands in Chatteris, by gift of his brother. By *Inquisition post mortem*, 47th Henry III. (1262), we learn that Baldwin de Insula, of the county of Devon, held, in the county of York, the manor of Harewood and

* The *Inquisition post mortem* of William de Fortibus, Earl of Albemarle, was taken in the 44th of Henry III., his next heir being his son Thomas, then seven years old, who was the last earl, and died, without leaving issue, before the 21st of Edward I. The widow of the above William de Fortibus, Isabella, Countess of Albemarle and Devon, and Lady De l'Isle, died November 10th, 1293.

the village of Lofthouse.* He was succeeded by his sister, Isabella de Fortibus, widow of William, Earl of Albemarle.

Warine, Lord Lisle of Rougemont, was living 13th Edward I. (1285). He married Matilda, daughter and co-heiress of Robert de Mucegros, and had issue—

Robert, eldest son and heir.

His other children were Margery, Warine, Gerald, John, Mary, and Joanne.

By *Inquisition post mortem*, 3rd Edward II. (1309), Warinus de Insula and Hugo de Courtenay, heirs of Isabella de Fortibus, Countess of Albemarle, held the manor of Harewood, the manor of Kirkby Oerblower, Lofthouse, parcel of the manor of Harewood, one messuage, and one carucate of land.

In *Nomina Villarum* (1315), Keswick and Kearby are entered together, of which Robert de Lisle was the lord.

Robert, Lord Lisle of Rougemont, son and heir of Warine, born in 1292, was summoned to Parliament in 1312, and again in 1316. He married Margaret Peverill, after whose death he took upon him the habit of a monk. He had issue—Robert, John, Peter, and others.

Robert de Insula, Lord of Rougemont, in the 18th year of Edward III. (1345), released all his manorial rights to his brother,

John de Insula, who became in consequence Lord of Rougemont. He was the most distinguished of his race. His father being disposed to give him one hundred marks, per annum, of land, to enable him to serve the king in his wars, with six men-at-arms. The king granted the said John license to give

* "31st Edward I., two and a half carucates in Kesewyk were of the fee of Baldwin de Insula, where ten carucates make a knight's fee."—*Knights' Fees, Surtees' Soc.*, p. 206.
"Towards the aid granted to King Edward I. on the marriage of his eldest daughter, Keswick contributed 10s."—*Ibid*, p. 295.

to his son the manor of Harewood, with other lands, to the annual value of four hundred marks, during his life, but afterwards to return to the heirs of the said Robert. His brother Robert, as above related, released to him and his heirs the said manor, and the advowson of the church there.* Being thus provided for, he attended the king in his first voyage into France, by way of Flanders, in 1340, and took part in the battle fought near Vironfosse. Two years afterwards he served the king in Aquitaine, and, in 1348, he attended the king in Bretagne, when they ravaged the country, and laid siege to Dinant.

For his good services the king granted him a pension of £200 per annum for his life, to support his dignity of banneret; of which sum £120 was assigned from the Priory of St. Neots, at Stoke, and £80 out of that of Eye; these were afterwards changed for other benefits.

He was one of the Knights of the Garter, on the first foundation of that order.

In 1852, the king made made him sheriff of the counties of Cambridge and Huntingdon, and granted him the custody of the Castle of Cambridge, for life.

In the expedition of Edward, the Black Prince, into Gascoigne, in 1855, John de Insula accompanied him, and had command of the main body of the army; but in the three days' march into the enemy's country he was wounded by a bolt, shot from a cross-bow, from the effects of which he died on the 11th of October, in the same year.

---

* "The figure of John, Lord Lisle, one of the first knights of the Garter, was remaining entire in the east window of the north chapel of Harewood Church, distinguished by the arms of his family—a fess between two chevronels on his tabard—till the church was repaired in 1798. This nobleman, however, from the style of the building, appears to have been the restorer of the church."—*Whitaker*.

From *Inquisition post mortem*, 80th Edward III., we learn that John de Insula, of Rougemont *(de Rubeo Monte)*, died seized in the county of York of the manor of Harewood, with its members, and lands in Carlton, Stokton, Helthway and Douteswyke (Healthwaite and Dunkeswick), the manor of Kirkby Orblawere, and *Sec* of Court in Spofforth.

During his lifetime, in 1853, he obtained letters apostolic, to appropriate the advowson of the church of Harewood to the priory of Bolton, on condition that the convent should grant to him and his heirs a rent-charge of £100 per annum, out of lands in Rowden, Wigton, and other places; and that a chantry of six priests should be founded at Harewood, or one of seven priests in the church of Bolton, to sing masses daily for the souls of his father, his mother, brothers and sisters, besides a special collect for the souls of himself and children. It is however doubtful whether this was carried into effect.

His wife was Matilda de Ferrars, by whom he had two sons and one daughter; the sons were

Sir Robert Insula, or De Lisle, Lord of Rougemont and Wilbraham, in Cambridgeshire; and

Sir William Insula, Lord of Cameldon and Shelford, who died without issue; the daughter was

Elizabeth, who married William de Aldburgh, to whom conjointly, Robert, Lord Lisle of Rougemont, in the year 1865, granted for the sum of £1,000, the manor of Harewood, with the appurtenances; and the said Robert paid £70 for license to do the same.

After this event, which transferred the manor of Harewood from the family of Insula to that of Aldburgh, we hear no more of the Lords of Rougemont; and as William de Aldburgh built the Castle of Harewood, and made it the residence of the lords of the fee, the probability is that Rougemont was abandoned

by its noble owners, and quickly went to ruin and decay. From
the appearance of the site, we suppose that the buildings were
entirely of timber; and in that manner only can we account for
the absence of all remains of any buildings. Had it been a
fabric of stone, like the adjoining Castle of Harewood, and
had it been pulled down and the stones taken away, large
mounds of lime and rubbish would have been left to mark
the site.

Although abandoned and neglected for the space of five
hundred years, the site of the home of the De Lisles is yet
strikingly obvious to all who come near it; situate at the south-
west corner· of the township, near the confluence of Weeton
beck with the river Wharfe. The latter stream, after wandering
among flat alluvial meadows (of its own formation), forms
a sharp curve, and rushes against a lofty cliff of reddish clay,
which as suddenly repels it, and again sends it winding among
level meadows. The top of this cliff is elevated about thirty
feet above the ordinary level of the river, and presents a
naked precipice to its waters—save where the water has
undermined the bank, and large patches have slid down,
with all their trees and brushwood. This is the only cliff
of earth for many miles along the river's course. The water in
front is apparently of great depth, but it is only for about
one hundred yards that it can be said to defend the position, and
that just at the bend of the stream. The buildings have
stood directly upon the highest part of this cliff, overlooking the
river and valley; and a pleasant situation it has been, commanding fine, though not extensive, views. Eastward, the
ridge of land on which the village of Kirkby Overblow stands
bounds the prospect in that direction; south-east are to be seen
the windings of the Wharfe, and the Castle and Park of
Harewood; in front, the hamlet of Weardley, the site of

Arthington Priory—the dwellers in Rougemont might hear the music of its bells—the fine wooded knoll, called Rawdon Hill, and the ridge of land on which Ecup, Adel, and Bramhope stand; westward, the view embraces the valley as far as the summit of Rumbald's Moor; and northward are Healthwaite Hill, Great Almes Cliff, and the Forest of Knaresborough.

The area which the buildings have occupied, as indicated by the hollows of the moat, is about eighty yards in length, along the river front, by sixty yards in depth. A moat has enclosed the whole, but the site is now so overgrown with trees, bushes, brambles, nettles, and all the rank undergrowth of a fat soil—not to mention a thicket of privet, which has been planted to form a fox cover—that any attempt at correct measurement is out of the question. In summer it will be completely impervious to man; in winter it is possible to creep through it, and trace the nearly filled hollows of the moat.

> "Change hath swept
> With wave on wave the feudal times away,
> And from their mightiest fabrics plucked the pride."

Outside the first is a second enclosure about 820 yards across, from east to west, and something less from north to south, surrounded on three sides by a moat and a mound. The mound in many places is forty feet across, and about ten feet in height; outside is the moat from which the soil has been thrown; at some time this mound has been covered with oak trees of a large size, the roots of which yet remain; a proof (if any were needed) of the great antiquity of the work.

The ancient name is yet partly preserved in the modern popular one—Ridgeman's, or Ridgeyman Scar. A footpath from Weeton to Dunkeswick passes through the outer enclosure, otherwise it is approached by no public road.

HEALTHWAITE HILL.

Healthwaite Hill* is a round detached mount, forming the northern part of the township of Dunkeswick. It is a pleasant well-cultivated district, on which are two large farm-houses and three or four cottages.

Soon after the foundation of Arthington Nunnery (A.D. 1154), Alice de Romillé, Lady of Harewood, gave to the nuns of that house a mediety of her lands at Healthwaite, which grant was confirmed by Warine Fitzgerald and William de Curci.

Isabel de Fortibus, Countess of Albemarle and Devon, and Lady Lisle, gave to the same house one messuage and a toft, with two carucates of land, in Healthwaite and Witheton, which grant was confirmed by King Edward II.

In the year 1505, on the marriage of Sir Robert Plumpton with Isabella, daughter of Ralph, Lord Neville, the lady's jointure was charged upon such lands as Sir Robert had purchased in Huby, Healthwaite Hill, near Harewood, and other places.

Early in the seventeenth century, Healthwaite Hill was the residence of a family of some consequence, named Maude; as, in 1631, Robert Maude, Esq., son and heir apparent of Robert Maude, of Healthwaite, was one of the parties to the indenture of Anthony Sawdrie's charity.

The village of Dunkeswick,† consisting of a group of well-built farm-houses and cottages, is situate in a warm and fertile

---

* This name appears to be derived from *Heal*, Hall, and *thwaite*, a clearing and the situation—that is the hall in the cleared or cultivated land on the hill—a name descriptive of the situation.

† Written at different times, *Chesvic, Dunsyke, Doutswicke, Donkeswyke*, &c. The derivation is probably from *Don*, a hill; *kaes*, water; and *wick*, a dwelling place—the dwelling place between the water and the hill—a name descriptive of its situation, between Healthwaite Hill and the river Wharfe.

spot, a short distance west of the place where the Leeds and Harrogate turnpike road crosses the river Wharfe at Harewood Bridge. It does not present any features of remarkable interest.

The Mallories, a family of considerable importance in early times, were located in this township.* In the year 1562, Peter Mallorie, a younger son of Sir John Mallorie, settled here; and his descendants still reside in the neighbourhood.†

At Harewood Bridge the road from Harrogate and the north crosses the river Wharfe. The bridge, a substantial structure, has been built at different times.‡ The last widening is commemorated on a stone inserted in the wall, with the following inscription—

"THIS BRIDGE WAS BUILT BY THE COUNTY, 1729."

Blind Jack of Knaresborough made five and a half miles of this road, for which he received the sum of £1,200.

Being entirely an agricultural district, the population is stationary. In 1811, it was 238; in 1821, 257; in 1831, 261; and in 1851, 249.

The annual value of this township as assessed to the county rate in 1849, was £1,860. As assessed to the income tax in 1858, £2,140: and to the poor rate in 1859, £1,953.

* In the parish register of Harewood is the following entry,—" Matthew Mallorie, Gent., a man greatly beloved by all men, who dwelt at Dunkeswick, and left most holy and comfortable precepts at his last end. Buried in Harewood Quire, 27th day of April, 1619."

+ " Jones' Harewood."

‡ In the will of "Robert Stanelay, rector of Kirkbyonerblawers," dated March 5th, 1441-2 (proved June 30th, 1442), occurs the following—" Item, do et lego ad constructionem pontis de Harwode, vjˢ. viijᵈ." Also in the will of "William Attegate de Kesewyk," made November 4th, 1427, we find the following bequest—" Lego at facturum pontis de Harwood, xxᵈ." The next item appears as though the testator had his eye on a feast on the day of his funeral,—" Lego ad distribuendum inter proximos et amicos die sepulturæ meæ, unum boviculum et tres oves."—*Testa. Ebor,* vol. i., p. 413.

WEETON.

WEETON,* formerly a township in the parish of Harewood, now
the head of a district parish of its own name, is situate in
a depressed or hollow part of the northern slope of Wharfedale;
the river Wharfe forming its southern boundary, Dunkeswick
adjoining it on the east, Castley on the west, and Rigton on
the north.

At the time of the Domesday survey Weeton was held by
the king, a king's thane, and Gospatric, and is thus entered—

"Lands of the king. Manor. In Widetune, Chetel had three
carucates to be taxed. Land to one plough and a half. Sixteen
pence."†

"Lands of the king's thanes. Manor. In Widetone, Ulchil
had two carucates and a half to be taxed. Land to one plough.
He has there three villanes and two ploughs. Value five
shillings."‡

"Lands of Gospatric. Manor. In Wideton, Gospatric, two
carucates and a half to be taxed. Land to two ploughs. There

* The first idea that strikes the mind when seeking for an etymology
of this place, is that of the Scottish verb "wee," little—that is, the little
town; but this is not feasible, as in early times the name is always written
Witheton, *Widetone*, or *Wythiton*, which seems to indicate the town of
Withes or Withies, *vulgo Ebor Widdies*,—that is, ropes made of twisted
willows, an article much more in demand formerly than now. The locality
is favourable to the growth of the willow.
† "Bawdwen's Dom. Boc.," p. 87.
‡ *Ibid*, p. 222.

are now two villanes and one bordar with one plough, and it pays seven shillings."*

In the Summary† we find—"In Widetun, the king, five carucates and a half. In the same place, Gospatric, two carucates and a half."

In very early times a family of some consequence derived its surname from this place, and probably resided here.

Adam and Robert de Wytuna are witnesses to a charter, by which Hugo de Creskeld gave certain lands to the nuns of Arthington.

Adam de Wytona is one of the witnesses to a lease from Kirkstall Abbey to Lawrence de Arthington, of lands on Arthington Bank.

William de Witheton is witness to a deed by which Nigel de Plumpton (about 1189) gave certain lands to Gamel, son of Elwin, his marshal.

William de Witheton was witness to a charter of Kirkstall Abbey, in 1189.

In 31st of Edward I., four carucates of land in Witheton were of the fee of Baldwin de Insula, where ten carucates make a knight's fee.‡

Weeton contributed one mark to the aid granted to the same king on the marriage of his daughter.

Isabel de Fortibus, Countess of Albemarle and Devon, Lady De l'Isle, confirmed to the monks of Bolton two carucates of land in this place and Healthwaite; which gift was confirmed by King Edward II., A.D. 1807.

* "Bawdwen's Dom. Boc.," p. 218.
† *Ibid*, p. 257.
‡ "Knight's Fees, Surtees' Soc.," p. 206.

According to the compotus of Bolton Abbey, in 1824, the lands in Wython paid the sum of £4 6s., and the land at Westecoch (Wescoe Hill), in Wython, paid 6s.

In the 45th of Edward III. (1372), the king committed to the custody of Richard de Rymington, one messuage and one carucate of land with the appurtenances, in Wytheton and Westcogh, in the county of York, which formerly belonged to Laurence Franke, of Wytheton, near Harewood.

Thomas, son of Henry de Scriven, gave to the nuns of Arthington, that land called Paynescroft, in Wytheton, lying near the road to Rigton.

In 1504, Sir Robert Plumpton had lands in Weeton and Huby, which he had purchased; and upon which lands there was a charge for the jointure settled on Isabella, daughter of Ralph, lord Neville, second wife of Sir Robert Plumpton, in 1505.

Since the year 1721 the greatest part of the land in Weeton has been held by the family of Lascelles, Earls of Harewood.

The church, dedicated to St. Barnabas, was built and endowed at the cost of the late Earl of Harewood. The foundation stone was laid on the 3rd of April, 1851, by the Bishop of Ripon; and the finished fabric was consecrated by the same prelate, October 12th, 1852. It is a beautiful specimen of the early English style of architecture, from designs by George Gilbert Scott, Esq., of London. It consists of a nave and chancel, between which, from a kind of transept, rises a large square tower, surmounted by a lofty octagonal spire, containing three bells.

The burial ground is large, and kept in the neatest order.

The living is a perpetual curacy, worth £100 per annum, in the gift of the Earls of Harewood.

The first incumbent was the Rev. James Palmes, B.A.; on whose resignation the Rev. T. H. Fearon was appointed, Nov.

14th, 1866; on whose decease the Rev. Christopher Wybergh succeeded, August 15th, 1867.

The parsonage, a large and elegant mansion in the Elizabethan style of architecture, near the church, was erected in 1858.

The schools and teacher's residence in the village were built in 1856, all at the cost of the Earl of Harewood.

The district, or parish, consists of the townships of Weeton and Dunkeswick, being that portion of the parish of Harewood situate on the north side of the river Wharfe.

The benefactions left to the poor of Weeton are—one close of ground, called Wescho-hill Close, lying at Wescho Hill, left by William Wade, in 1722; lets at £5 per annum.

To the poor of Weeton and Dunkeswick, the sum of 20s., to be paid yearly out of the estate of Mr. Robert Midgeley, lying at Weeton.

To the poor of the parish of Harewood, two closes of ground called Foxglove Close, and Straike-foot Ing, lying at Weeton; left by Anthony Sawdrie, parish clerk, in 1681. Also an allotment for the same, situate at Huby; the yearly rent to be used for putting out a boy or girl apprentice yearly within the parish of Harewood. This charity is so apportioned that every sixth year it belongs to Dunkeswick, and every ninth year to Weeton. None are to have the benefit but such as are born in wedlock, whose parents are inhabitants within the parish of Harewood. If within the space of ten years there should be no proper object within the said places, the money to be laid out in gray cloth, and given to the poorest there.

To the poor of Weeton, a house and garth at Huby, left by Thomas Harrison, of Stubhouse, which let for £8 a-year.

A legacy of £200 was left to the poor of this township, in 1851, by Lester Brand, Esq.; the interest to be distributed on the donor's birthday.

The Wesleyan Methodist Chapel, a large substantial building of stone, was built in the year 1796.

The village of Weeton is ranged east and west along the sides of a narrow road, and presents nothing deserving of particular remark.

A station on the Leeds northern branch of the North Eastern Railway, about half a mile west of the village, gives the inhabitants the opportunities of travel when they think proper to use them.

Wescoe Hill is a round-backed mount, composed of a mass of clay and shale, to the westward of Weeton. The railway passes completely through it, partly by a short tunnel, and partly by deep and wide cuttings on either side.

The name is evidently of great antiquity, probably of Norwegian derivation,* and is met with in very early documents. It also supplied a surname to a family, of whom the service of Henry de Westcoght was given, with the mill of Castley, by William de Castelai, to the monks of Fountains Abbey. The monks of Bolton had lands upon this hill. Two or three pleasantly situated farmsteads are now seated upon it.

Huby† is a cluster of small farm-houses, and small antique straw-thatched cottages, with a small Methodist Chapel, situate on the slope of a hill, a short distance west of the railway station.

Roger, son of Alexander de Huby, gave to the monks of Fountains Abbey one oxgang of land, with a toft and croft here.‡

---

* In this and in the adjoining hill, called Riffa, or Riff-how, we think we perceive, but slightly concealed, two of the Norwegian *Hoes*. The word "hill" is superfluous, and has been added by another people.

† This is evidently the *by* or homestead of Hugh, a Danish settler; as Newby is merely the new farmstead or home.

‡ "Burton's Mon. Ebor."

Newby, which close adjoins, consists of two or three farm-steads belonging to the Earl of Harewood.

The township contains 1,376 acres of land of variable quality. The population in 1801 was 287; in 1811, 297; in 1821, 810; in 1831, 822; and in 1851, only 800. The annual value as assessed to the county rate in 1849 was £1,846; as assessed to the property tax in 1858, £2,149; and to the poor-rate in 1859, £2,268.

CASTLEY.

CASTLEY* is a village and small township in the parish of Leathley. On the south it adjoins the river Wharfe, which, with an extensive curve, embraces it almost on three sides; the other adjoins to Leathley and Weeton. This township forms the south-western angle of the Forest of Knaresborough.

At the time of the Domesday survey (1086) it was in the hands of the king, and is thus entered—

"In Castlelai, Elwin had one carucate to be taxed, and Berne and Elflet had one carucate to be taxed. Land to two ploughs. Ebrard, a vassal of William de Percy, farms it, but William does not vouch for him. Value in King Edward's time —— shillings; at present sixteen pence.†

Afterwards it was held by a family to which it gave a surname,‡ many members of whom were benefactors to the

---

* The name is evidently derived from some *castra*, castle, or camp of the Romans, and *ley*, a field—that is the castle field. Within a very limited space around this village, we have evidence, in the names of places, of the different nationalities which have occupied or peopled the country. In Castley, we have Roman and Saxon; in Huby and Newby, we have Danish; in Weschoe and Riffoe, Norwegian.

† "Bawdwen's Dom. Boc.," p. 87.

‡ At the time of Kirkby's Inquest (1284) "Castelley" was held by Richard de Goldsburgh and William de Castley, as the fourth part of a knight's fee, of the heirs of Percy, and the same heirs held it of the king, *in capite.*—*Kirkby's Inquest, Surtees' Soc.*, p. 45.

In the list of knights' fees, 31st of Edward I., here was one carucate of land of the fee of Percy, where fourteen carucates make a fee.—*Ibid*, p. 203.

To the aid for marrying the same king's daughter Castley contributed 2s. 10½d.—*Ibid*, p. 298.

Abbey of Fountains, as will be seen by the following extracts from "Burton's Monasticon Eboracense"—

"Robert, son of Nigel de Castelay, gave one acre and a half of land here in Turneridding, and one acre and a half in Thieveridding."

"William, son of Gilbert de Castelai, gave two oxgangs of land, with his share of the mill and its pool, and the service of Henry de Westcoght for the said mill, reserving the right of having his corn grinded there muclture free; they, the monks, paying three shillings to the canons of Park."*

"Hugh, son of William de Lelay, quit-claimed to them the service of William, son of Gilbert de Castelai, for one tenement here."

"Roger, son of Henry de Castelay, gave a toft and a croft here, with one acre of land, and all his demesne in East-head of Hungerholme, upon the bank of the water."

"Alexander, son of William de Castelay, gave his land with this piece which Hamer de Castelay had, with a toft and croft, and half of the holme betwixt Cornhill and Werf, which did belong to John de Castelay, his brother."

"Then Alexander also confirmed to them the land called Ulframrode, as far as Tuinber-beck, with the land that is betwixt Ulframrode and the boundary of Buggerode, together with the land, toft, and croft, which Roger, son of Henry, his brother, held here."

"William de Uskelf quit-claimed a toft in this place, called Foulesikecroft, and eight acres of arable land in the same village."

"Francis de Cipria quit-claimed his right in the wood, betwixt Huby and Moseker."

"Malger, son of William Pouella gave all his land here, being three acres, on the east side of the way or ford called

* The Monastery of Healough Park, in the Ainsty.

Haldwadford, in Poolholme, in Castley, to the monks of Fountains; which was confirmed by Robert, son of William Bram de Powel."*

The mill mentioned above belonged to the monks of Bolton Priory, and not a vestige of it, or its pool, can be discovered at the present day.

"Isolda, daughter of Hugh de Lelay, gave six acres of land in Castelay, with one oxgang of land, with the service of Galfrid de Arthington, and of 4d. annuity to the nuns of the Priory of Nun-Appleton, which Sir Hugh de Lelay confirmed."†

In the year 1300, William Castleley was one of the jurors on the *Inquisition post mortem* of Roger de Mowbray.

In the grant of half an acre of land from Walter, the son of Hugo de Creskeld to the nuns of Arthington, the name of William de Castelay occurs as a witness.

In the *Nomina Villarum* (1315) William de Castellay is returned as lord of Castellay.

At what period the family of Castley ceased to be lords of this village we have no direct information. Afterwards it came into the hands of the family of Lindley, of Leathley, from them it passed to those of Hitch, Maude, and Fawkes; the Rev. A. Fawkes being at present the principal proprietor.

The village of Castley is placed in a most singular situation; more especially since the formation of the railway, the lofty embankment of which carries the road above the tops of the highest houses, so that the inhabitants, on looking up, can see between themselves and the sky the rapid rush of the fire-impelled chariots of the present iron age. The viaduct, which carries the railway across the Wharfe, consists of twenty-one arches, each sixty feet in span and ninety feet high in the

* "Burton's Mon. Ebor.," p. 191.
† *Ibid*, p. 227.

middle, containing upwards of 50,000 tons of stone; a most
stupendous piece of work to be constructed for the mere passage
of a road across it.

Castley Hall, now a farm-house, was built about the year
1700, by Mr. Robert Dyneley, second son of Robert Dyneley,
Esq., of Bramhope.

Riffa or Riffoe Wood is a hill covered with wood, and
strewn with blocks of hard coarse gritstone; on the top is a
gamekeeper's cottage, in a lofty and romantic situation. On
the western side runs Riffa-beck, one of the boundaries of
Knaresborough Forest.

The charities belonging to this township consist of fourteen
shillings, being the interest of £14, left to the poor by Mrs.
Ann Hitch, in 1769.

The area of this township is only 527 acres, and the
population about 80. In 1801 it was 82; in 1811, 96; in
1821, 110; in 1831, 118; and in 1851, 88. The annual
value as assessed to the county rate in 1849 was £777; as
assessed to property tax in 1858, £926; and to the poor rate in
1859, £990.

RIGTON.

RIGTON is a village and township in the parish of Kirkby Overblow, situate principally on a ridge of land extending east and west, whence it derives its name. Previous to the Norman conquest it was held by Gamelbar and Archil; afterwards by Gilbert Tyson and the king, and is thus briefly noticed in Domesday survey—

"Manor. In Ristone, Gamelbar had two carucates to be taxed. Land to one plough."*

Gilbert Tyson had this portion, but it was waste.

Again, amongst the lands of the king's thanes we find—

"Manor. In Ristone, Archil had two carucates of land to be taxed. Land to one plough. The same now has it, but it is waste. Value in King Edward's time, ten shillings."†

The family of Mowbray appear afterwards to have obtained some influence here, as, about the year 1120, there is a charter quoted by Dr. Whitaker, from Roger de Mowbray to a son of Gospatric de Rigton, who was father of Simon de Hebden, granting him free warren over thirteen townships, *quæ extendit usque in Werf . . hab. et tend cum om . . ad manerium meum di . . Kirkby Malapart.*

* "Bawdwen's Dom. Boc.," p. 194,
† *Ibid,* p. 228.

The monks of Fountains afterwards became possessed of a large portion of this township.

Hugh, son of Hugh de Lethley, gave to them a moiety of a mill in Rigton, which Adam, son of Hugh de Lelay, quit-claimed to him; he also gave the suit of a mill, with a free passage over his land, through his territory to and from the mill, obliging his tenants to repair the dam, &c.*

The said Hugh also gave one carucate of land, being a moiety of his land here, together with the whole village, and the service of the freeholders and their heirs, and the natives there, with their families and cattle, for which John, Abbot of Fountains, in A.D. 1244, gave to him one hundred marks, and in A.D. 1248, Sir William de Middleton, being High Sheriff of Yorkshire, gave security to indemnify the Abbot and Convent of Fountains from all suits belonging to Margery de Rypariis, and her heirs, or assigns, at her Court of Harewood, for what the monks had here of his granting.

Isabella de Fortibus, Countess of Albemarle and Devonshire and Baroness of Skipton, confirmed to them the moiety of this village. In 1284, Robert de Furneys and the heirs of William de Plompton held a mediety of the village of Rigton, for the second part of the fourth part of a knight's fee, of Roger de Mowbray, and the same Roger of the king, *in capite.*†

In *Nomina Villarum* (1315), the Abbot of Fountains and Richard Furneaux are returned as lords of the manor of Rigton.

In 1318, Rigton and the adjoining manor of Stainburn were so ruined by the plundering incursions of the Scots, that the Abbot of Fountains petitioned the king for a relief from taxation; which was granted.

* The only mill now in Rigton is called Burn Bridge Mill, and is situate on, and supplied with motive power by, the waters of the Crimple, which brook forms the northern boundary of the township of Rigton.
† "Kirkby's Inquest," p. 45. "Surtees' Soc., 1866."

In 1326, Richard Furneaux held in Rigton, on the demise of John de Mowbray, the fourth part of a knight's fee, worth 25s. per annum, pertaining to the manor of Kirkby Malzeard.

On the dissolution of the Abbey of Fountains, in 1539, the manor of Rigton was valued at £7 18s. 5¼d. per annum. At that time John Fowler was bailiff of the manor, and his annual fee was 20s.

The manor continued vested in the crown until the year 1556, when it was sold to Sir William Fairfax for £266 7s. 6d., in which* family it continued until 1716, when it was sold, under a decree in Chancery, to Robert Wilkes, Esq., from whom it descended to his grand-daughter, the only daughter and heiress of Charlton Palmer, Esq., of Beckenham, in Kent, and wife of the Rev. Dr. Thomas Pollock, from whom it was purchased by Lord Harewood, in 1796, in whose family it yet continues.

The village of Rigton is a cluster of farm-houses and cottages, ranged along the side of a road passing from north to south; many of them placed with a gable towards the narrow street.

---

* This manor is particularly mentioned in a codicil to the will of Thomas, Lord Fairfax, the great Parliamentary general, as follows—" I give to my uncle, Charles Fairfax, of Menston, Esq., and the heires males of his body, the sum of fifty pounds per annum out of these farmes followinge—in my manor of Rigton, in the county of York (that is to say) out of one farme, called the Spoute Farme, now in the tenure or occupation of Francis Ingle; and also out of one farme in Rigton aforesaid, called Mawson's Farme, now in the tenure or occupation of Thomas Topham, or his assigns; and of one other farme, called Hardesty's Farme, now in the tenure or occupation of Richard Hardestye, or his assigns; and also out of one other farme in Rigton, belonging to William Smith; and also the warrant upon the Common there. Dated Nov. 11th 1671." From the same document, it is also evident that this Lord Fairfax held the royalties of the Forest of Knaresborough on lease, as he gives the same to Henry Fairfax, Esq.,—"Also I give unto him all my right and interest of two leases of the royalties of the Forest of Knaresborough, in the county of Yorke."

On the highest ground in the village is a piece of land, now occupied by six cottages, called Chapel Hill.* In the back of one of the cottages is a piece of wall of great strength and thickness, which is supposed to have formed part of the chapel, which tradition declares stood here. The same authority also relates that here was a burial ground, and that human bones were found when a cellar in one of the cottages was dug.

As in almost all old villages, here is a small enclosure, bearing the name of the Hall Garth, where a building of some importance is believed to have stood.

The site of the ancient grange or manor house is yet to be seen on the south-east of the village, now called the Moat. It comprises a level area, thirty-three yards in width by fifty yards in length, surrounded by a moat, which, when complete, has been fifteen yards wide and ten feet deep. A draw-bridge would be necessary to reach the building thus enclosed, which building has been of timber, as not a fragment of stonework is to be seen around; and, on making a drain to take the water from the moat, a piece of squared oak timber was found, grooved in such a manner as shewed it to have been part of the framework of a large building.

The Wesleyan Methodists have a chapel here; a large substantial building of stone, erected in the year 1816.

A national school, with teacher's residence attached, was built in 1851, at the joint cost of the Earl of Harewood and the

* The only mention we have seen of a chapel here in any printed book is in "Jones' History of Harewood," p. 217, when speaking of Almes Cliff he says—"By others it is said to have derived its name from the distribution of almes, at certain times, agreeably to the tenor of legacies left to the chapel which stood there in the sixteenth century, and was at that time dedicated to the Virgin Mary. The site of the chapel now goes by the name of Chapel Hill." It is a pity that this writer was not a little more explicit about the legacies and the chapel. Chapel Hill and Almes Cliff are a mile apart.

Rev. Henry Blunt, M.A., rector of the parish. Divine service, according to the rites of the Church of England, is performed in the school once every Sunday.

ALMES CLIFF.

The most remarkable and interesting feature of this township is the lofty group of coarse gritstone rocks, known as Great Almes Cliff.* This group of rocks occupies the highest point of the ridge of land on which the village stands, and appears to be the highest and hardest portion of a great upheaval of the earth, extending from east to west; the strata dip to the south and east, and confront the west and north-west with a lofty and precipitous face; from this face huge masses of rock appear to have fallen at the time of its elevation, and become embedded in the earth below, presenting their *cleavage* in every variety of posture. The front is perpendicular, in some parts overhanging; the joints and beds crannied and worn, as if by the action of tidal waves, into all imaginable kinds of holes and crevices; the top is also covered with inequalities, many of them of a regular basin-like shape, whence it has been inferred that these rocks have been held sacred in ancient days, and made subservient to the rites of the Druidical religion. In short, we believe, it would not be difficult to show that, with the exception of the artificial temple or circle of stones, this place possesses all the accessories of that ancient worship, as, the

* Hargrove, in his history of Knaresborough, derives the name from the Celtic *Al*, a rock or cliff, and *mias*, an altar—that is, the altar cliff. This has evidently a leaning towards Druidical rites and ceremonies. The name is always locally pronounced *Almes* or *Omes Cliff*. A short distance eastward, the crossing of the Crimple brook bore the name of *Almesford*. We have sometimes seen it written *Orm's Cliff*; in that case it might be named from some owner in early times; or as *Orm*, in the Norwegian, signifies a serpent, this may be properly *the serpent's cliff*—a descriptive epithet.

grand karn or altar, the idols, in the shape of pyramids with
fluted tops, typical of the worship of the sun, the tolmen,
the cromlech, the sacred cavern, and the rock basins for catching
the pure water from heaven before it became polluted by
contact with the earth.   The altar is a large rock, about forty
yards south of the main group, upwards of one hundred feet in
length by thirty feet in breadth, and forty feet in height on the
southern side, while the northern is only slightly elevated above
the soil.   On the western portion of this rock is sculptured the
figure of a large tree, which we take to be the monogram of the
Celtic Jupiter, whose representative was an oak tree—the
fairest of the forest.   This is so distinctly marked that no
one can question its artificial origin.   In front of this is
what we style the tolmen, a huge misshapen stone, eleven
feet six inches in height, and twenty-two feet in breadth across
the top; not touching the ground, but resting upon six smaller
stones, placed in such a manner that there is a passage under
the upper rock between them.   At the north-western end
of the altar is a large triangular rock, now thrown down,
with a fluted or rayed apex, which we presume to have been
one of the idols sacred to the sun.   Two others of similar
shape and kind stand in a separate enclosure, towards the
south, and are close together; their tops marked with cup-
like indentations, with channels leading from them down the sides
of the stone to a considerable distance.   The length of the base
of this pair of idols is 20 feet, and the height 14 feet 6 inches.
Near the altar, towards the north-west, is the entrance to the
" Fairy parlour," a natural vertical joint or opening in the
rocks, eighteen inches wide by five feet in height.   It apparently
dips with the strata in a south-easterly direction, and is said
to have been explored to the distance of one hundred yards,
and egress made at another opening; other reports say that

a goose turned into this fissure, followed the passage underground, and came out near Harewood Bridge. Its name has always been associated with the fairy people, who were formerly believed to be all powerful on this hill, and exchanged their imps for the children of the farmers round about. This cavern might be made useful for the delivery of oracles in the olden day. With this exception, the openings into the rocks are carefully walled up, to prevent foxes from earthing in the deep dens and caverns within; and the fairies, being either walled in, or finding themselves walled out, have left the country—as they have not been seen lately in this neighbourhood. The cromlech is apparently of natural formation, and is situate in the fence between two enclosures; the most southerly portion of the group, and about eighty yards distant from the altar. It is composed of four large stones—three of which form the sides and one the cover; this last is nineteen feet in length by thirteen feet in breadth, and five feet in thickness; the cave below, open at both ends, is six feet in height and twelve feet wide. On the top of the main group are many rock basins, only two of which demand particular attention; one of them is three feet in diameter and eighteen inches in depth, the other is situate further to the north, and very near the edge of the cliff—it is neither so wide nor deep as the last, but has a greater reputation, and is known as "the wart well." To remove these excrescences from their hands the country people come here, prick them until they bleed, let the blood drop into the well, then wash their hands in the water, and, if they have faith, in a short time the warts will take their departure and be no more seen. Fires have apparently been kindled on many points of this group; most probably on the grand Druidical festivals, when the altars of the worshippers of fire blazed over all the land.

The rock basins are evidently natural formations, probably a little assisted by art, as similar kinds of rock present similar appearances all over the country. A narrow opening, fronting the south-west, cuts through the mass of rock, and divides it into two portions; another natural fracture runs from nearly south to north, and forms the boundary between the townships of Rigton and Stainburn, so that a portion of the rock is in each township. On the rock on each side of this fracture are deeply cut the letters T. F. and E. L. being the initials of Thomas Fawkes, of Farnley, and Edwin Lascelles, of Harewood —for here met the domains of these two "lords of broad lands," and which are yet held by their descendants. The Fawkes of Farnley might stand upon this rock, and looking west and south behold the townships of Castley, Leathley, Stainburn, Lindley, and Farnley—nearly all his own; the Lascelles of Harewood, standing on the same rock, and looking eastward and southward, would see on this side the river Wharfe, Rigton, Weeton, Dunkeswick, and Swinden—nearly all his own—and on the south of the river, Harewood, and many a fair domain beside.

The highest part of the precipice fronting the west bears the name of the "Lovers' Leap," not from any fancied suitability for that purpose, but from what might have been a tragical affair. In or about the year 1766, a young woman, daughter of a respectable farmer, in Rigton, of the name of Royston, being dis-appointed in love, determined to destroy herself, by leaping from a point of the rock, upwards of twenty yards in height; a strong wind from the west was blowing at the time, which inflated her dress in such a manner, that she made the descent com-paratively unharmed in the adjoining field; and instead of breaking her neck, only sprained her thumb. She made no attempt to repeat the experiment, which probably cured her hopeless passion, as she lived long afterwards, and died at Kirkby Overblow.

As this rock is completely isolated, the view from the top takes in the whole circle of the horizon; but the most interesting and beautiful part of the prospect is the valley of the Wharfe, which in rich variety of beauty lies stretched before the eye— from Grimston, the seat of Lord Londsborough, on the east, to the crest of Rombald's Moor on the west. To describe it is impossible—it must be seen to be properly enjoyed, and once seen, will not be readily forgotten.

> " Ever charming, ever new,
> When will the landscape tire the view ?
> The fountain's fall, the river's flow,
> The woody valleys, warm and low ;
> The windy summit, wild and high,
> Roughly rushing on the sky ;
> The pleasant seat, the ruined tower,
> The naked rock, the shady bower,
> The town and village, dome and farm,
> Each gives each a double charm,
> Like pearls upon an Ethiop's arm."

A summer sunset viewed from this place is highly beautiful; the vale itself is a picture of natural loveliness; and at such a time every object therein appears bathed in a flood of radiance, adding to its charms, and making beauty more beautiful; the hills appear higher, the valley more rich and varied; and the hues of the foliage that clothes them more distinct than in the full glare of day; the fine reaches of the Wharfe flash like mirrors of silver, when the sun wheeling downward touches the western hills, and then bids, almost reluctantly, the lovely scene farewell—

> " A pomp
> Leaving behind of yellow radiance spread
> Upon the mountain sides, in contrast bold
> With ample shadows, seemingly no less
> Than those resplendent lights, his rich bequest,
> A dispensation of his evening power."

At Horn Bank, on the crest of the hill east of Rigton, near a farm-house, are the remains of three camps—two of a square, and one of a circular form; they are probably of British and Roman origin. The situation is a lofty and commanding one; but the ploughshare has so often passed over them that they are nearly obliterated.

In 1787, a large boss of a bridle, and several fragments of gilt brass were found here;* and refuse from iron smelting works are abundant in the valley below. A fine spring of water was formed into a bath here many years ago, but the whole is now in a state of ruin.

BRACKENTHWAITE†

Is a hamlet in the township of Rigton, standing on an eminence between the brooks Crimple and Norbeck.

The first time we find this place mentioned is about the year 1170, when Henry de Brakenthwaite and Adam de Brakenthwaite were witnesses to a charter, by which Nigel de Plumpton gave certain lands in Little Ribstone to Robert, the son of Huckman. Hence we infer that at that early date this place was the home of some respectable yeomanry.

Sir Henry Byaufiz held the manor of Brackenthwaite and other lands, by the courtesy of England, of the inheritance of his wife, Cecilia, daughter of William de Plumpton (descended from Robert, son of Huckman, seneschal of the manor of Plumpton), and on his death, in 1325, this manor was settled upon Sir William Plumpton, of Plumpton, and Alice, his wife, daughter of the said Sir Henry Byaufiz, and their heirs, with remainder to Thomas, son of Peter de Middleton.

* "Hargrove's Knaresborough."
†The name is derived from *Bracken*, the fern *Pteris aquilina*; and *thwaite*, a clearing—that is, the clearing amongst the brackens; in early times, we have no doubt, a descriptive epithet.

Sir William Plumpton having no issue by the said Alice, who died about 1341, Brackenthwaite consequently reverted to Thomas de Middleton. It was however destined again to return by marriage to the family of Plumpton.

In 1468, on the marriage of Thomas Middleton, of Stockeld, Esq., with Jane, daughter of Sir William Plumpton, it was agreed in the marriage settlement, that William Middleton, Esq., father of the said Thomas Middleton, should settle an estate, in jointure, of lands and tenements in Brackenthwaite and Little Ribston.

The family of Beckwith also held lands here; the last portion of which was sold in the year 1758, by Mr. John Beckwith, of Knaresborough, to Edwin Lascelles, Esq. The same family —that of the Earls of Harewood—have recently increased their estate here by purchases from Andrew Montagu, Esq.

The few houses which constitute the hamlet of Brakenthwaite are situate almost on the crest of a hill, and some of them are of considerable age, substantially built and covered with thatch, showing the old-fashioned wide chimney inside, and windows divided by stone mullions. Over the doorway of one are the following initials and date, **B.M.S., 1687.**

Tatefield Hall and farm, now the property of Messrs. Benjamin and John Kent, is situate in the valley of the Crimple, on the northern side of the township. The hall has been built probably about two hundred years, but recently much modernized; sash windows have been substituted for the original mullioned ones, but even yet the home of the substantial English yeoman is to be seen in perfection.

The township contains 3,111 acres of land, of almost every quality; and in 1858 was assessed to income tax at £3,820. The population in 1801 was 414; in 1831, 451; and in 1851, 463.

STAINBURN.

STAINBURN* is a township and chapelry in the parish of Kirkby
Overblow, situate on the northern slope of Wharfedale, to the
west of Rigton.

In Domesday survey it is entered among the lands of the
king, counted as four manors, and held by four thanes, who had
five carucates of land to be taxed, of the annual value of
forty shillings.† It afterwards became part of the possessions of
the monks of Fountains Abbey. A few of the many grants and
confirmations by which they obtained and held it, are given
below, from "Burton's Monasticon Eboracense"—

"Malgar, son of William de Pouilla, gave two acres of
land here."

"Ysolda, relict of Rodger Peyteven (Pictavensis), daughter of
Hugh de Lelay, gave the whole village of Staynburn, containing
five carucates of land, as well in demesnes as in service, which
was confirmed by Roger Peyteven, the younger, her grandson,
and by Hugh, son of William de Lelay, as specified by the
boundaries."

"William de Plumpton confirmed the wood and moor of that
place, reserving the right of herbage in the wood for his men of
Brackenthwaite."

* This name is evidently derived from *Stain*, stone, and *burn*, water; a
term applicable to more than one watercourse, which pours its muddy
waters in winter, over a stony bed, from the heathy moors above into the
valley of the Wharfe.
† "Bawdwen's Dom. Boc.," p. 37.

"Robert de Lelay gave thirty acres of land, and pasture for two hundred sheep in this place."

"Margaret de Redvers, Countess of Devonshire, confirmed and quit-claimed to the monks all their suit of court, belonging to the Court of Harewood, for their lands, &c., in this place and Rigton."

"Eva de Lelay, daughter of William Palmar de Swillington, gave three oxgangs of land, with tofts and crofts here, which was confirmed by William, son of Ralph."

"William, the clerk de Staynburn, gave three acres of land here, and confirmed the thirty acres and common pasture for two hundred sheep, which Robert de Lelay had given before."

"The said William also gave certain lands, as described by the boundaries, with twelve acres and one rood of land, with six score sheep and their lambs, till the separation from their dams, and for twenty cows with their calves, till two years of age, and for ten oxen, together with estovers for firing and building, out of Staynburn Wood. He likewise gave land in Lavel-rode, towards the north of this land. He likewise gave one messuage here, with pasture for one hundred sheep, and common pasture of the same village, with all that he had on the west of the land of Robert de Lelay, and all his meadow about Eskelde."

"Alan, son of Alan de Weston, gave one messuage and a croft here, which William, son of William, son of Thore, had given him."

"William, son of William de Staynburn, gave one messuage and a croft, called Hesse Croft, and confirmed the grant of Alan de Weston."

"Jeremias, son of William, the clerk of Stayneburne, gave two carucates (or oxgangs) of land here, and confirmed what his father had given."

"Nigel de Plumpton gave five acres and one rood of land, which William, the clerk, confirmed."

"Adam, son of William, son of Mildred, gave one oxgang of land here, with a toft and croft, which Helias, son of Knute de Staynburn, confirmed."

"Adam, son of William de Staynburn, gave one oxgang of land here, with a toft, and croft, and meadow, in Thruskew."

"Robert, son of Uckeman de Plumpton, gave one oxgang of land here, with a toft and croft."

"Robert, son of Ranulph de Monketon, confirmed what Isouda, relict of Roger de Peyteven had given, and Helewise, his relict, confirmed the same."

"Helias, son of Knute de Staynburn, gave one oxgang, containing eight acres, with half an acre of meadow and waste ground, for one hundred sheep, eight oxen, and sixteen cows, with their calves of one year old, and one bull. He likewise gave his meadow ground, with all his land in Lincroft-ker, in Savel-rooker, with all his land called Wranglands, and three acres on the south of Buggerodes; and confirmed all that they held of his fee in Staynburn."

"Hagmeric, son of Gamel de Castelay, gave three acres here, which Alice, his relict, confirmed."

"Hugh, son of Fromard, gave a toft and a croft, and one acre and a half in Westcroft, and one acre and a half in Landpot, with the meadow adjoining, and one acre and a half in Clyveland, and one acre of the east end of Milnebeck, and a toft here. He also gave half an acre of meadow near the head of Savile-rode, towards the west, with one acre and one half abutting upon Stainburnbec, and half an acre in Spitelwath."

"Helias de Castlay, in A.D. 1267, quit-claimed all his right in Buggerode."

"Henry de Braithirne gave all his land here, which Agnes, daughter of Elin, sister of Henry Braithirne, confirmed."

"Isabel de Fortibus, Countess of Albemarle and Devonshire and Lady de Lisle, confirmed to them this village, with a moiety of Rigton, and one toft and one oxgang in Huby, of the fee of Harewood."

"King Edward confirmed the same, as did John, son and heir of Sir Robert de Lisle, Knight, Lord of Harewood."

In 1284, the Abbot of Fountains held the village of Stainburn, and a mediety of that of Rigton, for the fourth part and the half of a knight's fee of the Countess of Albemarle, and the same countess of the king, *in capite.*[*]

In the enumeration of the knights' fees, 31st Edward I., Stainburn is entered at four carucates, of the fee of Baldwin de Insula, where twelve carucates make a knight's fee, then held by the Abbot of Fountains.[†]

In *Nomina Villarum* (1815), the Abbot of Fountains is returned as lord of the manor of Stayneburn.

On the dissolution of the monastery of Fountains (1539) Stainburn was valued at £24 10s. 4d. per annum. At that time Ralph Lealome was bailiff, and his annual fee was 88s. 4d.

Afterwards the estate became part of the possessions of the Palmes, of Lindley. Ayscough Fawkes, Esq., of Farnley, is the present owner.

There is no village of the name of Stainburn; the houses being scattered nearly all over the township, but more particularly grouped in small clusters, near the road which winds its devious way from east to west.

The Norman Chapel and surrounding burial ground are situate in the fields, at some distance from any dwelling—

[*] "Kirkby's Inquest," p. 45. "Surtees' Soc., 1866."
[†] "Knights' Fees in Yorks." p. 204. "Surtees' Soc."

venerable, quiet, and lonely. The building is of the most
primitive kind; simple in form, and of rude masonry; composed
for the most part of stones which may have been gathered from
the neighbouring fields. It consists of a nave and chancel, with
a bell turret at their junction, pierced for two bells (now
only one), which has rather a singular appearance, as they are
generally placed at the west end of the nave. Two windows in
the south wall, about six inches wide, with circular heads
and deeply splayed insides, are of the same age as the building;
the others are modern insertions. The east window of the
chancel is of three lights, in the perpendicular style. At some
period the roof of the chancel has been of a higher pitch, as may
be seen in the dripstone of the bell turret. It is not improbable
that what is now the chancel at one time constituted the whole
church, and that the nave was erected some short time
afterwards. The windows are all filled with plain glass.

The arch between the nave and chancel is circular, and
without any kind of ornament.

In the chancel, within the altar rails, are two tombstones, one
with an inscription—"In memory of Thomas Weston, gentleman, born at Bilton, in the Ainsty of York; he died October the
3rd, in the year 1774, aged 85." On the other are inscriptions
(partly obliterated)—"In memory of John Robinson, of Castley,
in the parish of Leathley, who died Sept. 29th, 1810. Also of
Christopher Ramshaw, of Castley, eldest son of the Rev.
Christopher Ramshaw, and grandson of the above named John
Robinson, who died the 12th of January, 1817, aged 27. Also
of Hannah, wife of the above John Robinson, who died,
universally lamented, Dec. 11th, 1822, in the 92nd year of
her age."

Against the north wall of the chancel are marble tablets—
"Sacred to the memory of Jane, the wife of Daniel Foster,

of Otley, who died December 12th, 1809, aged 48 years;" and
"Ann Ramshaw, in whom were united the affectionate wife, the
tender parent, the good christian. She died lamented January
16th, 1798, aged 83."

Against the wall at the east end of the chancel is a tablet in
memory of Thomas Hutton, who was born at Stainburn, June
22nd, 1780. For upwards of sixty years he was a resident
of Newgate Street, in the city of London. He died at Balham
Hall, in the county of Surrey, 2nd of September, 1859, and was
interred in the cemetery at Norwood, in the same county.

The most interesting object in the church is the font, which
may be upwards of six hundred years old, or as old as any part
of the fabric in which it is sheltered. It is of a cylindrical form,
two feet seven inches in height. The upper half is ornamented
with an arcade of interlacing arches, and the upper edge around
the basin has a bead moulding worked in it. The bowl, lined
with lead, is about two feet in diameter. The cover is a rude
primitive oaken lid.

Many of the seats are plain oaken benches, with square ends,
and a narrow bar at the back; simple as they possibly can be.

Nearly in the centre of the churchyard, on the south side
of the church, is a block of gritstone about two feet square, into
the top of which is cut a cavity, fourteen inches square by eight
inches deep, as though it had been intended to receive the base
of a cross; tradition, however, declares that it was used as
a font in very early times.

Near this, on a slab of coarse gritstone forming the top of an
altar tomb, is cut lengthwise, in letters four inches high—
"Here lyeth the body of John Lynly, son of John Lynly,
of Snowden, 1686."

On another tomb of the same kind is inscribed—"Here lyeth
the body of Mary Bradley, 1686." Part of the inscription

on another altar tomb adjoining the last is, "Here lies Bryan Hodgson, 1686."

Very rarely do we find tombs in exposed situations so old as these.

A very small upright stone near the porch bears "A. A. D., aged 78, 1778." Obscure, but brief.

On the 1st of February, 1862, when the plague was ravaging the country, and people were afraid of contagion when crowded into buildings, the Archbishop of York granted a license to the inhabitants of Stainburn, to have service in the cemetery of their chapel during the continuance of the pestilence.*

The living is a curacy, in the gift of the rector of Kirkby Overblow, valued in 1536 as worth only £4 per annum, and that as a pension paid by the rector.

In the report of the Parliamentary Commissioners, made during the Commonwealth, it was recommended to be made a distinct parish; at which time the curate was allowed £20 per annum.

In 1775, it was augmented with £200 by lot; and in 1778 with £200, to meet a benefaction of a rent-charge of £12 per annum from the Rev. Charles Cooper, D.D.; and again in 1826 with £400 by lot. The present yearly value is about £66.

The charities are a rent-charge of £3 per annum, left by the will of Francis Dunwell, in 1729, to be distributed amongst the poor not receiving relief from the parish; and the interest of £3, left by the same donor.

An infant school, with teacher's house attached, in the Elizabethan style, was built in 1862, at the cost of Mr. Fawkes, a short distance below the church in one of the warmest spots in the township.

* "Raine's Fasti Ebor.," p. 461.

The Wesleyan Methodists have a small chapel here, built in 1836.

In Burscough Rig, on the eastern verge of this township, we have the Norwegian *hoe*. Here is also a large farmstead on the highest cultivated ground in the district (748 feet), close to the turnpike road leading from Harrogate to Otley. The trees which have been planted here for shelter, unmistakably tell us that the sycamore is the best adapted for that purpose in high lying situations.*

Near the northern boundary of this township is situate the rocky mount of Little Almes Cliff, the summit of which is 887 feet above the level of the sea, and from its situation commands a wide extent of country. The top of the main rock bears the rock basins and channels, which point it out as having been a carn or fire station in the Druidic day; there are also two pyramidal rocks, with indented and fluted summits, on the western side of the large rock. A beacon was also erected here in the year 1808, when the first Bonaparte threatened to invade England.

The township contains 2,910 acres of land, widely varying in quality; and was assessed to income tax in 1858 at £2,605. The population is about 300.

---

* A tragic event is connected with this place.—On the evening of January 25th, 1846, a young man named John Brotherton, of Beckwith-shaw, who for some time had courted a young woman who resided here as housekeeper to the farmer (who at that time was named Nathan Atkinson), goaded by the jests of his companions, who told him that he durst not go that night, went to the house sometime after its inmates had retired to rest, and, in an attempt to rouse his sweetheart, roused the farmer, who, suspecting that the noise proceeded from robbers attempting to break into the house, seized his loaded gun, and having called aloud and received no answer, fired; the whole charge struck the unfortunate youth, who managed to drag himself into a field about one hundred yards from the house, where he was found next morning quite dead.

LINDLEY.

As a small portion of the township of Lindley is situate within the bounds of the Forest of Knaresborough, it would be improper to omit all mention of it; yet we know very little of its early history, as it is not mentioned in Domesday, or in any of the ordinary sources of local history. Amongst its early owners was a family to which it gave a name, that of "Lindele, of Lindele." In the year 1240, the Archbishop of York granted to Falcon de Wakefield the marriage of William de Lindley, son and heir of William de Lindley, and that he should, when of the proper age, marry Alice, daughter of the said Falcon.

This marriage probably took place, and a son named Falcasius de Lindley was the issue thereof, as on July 18th, 1300, "Falkasius de Lyndeley" did homage and fealty to the Archbishop of York for possessions in Lindley, which were held by suit of court, and an annual rent of 18s. 2d.

Nov. 24th, 1818. "Faucus de Lyndelay" again made homage and fealty to the archbishop for possessions in Lindley, which answered for the sixteenth part of a knight's fee, held by the payment of the yearly rent of 18s., and suit of court at Ripon.*

In an enumeration of the knights' fees belonging to the Archbishop of York, made some time between the years 1266

* "Homages and Fealty." "Surtees' Soc.," p. 413.

and 1279, it is stated that Falcasius de Lyndeley held in Lyndeley two carucates of land by suit of court, and a rent of 18*s.* 2*d.* per annum.*

This Faucus de Lyndeley was probably progenitor of the family of Fawkes, of Farnley.

For a long time the hall was the abode of the ancient and honourable family of Palmes. A tombstone in Otley church gives their lineage for sixteen generations. It is only a skeleton, giving the heirs male and their intermarriages, beginning (*sans* date) with

```
William de Palma....with Waterton.
Nicholas............with Fitzhenry.
William ............with Mauleverer.
Nigelus ............with Russells ............1297.
William ............with Hammerton..........1300.
Nicholas...........with Moody..............1332.
William............with Charlton.
Brian .............with Plumpton.
Francis............with Dalbeny ............1393.
Thomas ............with Pykering...........1419.
William ... .......with Rockliffe ...........1454.
William ............with Hellerton.
Guy................with the heiress of Drew ...1516.
Bryan........with Mabella, heiress of Lindley ...1529.
Francis........ .....with Corbett ............1567.
Francis........with the heiress of Hadnall......1593.
```

Here the pedigree on the monument ends, with the figure of a man reposing on a couch, a ruff around his neck, a sword by his side, and his hands in the attitude of prayer. Beneath are half-a-dozen Latin verses,† signifying—

"Many of the race of Lindley have been laid within this temple, to the last of whom that of Palmes was twice joined.

* "Knights' Fees." "Surtees' Soc.," p. 389.
  † "Plurima Lindlorum templo conduntur in isto,
  Ultima Palmsorum corpora bina jacent.
  Gloria certa viri non est, sunt omnia vana
  Nec faciunt clarum stemmata clara virum.
  Hoc virtutis opus: justus ceu Palma verebit
  Nam dotes animi nulla sepulchra tegunt."

The glory of man is uncertain, nor can ancestry confer nobility. Virtue alone is true riches, and the just and gifted soul shall flourish like a *Palm-tree*, which no sepulchre can hide."

William Palmes, eleventh on the above line, married Ellen, daughter of Sir Guy Roucliffe, of Cowthorpe, recorder of York, and sister to Sir Brian Roucliffe, a baron of the Exchequer, whose second son,

Guy Palmes, Esq., was called sergeant-at-law Nov. 1st, 1504, made king's sergeant, May 9th, 1514, and died in 1516. He married Jane, daughter and heiress of John Drew, Esq., of Bristow, by whom he had issue—Brian, his eldest son and successor; John and Leonard, who both died unmarried; and Jane, the first wife of Sir Nicholas Fairfax, Knight, of Walton and Gilling.

Brian Palmes, Esq., of Farnley, in the parish of Otley, married Isabel, daughter and co-heir of Thomas Lindley, Esq., of Lindley, by whom he had issue—Francis, eldest son and successor; Leonard and Thomas, living in 1567, who both died unmarried; Maud, wife of Thomas Beckwith, Esq., of Clint, who died in 1575; and Jane, wife of William Catterall, Esq., of Rathmell, in Craven. By his will, dated October 2nd, 1528, and proved April 14th, 1529, Brian Palmes desires "to be beried in oᵣ Ladie where of the churche of Otteley dedicate to the honoᵣ of Alhallows, if I decesse there, in the parishe. A stone to be laide opon me, and an ymage of the Nativitie of oᵣ Ladie set opon the same, and an ymage of myself maide kneling under hir." To the chapel at Farnley he bequeaths 8*s.* 4*d.* After his decease his widow married (by license dated Jan. 12th, 1528 or '29) Sir Thomas Johnson, of Lindley, Knight, whom she survived eight years. By her will, dated April 1st, 1550 (proved April 16th, 1551), she desires to be buried at Otley; mentions her sons, Francis Palmes, Henry

Johnson, Thomas Palmes, and Arthur Johnson; and her daughters, Maude Beckwith, Jane Catterall, Margaret Johnson, and Frances Johnson; and her cousin, George Palmes, Archdeacon of York, whom she appoints supervisor of her will.

Francis Palmes, Esq., sometimes called a knight, married Margaret, daughter of Roger Corbet, Esq., of Morton, county Salop, by whom he had issue—Francis; and Elizabeth, or Isabel, wife of John Acclom, Esq., of Moreby. On his decease, in 1567, he was succeeded by his eldest son,

Francis Palmes, Esq., of Lindley, who was a justice of peace for the West Riding, and member of Parliament for the borough of Knaresborough, from 1586 to 1588, and died in 1593. He married Mary, daughter and co-heir of Stephen Hadnall, Esq., by whom he had issue—Guy, his successor; Thomas, William, Brian, and Andrew, who all died unmarried; Margaret, wife of Edward Nevile, Esq.; Ellen, wife of Edmund Griffin, Esq., of Waterley, county Northampton; and Ann, Jane, and Mary, who all died unmarried.

Sir Guy Palmes, of Lindley, Knight, was a justice of peace and high sheriff of the county of York in 1628. He married a daughter of Sir Edward Stafford, Knight, by whom he had issue—Brian, his successor; Stafford, William, and Francis, who died unmarried; Elizabeth, wife of William Leake, Esq., of Newark; Douglas, wife of John Vaughan, Esq.; Mary, wife of William Mallory, Esq.; and Anne, wife of Sir Thomas Browne, Bart., afterwards of Robert Sutton, Lord Lexington.

Sir Brian Palmes, Knight, of Lindley, married Mary, eldest daughter and co-heir of Gervase Tevery, Esq., of Stapleford, county Notts, by whom he had issue—William, his successor; Tevery, who died unmarried; Francis, Elizabeth, Mary, Anne, and Katherine.

William Palmes, of Lindley, Esq., lord of the manors of
Old and New Malton *(jure uxoris)*, which he eventually sold
to Sir Thomas Wentworth, married Lady Mary Eure, daughter
and co-heir of William, sixth Lord Eure, by whom he had
issue—Guy, who died in 1669, in infancy; Francis, who
died without issue in 1698; William, who married Elizabeth
Watson, and died without leaving issue in 1732; another Guy,
who also died without leaving issue; Maria and Katherine,
who died in infancy; Margaret, who died.unmarried in 1734;
and Elizabeth, eventually sole heiress, who married, in 1684,
Sir William Strickland, Bart., of Boynton, and died in 1740.

In the year 1702, Ralph Thoresby, the antiquary of Leeds,
stood upon the mount, called the Chevin, which overlooks Otley
and the valley of the Wharfe, "he saw the land that it was
good," as many others have done from the same point before his
time, and since. They viewed, and perhaps admired only—he
viewed, admired, and made a note of what he saw; and we
transcribe so much of his note as relates to our district and
its immediate neighbourhood.

"Between Farnley and Leathley, Washburn falls into
Wharfe. Leathley is the seat of Mr. Hitch, whose grandfather
was Dean of York; Lindley, of the noted member of Parliament,
William Palmes, Esq., my father's special friend, and yet
living in the south, to whom also appertains Stainburn. The
next thing in view are the two famous crags of Almes Cliff—
in some old writings called Aylmoys, *ut dicitur*—but have
seen nothing memorable of it saving its remarkable lofty
situation. Rigton, the possession of the Duchess of Buckingham, but in reversion my Lord Fairfaxe's."

The glory of the family of Palmes of Lindley has departed,
their names are remembered in Wharfedale tradition, but the
genealogist and biographer have not been busy with their

actions; their lands have passed into the hands of others, and the halls in which they so long dwelt have gone to decay. The site, and part of the fabric yet remain, and a more pleasant spot was never chosen by man on which to rear his dwelling. Though not deserving the name of a mountain, it is a piece of elevated ground on the northern side of Wharfedale, overlooking and commanding the country around; on the right, immediately adjoining, are the woods of Lindley and Farnley, clothing the sides of the valley of the Washburn; more distant are the hills, Beamsley Beacon and Rumbald's Moor, and a long stretch of the southern slope of Wharfedale, including Ilkley, the ancient Olicana, and its splendid modern hydropathic establishments. Immediately in front are Farnley and Leathley, with the confluence of the rivers Washburn and Wharfe; the town of Otley, with the long range of the Chiven, and the southern slope of the valley, finely varied with villas, fields, and farms; over Bramhope, to the wooded slopes of Harewood Park, and far beyond. Towards the east the view is only interrupted by the Wolds, the Howardian, and Hambleton hills, which rear their blue summits at an immense distance; to the north rises the ridge which bears the picturesque piles of rock named Little Almes Cliff and Fox Crag. Standing in front of the old hall, we look over some of the finest scenery in Wharfedale—perhaps in England—rendered illustrious by the homes, names, and actions of Middleton, Fairfax, Fawkes, and a host of worthies besides.

Only one wing of the old hall remains, now used as kitchen and granary. It is two stories in height; the lower presents only two windows, of five lights each, the heads circular; the upper has been far better lighted, as in the same space there has been six square windows, each of two lights, divided by a transom. The masonry is good—the stones being large, and

x

carefully dressed. There has been no entrance into this wing from the south; indeed it is evident that the entrance has been from an open court at the back, as may be easily seen from the remains of walls and gateways. A large portion was pulled down, and part of it rebuilt in a similar style as a farm-house, in 1852. Some of the gardens yet remain, surrounded by lofty walls. The barns and stables are of considerable antiquity, and with the hall, gardens, and other appurtenances, have been enclosed with a strong and high wall, enclosing an area of a square form, with something like projecting round towers at the angles; the entrance into which has been on the eastern side, through a lofty gateway, the pillars of which yet remain. The arrangement of the buildings, the strong enclosing wall, and the situation, all indicate that the builder had an eye to the defensive, as well as the picturesque.

The population of Lindley, in 1801, was 164; in 1831, 125; in 1851, 135; and in 1861, 108. The area is 1,789 acres, of almost every variety of land. On the side of the Washburn are some large woods of fine timber. The annual value as assessed to the county rate, in 1849, was £971; and in 1859, £1,219. The annual value of property assessed to income tax, in 1858, was £1,882.

HAVERAH PARK.*

THIS was formerly one of the royal parks of the Forest of
Knaresborough, and is now an extra parochial district, situate
about two miles to the west of Harrogate. At what time it
was first enclosed we have no direct information. Along with
the Honour of Knaresborough, it was granted by King Henry II.
to William de Stutevill, in the year 1177, who appears to have
dispossessed the men of Killinghall of a right of pasture which
they claimed therein; which seems to indicate that the park

* The name is probably derived from *Haie*, a hedge or enclosure,
and *wra* or *roe*, the roebuck—that is, the park or enclosure of the
roebuck. If this etymology be not satisfactory, we give a more popular
one, well known to the dwellers in the park, and which they learned from
their *fore-elders*, as follows—When John of Gaunt was lord of the
Forest of Knaresborough, a cripple, borne on crutches, of the name
of *Haverah*, petitioned the kind-hearted prince to give him a piece
of land, from which he might contrive to obtain a subsistence, who
at once granted his request in the following charter-like terms—

"I, John o' Gaunt,
Do give and do grant
To thee Haverah,
As much of my ground
As thou canst hop round
On a long summer day."

The stout-hearted cripple selected the longest day in the year (St.
Barnabas) for his exploit, commencing with sunrise, and keeping hopping
all day until evening, when just as the sun was setting, he had completed
the circuit of the park within such a short distance, that he threw
his crutches over the intervening space, to the point whence he had
started, and by so doing gained the land, which ever since has borne
his name. The spelling varies considerably, sometimes we find it—
Hawra, Haywras, Hayra, Hayrah, Awerray, Arerah, Avria, and many
others.

at that time was of recent formation. On their complaint, or petition, King Henry III. issued a mandate, dated December 3rd, 1227, to the Archbishop of Canterbury, commanding him, by good and lawful men of the soke of Knaresborough and Boroughbridge, who may best know, and are willing to speak the truth, to diligently enquire if William de Stutevill dispossessed the men of Killinghall of his own will, and whether the said pasture was in his lordship; and also whether the aforesaid men ought to have pasture therein. And, if it appear that the said William dispossessed these men solely of his own will, and that the said men have right of pasture therein, then he is to make seizure of the aforesaid pasture, for the above named men.*

We infer from the above that the park was formed by William de Stutevill, soon after his acquisition of the honour, and that a part of the land he enclosed had been previously grazed over by the cattle of the men of Killinghall—the common of which adjoined it on the north and east; and it was only when the star of the Stutevills had declined almost to its setting, that the deprived herdsmen petitioned for relief, which it is evident they did not obtain.

During the reign of Edward III., this park is frequently mentioned in royal grants and patents. At that time this, and the other parks belonging to the forest, were set apart for the purpose of breeding and grazing horses for the king's use, and a nobleman was appointed supervisor of the same.

In 1333, the king issued a mandate to the sheriff of Yorkshire, commanding him to repair the hedges, ditches, and pales of the parks in the Forest of Knaresborough, which were broken in such manner that the king's horses escaped therefrom, and were lost.†

* "Close Roll," 12 Hen. III.
† "Rot. Orig.," 8 E.1. III.

In the following year William de Nusom was appointed keeper
of the king's horses beyond Trent, and especial mention is made
of those in the parks of Haywray, Bilton, and Hay. Soon
afterwards Edmund de Thedmersh was appointed his colleague.

In 1342, the king appointed his valet, Roger de Normanvill,
custodian of the "*equoi, jumentui, pullanui,* and *equicii*" of his
majesty in the aforesaid parks.

In 1849, John de Barton received the like appointment,
with an allowance of ten marks per annum for his services.

In 1357, Thomas del Bothe was appointed to the same
office, in place of Roger de Normanvill. In 1359, the conqueror
of Cressy issued a mandate to John de Barton and Thomas del
Bothe, commanding them to select ten of the best draught
horses *(jumentui)* in the parks of Haywra and Bilton, by the
testimony of Henry de Ingilby and Richard de Ravensere, and
sell the same, and forward the money to William de Wykeham,
supervisor of the king's works at the castle of Windsor, to
be expended on the said works. In the following year is a roll
or receipt stating that the same has been done.*

In 1371, Haywra, along with the Honour of Knaresborough,
was granted by the king to his fourth son, John, Duke of
Lancaster; and long continued an appanage of that duchy, to
which it yet nominally belongs.

The park now appears to have been devoted more to the
grazing of deer than horses, as in 1489, when Sir William
Plumpton was seneschal and master forester of the Honour
and Forest of Knaresborough, there were one hundred and
sixty head of wild deer in the park, which had been viewed
by Thomas Beckwith, Ralph Beckwith, John Beckwith, and
others. Thomas de Thorp and Thomas Brigg at that time were
the park keepers.

* From " Rot. Originalium," temp. Ed. III.

In 1490, David Griffith, one of the council of Thomas, Earl
of Derby, held this park, and sub-let the same to Sir Robert
Plumpton, for a yearly rent of £8; and the same David Griffith
certified, October 5th, 1490, that he received of Gefferay
Townley, servant to Sir Robert Plumpton, £9, for his fee of
"Hawwarrey Park."

On the 26th of August, 1490, a lease was made between
David-app-Griffith of the one party, and Sir Robert Plumpton
of the other, whereby the office of keeper of the park of
Haverey, with the herbage, pannage, &c., were granted for
a term of six years to the latter, at a rent of £8, yearly, to
commence from Lady-day next coming; Sir Richard Langton,
and Sir John Langton, clerk, being sureties in £20, for the
performance of the covenants on the part of the said Sir
Robert Plumpton.

Some time previous to the year 1490, the park had been
held by Sir Randolph Pigot, of Clotherholme, near Ripon, as
he says in that year, in a letter addressed to Sir Robert
Plumpton, "I payd my palassis of Averey Park, during the
time I occupied xxx⁵ discharging one of the palas to the King's
Grace."*

In 1551 (6th Edward VI.), Thomas Skayffe was keeper of
Haverah Park, and the fortress therein, and was plaintiff in
a suit in the duchy court against Henry Atkinson and others
for trespass and breach of fences, in Haverah Park and Rigton.

In the 7th Elizabeth (1564), William Fleetwood, sergeant
of the duchy, was plaintiff in a suit against Ellis Markham,
concerning "herbage and pannage, deer and game, destruction
of the trees, and building of cottages in Haverah Park."

During some part of the reign of Elizabeth the park appears
to have been divided, and held by at least two parties; as, in

* "Plumpton Correspondence," p. 98.

the year 1589, we find Roger Darnbrooke, in right of Jervis
Markham and William Knolles, plaintiff in a suit in the duchy
court against William Redshaw,* claiming a moiety, the east
part of Havray Park and goods and chattels therein.

All disputes respecting ownership came to an end in the reign
of King Charles II., for that monarch granted to Sir William
Ingilby, Bart., of Ripley Castle, the whole of the park, with
all the rights thereto belonging; and since that time it has
been held uninterruptedly by the same family—Sir Henry John
Ingilby, Bart., being the present owner.

The park is of an oval form, the longer axis being about two
and three-quarters miles in length, and the shorter about one
and a half miles, and comprises an area of 2,245 acres, divided
into thirteen farms; all the houses standing singly; these are
generally good; most of them modern, though one or two
of them may probably have been built during the reign of the
second Charles.   There is no church, chapel, or place of public

* This family was long settled at Beckwithshaw, in the parish of
Pannal, adjoining Haverah Park on the south. Their names are of
frequent occurrence on the Court Rolls of the Forest of Knaresborough.

"May 24th, 1637. Probate of the will of William Redshaw, of Beckwithshaw, dated May 3rd, 1636; whereby he declared that William
Broadbelt, of Beckwithshaw, and William Atkinson, of Rossett, their
heirs and assigns, should stand seized of one messuage builded, and
twenty-three acres and two pennyworth of land, situate in the hamlet
of Beckwith-with-Rossett, and township of Killinghall, which he had
already surrendered to them, 'when it shall happen after my death,' until
William Redshaw, his eldest son, shall attain the age of twenty-one years,
then to surrender the premises to his said son, William, his heirs and
assigns for ever; and if his said son should die before attaining twenty-
one years, and leaving no lawful issue to, Thomas Redshaw, testator's
youngest son—then unto Grace Redshaw, testator's daughter."

"June 21st, 1654. William Redshaw, of Beckwithshaw, surrendered
one ancient building, and seven closes of land, called Two Moore Closes,
Parsacre Close, Stripe, Great New Moors, Little New Moors, and Geld
Pit, containing seven acres, in the hamlet of Beckwith-with Rossett—to the
use of Jane Leeming for life, &c."

"1613. Grace, daughter of William Redshaw, de Shawe, baptized
the 2nd day of May."—*Pannal Reg*.

worship within the district; some of the inhabitants bury their
dead at Hampsthwaite; some at Pannal; either place being
four miles distant. No line of public road passes through this
secluded domain, but the cartway—deep and dirty—winds
through it from farmstead to farmstead; and even this and the
few footpaths, which necessity or convenience have made across
it, are guarded, so that no stranger can enter without stating
who he is, where he is going, and what he intends to do; and if
the answers are not satisfactory, he is unceremoniously turned
back. The motives for such conduct we cannot divine, unless it
be to preserve the primitive virtues of the inhabitants from
contamination by contact with the outward world.

A shallow valley, running nearly east and west, divides it into
two parts, down which a rivulet flows, bearing the name of
Oakbeck, which rises at the top, and receives continual
accessions as it descends from runnels on either side. The
native woods yet cling to the sides of the valley; and here and
there may be seen a few oaks—aged and time-worn, remnants of
the original forest. The other trees are hazel, birch, and alder;
the ash is not abundant; the holly and white thorn are in
profusion, and often form magnificent masses. In some places,
near the sides of the brook, the woods are a tangled brake—wild
as when the roebuck roamed the dell, and the shaft of the roving
outlaw struck the royal deer, on the sides of the valley. Two
large patches of woodland, partly artificial, on the southern side
of the brook, bear the names of High and Low Boarholes, from
being the traditional haunts of that animal.* A long, narrow

* The following legend is connected with one of these places—"Once
a king of England was hunting in the Forest of Knaresborough, and, being
separated from his retinue, was attacked in this dell by an old wild
boar, which said boar paid so little regard to majesty that it snatched
the weapon from the royal hand, and appeared fully disposed to follow
up the advantage gained, by ending the fight and the king's reign at
the same time. A knight of the name of Ingleby, from Ripley, coming

plantation of firs runs outside the northern boundary of the park, and in some measure shelters it from the north and east winds.

Close to the most westerly farm-house, and very near the boundary of the park, are the very slender remains of the ancient peel or tower, called John o' Gaunt's Castle. When and by whom built we cannot state with certainty, though it is very probable that it was erected during the latter part of the reign of Edward I. King Edward II., in the seventeenth year of his reign (A.D. 1823), abode here for some days. From an itinerary of his, given in the first volume of the *Collectanea Archæoligica*, it appears that he was at Kirkby Malzeard from the 20th to the 22nd of September; at Haura and Rammesgill on the 23rd; at Bewerle, in Nidderdale, and Dacre on the 24th; at *Haywra* on the 25th and 26th; and at Skergill and *Hawray* on the 27th; all in the same year. If the castlet was not built at that time, where was the king lodged?

This royal visit is also mentioned by Mr. Hunter, in his tract on Robin Hood, who endeavours to identify with this progress that famous hero of the green wood, from which it is made to appear that he had been exercising his woodcraft upon the royal deer in this forest. Remote, lonely, and insignificant as the place now appears, we can truly say, when standing on its ruins and looking on the landscape around, that King Edward more than five hundred years ago gazed upon the same hills and valleys as we do now—standing on the same ground on which we now stand.

The earliest document in which we have seen this fortlet mentioned is in 1334, when King Edward III. gave the

to the rescue, made an attack upon the boar in flank, with such vigour and success, that he quickly stretched the would-be regicide dead on the ground; and as a reward for this very important service, the king gave to the Ingleby and his heirs the lands of Haverah Park for ever."

superintendence of the *fortalicii Regis Heywra*, and the works
then carrying on there, to Edmund de Thedmersh, for which
service he was to receive the sum of ten marks annually. He
appears to have been custodian until 1349, when the same king
committed the care of the said fortalice to John de Barton,
who had a like salary of ten marks yearly; he had also the care
of the king's horses, bred and grazed in the parks north of
Trent.

When complete, the castle has evidently been nothing more
or less than a forest lodge, for the residence of the park-keeper
and his assistant forest rangers; strong enough to repel the
attacks of any band of freebooters, or outlaws, which might
harbour in the forest, but of no importance whatever in a
military point of view.

The site is of a square form, surrounded by a moat, some
parts of which yet contain water; the north and southern sides
of the area within the moat, are about forty yards in length; the
west side thirty-three, and the east thirty-seven yards. The
building has not occupied the whole of this inner area, but
has stood about ten feet from the sides. Nothing but the
foundations are left, with the exception of a fragment on the
southern side, which has apparently projected from the main
wall, and formed the entrance or gateway; this piece is of
a square form, about six yards in length by three in breadth,
and in one part about five yards in height. The masonry
is of the commonest kind; the stones being such as are found in
the neighbourhood—untouched by the chisel, except near the
sides of doorways and windows, or rather loopholes. In the
centre of the area is a circular depression, where the well
has been for supplying the garrison with water. The situation
is high and commanding—overlooking the country east, west,
and north, to a considerable distance; towards the south the

ground quickly rises to above the level of the castle, so that it had no advantage for defence on that side. No relics of importance have been found on digging about the foundations. The popular story is that the castle was battered down by the cannon of Oliver Cromwell, from near a farm-house on the northern side of the valley—which needs no confutation. The narrow valley below, on the northern side, at some period has been formed into a pond of considerable size, by throwing a dam across it; portions of which yet remain. It has evidently always been of a marshy nature, and impracticable as a road for any purpose whatever. A hollow place below the dam bears the name of Beaverholes, and the stream which runs through it is called the Beaverdike. Was this place, in olden times, the haunt of the beaver, as well as the boar, as it is generally admitted that the beaver inhabited this island in Saxon times? The head of this valley forms the watershed: the streams to the eastward flow to the Nidd, while those on the west find their way into the Washburn.

Near the south-western extremity of the park, and about three-quarters of a mile southward of John o' Gaunt's Castle, is a large earthwork, or series of earthworks, called by the country people Pippin Castle, where, they say, was once a chapel and burial ground to John o' Gaunt's Castle. A burial place it has undoubtedly been, and that long before a stone was laid of the now ruined peel. It is situate on the western side of a narrow rugged valley, or rather at the junction of two shallow valleys, and consists of three large earthen mounds, adjoining each other. The largest of these is not remarkable for its height, nor the depth of the trench around it, and is probably a great deal of it the natural hill, assisted in the form and elevation by art; it is of an oval form, tapering to points at the longer axis, and measures eighty yards in that direction, by about forty yards, in the widest part, in another. The middle mound is very remarkable from the flat area on its summit, which does not appear to have ever been otherwise than as it is at present; it is also of an oval form, thirty yards across in one direction, by eighteen in the other; on the north side the ascent is composed of broken terraces, and fronts the valley; the trench around the other portion is at least fifteen feet deep, and upwards of ten wide, near the bottom, The smallest mound is close to the last—a barrow of the common conical form, about fifteen yards in diameter at the base, with a cup-like cavity in the centre of the top. The trench from which it has been thrown is equally deep with that of the last mentioned. A few stunted thorns grow upon the last, and gorse bushes on the others; the sides are pierced by the burrows of numerous rabbits, which rear their young within those ancient receptacles of the dead. How extraordinary it is to find such works of man in such a silent solitude as this! In this wild uncultured spot, where rarely at present a human being is seen, and where a human dwelling cannot be discerned nearer than at a mile's distance; at a period beyond the earliest records of our history, hundreds of anxious beings must have laboured in the formation of these mounds, and a numerous tribe must have resided in the neighbourhood, to render such funeral monuments necessary or possible; for we can say, without fear of successful contradiction, here are deposited

> "The patriarchs of the infant world,
> The powerful of the earth;
> Fair forms, and hoary seers of ages past,
> All in one mighty sepulchre."

On the opposite side of the valley to these tumuli, on a piece of rugged, uncultivated ground, the very remarkable phenomenon of an aerial army was witnessed on the 28th of

June, 1812, by Anthony Jackson and Martin Turner, two
farmers resident in the park, while attending to their cattle
on the evening of that day. They saw at some distance what
appeared to be a large body of armed men in white uniform;
in the centre of which was a person of commanding aspect,
dressed in scarlet. After performing various evolutions, the
whole body began to move forward in perfect order towards
the summit of the hill, passing the two terrified spectators
crouched among the heather at the distance of one hundred
yards. No sooner had this first body, which extended four
deep over an enclosure of thirty acres, attained the hill, than
a second body, far more numerous than the former, dressed
in a uniform of a dark colour, appeared and marched after the
first to the top of the hill, where they both joined, and passing
down the opposite slope, disappeared; when a column of thick
mist overspread the ground where they had been seen. The
time from the first appearance of this strange phenomenon to
the clearing away of the mist was about five minutes, as near
as the spectators could judge, though they were not in a "proper
mood of mind" for forming correct estimates of time or numbers.
They were men of undoubted veracity, and utterly incapable of
fabricating such a story. We never could learn that any similar
appearances, due to skyey influences, have been since seen on the
same ground. As this appearance took place during the Luddite
disturbances, might not a number of those men be practising
military evolutions amongst the West Riding hills, and their
forms, defined upon a body of cloud, again be mirrored here?
It is admitted on all hands that this class of phenomena are
produced by optical refraction and reflection.

On the southern side of this district, near the farm called
Haverah Park Lodge, is a reservoir belonging to the Harrogate
Waterworks Company, formed in 1866-7, covering about seven

acres, and capable of containing twenty millions of gallons.
The water is of excellent quality—being, as it were, filtered
through the millstone-grit rock. Almost close to this reservoir
is a fine group of rocks, among which are a Druidical idol and
altar, yet complete. These, taken in connection with the tumuli
at Pippin Castle, and the British dwellings called "The Bank,"
in Norwood, form an interesting study for the antiquary.

A festive meeting of the male population of the park takes
place at some one of the farm-houses once a year; when
a plenteous dinner is provided, and the appendages thereto are
all that the heart of a sturdy English yeoman can desire; for
the dwellers in the park generally are neither poor nor deficient
in hospitality. One peculiarity of this social gathering is, that
no ladies are permitted to partake of it—only one or two to
wait upon "those proud lords of creation" while they sit at
meat. This meeting, which bears the name of Haverah Park
Feast, generally takes place on the 25th of March; and probably
had its origin in some remote period when the park keepers
and foresters assembled together, and

> "Revelled as merrily and well
> As those that sat in lordly selle."

The population of this district is slightly on the increase:
in 1801, it was 71; in 1831, 96; and in 1861, 100. The
valuation to the income tax, in 1858, was £1,323; and to the
county rate, in 1866, £1,297.

KILLINGHALL.

KILLINGHALL* is a township in the parish of Ripley; bounded on the east and north by the river Nidd; on the west by Hampsthwaite; and on the south by Oakbeck, which divides it from Harrogate.

This place is very imperfectly described in the Domesday survey. Amongst the lands of the king, after the description of the manor of Burc, or Aldburgh, occurs—"To this manor belongs the soke of Chenehalle, one carucate."† Again, among the lands of the Archbishop of York, in the enumeration of the berewics belonging to the Leuga of St. Wilfrid of Ripon, we find "Kilingala," which certainly means this place. Afterwards, in the summary, we find the archbishop's portion stated to be one carucate. The whole of it subsequently formed part of the Forest of Knaresborough, and consequently always passed with that fee; and at present is divided among many owners.

This village was for a long time the seat of a branch of the ancient and respectable family of Pulleine,‡ the present

* Written at different times, *Chenihalle*, *Kelengala*, *Kellingholm*, *Kellingale*, *Kelinghalle*. Though many different derivations have been given, it is evidently a compound term, descriptive of the Saxon manor house, and its situation—the *hall* by the *keld*, or spring, in the *ing*, or meadow.

† "Bawdwen's Dom. Boc.," p. 16.

‡ This family, under the different spellings of Pulleyne, Pulane, Pullaine, Polleyne, Pullan, Pullen, &c., are a numerous race in and around the Forest of Knaresborough, and have been so from very early times.

representative of which is James Pulleine, Esq., of Crakehall
and Clifton Castle. The pedigree begins with Richard Pulleine,
of Killinghall,* who married Eleanor, daughter of John Rudd,
of the same place, and had a son,

John Pulleine, who was Recorder of York from 1533 to
1537.† He married Jane, daughter of Thomas Ros, of
Ingmanthorpe, by whom he had four sons and six daughters—
James, his heir.

Marmaduke, in holy orders, Rector of Ripley from 1552
to 1554, when he was deprived.

Richard and Thomas; both died unmarried.

---

* We suspect that "Dom. Joh. Pulleyne," vicar of Fewston from 1545 to
1583, and his successor Henry Pulleyne, who held the same vicarage from
1583 to 1591, were both of this family, though not mentioned in the
pedigree. In one of the windows of Newhall, in Little Timble, close
to Fewston, the crest of the family of Pulleyne, in stained glass, yet
remains.

† The following extract from the minutes of the Corporation of the city
of York, will show the importance of the recorder to the city, as well as in
his own estimation—

"31st Jany., 28 Hen. VIII. *Item*, it is agreyd that Mr. Pulleyn,
Recorder, shallbe sent for in all the haist posyble to come to this Citie, in
all haiste convenyint, to give his counsell in dyverse and especiall bisynes
concernying this said citie."

"Saturday, 10 Feby. (following). Md· ther was a letter sent unto Mr.
John Pulleyn, Recorder of this Citie, from my lorde Mayer and his
Brethren, that he shuld in any wyse com to this Citie in all the haist
convenyent, to gyve his counsell both as concernyng the late Eleccion of
two Aldermen of this Citie, and also for other thinges concernyng this said
Citie, orells they wold seke further counsell if that he can not. And
therrupon he sen a letter of his aunswer therin, the tenor whereof herafter
folowith—

'To my lorde Mayer of the Citie of Yorke.

My lorde Mayer, I recomend me unto you with knawlege that I have
resavyd yoᵣ letter, whereby ye wold have had me to be wᵗ you this
mornyng. My lorde, I dowt not ye have in yoᵣ remembrance that I was
wᵗ yoᵥ V. days laitlie, to my charge nee iiij nobles wᵗout recompence, and
ever sens my comyng home I myght not stond streyght up in my buke.
Therfore, seyng I am agyd and may not well labor, ye may at yoᵣ pleasor
taike suche counsell as will serve you to the worship of this Citie,
according to yoᵣ letter, in the name of God. At my power howse at
Kyllynghall, this present Fryday, in the mornyng. Yoᵣs, John Pulleyn.' "
—*R. H. Scaife.*

Cecilia, married to Thomas Swale, of South Stainley.

Agnes, married to George Tomlinson, of Birdforth.

Grace, married to Robert ——, of Ravencliff.

Maud, married to Marmaduke Coghill, of Knaresborough.

Isabella, married to Robert Gibson.

Ann, married to William Tankard, of Boroughbridge.*

James Pulleine, the eldest son, married, first, Frances, daughter† of Sir William Ingilby, Knight, of Ripley, by whom he had a son, John, and a daughter, Cecilia, who died unmarried. He married, secondly, about 1570, Frances, daughter of Walter Pulleine, of Scotton, by whom he had three daughters and four sons.

John Pulleine, eldest son and heir, married Agnes, daughter of William Vavasour, of Weston, Esq., by whom he had a son and successor—

John Pulleine, who married Isabella, daughter of Thomas Busfield, of Rishforth and Leeds, and had, with other issue, a son,

Thomas Pulleine, who was master of the stud to king William

† Recorder of York from July 9th, 1537, till his death in 1573. By his will he did "give and bequeth to the Maior and citysyns of the cyttie of Yorke, a silver pott, with a cover, double gilt." He was son of Hugh Tancred, of Boroughbridge, by Anne, daughter of John Slingsby, of Scriven.

† Thirty-six of Henry VIII. "Jacobus Pulleyne, de Kelinghall," surrendered, &c., the mediety of three messuages and six oxgangs of land, to the use of Frances Pulleyne, wife of the said James Pulleyne, pro termino vitæ suæ.

In the same year, John Palicer, clerk, Vicar of Kirkhamerton, surrendered one cottage, one orchard, and three acres of land, in Grafton, to the use of John Pulleyne, son and heir-apparent of James Pulleyne, Gent.

Thirty-seven of Henry VIII. June 10th, "Jacobus Pulleyne, de Kelinghall, et Francise, uxor ejus," surrendered, &c., a mediety of three messuages and six oxgangs of land, in the towns and fields of Grafton, then in the occupation of William Readman. to the use of "William Tancard, de Burghbrig Armigeri," his heirs and assigns, &c.—Court Rolls of Grafton-with-Grindale.

III., and high sheriff of Yorkshire, in 1697 and 1704.* This
gentleman purchased Carleton Hall, in Cleveland, to which he
removed, and the family residence at Killinghall, being deserted
and neglected, became ruinous. Hargrove, in his "History of
Knaresborough," says—"The mansion of the Pulleynes, with
some other stately buildings, formerly at this place, have been
suffered to decay, and out of their materials farm-houses and
their offices have been erected. Heaps of ruins covered with
grass mark the place where two of these mansions stood. A
porter's lodge is seen at the east end of a barn; the lower part
of which, being thirteen feet square, and having two arched
gateways, is now converted into a cowhouse, while the chamber
above, with an ornamental ceiling, serves the purpose of a
dovecote."

The ruins mentioned above have been cleared away, and a
neat modern villa, called "The Manor House," was erected on
the site by Mr. Cautley in 1857.

The arms of Pulleine are—*Azure*, on a bend, cotised, *argent*,
three escallops, *gules*, on a chief, *or*, three martlets of the field.

Crest—A pelican feeding its young.

Motto—*Nullá pallescere culpá.*

The family of Strother have been landowners and residents in
this village for some generations. The family is of considerable
antiquity, and was settled for several centuries in the county of
Northumberland. Sir Henry Strother, of Kirk Newton, in
Glendale, held the manor there in the reigns of Edward II. and
Edward III., and was Sheriff of Northumberland in the years

---

* "March 4, 1702. The Vicar (of Leeds) preached the funeral sermon
of old Mrs. Pullan, mother of the late high sheriff, who was born here,
and where his father is yet living, and can read without spectacles (which
he formerly used), though 92 years of age. *Poulain*, in French, signifies
a colt. And his son, Thomas Pullain, Esq., stud-master to his majesty,
rose from small beginnings to a great estate by horses."—*Thoresby's
Diary*, vol. i., p. 353.

1858 and 1859, and again in 1868, and for several years following. His sister Joan was married to John de Coupeland, the
celebrated Northumberland Esquire, who, at the battle of
Neville's Cross, Durham, fought October 17th, 1846, took David
Bruce, King of Scotland, prisoner; for which King Edward III.
created him Knight Banneret, and settled upon him and his
heirs £500 a-year.

Alan Strother, of Kirk Newton, was Sheriff of Northumber-
land in 1856 and 1857, and in the year 1864 he was appointed
Warden of the castle of Roxburgh, and Sheriff of the county of
Roxburgh, in the place of John de Coupeland, deceased.

William Strother, Esq., was M.P. for Newcastle-upon-Tyne,
in the year 1859.

The Manor of Kirk Newton was held by William Strother,
Esq., in the reign of King Edward VI., and by Mark Strother,
Esq., Sheriff of Northumberland, in the first year of the reign
of King George I.

John Strother, Esq., settled at Ripon in the seventeenth
century, and was Mayor of that town in 1681, and again in
1697. He was offered the honour of knighthood by King
Charles II., but declined it. He died in 1709, leaving four
sons and several daughters. Wilfrid, his eldest son, left issue.
Thomas, his second son, also left issue, from whom the present
family at Killinghall are descended. Thomas, his eldest son,
became the owner, by purchase, in 1738, of Killinghall Mills,
and, in 1740, of other property in that township. He settled
his Killinghall property upon his son John, who made it his
place of residence. John died in 1808, and was succeeded by
his second son Richard, who resided there until his death in
1834; since which time the Killinghall estate has been in the
family of William Strother, the brother of Richard, and his
descendants.

Thomas Strother, Esq., the son of William, became the owner, by purchase, of Westfield House, where he now resides ; and his son, William Strother, Esq., now occupies the old family residence.

The arms of Strother are—Gules, on a bend, *argent*, three eaglets, *azure*. Crest—An eagle. Motto—*Ad alta*.

In the beginning of the last century William Armytage, Esq., fourth son of Sir Francis Armytage, of Kirkless, Bart., resided at Killinghall. and married Elizabeth, daughter of Francis Trappes Byrnand, Esq., of Nidd.

The village is clean, well built, and respectable in appearance; the houses generally stand back from the street, and are mostly surrounded by gardens and orchards. The turnpike road from Harrogate to Ripon runs directly through it.*

Here is a school built by public subscription in 1857, in which occasional lectures are given by the rector of Ripley, or his curate.

The Wesleyan Methodists have a chapel here, erected in 1793.

Fragments of the village *Stocks*, and the base of an ancient cross, stood near the middle of the village, until a few years ago.

* "August 15th, 1663. Before John Tempest, Anthony Byerley, Samuel Davison, and Stephen Thompson, Esqrs., John Williamson, of Rawdon, clothier, saith, that himselfe, with his servant and daughter, were travailing from his house at Rawdon, on the 5th instant, towards Rippon, about his profession of a clothier; and that as he was going on Killingshall Moore they were overtaken by three persons, who did assault them, clapping a pistoll to his brest and bade him deliver his money, or he should dy for it. Whereupon he was forced to submitt to them, and one of them, who, as he now understands, calls himselfe John Smyth, who likewise clapt the pistoll to his brest, did search his pocketts, and took out 14s. and one penny. Another of the said persons did thereupon cutt the wametow and tooke off the pack cloaths which were upon a driven horse, and out of them tooke £40, which he gave to a person, who, as he understands, calls himselfe by the name of Thomas Lightfoot. The said Thomas Lightfoot did search the informant's daughter Sarah, in a very rude and uncevell fashion, and did take out of her pockett a letter box, wherein there was 1s. and threepence. It was about ten of the clocke in the fore- ١ oone."—*Depositions, &c from York Castle, Surtees Soc.* 1861.

Smith and Lightfoot were convicted at the York Assizes, and both executed.

Hazelcroft, on the eastern side of the village, is an elegant modern mansion in the Elizabethan style of architecture, built in 1857, the residence of Mrs. Elizabeth Lloyd, widow of the late George Lloyd, Esq., of Cowesby, near Thirsk.

About half a mile north of the village, the turnpike road crosses the river Nidd by a substantial bridge of stone. On the right of which are the Killinghall Mills, which were probably built about the year 1500, by Ralph, Lord Greystock, who held lands here, as well as in the adjoining parish of Nidd; as inquisition was made in that year of the amount of damage done by the building of a fulling mill on the water of Nidd, "vocat Nydd Walk Milnes in Kelynhall de Honore de Knaresburgh."* They have not been employed in the fulling of cloth for a very long time, but as corn and saw mills.

In the year 1715, these mills were sold by Ellen Burton, of Knaresborough, widow, and Elizabeth Burton, of Haton, spinster, to Edward Jackson, of Aberforth, miller.

In 1788, they were purchased from William Whitelock, of Leeds, gentleman, and others, by Thomas Strother, Esq., great-grandfather of Thomas Strother, Esq., the present owner.

Owing to the dam above the bridge, the river Nidd fills its wood-fringed bed, and has the appearance of a deep, quiet water; below, it runs rapidly between steep banks, with the millstone grit rock coming out prominently on the right, and a mass of yellow, marly, magnesian limestone on the left. Immediately on the north side is the Nidd Valley Railway, and the station for Ripley and Killinghall.

In Lund Lane, about a mile from the village, in a westerly direction, is an antique farm-house called Leavens' Hall, which is chiefly remarkable as having been at one time the residence of Captain John Leavens, who lived during the times of Charles I.,

* Cal. of Inquisitiones in Duchy of Lancaster.

the Commonwealth, and Charles II. He is said to have fought
on the side of the Parliament during the great civil war; but,
on becoming a convert to the tenets of George Fox, founder of
the Society of Friends, he retired to this place, and built the
house which yet bears his name. He appears to have been a
prominent leader among his party, and suffered much persecution during his life-time on that account. In 1661 he was committed to prison in York Castle for refusing the oath of allegiance.
In the following year he was again imprisoned, and tried at York
for a similar offence. During the short Protectorate of Richard
Cromwell, a petition was presented to him by "The Justices,
and others, well-principled inhabitants of Leeds, Wakefield, and
Bradford," against the people called Quakers, stating, among
other matters, that "there is now of late one John Leavens,
once a captain, who is now again, after his releasement, at the
head of this giddy party." What answer Richard made to this
we know not, but Leavens lived long after his short lease of
power was ended, and for some time during the licentious reign of
his successor. He died in 1688, and was buried in his own
orchard, by the side of two of his children. The tombstones
placed above the graves yet remain, massive slabs of coarse gritstone; that of the father, large as life, and one smaller, as of a
youth; the place of another is indicated by a pile of stones
which have belonged to it, but the cover is gone. Tradition
says these stones once bore inscriptions, but these are now completely worn out; yet some depressions across the middle of the
largest stone give credibility to the report.

The ground, though now used as a stackyard, has evidently
been a garden, as, by the sides of the fences are gooseberry
bushes run wild through want of culture; some fragments of
apple trees yet remain, and a large bush of the buckthorn, the
berries of which were formerly much used in medicine. The

house is probably of the same age ; the front windows have been modernized, but the back, adjoining the road, yet remains as it was built, with stone mullions dividing the windows into different lights.

Peaceful be the rest of the heroic John Leavens! May no rude hand disturb his ashes, nor remove the stone which covers his grave!

The following copy of his will throws more light upon the character of this extraordinary man, as well as shows his social standing among the yeomanry of the forest :—

" I, John Leavens, of Killinghall, in the Forest of Knaresbrough, Gentman, being sicke in body but in sound and perfecte remembrance, doth make and ordaine this my last Will and Testament in man^{r.} and forme following—that is to say—for all my personall estate I doe hereby give and bequeath the same to Grace, my now wife, shee discharging my just debts and funeral expences. And whereas I have, accordinge to the custome of the Forest of Knaresborough aforesaid surrendred one cap^{tall} messuage and tenement wherein I now live in Killinghall afore^{sde} and ten ackres, halfe an akre, one penniworth and halfe a peniworth of land to the same belonginge, bee they more or lesse. One other messuage called the Potthowle,* and eleaven acres of lande theirunto belonginge, and likewise one antient buildinge and eight acres of land theirto belonginge, called Ashwoods and Kardall† Farme, lyinge and beinge in Killinghall aforesaid, to the use and beehoofe of Henry Atkinson, of Rippan Parke, in the said county, Esq., John Stables, of Nostropp, George Watkinson, of Scotton, and Joshua Dawson, of Jackhowle, in the said county, Gent., and their heyrs, to such uses only as

* This was probably at Pott-bridge, near to the eastern boundary of Haverah Park.
† These places probably adjoined the last, Oakbeck only parting them.

shall be declaired in this my last will. Now, my minde and
will is, and I doe hereby request and give power to my said
feofies, with consent of my wife, that they, and the surviv^{rs} of
them, after my death, shall sell and dispose of all ye surrendred
premises with the appurtenances and every part of them, for the
resynge and payinge of fower hundred pounds of lawfull moneye
to Emanuel, Roger, Pheby, and Grace Leavens, my younger
sons and daughters, and the remainder of the monye which
shall be given for the purchase of the said lands, I do hereby
give unto Grace, my said wife. And my further will and minde
is, if either of my sonns or daughters shall happen to dye before
they accomplish the age of one and twentye yeares, that then
such parte (to wit, one hundred pounds not beinge paid and discharged), an p'portion shalbe given and paid to John Stables
abovesaid ; and in case any oth^r of them shall happen to dye as
aforesaid, then such parte and p'portion as did belonge unto any
of them deceased, I doe hereby give it to the survivr^e of them.
And that my said feofees, and the survivors of them, shall pay
to my fower younger sons and daughters their respective and
equal p'portions of the said fower hundred pounds, when they
shall accomplishe the age of twenty and one yeares, together
with consid'on for soe much belonging to any of them from the
time of the purchase. And whereas, I am seized to me and my
heyrs of, and in seaven acres of freehould lande, meddow, and
pasture in Killinghall aforesaid, comonly called Rainridding, in
a place their called the Westholmes, which said seaven acres of
lande, together with all its appurtenances, I doe hereby give and
bequeath the same to John Leavens, my eldest sonn, to him and
his heyres for ever : further . . . . . my will is that my said
feofies, imediately after the receipt of the purchase money for the
said copiehold^e lands, shall yearely pay the considon and interest
of the said fowre hundred pounds to my said . . . . . children,

their equal p'portions for, and towards their educaon and maintenance, and if ether of my . . . . . do marrye before they
attaine their respective ages of twenty and one yeares, with
consent of . . . . wife and feofies, that then my said feofies
shall pay to such soe marryinge, their parte and p'portion of the
said sume, givinge them a lawful discharge for the same. And
I doe hereby nominate . . . . Grace, my said wife, sole
executrix of this my last Will and Testament. In witness
hearof I have hereunto set my hande and seale the twenty-
seaventh day of the tenth month, comonly called Decemb[r]· one
thousand six hundred sixty and eight.—John Leavens, L.S.
Sealed, signed, and published to bee my last Will and Testament,
in the p'sence of these whose names are und[r]written, whom
I have desired to bee witnesse hereof.—Thomas Wardman,
Ann ⨯ Carr."
  her mark.

A short distance further west, on the right of the same
road, is "The Hollins," a modern mansion, erected by the
late John Williamson, Esq., about the year 1818; it was
sold by his grandson in 1866, to Captain Holdforth, of Leeds,
who, in 1868, disposed of the same to John Field Wright, Esq.,
the present owner. This mansion is situate on a gentle
eminence, on the southern slope of the valley of the Nidd,
and overlooks some pretty scenery.

Sprusty Hill is a hamlet on the southern side of the township, pleasantly situate on a hill, overlooking the valley of
the Oakbeck, as well as that of the Nidd. In the year 1299,
we find it written Sprokesby;* afterwards it gave name to a
resident family of the name of Sprustoe—the last of whom

  * This place is mentioned in the will of Joan, widow of Sir William
Ingleby, Knt., of Ripley Castle, dated October 12th, 1478; in which, after
sundry bequests, she says—"I give to Katherine, my daughter, all lands,
&c., in the villages of Hutton-Wandsley, Killinghall, Sprusty, Maunby-
upon-Swale, Kirkby-upon-Wiske, and Skelton, near York.

appears to have been "Georgeii Sprustoe, Armiger," whose daughter, Ann, was married to John Pallisser, of Burthwaite, and died in 1675.

In 1648, it was occupied by Henry Tankard, Esq., second son of Charles Tankard, of Whixley, Esq., by his wife, Barbara, daughter of William Wyvill, of Osgodby. He married, first, ——, daughter of —— Fletcher, of Killinghall, and. secondly, a daughter of Richard Atkinson, of Whixley, by whom he had issue—Maria, who died in 1705, aged 37.

In 1692, Charles Wilkinson, of Boroughbridge, Gent., surrendered the reversion of five messuages and forty-seven and a half acres of land in Sprusty, within the township of Killinghall, after the death of the said Charles Wilkinson and Deborah, his wife, to the use of Andrew Wilkinson, Esq., and John Pomfret, clerk, to the use of the said Charles and Deborah, for their lives, with remainder to their heirs. At the same time he surrendered one messuage and sixteen acres of land in Bilton-with-Harrogate, after the death of Clara Cholmley,* widow, to the same trustees, for the same uses.

From the family of Wilkinson the estate passed to that of Lawson, and was sold by the late Andrew Lawson, Esq.

In 1888, this estate belonged to Mr. Thomas Jamison, and,

---

* Clare Cholmley was the widow of Richard Cholmley, Esq., of Sprusty. They were only married in 1687 (probably she was a second wife), as we learn from the Ripley parish register, where are the following entries belonging to this family—
"Mr. Daniel Hoare, of Hull, and Mrs. Hannah Cholmley, of Killingham, marr. 8. Oct. 1685."
"Richard Cholmley, Esqre., and Clare Colling, of Killingham, marr. 16. Dec., 1687."
Thoresby, the Leeds antiquary, notes in his *Diary*—"A.D. 1683. March 1st. London. Evening; at funeral, and a bearer of young Mr. Cho'mley, who yesterday sevennight, when I first was with him at Mr. Stretton's, was, I thought, much likelier for life than myself."—Vol. i., p. 158. The editor adds in a note—"The son and hair of Richard Cholmley, Esq., of Sprusty, in the Wapontake of Claro. He was supposed to have died of the plague."

in 1848, was purchased by William Sheepshanks, Esq., the present owner.

At the Warren farm are the remains of a Roman camp, now nearly obliterated by the plough; it can, however, be distinctly traced. Its dimensions are about 130 yards by 110; the south front has been slightly circular, and the entrance on that side protected by a covered way. The peaceful husbandman now builds his corn stack where once the Roman eagle shone—that proud bird of conquest,

"With glittering wings expanded to the sun."

On the enclosure of the Forest of Knaresborough, the rector of Ripley received, in lieu of tithes in this township, an allotment of 544a. 3r. 2p. of land on Killinghall Moor, between Oakbeck and the Otley and Ripley turnpike road, and another allotment of 61 acres near the Warren, and money payments for many small encroachments made, amounting to 18s. 2d. annually. Another allotment was also awarded in this township, of 9a. 3r. 25p., either to the rector of Ripley or the vicar of Hampsthwaite.

The charities consist of 30s., annually distributed by the overseer, being the interest of £34, left by the will of a Mr. Pullan—period unknown; and 9s., being the interest of £10, left by the will of Robert Clarkson, in 1757.

The population in 1801 was 462; in 1811, 485; in 1821, 519; in 1831, 545; in 1841, 559; in 1851, 569; in 1861, 746.

The annual value of this township as assessed to the county rate in 1849 was £3,763; in 1859, £4,039; and in 1866, £4,656. Amount assessed to property tax in 1858, £4,482.

CLINT.

CLINT is a township in the parish of Ripley; bounded on the east by Ripley Park, on the west by the Munk wall, which divides it from Hartwith-with-Winsley, on the south by the river Nidd, and on the north by Thornton beck, which separates it from Bishop Thornton; and includes within its limits Clint, Whipley, and Burnt Yates.

Clint is not mentioned in the Domesday survey; and only a small portion of this township is entered in that record under the head of Whipley. First, amongst the lands of the king—

"In Wipelei, one carucate. Waste."*

Next, among the lands of Ernegis de Burun—

"In Wipelei and Bemeslai, Gospatric had one carucate of land to be taxed. There is land to half a plough. Ernegis has it and it is waste."†

Again, among the lands of the king's thanes—

"Manor. In Wipelei, Archil had half a carucate of land to be taxed. Land to two oxen. The same has it, and it is waste. Value in King Edward's time, two shillings and eightpence."‡

. In the summary of lands in the Wapontake of Claro, we find the quantities given, thus—

"In Wipelei, Erneis half a carucate. In the same place, the king one carucate and a half."§

* "Bawdwen's Dom. Boo.," p. 17.
† *Ibid*, p. 207.
‡ *Ibid*, p. 228.
§ *Ibid*, p. 256.

This quantity includes the king's own carucate, and the half carucate held by Archil.

Whipley is now confined to a small district adjoining to Ripley. On the road leading from Scaro Bridge to Burnt Yates is Whipley Moor; otherwise the name appears to be forgotten. In the same neighbourhood is a place called Archil or Arkell Nook.*

This township is chiefly memorable as having been the residence of the family of Beckwith. Early and long were they seated in Knaresborough Forest, and the manors of Beckwith and Beckwithshaw, as well as "the lordship of Clynt, bounded of the north side of Nid juxta Hampsthwaite," were theirs. To those who delight in tracing long ancestral lines, it will be a pleasure to trace the descent of this family through the course of time for the last eight hundred years, and find the current of life yet running with undiminished vitality, though diverted from its original dwelling-place. The line begins so early that its origin is lost in the mists of antiquity. Some derive their descent from Gamelbar, a large landowner in this district before the conquest. This is probable, though neither certain nor proveable.

The pedigree is deduced by genealogists from Hugo de Malebisse, who held lands in Yorkshire in the time of William the Conqueror, from whom descended—

Sir Hercules Malebisse, who changed his name to Beckwith, on his marriage with the Lady Dame Beckwith Bruce, daughter of Sir William Bruce, of Skelton, in Cleveland, in 1226. Their son,—

* In a list of Romish recusants, in 1745, we find the name of "Christopher Maltas, Arkell Nook, in Clint, spurrier." Did this place derive its name from the Saxon thane, Archil, or from a copious spring of water called *Ar*, or *Har keld*—that is, the soldier's well? We incline to the latter opinion.

Sir Hercules Beckwith, married a daughter of Sir John Ferrars, of Tamworth Castle, by whom he had—

Nicholas Beckwith, who, by a daughter of Sir John Chaworth, had a son,

Hamond Beckwith, Esq., who, in the year 1339, took upon him a coat of arms incident to John, Lord Malebisse. He was seized of the lordship of Clinte,* near Hampsthwaite, Ugle-barnby, in Whitby Strand, lands in Pickering and Roxby, with the manors of Beckwith and Beckwithshaw. He married a daughter of Sir Philip Tilney, and had issue—

William Beckwith, who had to wife a daughter of Sir Gerard Usflete, by whom he had a son and successor,

Thomas Beckwith, of Clinte, who held the manors of Magna Otterington and Hornby juxta Thirsk, of John, Lord Mowbray, 4th of Richard II. (1380). He married a daughter of John Sawley, Esq., of Saxton, by whom he had issue—

Adam† Beckwith, de Clinte, who, in 1364, married Elizabeth, daughter and co-heiress of Thomas de Malebisse, Knight, and thus the older and younger branches of the family of Malebisse became united in their son,

William Beckwith, de Clint, who married a daughter of Sir John Baskerville, whose son,

Thomas Beckwith, married the daughter and heiress of Sir William Hasterton, and in her right enjoyed the third part of the manors of Filey-Muston and Thorpe; they had issue—

---

* 16th Edward III. (1342). John de Bekwyth surrenders "j. acram terræ in Rakis de Hamesweyt," to the use of John Littister.—*Knaresborough Court Rolls.*

† This was not the first or only Adam in the family of Beckwith, as we learn from the Court Rolls of Knaresborough Forest, that Agnes, widow of Adam de Becwith was living in the 25th of Edward III. (A.D. 1351); and also that on the 18th May, in the same year, John, son of Adam de Bekwith, is presented by the constable of Bekwith, and fined 12s. for having drawn blood from Henry, son of Richard atte Kirke.

William Beckwith, Esq., afterwards Sir William Beckwith, Knight, who married Elizabeth, daughter of Sir William Plompton, of Plompton. The marriage contract bears date October 15th, 1455; wherein it is agreed that William, son of the above Thomas Beckwith, shall take to wife Elizabeth, daughter of the said Sir William; the said Thomas to give jointure to the yearly value of £10 3s. 4d.; and to bind himself that all lands, tenements, &c., of which he stood sole seized, betwixt the waters of Nidd and Thornton Beck, and in the towns of Muston, Filey, Halneby, Little Aiton, and South Otterington, within the county of York, should descend to his son William and his heirs; and also all other lands, &c., of which Elizabeth, the wife of the said Thomas, was jointly enfeoffed with the said Thomas, in like manner; and the lands held by feoffees to his use, to go to the said William and his next heirs male. The marriage portion was fixed at £123 6s. 8d., to be paid by instalments; and if the said Elizabeth should die without issue male, had by the said William Beckwith, then Sir William Plompton to be discharged of the surplus, if any remaining unpaid. The moderate sums mentioned for jointure and marriage portion, are proofs of the scarcity of money among the gentry at that time. The marriage was issueless; and Sir William married, secondly, a daughter of Sir John Ratcliffe, but died without issue, and was succeeded by his nephew,

Thomas Beckwith, who married Maude, daughter of Sir Henry Pudsey, of Barforth.

By *Inquisition post mortem*, taken at Wetherby May 25th, 2nd Henry VIII., Thomas Beckwith, deceased January 20th, 10th Henry VIII. (1518), at the time of his death was seized of one messuage, six oxgangs of land, and ten acres of meadow in Clint; and by Indenture, dated at Clynt, 28th July, 9th Henry

VIII., he enfeoffed Henry Pudsey, Esq., Thomas, son of Ninian Markenfield, Knight, Henry, son of Thomas Pudsey, Ralph Berton, Gent., Thomas Ingleby, Esq., Christopher Wandesford, Esq., and Henry Pudsey, Gent., by the name of the manor of Clint, and of all lands and territories, with all the appurtenances in Clint, to the use of the said Thomas Beckwith and Maude, his wife, for their lives, and after to the use of the right heirs of the said Thomas. The manor of Little Ayton was conveyed to other trustees. Henry Pudsey and Robert Skayf were also enfeoffed of the manor of South Otterington to the use of the said Thomas Beckwith, and his heirs, &c. Thomas, Henry, Lambert, and Agaypt, were his younger sons.

The lands and tenements in South Otterington were of the annual value of 26s. 2d., together with the advwoson of the church of South Otterington. The said lands being held of the abbot of Byland. William Beckwith, Esq., his son and heir, was then of the age of twenty-four years and upwards.

William Beckwith, eldest son and successor, married Johanna, daughter of Sir John Mallory, of Studley, but died without leaving issue.

By *Inquisition post mortem*, taken at Newburgh, Nov. 12th, 13th of Henry VIII. (1521), the marriage settlement and will of William Beckwith, Esq., of Clint, are recited at length. Robert Skayffe and John Hardcastle are called his servants; the former had an annuity of 40s. per annum for term of his life, and the other of 20s. by indenture annexed to his will, called his will indented. This is dated Feb. 12th, in the 12th of Henry VIII. His solemn will, made Feb. 14th, 1521, orders a trental of masses to be said for his soul on the day of his burial, and " an honest prest syng for my soule, my father's soule, and all my frends' soules, at the parish church of Ripley," for a year. " *Item.* I will that the masses of *Scala Celi* be sung and saide for my soule, my father's soule, and all my frends' soules." Mentions Johanne, his wife, but no relations. Was seized in fee of certain lands in South Otterington of the annual value of 26s. 8d., and of the advowson of the church of South Otterington. The said William Beckwith died 14th February, 13th Henry VIII., and was succeeded by his brother and heir, aged twenty-two years and upwards,

Thomas Beckwith, who became seized of Clint, and married Elizabeth, daughter of William Tyrrell, of South Ockden, Essex.*

By *Inquisition post mortem*, on the death of Thomas Beckwith, late of Clint, Esq., who held of the king and queen, in free socage, as of their Honour, Manor, or Castle of Knaresborough, parcel of the Duchy of Lancaster, a capital messuage in Clynt, called Clynt Hall, four other messuages there, a certain parcel of land there called Clynt Park, one close called Mytting Close, another close called Height Field, another close called Derby Field, another close called New Close, another close called Horse Close, another close called Tott Holmes, another close called Sail Holmes, one virgate of wood called Cloyling Spring, lying in Clynt, aforesaid, which said parcel and closes of land contained in the whole two carucates of land at the time when the inquisition was taken; after whose death came Thomas Beckwith, junior, as son and heir of the aforesaid Thomas Beckwith, senior, and claimed the same by service, and by two shillings annual rent, by fealty and suit of court, at the Castle of Knaresborough, every three weeks, and paid to the aforesaid king and queen 2s., rendering fealty, and was admitted as free tenant.

Thomas Beckwith, born in 1503, married Maud, daughter of Brian Palmes, of Lindley; and after her decease, Catherine, daughter of William Tancred, Esq., of Boroughbridge.

* "Knaresborough Court Rolls." 5 and 6 Phillip and Mary (1558).

z

By *Inquisition post mortem*, taken Aug. 28th, 20th Elizabeth, it was found that Thomas Beckwith de Clint, Arm., before his death, was seized of the capital messuage of Clint Hall, and of 20 messuages, 10 cottages, 100 acres of arable land, 200 of meadow, 500 of pasture, and 2,000 of moor, in Clint ; and of the manor of Little Ayton, and 12 messuages, 10 cottages, 30 oxgangs of land, 200 acres of meadow, 600 of pasture, and 1,000 of moor in Little Ayton. The jurors say that William Faule, Elizabeth, his wife, in right of the said Elizabeth, who is now living at the time of the death of the said Thomas, were seized for the life of the said Elizabeth, in the manors of Muston and Filey, and of 40 messuages, 20 cottages, 500 acres of meadow, 1,000 of pasture, and 1,000 of moor, in Muston and Filey, of which the reversion appertained to the said Thomas Beckwith, and to his heirs, at the time of his death. The said Thomas died 30th November, 18th Elizabeth. Capital messuage and premises in Clint, worth yearly 18*s*. 4*d*. *(sic)* beyond reprises, are held of the queen of the Honour of Knaresborough, in free socage and not in capite. The manor of Ayton and premises, worth yearly £6 18*s*. 4*d*. is held of the queen, as of the Honour of Hay, by military service. Manors of Filey and Muston, worth £10 per annum, held by the heirs of Gaunt, as of the fee of Gaunt, by military service. William, son and heir of the said Thomas, is now aged 26 years and more.

William Beckwith, of Clint, married, first, Ann, daughter of William Tancred, Esq., of Boroughbridge, sister of his father's second wife, by whom he had a son, named William (who died without issue), and two daughters, Elizabeth and Anne. After this marriage clouds of misfortune began to gather over the old and honourable family. While serving in Ireland, as a captain in the army, his wife proved unfaithful to him. On his return he repudiated her,* and during her lifetime, married Mary, daughter of Anthony Salmon, of Annesley Woodhouse, in Nottinghamshire, by whom he had a son, named Huntingdon, his successor, and two other sons, William and Henry,† and two daughters, Catherine and Isabel. On his decease, in 1607, he was succeeded by

Huntingdon Beckwith, Esq., of Clint, who married Margaret, daughter of Thomas Mering, of Mering, in Nottinghamshire, who became insane, and having survived her husband, died in 1655,‡ when

Marmaduke Beckwith, of Aikton, succeeded to the estate in Clint; great-grandson of Robert Beckwith, of Broxholme,

* Mr. Walbran has the following note on this unhappy event—"Whether he was separated from her legally or not I cannot as yet tell; but when her father made his will, in 1573, she appears, either through absence or otherwise, to have been insufficiently maintained by her husband. After bequeathing to her a silver salt, with a cover gilt, and the sum of £3 6s. 8d., he says—'I do will and require Thomas Tanckard, my sonne, whome I make my executor, to dispose and give to Jaine Beckwith, my said daughter, xxli. at such time as he shall think it convenient in her necessity. *Item,* I give and bequethe to the said Jaine Beckwith, my wife best gowne, her best kyrtle, and her best peticote.'"—*Memorials of Fountains,* vol. i., p. 323.

† In the Knaresborough Court Rolls, for the year 1609, we find the will of Henry Beckwith, of Clynt, Esquire, dated 30th of November, 1608, (he was buried at Ripley, January 2nd, 1608-9,) whereby, after reciting that the Right Hon. Gilbert, Earl of Shrewsbury, stood possessed of all the right, title, &c., then in the testator's possesion; and the said earl was bound by obligations to surrender unto the said testator, as right heir unto the same. His will was, that the said earl should surrender unto Charles Clapham, Richard Slater, and John Flesher, upon trust, to receive the rents and profits of the same, until they should amount to the sum of the testator's debts, funeral expenses, &c.; and then to surrender the same to Daniel Beckwith, *alias* Bellingham, his brother, and his heirs, with remainder to his cousin, Charles Clapham, and his heirs.

‡ "In the life-time of his parents, and in 1589, Huntingdon, their eldest son, married Margaret, daughter of Thomas Mering, of Mering Co., Notts, Esq., a family previously related to the Beckwiths. But thereby one misfortune followed another; she became of unsound mind, and having, on failure of issue, had this estate at Clint left to her by her husband, she sold it to Sir John Saville; and, after existing to an extreme age, was buried—as a note mournfully records opposite the registration of her marriage—'in great poverty, at Ripley Church, 4th of May, 1655. The family of Beckwith both gone, and Mering.'"—*Memorials of Fountains,* vol. i., p. 323.

who married Anne, daughter of Robert Dyneley, of Bramhope, Esq., by whom, among other issue, he had a son,

Roger Beckwith, Esq., who, in the year 1597, sold all his lands in Clint, and purchased the manor of Aldborough, near Masham.* Thus the main line of the family ceased from Clint Hall, after having held possession thereof nearly four hundred years.

Roger Beckwith, of Aldborough, died January 19th, 1684.

Arthur Beckwith, Esq., his son and successor, was a captain in the Parliamentary army, and slain in action in 1642.

Sir Roger Beckwith, son and successor of Arthur, was created a baronet, April 15th, 1681. He died October 6th, 1700.

Sir Roger, the second baronet, eldest son of the above, died in May, 1748. His two sons, Roger and Edmund, died unmarried, and the direct male line became extinct.

They bore *argent*, a chevron between three hinds' heads erased, *gules*.

Crest—An antelope, proper, with a branch in its mouth, *vert*.

Motto—*Joir en bien.*

Besides the main line of the family at Clint, strong and vigorous branches from the parent stem are to be found in many places,—as at Stillingfleet, one member of which, Sir Leonard Beckwith, was Sheriff of Yorkshire in 1550. He had served King Henry VIII. in his French wars; he was also in the service of King Edward VI., from whom he had a grant of

---

* The inscription on a stone, yet remaining to his memory, in Masham Church, states that—" He was the son of Marmaduke Beckwith, of Acton, by Anne, daughter of Mr. Dyneley, of Bramhope; which Marmaduke was the next in descent to Huntingdon Beckwith, of Clint, where the family had continued from the tenth year of King Henry III., A.D. 1226, until the year 1597, when the aforesaid Roger Beckwith sold his lands in Clint, and purchased Aldborough."

the Abbey of Selby;—at Aikton, near Pontefract;—at Trimdon, in the county of Durham, which yet survives in vigorous prosperity; and the name is yet kept up in many other places in and around the Forest of Knaresborough,* while, by means of the female branches, the blood of Beckwith yet flows in the veins of some of the noblest families in England.

Notwithstanding their long family life they were not a race which avoided danger. Like many others of the north country gentry, they were feedmen or retainers of the Earls of North-umberland, and, as such, followed them to the battle and the banquet; bore a share in their perils as well as in their pageantry; and sometimes took a part in frays, without their liege lord's permission, as, in 1441, they were prominent leaders in the "feud of the forest, against the men of John Kemp, Archbishop of York," particulars of which we have already related. Sir William Beckwith was one of the knights who rode along with the noble company of thirty-three knights, all his feedmen, besides esquires and yeomen, who attended the Earl of Northumberland to meet King Henry VII. in his progress towards York, in the first year of his reign, "in Barnesdale, a little beyond Robyn Huddes Ston."

Few families located in the Forest of Knaresborough have had a longer life than that of Beckwith. The name, descriptive of the situation whence it is derived, carries us back to very early times—*Beck*, a brook, and *with*, a wood or forest—the wood by the side of the brook; a correct description of the upper part of the valley of the Crimple, in the parish of Pannal; now, as at the time of the Domesday survey, nearly

* "Feb. 18, 1503. Antonius Beckwith de Clynt, parochia de Ripley. Ebor Dioc. Came to the cathedral church of Durham, and there sought sanctuary for having, in the west part of the park of 'Magistri Ynglisby,' unfortunately caused the death of John Parker, by striking him on the leg with a sword, in such manner that he died."—*Sanctuary Roll*, p. 40.

800 years ago, bearing the name of Beckwith. Originating thus early from Saxon or Danish parentage, this family lived through the Wars of the Roses, which struck down the nobles of the land like grass before the mower's scythe; the grand rebellion of the seventeenth century, when confiscation and the sword carried beggary and death to the homes of many; and through all the social and commercial revolutions since, which in numberless instances have pulled down the lofty and lifted the lowly. Though the titled branch became extinct, many vigorous minor ones continued to flourish, and the name is yet widely spread, and not likely to be one that will suddenly die out. Their station in society was certainly not the highest —they were not the oaks at which the thunderbolt is most frequently aimed; yet they were men of high standing in their neighbourhood; allied themselves with the best families; took an active part in the business of the great world, and comported themselves as men of bravery and worth.

From the family of Beckwith the Clint Hall estate passed to that of Swale, of South Stainley, in which it continued until about the year 1733, when Sir Solomon Swale, Bart., sold the same to John Aislabie, Esq., of Studley Royal, after whose decease, in 1742, his son, William Aislabie, Esq., was admitted to the same, at a court held February 16th, 1742. By his will, dated April 5th, 1776, the said William Aislabie gave all his estate at Clint (except the wood growing thereon) unto his son-in-law, William Lawrence, who was admitted to the same, October 25th, 1781. On his decease, in 1785, the estate passed to his daughter, the well-known Mrs. Elizabeth Sophia Lawrence, whose munificent charities will be long gratefully remembered by Ripon and the neighbourhood. On her death, July 30th, 1845, she bequeathed the same to her relative, Harry Edward Waller, Esq., of Lemington, Gloucester-

shire, and from whom the same was purchased, in 1861, by
John Greenwood, Esq., of Swarcliffe Hall, the present owner.

Clint Hall stood on the northern side of the valle of the
Nidd, on a commanding eminence, overlooking an extensive and
beautiful prospect; down the vale of the Nidd, eastward, finely
varied by hill and dale, plain and woodland; to the south the
Forest of Knaresborough, with all its hamlets, woods, and
wastes, the windings of the Nidd, and deep down below, the
humble church and village of Hampsthwaite; on the west, the
hills of the upper Nidd, and the Craven Fells are seen, peeping
over each other's heads; to the north, the Roman camp on
Nutwith is visible; and along the north-east and east, the view
is only interrupted by the Hambleton and Wold Hills; and, on
the south-east, as far as human vision can discriminate objects.

The site is a projecting knoll, from which is a descent on three
sides—east, south and west. On the northern side the land
rises above it. A moat has surrounded it, but whether it has
contained water or not is questionable. The building or Manor
House has been of the Tudor age, judging from the fragment
which remains; which is merely the wall enclosing three sides
of one room, which has been about eighteen feet square; the
walls are about fifteen feet in height; on the south has been
a large window of three lights, divided by a transom. The
beams supporting the floors have not been inserted in the walls,
but rested on projecting corbels, which yet remain. The whole
of the remainder of the house, and its appurtenant offices have
entirely disappeared, and left not a wreck behind. Indeed the
greatest part of the site has been under the plough, and this
insignificant fragment is all that remains to point out the place
where the home of the family of "Beckwyth of Clynt" once stood.

The traveller by the Nidd Valley Railway may catch a glimpse
of this tiny ruin, by looking up the hill to the north-east, when
the train is at a stand at Birstwith Station.

The hamlet of Clint,* which gives name to the township, consists of about half-a-dozen old houses, situate on the sides of the road leading from Clint Hall to Ripley ; four of them, at the period of their erection, have belonged to the better class of yeomanry, as is evident from the substantial manner in which they have been built ; and they are probably upwards of two hundred years old. The most interesting object is an ancient cross situate on one side of the road, which consists of a platform of masonry, the summit raised three steps above the surface ; upon the upper step is a block of stone about two feet square, into which has been inserted a slender shaft of stone (now removed), about nine inches square. Nothing is known of the time of its erection, or of its use. It could not, from its situation, be placed to mark a boundary, as the limit of no manor, township, or district passes near it. The inhabitants have a tradition that their now humble hamlet was once a town

---

*Probably from *Clied, Clent* (A. S.), a piece of rock. Gawain Douglas has "clints of rock." We have heard the masses of hard blue limestone, sometimes to be seen in the bed of the Nidd, in the higher part of the valley, called "clint." Drunken Barnaby, at Hardrow, in Wensleydale, saw—"Barraine cliffs and *clints* of wonder."

This township gave name to a family of some distinction and wealth in early times ; of whom William and John respectively founded chantries in the collegiate church of Ripon.

John, son of Robert de Clint, gave half an acre of meadow to the monks of Fountains Abbey, lying between Ripley Beck and Barthenge.

William Clint, S.T.P., was Vicar of Masham, from 1898 until his death in 1425. He attended the General Council of the church at Constance, in 1414. He is mentioned in the will of John de Harwod, an advocate in the Court of York, in 1406, as—"Magistri Willielmo Clynt, vicaria de Masham," to whom he bequeaths "j parvum calicem. *Item*—j peciam argentum coopertam cum pedibus bonum et ynbretest. *Item*—optimum equum meum quem habui ex dono ejusdem."—*Testamenta Eboracensia*, vol. i., p. 341.

In 1471, Margaret Clynt, late a serving sister in the Hospital of St. Leonard, York, is mentioned in the will of John Pickering, of York, to whom he bequeaths a plain silver ring.

A family named Clint was resident in Pannal from 1550 to about 1620.

This family name is not yet extinct ; as, on Oct. 14th, 1869, John Clint, linen manufacturer, died at Harrogate, aged 92.

of importance, and that this was the market cross,—a tale
which is not very probable. It has been suggested that it may
have marked the limits of some sanctuary belonging to Ripley
Church, as the base of a very singular cross is found in the
churchyard there, and roadside crosses either now exist, or did
some time ago, at Scaro, and in Killinghall, all in this parish.

Near to the old cross may be seen a portion of that antique
instrument of punishment, the village stocks.

At the gaol delivery at Knaresborough, 18 Edward II. (1325),
William, son of Adam de Clint, was arraigned for the death of
William del Ridding, of Clint. The jurors of the Liberty of
Knaresborough say that the men were together in a tavern in the
"villa" of Clint, kept by William del Sayles, on the Sunday
next after the Epiphany, 17 Edward II., and quarrelled there.
William Clint, fearing the malice of the said William del
Ridding, went out of the house, and the said William del
Ridding took his bow and arrows, "et alia arma," and followed
him to the house of a certain Agnes Serveys, where he shut the
door, wishing to hide himself. William del Ridding, however,
broke in upon him, when he fled by another door, his pursuer
following him with his bow strung across divers "sepes," to the
head of the village of Clint, shooting at him as he went; and
thus "viriliter" did he pursue him for the space of two miles,
" usque ad magnum fossatum plenum aquæ, et quædam sepes
fuit superposita ubi dictus Willelmus fil. Adæ nullo modo
præterire potuit, et reversit se versus prædictum W. del Ridding,
te defendend, percussit eum cum quadam sagitta in pectore unde
obiit." The jury being asked if the said W. fil. Adæ could not
have fled further, say that " W. del Ridding fuit fortior et
velocior;" andt hat the said " Will. fil Adæ " was so wearied
"quod ulterius fugere non potuit." Jury also say that said

Will. never withdrew himself on account of this death—" Ideo remittitur prisonæ ad gratiam dom. regis exspectandum."*

BURNT YATES.

This is the most populous part of the township; the houses are arranged along the sides of the road leading from Ripley to Pateley Bridge; it has also a much more modern appearance than Clint.

Here is a free school, built and endowed by many benefactors.

The first school was built by a public subscription of the inhabitants, about the year 1750.

William Coates, in 1751, left, by will, to the school at Burnt Yates, the annual proceeds of the sum of £150. The trustees were the Rector of Ripley, Rev. Mr. Roundell, Rev. Mr. Fletcher, William Williamson, Mr. Tuton, and Charles Long.

Rear-Admiral Robert Long, in the year 1760, by deed, endowed the said school with the Flask House Farm, in the township of Hartwith, and other lands in the townships of Hartwith and Clint,| of the annual value of £45. By the deed of endowment thirty poor boys of the townships of Clint and Winsley are directed to be taught reading, writing, and arithmetic, and thirty poor girls to knit, sew, and spin, free; and it is directed that all persons resident in the said townships, who might rent a farm of £30 a-year, or possess property of the annual value of £10, do pay for the instruction of their children. Children of the name of Long to have preference before others. The trustees appointed were the Rev. Samuel Kirshaw, Rector of Ripley, the Rev. Matthew Metcalfe, Curate of Hartwith, Danson Roundell, Esq., of Spring House, Charles

* R. H. S.

Long, of Winsley Hall, Gentleman, William Mountaine, of the parish of St. John's, Southwark, in the county of Surrey, Gentleman, and John Williamson, of Ripley.

William Mountaine, F.R.S., in 1778, left by will, after the death of Thomas Grayson and his daughter Margaret, to the Rector and Churchwardens of Ripley, the sum of £50; and also, by the same will, after the death of Thomas Grayson and his son, William, the sum of £140. The whole bequest was £200, to be distributed annually among the poor scholars attending the school. He also gave his library to be deposited in the school.

In 1778, the commissioners for the enclosure of the Forest of Knaresborough awarded 8a. 2r. 19p. of land to Clint School.

William Lawrence, Esq., in 1788, gave, by deed, to this school, about five acres of land.

Of the lives of these public benefactors very little is known. Of the first of them, William Coates, we know nothing but the name.

Robert Long is said to have been born at Winsley Hall; the brother of Charles Long, appointed one of the first trustees of the school. In the deed of endowment he is described as "Robert Long, of the parish of Marylebone, in the county of Middlesex, Esquire, brother and heir of William Long, late of the same parish, deceased." Traditions preserved in the families of Long (now resident in the Forest of Knaresborough), relate that the admiral once came from London to visit the place of his birth, and that all of the name of Long, with whom he had any relationship, met him at Ripley, to welcome him home. The same authority states that he was buried at Langleybury, in Hertfordshire. However this may be, all that is known of his life serves to prove that he was closely connected with this place, and one of its greatest benefactors.*

William Mountaine was a native of Clint, born in a small farm-house, yet existing, at the bottom of the hill, on the right of the road leading from Scarobridge to Burnt Yates. He was a self-taught genius, and rose to considerable eminence as a mathematician. On the title page of one of his publications he is styled "Mathematical Examiner to the Honourable Corporation of Trinity House, of Deptford Strond, and F.R.S." Of the Royal Society he was an active member—often one of the Council, and a frequent contributor to its transactions. His papers are chiefly on mathematics, applied to astronomy and navigation. Amongst kindred subjects, the variation of the compass appears to have engaged much of his attention. The rectification of the lines drawn upon "Gunter's Scale" was another of his labours: this tract is enriched with much biographical and historical matter on the subjects therein

* The following extracts relative to the family of Long, and the estate called Flask, are from the Knaresborough Court Rolls.—

28th July, 1708. "Willelmus Ingleby de Raventopps, generosus," surrendered "unum messuagium et sex acras terræ, et prati, per estimationem, cum omnibus ædificiis et pertinentiis, vocatis le Flaske house, jacent infra villam de Clint." Then in the occupation of Philippa Long, widow, "ad opus et usum prædictæ Phillippe Long, hæredum et assignorum suarum imperpetuum." Admitted, and paid a fine of 3s. 4d.

28th July, 1708. Philippa Long, widow, surrenders the above to the use of John Dodsworth, his executors or assigns, for the term of seven years, from the 25th of March, last past, he paying the said Philippa Long £34 per annum.

27th March, 1723. "Barnabas Long de Clint, in periculo mortis," surrenders "unum messuagium, unum horreum, unum pomarium, et octo clausa, vocata Leeminghill, Cow Pastures, Well Close, Middle Close, Farr Pasture, and Moor Close, in the hamlet of Clint, containing thirteen acres, to the use of Thomas Long, of Winsley Hall, gent., in trust, "to and for the only proper use and behoof of his (the said Thomas) only daughter, Sarah Long," then a minor; and also to pay £7, quarterly, after the decease of the said Barnabas, to Lucy Long, wife of the said Barnabas.

"Robert, the son of Mr. Robert Longe, of Winsley Hall, was baptized the 17th day of March, 1663-4."—*Par. Reg. of Kirkby Malseard.*

mentioned. The best history of his life would probably be that
of his writings, which might be drawn from the transactions of
the Royal Society. We only regret that we can give no fuller
account of his life, as he ranks deservedly high amongst the
worthies of our district.

William Lawrence was father of the late Mrs. Elizabeth
Sophia Lawrence, of Studley Park, and at the time of making
the bequest to this school was owner of a considerable estate in
Clint, now belonging to John Greenwood, Esq.

The career of the school has been one of general prosperity;
and, contrary to what has taken place on similar foundations
elsewhere, the revenue has exceeded the expenditure, which
last keeps continually increasing, and consequently extending
the benefits of the establishment.

The money given by John Coates, with some savings of
income, was laid out in the purchase of a house, three cottages,
and twelve acres of land, at Hunslet, near Leeds.

In 1801, the trustees purchased the Winsley Hall estate
for £2,000, derived from the savings of income and the sale of
timber.

In 1864, they purchased Dixon's Farm in Clint for £1,200,
derived from similar sources.

At present (independent of the Hunslet estate) the trustees
are possessed of 49 acres of land in Clint, and upwards of
222 acres of land in Hartwith-with-Winsley, producing an
income of upwards of £800 annually.

The freedom of the school is now extended to all children
within the townships of Clint and Winsley, without distinction.

In 1855, the benefits of the charity were further extended by
the erection of an infant school, about half a mile distant
from the other.

The number of children, for many years past, receiving education in this establishment has been upwards of one hundred.

Divine service is held once a week in the school-room, and there is no other place of public worship in the township.

The trustees are six in number, the Rector of Ripley, the Incumbent of Hartwith, and the owner of Spring House, by virtue of their offices and estate; the others may be styled elective, and are John Greenwood, Esq., of Swarcliffe Hall, John Yorke, Esq., of Bewerley Hall, and John Williamson, Esq.

The masters since the foundation of the school have only been four—

```
Robert Leeming .....................about 1764.
Robert Cundall .....................————.
William Cockett..........................1811.
James Clark ...........................1856.
```

The school premises are situate on the north side of the road, near the middle of the village, and have evidently been built at different times: first, is the original structure, built before Admiral Long's endowment was given; next, the school-room, added immediately after that period; then the large room over the first erection; in which the meetings of the trustees are held, and in which William Mountaine's library is deposited; and, lastly, the new school-room built in 1849, which stands at an angle to the others. Over the entrance is inscribed,—

" This school was erected Anno Domini 1849, by the trustees, under the provisions of the will of Rear-Admiral Long, the founder of this charity."

Over the entrance of the old school-room, on a slab of white marble, is inscribed,—

" This school was erected and endowed in his lifetime, by Robert Long, Esquire, a Rear-Admiral in his Majesty's Royal Navy, Anno Dom. MDCCLX."

Above, are the founder's arms—a lion rampant, with eight crosslets in the field. Crest, a lion rising out of a ducal coronet.

The room containing the library is lofty and spacious with a pleasant look out towards the south. In the centre are the mahogany table and arm-chairs used at the meetings of the trustees. On the left hand are full length portraits of King Charles II. and Queen Caroline ; on the back of the first, near the top, is inscribed :—" The gift of William Mountaine, Esqre., F.R.S., to Clint School, in par. Ripley, Com. Ebor. Aug. 26, 1771." Near the bottom, " K. George 2nd. An original by Maingaud, Sergeant Painter to King George I." The word " original " is struck out. The queen's portrait has the same inscriptions, retaining the word " original." These paintings have become much faded, and the frames tarnished. At the east end of the room are half-length portraits of William Mountaine and his wife, by " Highmore," senr. These are in good condition, having been recently cleaned and renovated by order of the trustees. The library consisted originally of 57 folios, 101 quartos, 844 octavos, 19 duodecimos, 20 miscellanies, 15 pamphlets, and 18 manuscripts*—in all, 569; besides a pair of globes, two telescopes, and other instruments. Time has spoiled the globes, the telescopes have lost their lenses, but the books yet remain, generally in a good state of preservation. Inside every book is printed, " The gift of W^{m}. Mountaine, Esqre., F.R.S., to Burnt-Yates School, Par$_{h}$. of Ripley, W.

* Some of the folios are ponderous affairs, consisting of nautical diagrams and charts, which have probably belonged to Admiral Long. The manuscripts are Dunstan's Juvenal, 8 vols.; Dunstan's Horace, 8 vols.; Terence, 8 vols.; Homer, 1 vol.; Ovid, 1 vol.; all by Dunstan. Dunstan's Catalogue, 1 vol.; and Catalogue of Discourses for and against Popery, in the reign of James II. Among others, we noticed Cowley's Works, Chaucer's Works, Pembroke's Arcadia, Harris's Universal Lexicon, Cary's Chronology, &c., &c. For much information on this school, we are indebted to Mr. Clarke, the present master, to whom we take this opportunity of offering our sincere thanks.

Riding Ebor, 1775." Amongst them is a complete set of the
"Transactions of the Royal Society," until the year 1778.
There is not much light reading among them ; but, on the whole,
they are such as we might expect to find in the possession of a
hard-working mathematician. The books may not be much read
in the place where they are deposited ; but have not Long and
Mountaine set a noble example to great and learned men, in the
height of their dignity and intellectual greatness, to remember
and provide for the wants of the humble hamlets where they
were born ?

The Infant School, a substantial building of stone in the Tudor
style of architecture, is situate about half a mile to the eastward
of the other. Over the entrance is inscribed—" Infant School,
built A.D. 1855, by the Trustees of Burnt-Yates School,
founded by Admiral Long, R.N., A.D. 1760."

The charities consist of the rent of 4a. 2r. 0p. of land,
called the Hop Bank; Nelson's rent-charge of 20s. per annum,
payable out of a piece of land, called Nelson's Land, near
Shaw Mill; and William Mountaine's gift, in 1778, of the
interest of £100,—the last to be distributed amongst twelve
poor widows.

The Munk Wall passes close to the western end of Burnt
Yates, and forms the boundary between the township of Clint
and that of Hartwith-with-Winsley; it also formed the boundary between the lands of the monks of Fountains and the
Forest of Knaresborough. The road passing through it at this
point would necessitate the putting up of gates or *yates*, and
some fray between the men of the monks and the foresters, in
which the *yates* were torn down and *burnt*, probably gave name
to this place.

There is a small payment, called *Geld*, made to the tax
collector of Clint, by Sir Henry Ingilby, Bart., of Ripley Castle,

of 2d. each on two homesteads or farms in Scaro, the same
number in Burfitt, and on three in some other part of Ripley.
This *Geld* or tax we believe to be the old acknowledgement
paid by the owners or occupiers of those particular farms,
for the right or liberty of grazing their cattle on the unenclosed
grounds of Knaresborough Forest. A note in "Burton's
Monasticon Eboracense" appears to prove the antiquity of
this payment, and also to indicate its origin—

"The tenants of the Abbot and Convent of Fountains
residing in Ripelay, Byrthwaite, Grawra (Scarah or Scaro) and
Broxholme, whether within the lordship of Ripelay or the
village of Clint, pay their tax with Clynt, and make their
constable with Clynt, and go with the men of Clint to the court
of Knaresburgh, and are free from paying tolls at York and
Burrough-bridge, and in all other places where the men of
the forest have any such liberty; neither are they bound
to attend to the customs of the lordship of Ripley. They
had likewise liberty of getting turf at Bentwray, with a common
right in the forest, as other foresters have, and therefore they
pay the Rekpennys; and, except as above, they are not any
way to interfere with the village of Clint."

The *Geld* and the *Rekpenny* are synonymous terms, both
signifying a tax, or payment for some particular purpose.

The population of this township in 1801 was 480; in 1811,
395; in 1821, 412; in 1831, 404; in 1841, 393; in 1851,
434; and in 1861, 481.

The value of this township as assessed to the county rate in
1849 was £2,150; in 1859, £2,726; and in 1867, £3,140.
Amount assessed to property tax in 1858, £2,978.

HAMPSTHWAITE.

THIS parish occupies a large portion of the northern side of the
Forest of Knaresborough, and includes within its limits the
townships of Hampsthwaite, Felliscliffe, Birstwith, Menwith-
with-Darley, and Thornthwaite-with-Padside, which now form the
three parishes of Hampsthwaite, Birstwith, and Thornthwaite.
Hampsthwaite and Felliscliffe are in the Knaresborough Poor-
law Union; the others are in that of Pateley Bridge. The
Domesday survey of this parish is very imperfect; indeed, the
township of Hampsthwaite, under its present name, is not mentioned at all; though it probably appears as a berewic belonging
to the manor of *Burc*, under the name of Hilton or Elton.*

The Roman road from Isurium to Olicana passed through the
village, therefore, it could not be unknown to that people, and it
is likely they would have some post-house, or small settlement
at the point where the road crossed the river Nidd, which was
probably only of a temporary kind, as no Roman remains have
ever been found here.

---

* In Birstwith, in this parish, and nowhere else in the manor of *Burc* or
Aldburgh, is a place known as *Elton*, that is, the old-ton or town, where,
at one time, stood a maypole and the village stocks. This we conjecture
to have been the Hilton, or Elton of Domesday. As the manor of *Burc*,
with its berewics, contained thirty-four carucates of land, there would be
somewhere about 1,000 acres to reckon for Helton. The term Hampsthwaite appears to be of Saxon origin, and compounded from *Ham*, home,
and *thwaite*, an open field, or cleared space of ground; that is, the home in
the clearing.

On the formation of the Forest of Knaresborough the whole
district was thrown into it, and ever afterwards formed a portion
of that fee.

The following document has reference to lands here; it is
dated 6th of Henry III., A.D. 1222.

" The king to Brian de Insula, greeting :—

We command you that, respecting the forty-two acres of
(arable) land, and the three acres and three perches of meadow,
with their appurtenances in Hamestweit, of which Richard de
Alneto was seized in demesne, and, according to the inquisition
fully made to us, that except there be nearer heirs, you will give
full possession of the land to Emma de Alneto, the daughter of
the said Richard, unless she has done anything in the meantime
on account of which she ought not to be put into possession of
the said land. She obtained possession of the lands Jan. 3ᵈ·,
1223."

About the year 1258, Richard, Earl of Cornwall, granted to
the newly-founded, or enlarged monastery of the brethren of
St. Robert of Knaresborough, the advowson of the church and
pasturage for twenty cows with their calves for three years, in
Hampsthwaite.

In the inquisition on the death of Edmund, Earl of Cornwall,
A.D. 1299, we find all the townships in this parish mentioned,
as Pateside, Thornthwaite, Derlemonewith (a rolling of two
places into one, now known as Darley and Menwith), Felliscliffe,
Berscate (Birstwith), and Hampsthwaite.

In the 12th of Edward II., A.D. 1318, Richard de Aldburgh,
of Aldburgh, held to farm of the honor of Knaresborough,
Hampeswate, Derlay, Menwiche, Berstok, and Fenniscliff, all in
this parish.

The church, dedicated to St. Thomas à Beckett, was in
the patronage of the Stutevilles, Lords of Knaresborough,

and afterwards in that of Richard, Earl of Cornwall, who gave it to the brethren of the house of St. Robert of Knaresborough, to whom it was appropriated, and a vicarage ordained therein, August 5th, 1257.

The following account of this chapel and church is from Torre's MSS., in the library of the Dean and Chapter of York.*

"The chapel of Hampsthwaite, as appendant to the mother church of Burgh, by composition was to pay thereunto three bezants per annum, at Pentecost, by the clerk thereof, presentable by William de Stuteville and his heirs.

The church or chapel of Hampsthwaite anciently belonged to the patronage of the Stutevilles, Lords of Knaresburgh, and after of Richard, Earl of Cornwall, who gave the advowson to the house of St. Roberts.

And on 5 Id. Aug., A.D. 1257,

The king being then patron of it (at the instance of Richard, Earl of Cornwall and King of the Romans), Sewallus, Archbishop of York, by the consent of his Chapter, made this ordination of it, viz.—He appropriated it to brethren of the Order of St. Trinity (scil. of the house of St. Robert, juxta Knaresburgh), giving them the tithes, garbs of the church, and the whole land belonging. Reserving the residue of the profits thereof, with the tithe hay, and a competent mansion, etc., to the vicarage, which he hereby ordained, and appointed that the vicar should be for the future presentable thereunto by the said brethren, to the archbishop, and his successors to be instituted, who shall receive all the profits of the church (excepting garbs and lands), for which he shall administer in the same church, and cause it to be faithfully served by able ministers, and bear (at his own cost) all ordinary and accus-

* "Archdeaconry of York," p. 195.

tomary burdens (excepting the annual pension of 6s., payable by the said brethren to the Chapter of York).

Which ordination was confirmed by the Dean and Chapter of York, Prid. Non. Nov., 1257.

And on 28th Decbr., A.D. 1848,

Licence was granted to the minister and brethren of the house of St. Robert, juxta Knaresburgh, to present one of their fellow-brethren, expressly professed and constituted in priest's orders, to the vicarage of this church of Hampsthwaite.

There was a chantry founded in this parish church of Hampsthwaite at the altar of St. Mary Virgin and St. Anne.

Chantry priests hereof.

Dns. Tho. Beckwith, cap........................p. mort.
8 May, 1509. Dns. Xpher. Back, cap..... Thos. Beckwith de Clynt, ar."

In the *Valor* of Pope Nicholas IV., A.D. 1292, the vicarage was valued at £5; and in the *Nova Taxatio*, A.D. 1318, it was worth nothing, owing to the ravages of the Scots.

In *Valor Ecclesiasticus*, about 1536, the rectory was valued at £7 per annum; of which the tithes of corn and hay were worth £5, and the house and rectorial glebe £2. At the same time the vicarage was returned as worth £13 6s. 8d., made up as follows—

	£	s.	d.
Tithe of lambs, average of years, £2; wool do. £3 9s...........	5	9	0
Calves, 18s.; fowls, 8s. 4d.; eggs, 1s.	0	17	4
Oblations on the day of St. Thomas the Martyr, 16s.; Nativity of our Lord, 16s.; and Easter-day, average of years	2	8	0
Oblations on purification, 2s. 4d.; weddings, 2s. 8d.; funerals, 4s.	0	9	0
Quadragesimal tithes	4	0	0
Tithes of hay in the fields of Hampsthwaite and Orton	0	3	4
	£13	6	8

The particulars of this living are given in the following copy of "A true Terrier of all the glebe lands, messuages, tenements, portions of tithes and other rights belonging to the vicarage

and parish church of Hampsthwaite, in the county and diocese
of York, and now in possession of Mr. Edward Bainbridge,
vicar; there taken according to the old use and custom, and
knowledge of the ancient inhabitants; and exhibited at the
primary visitation of the most Rev. Father in God, Thomas,
Lord Archbishop of York, holden at Leeds, June 23rd, 1743."

"*Imprimis.*—There is a vicarage house, twenty-four yards in
length, and ten in breadth; also one barn, with a stable and
cowhouse under the same roof, in length fifteen yards, and
breadth five yards; one henhouse, two gardens, one orchard,
with about half an acre of glebe land on the north side,
adjoining and abutting upon a little close, now in the possession of Mary Umpleby, widow. The vicar is possessed of the
hay tithe of several closes or parcels of land lying and being in
the township or hamlet of Hampsthwaite; and likewise of a
modus of four shillings a-year, payable yearly on the feast of
St. John Baptist, by the proprietor or tenant of a farm, called
Hall Garth, in lieu of the small tithes issuing therefrom.

Item.—The vicar is possessed of a modus of six shillings and
eightpence, payable at Easter, yearly, by the owner or tenant
of a mill called Wreaks Mill, in lieu of the tithe of the said
mill, which is now in possession of Henry Avison.

Item.—Of a modus of four shillings, payable yearly, at Easter,
by the owners or tenants of a mill, called Darley Mill, in lieu
of tithe of the said mill, which is now in the occupation of
Robert Hall.

Item.—The vicar is entitled to the payment of one halfpenny
an acre, according to estimation, in lieu of hay tithe of the
copyhold grounds throughout all the other parts of the parish.

Item.—The vicar is entitled to the tithe of lambs, wool,
pigs, geese, ducks, turkeys, chickens, apples, pears, plums, and
cherries, and all other kinds of fruit, as well as all manner

of ecclesiastical rights and dues, so far as the hay tithe extends (excepting tithe corn). In the hamlet of Hampsthwaite, where the hay tithe and petty tithes are payable in kind, the vicar is entitled only to one penny, called custom penny; and every house, messuage, or tenement, is obliged to pay to the vicar at Easter fourpence, called custom pennies, in lieu of tithe fruit and eggs.

Item.—The vicar is entitled to the tithe of lambs, wool, pigs, geese, pigeons, and all other vicarage tithes and rights whatever throughout the parish.

Item.—For every lamb under the number six, there is due to the vicar one penny; at six, half a lamb; at seven, a whole lamb, payable to the owner threepence; and at ten, a whole lamb, without deduction. The same in tithing wool—only for every fleece under the number of six there is due to the vicar one halfpenny, and for every fleece at and above that number seven; when taken in kind there is due to the owner one halfpenny for every odd one. For a tithe calf there is due to the vicar three shillings and fourpence; for every foal, two-pence. Twopence for every communicant at the age of sixteen. For every cow with calf, usually called in milk, one penny halfpenny; for every cow unrenewed, one penny. For a swarm of bees, one penny. For keeping a plow, twopence. The vicar is entitled to the payment of mortuaries."

A note made by the Rev. Joseph Wilson, in 1786, states that the vicar's dues on Easter Tuesday are 4s. 6d. and 4s. Clerk's dues are, for winding up the clock, 10s.; sweeping the church, 5s.; washing the surplices, 8s.; communion bread, 5s. Sexton's wages, 10s.; cleaning the churchyard, 1s. Ringers' wages, 8s. 4d. each; allowance on Easter Tuesday, 12s. Per-ambulation, 18s. 4d., 5th Nov.—10s. was 5s. Visitation four times, 10s. Court fees, about 6s. or 7s., deducted. To the balance the chapel contributes an equal share.

In the same year a rate was made on the 2nd day of April, "for the repairs of the church, and other imbursements," as follows—Hampsthwaite and Hollins, £8; Felliscliffe, £8; Birstwith, £8; Menwith-hill and Darley, £8.

On the enclosure of the Forest of Knaresborough, the following allotments were made to Thomas Shann, rector, in lieu of tithe—

	a.	r.	p.
In Felliscliffe	111	0	28
In Clifton, near Nesafield	74	0	27
In Birstwith	92	3	12
In Darley	198	3	16
In Timble	285	1	24
In Thruscross	561	0	21
Total	1323	2	8

To the vicar, at the same time, in lieu of his claims, was allotted—

	a.	r.	p.
In Killinghall	263	2	38
In Felliscliffe	390	0	22
In Clifton	18	1	29
Total	672	1	9

In 1831, the vicarage was returned at £264 per annum. Patron, the Rev. Thomas Shann.

There were two chantries in this church; one dedicated to St. Osithe, or St. Sythe, which some accounts state was in Thornthwaite; the other to the Virgin Mary and St. Anne. One of these appears to have been dependant on the church at Burgh, or Aldburgh, and to have paid a pension thereto. The other, at the time of the Reformation, was in the incumbency of Richard Buller, and worth £4 18s. 4d. per annum, arising from the

rents of divers lands and tenements, out of which a rent of
10s. yearly was paid to the king.*

The church is situate at the northern extremity of the village,
close to the river Nidd, and comprises nave and chancel, a south
aisle, a projecting vestry at the east end, and a square tower at
the west. With the exception of the tower, the whole was
rebuilt in 1821. The lower part of the tower is in the early
decorated, the upper part in the perpendicular style of architecture; the large window, on the western side, is a later inser-
tion. When pulled down in 1820, it was evident that the nave
had been three times previously enlarged or altered. At first it
had been a long and narrow building, with the roof of a high
pitch; the first alteration had been the removal of the south
wall, and the erection of an aisle on that side, substituting in place
of the wall a row of octagonal columns, bearing pointed arches,
with a clerestory above; the roof of the aisle being flatter and
of the lean-to kind. The next alteration destroyed the clerestory,
and covered the whole building with one wide, unsightly roof,
somewhat similar in appearance to the present one. The interior
was open timber-work—the outside covered with lead. It would
not be easy to determine the exact date of any of these alterations without documentary evidence. A church existed here
previous to any of them, as was shown when the old walls were
pulled down to the foundations, which were found to consist
mainly of stone coffins, the spoils of some former church, which

* In the 35th of Elizabeth, 1590, there was a suit in the Duchy Court
between Thomas Phillips, as the queen's lessee, and Richard Gascoigne,
John Ellis, Francis Slingsby, Christopher Boys, Wm. Ingleby, Francis
Tankard, and William Kellingbeck, claiming, by letters patent, certain
chantry lands, amongst which were those of St. John and St. Mary Mag-
dalen, of Knaresborough; St. James, of Pannal; and St. Osythe, or St.
Sythe, in Hampsthwaite. The lands were situate in Killinghall, Bylton,
Clynt, Scryven, Arkendale, Fellycliff, Rydon, Beckwith, Bosfatt, Grafton,
Menwith, Birscliff, Thornthwaite, Aldbrough, and Harrowgate. From the
above names we may learn into whose hands the chantry lands passed.

were all allowed to remain, and form the support of the present structure. At the east end of the aisle was a piscina, above which were two brackets inserted in the wall, as if for the support of an image, thus marking the site of one of the chantries. The walls had been ornamented with paintings and texts of scripture.

The basements and part of the shafts of the old columns which divided the aisle and nave yet remain, surmounted by slender shafts of a different character.

The font is very old, in the form of a massive cup, large enough for baptism by immersion, and probably coeval with the foundation of the church.

The present fabric does not belong to any acknowledged style of architecture ; the windows are glazed with large squares. The sittings are pews, many of them composed of old carved oak.

The chancel is properly only a small portion of the east end of the nave, raised two or three steps above the rest. The walls of the portion enclosed by the altar rails are panelled with carved oak. Within the rails are two carved oak chairs of antique pattern.

The monuments are not numerous, nor any of them very old. A portion of a mutilated brass, now preserved in the vestry, bears the representation of a bearded figure, with belt and sword, upon which are scratched, rather than cut, the following words—

"Praye for the soule of John Dixon, uncle to Vicar Dixon, 1570."

Rather strange to find an inscription of this kind during the reign of the protestant Queen Elizabeth!

In the cross aisle at the west end of the nave is the following curious inscription, in rude antique capitals, on a block of gritstone—

"Feb. 18, A.D. 1658.

The. earth. my. mother. was. my. mother. is. and. thine. shall. be.
Oh. thinke. it. not. amise. her. to. obey. I. was. a. man. like. the.
Repent. feare. God. love. all. &. follow. me.
FRANCIS JEFFRAY."

In the cross aisle in front of the chancel are the following two inscriptions—

"Here lyes the body of Mr. Lawrence Danson, of Winsley, who dyed the 24th day of February, Ano. Dni. 1729, in the 73rd year of his age."

"Here lieth interred Mrs. Mary Leuty, relict of Mr. William Leuty, of Holm, Gentleⁿ· She died the 16th of December, 1768, aged 76."

Against the north wall, within the chancel, on a tablet of white marble, is inscribed—

"Sacred to the memory of Timothy Metcalf Shann, M.A., who was for many years vicar of this parish, and who died on the 3rd day of June, 1839, in the 74th year of his age."

On the same side of the church as the last, but more to the westward, is the memorial tablet of another vicar, inscribed—

"Beneath lyeth the body of Thomas Atkinson, A.B., and vicar of this place 27 years. He was born in the parish, and descended from an honest and antient family therein. He was every way qualified for the sacred function, and performed his duty with great care, zeal, and diligence. He lived beloved, and died lamented by all his parishioners and acquaintance the 14th of February, 1788, aged 62 years.

Likewise the body of Alice, his wife, a woman every way amiable, and in all respects worthy of such an excellent husband. She died the 30th of September, 1788, aged 64 years. *Ens entium eorum miserere.*"

Another tablet on the same wall is inscribed—"Sacred to the memory of Mary, the affectionate and beloved wife of John

Crosby, surgeon, and only daughter of Thomas and Sarah Ingle, late of Knaresborough, whose bodies lie in this churchyard. She died with truly christian resignation, July 12th, 1825, aged 24 years and 9 months. And according to her desire was buried at Overton, near York. Her unaffected piety, disinterested friendship, and engaging manners, flowing from a kind and feeling heart, greatly endeared her to those who knew her, and most of all to him who knew her best. Invidious grave, how dost thou rend in sunder whom love has knit and sympathy made one!"

The next is a mural tablet, principally composed of Caen stone, in the early decorated style, with foliated crockets, pinnacles, and a richly carved centre finial; the shafts supporting the inner arch are grey fossil marble; the ground is highly polished black marble, and on a slab of Carrara statuary marble is inscribed—

SACRED TO THE MEMORY OF
THE REV. JOSEPH WILSON, B.A.,
SOME TIME VICAR OF THIS PARISH,
WHO DIED DECEMBER 6, 1810,
AGED 88 YEARS.
AND OF HIS WIFE,
MARY WILSON,
WHO DIED DECEMBER 18, 1806,
AGED 70 YEARS.
AND ALSO OF THEIR ONLY SON,
BILTON JOSEPHUS WILSON,
WHO DIED JANUARY 28, 1866,
AGED 87 YEARS.

On a piece of oak below the gallery is carved in relief—"Samuel Sugden, Vicar, 1671. Jo. Birkhead, Li. Randall, Will. Hardisty, Jo. Light, Churchwardens."

On the front of the gallery is inscribed in gilt letters—"Mr. Thomas Leuty built this Loft at his own charge, A.D. 1725. T. Atkinson, Vicar."

Against the south wall of the nave, on a large slab of white marble, is the following singular inscription—

"Sacred to the memory of William Simpson, of Gilthorn and Felliscliffe, in the parish of Hampsthwaite. He died in September, 1776, aged 65 years, and was interred in this burial ground.

William Simpson was the twenty-sixth in direct descent from Archil, a Saxon thane, who, in the reign of Edward the Confessor, King of England, possessed very considerable estates in the north and west ridings of Yorkshire, amongst which was Wipeley, now a hamlet in the township of Clint, and which he held as a king's thane. Before the Norman conquest Archil resided in York, but after that event, being dispossessed of the greatest part of his estates, he retired to Wipeley, where he died in the reign of William the I., King of England. But his posterity appears to have continued to reside at Wipeley, until the year 1698, when Thomas Sympson sold the remnant of Wipeley—the last of the possessions of Archil, to Sir John Ingilby, Bart., of Ripley.

Also to the memory of Sushannah, eldest daughter and co-heir of Anthony Pulleyne, gentleman, of Timble; descended from the ancient family of the Pulleynes of the Forest of Knaresborough, and wife of the above named William Sympson. She died 1741, aged 80, and was here interred.

John Simpson, Esq., of Knaresborough, great-grandson of the above William and Sushannah Simpson, caused this monument to be erected to the memory of his ancestors."

Well do we love "a tale of the times of old;" and a long pedigree carefully substantiated is particularly interesting—it is

like a ray of golden sunshine flashing through surrounding
darkness. But where are the registers which prove the death of
Archil at Wipeley? And where are the documents which trace
the line of his posterity for the first three hundred years
after the conquest? Has not imagination supplied many links
in the chain of this wonderful pedigree?

On the same side of the church, beneath a brazen foliated
cross, on a slab of white marble is inscribed—

"In memory of Edwin Greenwood, of Swarcliffe Hall, Esq.,
born 11th of April, 1798; died 28th of September, 1852. 'Be
ye also ready: for in such an hour as ye think not the Son
of Man cometh.'"

At the east end, over the vestry door, on a marble slab
is inscribed—

Benefaction to the Poor of Hampsthwaite.

THE BILTON WILSON SCHOOL FUND.

On the 25th day of January, A.D. 1865, Bilton Josephus Wilson,
of this place, son of the Rev. Joseph Wilson, B.A., formerly vicar
of this parish, transferred the sum of £1,500, new 3 per cent.
annuities, to four trustees, in order that the yearly interest of the
said sum might be employed by them and their successors in the
trust, according to such rules and regulations as they may from
time to time see fit to make, for the purpose of maintaining a
school in this parish, for the education of the poor, in connexion
with the United Church of England and Ireland. The trustees
are the Vicar of Hampsthwaite, and his successors for the time
being; the Incumbent of Thornthwaite, and his successors for the
time being; Thomas Shann, M.A., sometime Vicar of this parish;
and Thomas Strother, of Killinghall, gentleman. Vacancies in
the number of the trustees are to be filled up by the remaining
trustees. For the better remembrance of the above recorded
facts, which are recited in the Trust Deed, dated the 2nd of
February, 1865, one of the landowners of the parish has been
permitted to put up this memorial of the benefaction.

The registers begin—baptisms and burials in 1603, and
marriages in 1604. The first marriage entry is as follows—

"1604. *Imprimis.*—William Winterburn and Jane Tanfield,
marr'd xxx. Octob. anno predicti."

Many names yet existing in the parish are to be found on the first pages of the register. Bramley occurs in 1604; Pullain in 1605; Gill in 1606; Day in 1604; Yeates in 1608; Leuty in 1618; Andrew in 1610. The names of Hardesty and Scaife are of very frequent occurrence.

The books have been generally well kept, and are in good condition. The following extracts are from the older ones.—

"1677. Mr. Matthew Bland, curate at Thornthwaite Chapell, buried Nov. y⁰ 4th."

Inside the cover of the first book is written—

"The Rev. Samuel Sugden, Master of Arts, and Vicar of Hampsthwaite, was inducted into his living Michaelmas Day, Anno Domini 1670." Below—"And came from Burton Leonard to reside, Aprill 4, 1671."

"Mr. Samuel Pawson, Vicar de Hampsthwaite, and Francis Burton, of the parish of Ripley, by virtue of a license out of the court of Richmond, were lawfully married 30th Aprill, in the year of our Lord 1665, by Matthew Bland, minister de Thornthwaite."

The Rev. Joseph Wilson, when vicar, has entered on the last page of his register the names of all those who were either excommunicated or did penance; and upwards of thirty suffered in this manner for their fleshly sins.*

During the eighteenth century, when the occupations of the different parties are given, besides the yeoman, farmer, and ordinary village tradesman, we find another class composed of weavers, sievers, dish-makers, spurriers, lorimers, and white-smiths. The two last appear to have been numerous in the higher parts of the parish, indicating a large amount of manu-

* A private note by the same vicar gives the following as the cost:—
"A private penance at York, £1 12s. 4d.; public penance, 10s. 6d.; 2s. less if they go themselves."

facture of that kind. We have been told that a great part of the articles made by these artizans were sold at Ripon, and that a majority of the famous "Ripon rowels" were made in this parish.

From 1780 to 1800 inclusive, 1,845 baptisms are entered in the register, of which 684 were males and 661 females. During the same period were 815 burials, of which 407 were males and 408 females. From 1754 to 1800 inclusive, 641 marriages took place at this church.

In the ten years 1811 to 1820, there were 788 baptisms, of which 402 were males and 386 females; 481 burials, 251 males and 230 females; and 168 marriages.

On the 6th of August, 1785, Matthew Mason was executed at York, for sacrilegiously breaking into the parish church of Hampsthwaite, and stealing therefrom seventeen shillings, some copper, and two silver cups—which last were found, broken to pieces, in his possession.

In the tower are three bells. On the least is inscribed—

EDWARD BAINBRIDGE, Vicar.
JONA. HUTCHINSON, } Churchwardens.
HEN. RANSOM,
1738.
Deo Gloria.

On the next is—

Soli Deo Gloria, 1626.

The other bears—

To God that doth dispose all things,
To him all glory and praise we ring.
1620.
Soli Deo Gloria.
W. O.

In the churchyard, inscriptions on altar tombs of coarse gritstone commemorate the ancient family of Day, of Day Ash, in Menwith—as, William Day, who died in 1661; Francis Day, his son, who died May 4th, 1696; Hannah, wife of Francis

Day, who died April 1st, 1699, aged 54; and the following—
"Here lyeth interred the body of William Day, of Menwith-Hill, in yᵉ parish of Hampsthwaite, who departed this life in the year of our Lord MDCXL.

Adjoining to which lyeth the body of Elizabeth Day, great-grand-daughter to the said William. who departed this life the 9th day of May in yᵉ year of our Lᵈ 1744, and in yᵉ 79th year of her age.

And in the grave of his great-grandfather, by his own order, lyeth interred the body of John Day, of the above mentioned Menwith-Hill, who departed this life the 29th of July, in the year of our Lord MDCCXLV., and in the 78th year of his age."

On the western side of the burial ground a headstone bears the following inscription—

"Sacred to the memory of Edwin Greenwood, of Swarcliffe, Esquire, born 11th April, 1798; died 28th September, 1852."

Another headstone in front of the church bears—

"In memory of Jane Ridsdale, daughter of George and Isabella Ridsdale, of Hampsthwaite, who died at Swinton Hall, in the parish of Masham, on the 2nd day of January, 1828, in the 59th year of her age. Being in stature only 81¼ inches high.

> Blest be the hand divine which gently laid
> My head at rest beneath the humble shade;
> Then be the ties of friendship dear;
> Let no rude hand disturb my body here."

On a pillar in the churchyard is a sun dial bearing the date 1672.

The following is the most correct list of vicars we have been able to obtain. Down to the year 1686 the names are from Torre's MSS.;* the others are from the parish register—

* "Archdeaconry of York," p. 195.

2ʙ

Kal. Maii, 1280.	Dns. Joh. dict. Flour, pbr. minister et Fratres. Sci.	
		Robti. de Knaresburgh.
2 Kal. Aug., 1292.	Dns. Ric. de Kinton, cap............	,,
6 Junii, 1307.	Dns. Ric. de Beston, pbr.	,,
7 Kal. Sep., 1322.	Dns. Gilbt. de Sheryngton, pbr.	,,
	Dns. Joh. de Burton, pbr...........	,, ...p. mort.
21 Sept., 1349.	Fr. Alan. de Scardeburgh, frater,	
	domus Sct. Roberti	,, . ..p. resig.
12 April, 1351.	Fr. Joh. de Rillington, confrater, &c.	,, ...p. resig.
26 Nov., 1368.	Fr. Allan de Scardeburgh, etc.......	,, ...p. mort.
9 Oct., 1369.	Fr. Will. de Spofford, etc.	,, ...p. mort.
Ult. May, 1378.	Fr. Joh. de Killingwyke, confr., &c.	
	Fr. Will. Risheton.................	,, ...p. resig.
27 June, 1421.	Fr. Wm. Lindessey, pbr.	,, ...p. resig.
9 Nov., 1422.	Fr. Will. Rysheton, (obit. 1431)	,,
	Fr. Joh. Harwood	,, ...p. mort.
9 Aug., 1455.	Fr. Joh. Hudson, cancus dom.......	,, ...p. mort.
26 Feb., 1486.	Fr. Rob. Tesh, frat. dom...........	,, ...p. mort.
1 Oct., 1499.	Fr. Joh. Whixley, frat. ibm.........	,, ...p. mort.
	Fr. Joh. Wilkynson	,, ...p. mort.
17 May, 1524.	Fr. Rob. Tash. fi. domous	,, ...p. mort.
20 May, 1525.	Fr. Oswald Benson, minister domus	
	Sti. Robti ....assignati domus St. Robti...p. resig.	
21 Oct., 1525.	Fr. Tho. Dacre, pbr...............	,,
	Dns. Tho. Dickson	,, ...p. mort.
~4 March, 1587.*	Christ. Lyndall, cl., M.A........Eliz. Reg...p. resig.	
18 Aug., 1603.	Ric. Slater, cl. M.A.................Jac. Rex.	
19 Feb., 1662.	Samuel Pawson, cl.......................p. mort.	
27 Sep., 1670.	Samuel Sugden, cl. ....Elena Hardish..p. mort.	
17 July, 1686.	Benjamin Holden, cl. ....p. resig.	
24 Nov., 1715.	Thomas Atkinson, A.B., ...Thomas Atkinson,	
	of Winsley, yeo. ....p. mort.	
9 Aug., 1738.	Edward Bainbridge, A.B. ....Wm. Woodburn,	
	Knaresbro,' gent. ....p. resig.	
12 Dec., 1771.	Joseph Wilson, cl. .... Thos. Shann,	
	Tadcaster, surgeon ....p. resig.	
11 July, 1790.	Timothy Metcalf Shann, A.B.,..Thomas Shann p. mort.	
	1839.	Thomas Shann..............T. M. Sham ..per resig.
	1845.	John Mare Ward ....per resig.
	1862.	Henry Deck ....present vicar.

The charities consist of the rent of lands left by William
Pullein, in 1691; —— Thompson, Francis Jeffrey, and Sarah

* There are evidently some names wanting here, which we have not the
means of supplying. On the 6th day of October, 1536, Robert Beckwith,
of Dacre, made his will, and among other bequests, made the following,—
"I gyve to Sr William Sothern, chapleyne at Hampesthwaite, to sing a
trentall of messes for my saule, and all cristen saules, v&." Sr Thomas
Dacre, vicar of Hampsthwaite, was one of the witnesses.—*Memorials of
Fountains*, vol. i., p. 354.

Newall, in 1655. These consist of 2a. 1r. 5p. called the Poor
Folk's Land, situate near Hampsthwaite; two closes containing
5a. 1r. 1p., near the Wreaks Mill, in Birstwith; and one-half
the rent of 3a. 1r. 21p., also situate in Birstwith. (The other
portion of this piece of land belongs to the parish of Fewston).
The amount of these rents is received by trustees, who pay
the same to the churchwardens of the respective townships,
by whom it is distributed to the poor at Christmas.

John Turpin, by his will, dated April 23rd, 1763, gave
to the poor of Hampsthwaite 20s. a-year, for ever, to be
given in bread on sacrament days.

William Ridsdale, by his will, dated Nov. 21st, 1711, devised
to his eldest brother, Edward Ridsdale, "the messuage house
and garth commonly called Vail's House, one garth called
Thompson's Garth, and one house anciently called his Farm
House, and the garth belonging to it, to the use and behoof
of teaching six poor boys, within the township of Hampsthwaite,
only from the primer to read well in the bible." Owing to
want of precision in the wording of the will only 42s. annually
has been paid towards the education of the said six poor boys.

An account of the donations belonging to the parish of
Hampsthwaite and the township of Fewston; to whom, let and
how distributed on the 25th of December, 1800, by the
then minister and churchwardens of the aforesaid parish.*

Lands let at the following rents—

	£	s.	d.
To Robert Milner, of Clapham Green, at	7	11	0
Thomas Metcalfe, of Hampsthwaite	6	16	6
Thos. Ranscm's widow, of Birstwith	3	10	0
Richard Umpleby, of Felliscliffe, and Mr. Day's Interest—£1 1s.	1	11	0
	£19	8	6

* From a Diary of the Rev. J. Wilson, Vicar of Hampsthwaite.

Distributions—

	£	s.	d.
To Hampsthwaite, Felliscliffe, Birstwith, Menwith-hill, and Darley ....each	4	8	4¼
Fewston (being one moiety of T. Ransom's wid.) ..	1	15	0

The village of Hampsthwaite is situate on the southern
side of the river Nidd, over which there is a narrow stone bridge
of three arches; two brooks from each side of the village
here flow into the river. The church is situate on the right
hand, on a piece of ground at some period left by the waters
of the Nidd. Like the other old churches of the forest, it
is as near the outside of the parish as it is possible to place
it. Viewed from the bridge in connection with the river,
the village and church form a very pretty picture.

Outside the churchyard wall formerly stood the stables for
the pack-horses, whose route from York to Skipton and
Lancashire lay through this village. They were demolished
some years ago.

In front of a cottage near the Lamb Inn is an old sepulchral
slab, now used as a stone bench; it is about seven feet in
length by about twenty inches in breadth; down the middle
of which is carved a highly floriated cross, on the right side
of which is the figure of a sword, three feet two inches in
length, and on the other a short, broad, pointed weapon,
something like a hunting knife or dagger. This stone came
from the church when it was rebuilt in 1820-1.

The next building is the Lamb Inn, which has been an
hostelry from time immemorial. A few years ago it was
a curious old building, thatched with ling and straw, with
low walls, narrow windows, wide chimneys, and fire places
still wider. Could its old walls relate all they have *seen*
and *heard* what a curious history they would reveal! Alas! for
the mutability of things in this world, the old Lamb has

been partly rebuilt; and the interest which attached to it as a memento of the past is gone for ever. A curious old weapon is preserved as a kind of fixture in this house, and has been beyond the memory of the oldest inhabitant. It is a kind of dagger; the handle and blade being 17½ inches in length; on each side of the handle is a guard projecting about an inch, and terminating in the figure of a human head. It is not known whence it came.

A short distance further south, on the right hand, is the residence of the late Mr. Bilton Josephus Wilson, who was an extensive landowner in this district, as well as the most munificent benefactor the parish of Hampsthwaite ever had. On the mother's side he was descended from the old and respectable family of Bilton, who have been landowners in the Forest of Knaresborough from a very early period.

Richard Bilton married Isabel, daughter of William Leuty, of Holme, and on his decease Dec. 9th, 1628, was succeeded by his only son,

William Bilton, who, on the 28th of July, 1655, married Isabel Leuty, by whom he had one son and three daughters—

William, bapt. March 6th, 1657.

Eling, bapt. Aug. 5th, 1660; buried Dec. 23rd, 1688.

Elizabeth, bapt. March 16th, 1662; buried March 7th, 1704.

Mary, bapt. Dec. 17th, 1665, was married to William, son of Thomas Smith, of the Hurst, June 18th, 1696.

This William Bilton built the house at Clapham Green, in Birstwith, as appears by a stone over the door, inscribed, **W. 1677. B.** He was buried October 12th, 1688, when he was succeeded by his only son,

William Bilton, who by his wife, Mary, had issue—

William, bapt. Feb. 3rd, 1694, and—

Richard, bapt. Nov. 18th, 1698. He was of Tang in

Birstwith, and built the house there, as appears from a
stone over the door, inscribed, "This building was erected
by Richard Bilton, Anno Dom. 1754." He was never married,
and died Aug. 24th, 1769.

William Bilton, the elder, died Feb. 29th, 1785, and was
succeeded by his eldest son,

William Bilton, who died September 5th, 1749; he married,
November 6th, 1785, Ann Wade, of Pannal, by whom he had
issue—

William, bapt. November 19th, 1788, who was never married,
and died at Tang, June 4th, 1806;

Ann, bapt. August 16th, 1741, never married, died at Tang,
August 12th, 1819; and—

Mary, bapt. September 10th, 1768, who on June 5th, 1771,
married the Rev. Joseph Wilson, vicar of Hampsthwaite.

The Rev. Joseph Wilson was descended from an ancient
Cumberland family of yeoman rank, long settled in the parish
of Kirkoswald, in that county. Reuben, son of John Wilson,
married Ann, a younger daughter of Thos. Hodgson, of Lazenby,
in the same county, and sister of the Rev. Thomas Hodgson,
Vicar of Brough, in Westmorland, by whom he had, along with
other issue, a son Joseph, born at Blunderfield, Kirkoswald,
in 1722—who was brought up to the church; was ordained
deacon at Richmond, Yorks, by Dr. Keen, Bishop of Chester;
and after serving curacies at Market Weighton, and Littleport
in the Isle of Ely, he returned to Brough to assist his uncle
in his ministerial duties. He was instituted vicar of Hampsthwaite, December 21st, 1771; and died October 6th, 1810.
By his wife, Mary Bilton (who died December 18th, 1806),
he had one son—

Bilton Josephus Wilson, bapt. July 4th, 1778; and who
on October 22nd, 1806, married Sarah, third daughter of John

Simpson, of Dacre Banks, yeoman, and Ann, his wife, eldest
daughter of John Hawkridge, of Brearton, and grand-daughter
of John Strother, Esq., of Killinghall. He died January 28th,
1866, leaving no issue. His widow survived him three years,
and died March 28th, 1869.

Mr. Wilson was educated for the medical profession, but
never practised, except among his poor neighbours, to whom
(before a doctor settled in the village) he freely gave his advice
and medicine. During the whole of his life he was remarkably
benevolent and kind to the poor. He died somewhat suddenly,
though slightly indisposed; he took tea as usual on the day
of his death, when a fainting fit came on, from which he never
recovered. When the school in Hampsthwaite was built he
was the largest subscriber; and on the 25th of January, 1865,
he transferred £1,500, new three per cent. annuities, to four
trustees, to form a perpetual endowment for the said school.
By his will he bequeathed £100 to the Leeds Infirmary, £100
to the Harrogate Bath Hospital, £100 to the Church Missionary
Society, £100 to the Society of Oddfellows at Hampsthwaite,
and directed his executors to distribute his annual gift of £40
to the poor of the village, on the New Year's Day next after
his decease.

Passing up the village street, is the cottage of Peter Barker,
the blind joiner, a most extraordinary man, who can make
almost anything which is made of wood, and that in a
workmanlike manner. He was born in the year 1808, and
lost his sight when about four years old, by an inflamation
of the eyes; since then he has been

> "——— dark, amid the blaze of noon
> Irrecoverably dark; total eclipse
> Without all hope of day."

Though deprived of sight, the spirit of enterprise was strong
within him; he joined in the games and plays of other boys

with a confidence and skill equal to their own, and was, not
unfrequently, a contriver and ringleader in their petty mis-
chievous pranks. If any one played a practical joke upon
the blind boy, he was pretty certain, before long, to have
it returned in kind. Having an ear for music, he became
a performer on the violin, and, as he grew to manhood,
frequented dances and merry-makings all round the country, as
a performer on his instrument. From frequenting these jovial
assemblies he began to have a love for strong drink, but his
moral nature was too strong to be overcome by these temptations.
He suddenly formed a determination to abandon the musical
profession, as well as the companions with which it had brought
him in contact, and beg his bread rather than obtain it in such a
manner. The idea entered his mind that he would be a joiner,
and he fell to work as a chairmaker, succeeding at the first
attempt, and since then has followed the occupation of a
joiner. He served no apprenticeship, received no instructions
or ideas from others, and yet, he says, he can make anything
that is made of wood, from a stackbar up to a chest of drawers.
The only peculiarity observable in any of his tools is in the foot
rule with which he makes his measurements, the lines on which
are marked by small pins, in different numbers, at different
lengths on the rule.

Like all enterprising men of the world, Peter Barker married
a wife, by whom he had a son, who was the constant companion
of his father, and, to his bitter sorrow, died January 19th,
1868, at the age of seventeen years. His wife died June 3rd,
1862, so he is now a widower, and an aged relative superintends
his domestic affairs.

He is tall and athletic in person; ready and quick in
conversation; plain, straightforward, and honest in the account
he gives of himself and his performances. He assumes no

superiority over ordinary men on account of the abilities
he possesses, but says it was Providence which gave him his
talents, and the same Providence has supported him through
life. He is held in high estimation by all his neighbours,
and, without considering his situation, he appears as happy,
cheerful, and comfortable, as any man we ever met with.

It has been settled beyond the reach of reasonable doubt that
Hampsthwaite was the original home of the family of Thackeray,[*]
which has been raised to high distinction by the talents of some
of its members, but more particularly by the brilliant literary
career of William Makepeace Thackeray, whose sudden death
cast such a gloom over the world of letters near the close
of the year 1868. The old hive whence the swarms of
Thackerays issued yet remains, opposite the vicarage. It
consists of three distinct tenements, two storeys in height
in front, but only about eight feet in height at the back. The
northern gable, with a large projecting chimney, is a piece
of excellent masonry, and is probably older than the side walls.
The roof is covered with thatch. A day of renovation or
rebuilding will come at no distant date, and when it does come
we humbly petition the owner to spare the northern gable,
and it will long serve as a memorial to mark the dwelling
of the great-grandfather of William Makepeace Thackeray,
the author of "Vanity Fair."

The family whence he sprung were of yeoman rank, owners of
land which they cultivated with their own hands. Walter
Thackeray, of Hampsthwaite, who died in 1618, had a son
named Robert, which said Robert had a son named Thomas,
born in 1628, who by his wife, Margaret, had a family of
seven sons and two daughters. The sixth of these sons, named

* By the pedigree given in the "Herald and Genealogist," by Mr. R. H
Skaife, of York, and Mr. J. G. Nicholas, of London; published in 1864.

Elias, became rector of Hauxwell, and appears to have been the first of the family to rise to distinction. The fifth son, named Timothy, born in November, 1664, became parish clerk in his native village; he had a family of seven sons and four daughters. Thomas, the eldest son, became head master of Harrow School in 1746; D.D. in 1747; and Archdeacon of Surrey in 1753. He was great-grandfather to the celebrated William Makepeace Thackeray, who died suddenly December 24th, 1868, at the early age of 53. He had, however, done enough to live in the memory of posterity.

To return to the Thackerays at home in their quiet nest in the forest village. Elias, the third son of Timothy, succeeded his father as parish clerk, and, on his decease, in July, 1725, Joseph, a younger brother, succeeded to the office, which he probably held till his death, on the 4th of January, 1771, when his son, Thomas Thackeray, succeeded, and held the situation thirty-three years, closing his career in January, 1804,* and was the last of the family who resided at Hampsthwaite.

Thackerays are numerous in and around the Forest of Knaresborough. There is scarcely a village that does not contain one or more families of that name. Near Fewston is an ancient homestead called Thackeray, and a brook in the same locality bears the name of Thackeray-beck. From these and other circumstances, we do not suppose that we

---

* A brass plate, inserted in the face of an older altar tomb in the church-yard, bears the following inscription to his memory,—" Here lieth the body of Thomas Thackwray, of this town, son of Joseph Thackwray, clerk of this parish, who departed this life the 21st of January, 1804, aged 56.

> Farewell, vain world, I've had enough of thee;
> I'm careless, therefore, what thou say'st of me;
> Thy smiles I court not, nor thy frowns do fear,
> My cares are past, my bones lie quiet here;
> What fault thou found'st in me take care to shun,
> Look well at home, enough there's to be done."

should err far in placing the original home of all the Thackerays in this neighbourhood.

The national school was built by public subscription, in 1861. It is an elegant and substantial building of stone, in the Elizabethan style of architecture; comprising schoolroom, with classroom, and master's house attached. In order to make this establishment of permanent benefit to the parish, the late Bilton Josephus Wilson endowed it with the interest of £1,500, on the 25th of January, 1865. The memory of such actions ought to go down to posterity in everlasting letters.

On the opposite side of the village street is the vicarage, a large, plain, comfortable looking building, situate in its own grounds.

The open space in front of the vicarage bears the name of Cross Green, where tradition says there formerly stood a cross, and that regular markets were held here.*

A short distance west of the church, on the brook called Tang beck, formerly stood a corn mill; it was also a soke mill, and in 1575 was held by Catherine Beckwith, with reversion to the queen. In which year she was plaintiff in a suit in the duchy court against Richard Lewty, and other copyhold and customary tenants, for suit and mulcture of a water corn mill, called Hampsthwaite mill. Twenty-one years afterwards there was another suit in the same court, in which the attorney-general, at the suit of Richard Loftus, was plaintiff, and Marmaduke Atkinson, Hewage Lapage, Richard Skaiffe, and others, tenants of the hamlets of Hampsthwaite and Rowden, defendants —concerning the right of repairing the mill dam of the mill of Hampsthwaite, then newly erected at a place called Clynts

---

* Does the following extract support the tradition?—"33rd. Ed: I. Claus. Panhall hamlet, Hamestwait hamlet, quæ sunt, &c., membræ maner de Knaresburgh, mercat, feria."

Wreaks. This appears to have reference to the removal of the mill to a new site; and the tenants who had repaired the dam at one place did not deem themselves bound to maintain it in the other. Nearly all traces of the mill on this stream are now obliterated.

In the field called the Hall Garth, adjoining the village on the west, are traces as if some important building had formerly stood there. The name also is suggestive of some such erection. The farm to which it belongs is sometimes called the Manor Farm; it is of freehold tenure, and was purchased by the late Mr. B. J. Wilson from C. H. Elsley, Esq., late Recorder of York. These lands at one time belonged to the Priory of St. Robert's of Knaresborough. In 1869, this farm was purchased by William Sheepshanks, Esq., of Leeds and Harrogate, the present owner.

The Wesleyan Methodist Chapel, erected in 1818, is situate a short distance east of the village. It is a substantial building of stone, and will accommodate about 200 hearers.

Rodon,* or Rowden Lane, is a hamlet situate on the slope of the hill, a short distance to the southward of Hampsthwaite village. Though now consisting merely of a few scattered houses, at the time of the Domesday survey it was of such importance as to obtain a separate entry. At that time it was in the hands of the king, and contained two carucates of land. It is mentioned again in 1299, as having been among the lands held by Richard, Earl of Cornwall, and appears to have been of much more importance in ancient times than at present.

A family named Parker resided here in early times; one member of which at least rose to wealth and distinction by

* The name Rodon is evidently from *Roe*, the roebuck, and *don*, a hill—the hill of the roe; a fine poetical epithet, descriptive of itself and its early tenantry.

his learning or talents, or both. A few extracts from his will*
will show his station in society, as well as his connection with
this place and parish.—

"Testamentum Magistri Johannis Parker, Doctoris in Medi-
cina." It is dated the 26th of November, 1406. He describes
himself as John Parker, of York, clerk, who, intending to visit
remote parts, made his will before setting out. He gives his
soul to God Almighty, the Holy Virgin, and All Saints, and
his body to be buried where God shall dispose it. He gives
three pounds in gold for the expenses of entertaining his friends
at his funeral, from the day of his death until eight days afterwards. He gives twenty marks in gold unto an honest priest,
to be selected by his executors, to celebrate mass for his soul,
the souls of his parents, and the souls of all the faithful dead,
for the space of three years next following his. death. He gives
ten marks to be distributed among the poor in the city of York.
After several bequests to churches and chapels in York, he gives
to Evota, daughter of John Dickinson, of Clint, 20s. in gold, on
her marriage. He gives to Robert Fellescliff, chaplain, 26s. 8d.
He gives to John, his clerk, one bay horse, with a new saddle,
and a bow and arrows. To John Killyngall, vicar of Kirkby
Stephen, a girdle with a gilded "baslardo." To Agnes Parker,
his mother, a gown of russet, furred with "fuyns." To Thomas
del Dam, spicer, his long sword and a harp *(citherâ)*, then in
the keeping of Robert, clerk of St. Martin's Church, in Coney
Street. To Robert Bird, one helmet *(wyrehatt)*, with one
Carlisle axe. To the vicar of Hampsthwaite, one book, called
"Circumstans." To Robert Fellescliff, chaplain, a gown of a
red colour, in the care of the vicar of Hampsthwaite. To
"domino Hugo de Hampsthwaite," one little psalter, and a
bow and arrows, then in care of his mother, in Rawdon. To his

* "Testamenta Eboracensia," p. 342-3. "Surtees' Soc.," 1836.

sister, Katherine, one vase and tablecloth, which he had of the gift of his father. He then orders William Rishton, vicar of Hampsthwaite, Agnes Parker, his mother, and William Schutt, after his decease, to sell all the lands and tenements which he had in Rawdon, with all belonging thereto, for money; and afterwards dispose of the same in masses, orations, alms, and other charitable works, for the salvation of his soul and the souls above mentioned. He also orders that his lands in Clint, of which Mr. John de Scotton was seized, should remain in his possession during his lifetime; and all his lands, tenements, rents, and services, with all pertaining thereto, in the villages and territories of Colton, Steton, and Acome, shall be sold by his executors. He appoints Robert de Otley, rector of the church of St. Martin, in Coney Street, in York, Robert Clifford, and Robert Fellescliff, chaplain, his executors, to whom he leaves the residue of his estate.

In a codicil he directs that the three pounds in gold, given in his will for the expenses of his funeral, may be given to defray the cost of recasting one of the bells of Hampsthwaite Church, the same being broken, should the vicar think proper to receive the same.

Probate was granted January 6th, 1406; so that the testator did not visit the remote places mentioned in the beginning of his will,—or perhaps he meant the unknown world beyond the grave.

The brook Cock, or Ock-beck flows past this place; one of its tributaries, entering from the east, has worn a great gully in the hill side, which has received the name of Hell-hole. In this gully is a bed of ironstone, in large nodules, enclosed by masses of shale. We believe that iron has been extensively mined along the edge of this brook in very early times, and removed to other places to be smelted.

Saltergate* Hill is a small hamlet on the Knaresborough and Skipton road, occupying the highest land in the township. One respectable house on the top of the hill is of considerable age. This estate, comprising nearly sixty acres, belongs to the poor of the parish of Adel, being purchased for that purpose with part of a legacy of £800, left by the will of Thomas Kirk, Esq., in 1701. The soil here is of superior quality to much of that around, owing to the presence of a bed of transition limestone full of fossils, the decomposition of which forms a good soil,

The population in 1801 was 439; in 1811, 418; in 1821, 490; in 1831, 445; in 1841, 455; in 1851, 445; and in 1861, 518.

In 1782, the estimated rental of the township was £728 10s., and the number of landowners 55. In 1857, the annual value, as returned by the overseers, was £1,046. Amount assessed to income tax in 1858, £1,790. Value assessed to the county rate in 1849, £1,088; in 1859, £1,627; and in 1869, £1,822.

In 1801, the following return was made of the agricultural produce in the parish of Hampsthwaite:—Wheat, 168 acres; barley, 112; oats, 909; pease, 88; beans, 18; potatoes, 56; turnips, 93; rye, 12.

The whole parish contains 11,908a. 2r. 6p., of which 41a. 1r. 8p. are water.

---

* This is probably derived from *Saltus terra*, forest land; which, if written contractedly, according to ancient custom, would make the word *Sal. ter*. *Gate* simply means road.

FELLISCLIFFE.

This township is bounded on the east by Hampsthwaite; on the north by Tang-beck, which separates it from Birstwith; on the south and west it abuts on the parish of Fewston. It is a picturesque, undulating, upland district, occupying the centre of the old forest, and comprising the hamlets of Swincliff, West Syke Green, and Kettlesing.

The Roman road from Isurium to Olicana passed right through this township from east to west, and, with trifling exceptions, along none of the present carriage roads. After ascending the hill from Hampsthwaite to Swincliff Top, on nearly the present line of road, it passed along the high ground, on what is now known as Long Lane, which Long Lane is merely a bridle road to Whitwall Nook, where a piece of the genuine lane yet remains. Further westward the ancient right of road is merely preserved by a footpath, which appears to keep upon the Roman stratum, or very close to it, as far as the Kettlesing Head toll-bar, when the old road runs parallel with the Knaresborough and Skipton turnpike road.

This township yields but very little matter to the local historian; it is, however mentioned in the Domesday survey, among the lands of the king, as *Felgesclif*, and containing three carucates of land pertaining to the soke of the manor of Burc.*

* "Bawdwen's Dom. Boc.," p. 16.

Swincliffe occupies the most easterly portion of the township, and evidently derives its name from the *Swine's-cliff*,—the *cliff* yet remains, but the *swine* have departed or become domesticated. This consists of a mass of millstone grit in a plantation of firs, facing the west, and commanding a fine view of the valley of the Tang Beck. On the top of this cliff a few years ago was a large rocking stone, which has been cut to pieces and removed, and the place is occasionally used as a stone quarry. On the north of this cliff, sloping down to Tang Beck, is a piece of land yet in a state of nature—a remnant of the old forest day—a matted thicket of underwood, gorse, heath, and ferns; while a part of it, called Gormire Wood, is a thick growth of native forest trees, amongst which the holly predominates.

At Swincliffe Top (the small cluster of houses on the hill) there exists a tradition of an archer named Smith,[*] who having bent his bow, by means of his hands and feet, against a large stone, shot an arrow over the village of Hampsthwaite, nestled in the valley below, over the river Nidd, into the township of Clint. A most extraordinary shot, which well entitled him to rank among those who

> "Well could hit a fallow deer
> Five hundred feet him fro."

The stone near which the archer stood is a natural rock, four or five feet square, level with the surface of the ground, quite flat and smooth, with a number of circular holes cut in it; these holes were cut for the purpose of playing the game of skittles or nine holes—this being the place where the youths of the neighbourhood met to play that game.

Over the door of a farm-house called Cote Syke, is the

[*] The following entry from the parish register of Hampsthwaite, is said by tradition to belong to this famous archer—"Burials. April 7th, 1780. Thomas Smith, Heckler, aged 57;—weighed 19 stones;—Papist."

following inscription. Who placed it there we know not, but he must have been much unlike the forest farmers around him.

17 S 85

W.S.

Omnem crede diem
tibi diluxisse supre-
mum grata superv-
eniet quæ non spe-
rabitur hora.

The above is on a slab of slate; some of the letters slightly defaced; on the door-head below is cut, **E.R., 1702,**

A family named Smith occupied lands in this township from early times; previously to the year 1700, Christopher Smith was settled here, and on his decease, in 1751, John Smith, his eldest son, was admitted to a moiety of a messuage, fourteen acres and two pennyworth of land, situate in the hamlets of Hampsthwaite and Felliscliffe, and also to two acres lying in the township of Birstwith; and on the decease of his mother, in 1754, he was admitted to the other moiety. He married, and had two sons, John and Thomas. John was never married, and died in 1794.* Thomas, the younger, had three sons, Thomas, John, and Christopher. Christopher married Helen Henson, by whom he had issue three daughters,—Mary, who died in infancy; Elizabeth, who married Charles Powell, Esq., solicitor, Knaresborough; and Emma Louisa, who married Francis Bolland, Esq., of Leeds.

At West Syke Green is a school, founded under the will of John Richmond, in the year 1711, by which £14 per annum

---

* From a schedule of his "goods and chattels," dated 19th April, 1794, he appears to have been a well-to-do yeoman—with good debts owing to him, apparently on note or bond, amounting to £919. His funeral expenses were £30; and the stock on the farm and goods in the house were worth £143 11s. 0d. Over the door of his house is inscribed on a stone slab—"This house was rebuilt by John Smith in the year of our Lord 1784."

is paid to a master, who instructs thirty free scholars of Birstwith and Felliscliffe, in reading, writing, accounts, and the church catechism.

The school room, as originally built, was only one story in height, with three windows on each side; afterwards the building was raised an additional story, and the lower divided, so as to make a dwelling for a master. The building is situate in an open, airy situation, commanding a fine view of the valley and the country to the east and west.

Kettlesing is the name applied to the upper part of the township, lying between the toll-bar on the Knaresborough and Skipton road, which is called Kettlesing Head, and the head of Tang Beck, which is called Kettlesing Bottom. Though the name reminds us of the *singing* of that useful domestic utensil, the tea kettle, before it boils, the derivation is probably from an early Saxon owner of the name of Chetel, or Ketel, and *ing*, a meadow.*

The shortest and most suggestive will we ever saw was made by a resident of this district, as follows—

"22nd May, 1587. Robert Thackwrey, of Kettlesinge, within the parishe of Hampestwate, mylner. I give my soul to

* This name is not of unfrequent occurrence in this neighbourhood. In the parish of Ripley we have *Kettlespring*—the name of a farm-house and fine spring of water. In Kirkby Malzeard, *Kettlestang* is the name of a large hill. In the Domesday survey *Chetel* is returned as a landowner at Appletrewick, Hebden, Coneston, and other places in Craven, in which district is *Kettlewell*, which Whitaker says is the *well of Ketel*.

There was also a family, which took its name from this place, flourishing in very early times. In the 16th of Edward III. (1342), "Johannes, filius Margaretæ de Kettilsyng," fines in 36s. 8d., for entry into one messuage and eighteen acres of land in Kettelsyng, which had been held by his said mother, Margaret.—*Knaresborough Court Rolls.*

In the Calendar of Pleadings, in the Duchy Court, we find, 19th of Elizabeth, Thomas Kettlesyne claiming, through William Arthington, a close of land at Markington. His name also occurs in the following year as alive and again engaged in law. A George Kettlestringe, in 25th of Elizabeth, is plaintiff against William Preston and others, for distraint of goods at Ripon.

Felliscliffe was also a personal surname in early times.

Almyghtie God, and I give all my goodes to Alison Swaille my wyfe betroythed, whom I make my full executrix." Proved 18th February, 1587-8.*

The Wesleyan Methodist Chapel at Kettlesing Bottom was built about the year 1790. It is the oldest Wesleyan Chapel in the parish of Hampsthwaite. There is a tradition that John Wesley himself preached within it, which we have not been able to authenticate. It is a plain building, in a low situation, and will accommodate about 200 hearers. A Wesleyan Sunday School was built on a piece of waste ground at a short distance from it; over the entrance of which is inscribed—"This school built by subscription in 1831." Correctly speaking both this chapel and school are in the township of Birstwith.

Tang Beck is a rivulet formed by the junction of two streams immediately adjoining the Wesleyan Chapel, thence flowing eastward, forms the boundary between the townships of Felliscliffe and Birstwith, and after passing Water Hall, Tang House, Birstwith Hall and Hirst Grove, empties itself into the Nidd. There were formerly many bleaching grounds upon this stream, and a large quantity of linen was manufactured in this valley previous to the introduction of the factory system.

The population in 1801 was 424; in 1811, 397; in 1821, 382; in 1831, 351; in 1841, 363; in 1851, 382; and in 1861, 347.

The annual value of this township as assessed to the county rate in 1849 was £2,349; in 1859, £2,582; and in 1869, £2,598. Amount assessed to property tax in 1858, £2,808.

* R. H. S.

BIRSTWITH.*

BIRSTWITH is of a triangular form; the Tang Beck forming its southern, and the river Nidd its northern boundary; an imaginary line drawn across high lands separates it on the west from Darley. This is the most beautiful and best cultivated district within the Forest of Knaresborough.

Birstwith is twice mentioned in the Domesday survey. First, among the lands of the king, we find—"Manor. In Beristade, Gamelbar had one carucate to be taxed. Land to half a plough. Five shillings."†

Again, among the lands of Gospatric,—"In Beristade, one carucate to be taxed. Land to half a plough."‡

In very early times this township became divided among a great number of small landowners;§ each residing on, and culti-

---

* Written at different times *Beristade, Birscale, Birscate, Berstok, Birstith,* and finally *Birstwith;* and is probably derived from *Ber,* water, and *with,* a wood or forest—that is, a land of wood and water.
Swarcliffe is probably the dark or tawny cliff.
†"Bawdwen's Dom. Boc.," p. 37.
‡*Ibid,* p. 217.
§ One of whom was a branch of the family of Skaife, as is evident from the following *Inquisition post mortem,*—"Inq. p. m. Thom. Skayfe, nuper de Burstith, 14. July. 2. Jac. I. 1604. When he died he was seized in his demesnes as of fee, of and in a messuage or tenement in Wynnesley and Hartwith, and also of a fourteenth part of a common pasture called Wynnesley Moor, or Pasture, into fourteen parts divided, appurtenant to the said messuage, and containing 37 acres. The premises were held of the king *in capite,* by knight's service, and are worth 20s. yearly. The said Thomas died 19. Dec. last (1603), and Elizabeth, his wife, now living at Wetherby, holds for life a third part of the said premises. Robert Skayfe, son and heir, was aged thirteen years and eight months old when his father died."
Notices of the Biltons will be found under Hirst and Hampsthwaite, and of the Days under Menwith.

vating his own farm. In the seventeenth century the family
of Bilton appears to have acquired a more than average share
of wealth and importance, as we find them subsequent to that
time settled at Elton, Hurst, and at Tang House, all holding
the rank of good substantial yeomen. In the eighteenth century
the family of Day, then resident at Day Hall (now Birstwith
Hall), gained a position somewhat elevated above their neighbours. During the present century the family of Greenwood
has acquired considerable estates here, and added much to the
wealth and beauty of the district.

Swarcliffe Hall, seat of the family of Greenwood, stands partly
upon the site of an old house, which had borne that name from
time immemorial, and was formerly the property of a family
named Blesard, who held it until July, 1800, when it passed
into the hands of a Mr. Arthington, who, in April, 1805, sold
the same to John Greenwood, Esq., of Knowle, near Keighley,
who considerably enlarged the estate by additional purchases;
rebuilt the hall, and nearly all the houses in the village below,
as they became by successive purchases his property; and since
that time every owner has done something to enlarge and beautify
the estate.

After rebuilding the hall, Mr. Greenwood formed gardens,
laid out grounds, and at once converted it into a gentleman's
residence. In 1848, the mansion was enlarged and partly
rebuilt by Mr. Edwin Greenwood, on a more extensive scale,
from designs furnished by M. R. Hawkins, Esq., of London.
The work was scarcely finished at his death, in 1852; when
the estates passed into possession of his brother, Mr. Frederick
Greenwood, who died in 1862, and was succeeded by his son,
Mr. John Greenwood, the present owner. Again extensive improvements were made in the gardens and grounds, and large
additions made to the house and estate.

Armitage & Ibbetson.

Bradford.

SWARCLIFFE HALL.
THE SEAT OF MAJOR GREENWOOD

The hall is now an elegant and substantial building, in the Tudor style of architecture, consisting of a centre and wings; the former surmounted by a tower and spire. It stands pleasantly on a hill, surrounded by its grounds and gardens, overlooking a most beautiful home prospect; a park-like range of land, studded with ornamental and timber trees, slopes gently down in front. A little lower, near the centre of the picture, stand the church, the parsonage, and village of Birstwith; the river Nidd winds along at the bottom of the valley—now and then seen shining through its fringe of lofty timber trees; the railway runs along the foot of the opposing slope, and adds to the variety of the prospect. On the top of the adjoining hill may be seen the diminutive ruin which marks the site of the manor house of the Beckwiths of Clint; a family which for centuries were lords and masters on forest soil. From the windows of the dining room a wide expanse of country can be seen, extending from the rock-crowned mount of Brimham on the north-west, to the blue summits of the Hambleton and Wold Hills on the east.

On a plateau south-west of the house are the gardens, laid out with taste and judgment, and kept in the neatest order. The mansion, as well as all the appendages around, are built of the best materials, and in the most substantial manner. In no part of the Forest of Knaresborough have the beauties of nature been so assisted by the hand of art as at this place.

This branch of the family of Greenwood derives its pedigree from James Greenwood, of Keighley, whose son,

John Greenwood, born July 6th, 1737, died March 10th, 1807; by his wife, Ann Barwick, he had a son,

John Greenwood, born September 8th, 1768; died October 11th, 1846; by his second wife, Sarah, eldest daughter of William Sugden, Esq., of Keighley, he had issue—

Frederick, born January 15th, 1797, of whom hereafter.

Edwin, born April 11th, 1798; died, unmarried, September 28th, 1852.

Anne, born 1795, married, in 1822, the Rev. Theodore Dury, Rector of Keighley, by whom she had a family of seven children.

Matilda, born December 19th, 1799, married Rawdon Briggs, Esq., M.P. for Halifax; died August 10th, 1882.

Sarah Hannah, born 1805, married John Benson Sedgewick, Esq., of Stone Gapp, Yorks.

Frederick Greenwood married, May 31st, 1828, Sarah, only daughter of Samuel Staniforth, Esq., of Liverpool, by whom he had issue—

John, of whom hereafter.

Mary Littledale, married August 4th, 1858, to Major Rhode Hawkins, Esq., of Oakley, Kent.

Emily, born September 26th, 1831; died November 19th, 1834.

For twenty years after their marriage Mr. and Mrs. Greenwood resided at Ryshworth Hall, near Bingley, but in 1848 removed to Norton Conyers, near Ripon. In the spring of 1858, when returning home from Leeds, he met with an accident on the railway by the overturning of the train. At first the effects seemed so slight as to cause no alarm, but gradually the effects of the shock his nervous system had received developed themselves, by an occasional loss of power in his limbs, which after a time became permanent. Every means which skill and kindness could suggest were tried to restore to him some portion of his former health, but in vain—he died at Norton, August 28th, 1862.

His amiable qualities endeared him to a large circle of friends and acquaintance, while to his family and dependants he was affectionate, kind, and considerate.

John Greenwood, the present owner of Swarcliffe Hall, was
born February 20th, 1829, at Ryshworth Hall; educated at
Eton and Christ Church, Oxford, where he graduated B.A.
in 1851, and M.A. in 1860. He married, February 19th,
1852, Louisa Elizabeth, eldest daughter of Nathaniel Clarke
Barnardiston, Esq., of the Ryes, Suffolk, by whom he has
issue—

Frederick Barnardiston, born at Swarcliffe, January 3rd, 1854.

Charles Staniforth, born May 1st, 1857.

Edwin Wilfrid, born June 28th, 1861.

Clara Louisa.

Mr. Greenwood was elected M.P. for Ripon on the 27th
of March 1857, and again on the 30th of April, 1859; both
general elections. He is a magistrate, and deputy-lieutenant for
the west and north ridings of Yorkshire.

Arms—Party per fesse, *sable* and *argent*, a chevron, *ermine*,
between three cross saltires, counterchanged, *argent*.

Crest—A tiger sejant, *or*.

The village of Birstwith is situate on the northern bank of the
Nidd, over which is a substantial bridge of stone, near one
end of which is the Birstwith Station, on the Nidd Valley
Railway. A short distance below the bridge are the gas works
and a corn mill, which last probably occupies the site of one
erected in 1596, at a place then called Clynts Wreaks,* in lieu
of an older one, which had stood on Tang Beck, near Hampsthwaite. A few years ago here was also a large factory for
the spinning of cotton, which has been removed. The village is
principally composed of stone-built cottages—substantial and
comfortable—most of them with gardens attached, which are
kept in very neat order. In the centre of a group called the
Square is an elegant fountain, consisting of a square pillar, with

* See page 411.

spiral columns at the corners, surmounted by a pediment, erected in 1859, for the purpose of supplying the inhabitants with water—a combination of the useful with the beautiful. On the southern side is inscribed—

ERECTED A.D. 1859.
F. G.

And on the front of the trough which holds the water—

Quæ dat aquas saxo latet hospitia nympho imo,
Sic tu quum dederis dona latere velis.

(From hidden springs learn thou the way
To give, and not thyself betray.)

On the east side—

"O Lord, how manifold are Thy works!"

On the north side—

"In wisdom hast Thou made them all!"

On the west side—

"The earth is full of Thy riches."

Another fountain, with drinking cup attached, further up the village, offers its crystal current to the wayfarer up the valley of the Nidd, with the following inscription—

Whoso comes here to drink, again shall thirst;
But One has living water; seek Him first!

A short distance beyond, on the road leading to Darley, is the school, built and supported by the family of Greenwood.

On the right of the road, between it and the river, is the Moss, a nicely secluded mansion, now occupied by Mr. John Dury.

In 1857, a church was built and endowed here by the late Frederick Greenwood, Esq. It stands pleasantly on an eminence on the southern side of the village. It is in the decorated style of architecture, and consists of a nave, with aisles, chancel, porch on north side, and a square tower at the west end, surmounted with a spire one hundred feet in height. It is a most beautiful and carefully finished fabric, and forms a highly interesting feature in the landscape. At the east end of the chancel, outside, is inscribed—"To the glory of God, and in affectionate memory of a dear father and brother, this church of St. James, the apostle, was founded and built by Frederick Greenwood, A.D. 1857."

The interior is fitted up with oak seating throughout, and will accommodate three hundred hearers, besides the school children. All the seats are free and unappropriated. The chancel is elaborately painted in colours; and round the nave a dado in Indian red is carried to the height of four feet, giving a rich, warm appearance to the whole. The east end of the chancel is enriched with an oak reredos.

The walls are decorated with texts from scripture. Many of the windows filled with stained glass, are memorials of different members of the family of the founder. One of two lights at the east end of the north aisle is—"In memory of John Greenwood, born Sep. 8th, 1768, died Oct. 11th, 1846; and of Sarah, his second wife, born April 20th, 1777, died Feb. 25th 1808." A single light on the north side of the chancel is—"In memory of Mary Staniforth, born May 19th, 1778, died Aug. 24th, 1846." The next, on the same side, is—"In memory of Samuel Staniforth, born Feb., 1759, died April 5th, 1851." The east window is of three lights, representing different scenes in the life of our Saviour. A single light on the south side of the chancel is—"In memory of Sophia Barnardiston, born January 31st, 1807, died May 6th, 1855." The east window of the south aisle, of two lights, is—"In memory of Edwin Greenwood, born April 11th, 1798, died Sept. 28th, 1852; and of Matilda Briggs, his sister, born Dec. 19th, 1799, died Aug. 10th, 1882." The next window in the south aisle represents different events in the history of David and Jonathan, and is inscribed—

"In memory of two departed friends of my youth, Martin W. J. Marsh, who died at Athens, from dysentery, Aug. 10th, 1845, aged 20. Also of Harry Denison, captain in H.M. 90th Light Infantry, who died of his wounds received before Lucknow, whilst fighting against the Indian mutineers, Oct. 29th, 1857, aged 28."

These windows are all of exquisite design and execution, and (with the exception of one by Messrs. Clayton and Bell, London) are all from the manufactory of Messrs. Ward and Hughs, Frith Street, Soho, London.

In 1869, another memorial window was added in the south aisle, facing the north entrance. It consists of two lights; and the design is intended to represent the story of Christ stilling the tempest. Beneath is inscribed—"By his sorrowing brothers and sisters of Hardcastle Garth, Hartwith, this window is placed in sacred memory of Thomas Ambrose Oxley, who, at midnight, fell from the ship Albert William, of Liverpool, and was drowned off the river Plate, on June 17th, 1868. Also in grateful memory of Malcolm Malcolmson, second mate, who nobly perished by jumping into the sea to save the above. 'Greater love hath no man than this, that a man lay down his life for his friends.'—St. John xv., 13." This window was by Hardman, of Birmingham.

The communion plate was the gift of Mrs. Greenwood. The whole fabric was from designs furnished by M. R. Hawkins, Esq., of London, under whose direction the whole of the works were executed. It was consecrated August 20th, 1857, by the Right Rev. Robert Bickersteth, Bishop of Ripon.

The churchyard is laid out in walks, and ornamented with shrubs, and a refined taste appears to preside over the whole.

The living is a vicarage, in the gift of the Greenwood family, and the Rev. George Hales was appointed first incumbent.

The district attached to this church includes the whole of the township of Birstwith, with the exception of a small portion at the eastern corner, nearest to Hampsthwaite, which yet remains attached to that parish. The boundary commences at the footpath near the corn mill, at a stone marked **A**, proceeds thence along the footpath up to the Hampsthwaite Lane, and then down the centre of the road leading to Swincliffe, until it reaches Tang Beck.

The charities of this township or parish consist of the rents of a house and garth at Longscales, containing 1a. 3r. of land; an allotment of 5a. 2r. at Coldcotes, in Felliscliffe, awarded by the commissioners on the enclosure of the Forest of Knaresborough; a close called the Poor Folks' Close, situate near the Wreaks Mill, containing 3r. 20p.; and a cottage with a small garden, about ten perches of land.

These rents are distributed by the churchwardens and overseers amongst the poor at their discretion.

Meg-yate is the name of a hamlet situate a short distance southward of Swarcliffe Hall. It has probably obtained its name in early times from being a *yate* or entrance into the unenclosed forest. Here was formerly an open "green," as well as a Maypole, and the village stocks; all of which have departed except the last. Here is also the only public-house in the district or parish.

Here is also a Wesleyan Methodist Chapel, erected in 1857. It is a substantial stone building, and will accommodate about 120 hearers. The land on which it stands was presented to the society by Mr. John Bramley.

Coal has been often obtained in this neighbourhood, but of indifferent quality. About the year 1820, a shaft was sunk near Meg-yate, and the workings continued for some time, but were eventually given up as not profitable. In the year 1830,

a company was formed for the purpose of winning the coal
here; they sunk three shafts, and put up an engine; but all
was in vain—the seam would not pay the cost of working.
After the capitalists had abandoned the undertaking, a collier
named Bill Ward, without purchase of royalty or other useless
ceremony, worked the seam in the river bank below the mill,
and his customers fetched away the result of his labour in
baskets and barrows. The river sometimes drove him from his
works, and finally the owner of the land drove him away; and
with him ended the coal trade of Swarcliffe. When it began
we have no certain information, but old people tell tales of
the great lumps of coal which were got when they were young,
some seventy years ago. The Hampsthwaite parish register is
evidence, in the following entry, that these pits were worked
more than a century ago.

"1748. Mr. James Car, steward to yᵉ Colliery of Swarcliff.
Buried April 7ᵗʰ."

In June, 1858, a large quantity of small copper coins was
found by the workmen, in digging the foundations of a building
here. They were in a chest, and weighed upwards of two
hundred weight; their number was so great that to count them
was out of the question. On one side is the representation of a
crown, and the legend CARO. D. G. MAG. BRIT.; on the
other a crowned harp, and FRA. ET. HYB. REX. They
resemble farthing tokens, struck out of thin sheets of copper in
a careless, rough manner. They are evidently of the age of
a Charles, and from the crowned harp (the ordinary reverse
of Irish coins, from the time of Henry VIII. to a late period)
intended for circulation in Ireland. King Charles I., soon after
his accession, granted a patent to Frances, Duchess Dowager of
Richmond and Lennox, and Sir Francis Crane, Knight, for
the term of seventeen years, empowering them to strike copper

farthings. In size and appearance these coins were like those found at this place, but the legend was slightly different. Charles II. also coined a farthing token of this kind, which was not put into circulation, which was evidently the fate of the coins found here. These have been pronounced by competent authority to be counterfeits, and certainly they have not been struck by a skilful workman, who got the only reward he deserved—his labour for his pains.

Elton is the name of a small hamlet east of Meg-yate, and the road leading from Clapham Green to the village of Birstwith bears the name of Elton Lane. This name is evidently of Saxon origin, and means the *Old-town*. We have an idea that this place was the *Hilton* of the Domesday survey; and at that time was the head of the parish or district, as Hampsthwaite was in more recent times. An old house at the top of this lane has inscribed on the lintel, **W. 1677. B.** These are the initials of William Bilton, who died in 1688. He built the house, and was owner of a small estate around it, which was held by his descendants until quite a recent period. It formed part of the estate of the late Mr. Bilton Josephus Wilson, of Hampsthwaite, from whose devisees it has recently been purchased by John Greenwood, Esq., of Swarcliffe Hall.

Elton Spring and the fields adjacent present some splendid specimens of oak timber—some of them old, pollarded, knotty, "gnarled, and unwedgeable" patriarchs of the old forest; others, young, tall, and straight, have grown up in their shelter, and indicate a soil suitable to the sustentation of the monarch of the British woods. One oak, felled in the spring of 1867, presented a perfectly straight trunk of fifty-one feet in length—the first thirty feet without a single branch; at the ground the girth was ten feet three inches; at thirty feet it was six feet ten inches. A finer specimen of oak timber has been seldom seen of native growth; and the quality of the timber grown here cannot be surpassed.

At the lower part of the district, on the left of the road leading from Hampsthwaite, is another remarkable tree of the oak species; at five feet above the ground it is twenty feet in circumference; at nine feet it divides into three main branches, and afterwards into many more. Its trunk is gnarled and knotted in a most singular manner. It is evidently of great age—a genuine relic of the old forest day.

> "Time was, when settling on thy leaf, a fly
> Could shake thee to the root.—And time has been
> When tempests could not.
> Time made thee what thou wast,—king of the woods,
> And time has made thee what thou art—a cave
> For owls to roost in."

Clapham Green is another hamlet or district near the top of Elton Lane. Within living memory a row of cottages stood on the northern side of the road, and here was also a piece of waste land, called the Green, but the cottages have been removed and the Green enclosed.

The Primitive Methodists have a chapel here, built in 1838, which will accommodate about one hundred hearers. The land on which it stands was presented to the society by Mr. James Swales, of Rougharlington.

A short distance south of Clapham Green is Hirst Grove,* situate in the valley of the Tang Beck. This is a place nicely secluded from the world, yet warm and comfortable, amid fair fields and woods. In the old monastic day it would have made a choice site for a small religious house. In front rises the ridge of Swincliffe—part of the slope yet clothed with native

---

* This name is a pleonasm; Hirst or Hurst being Saxon for a grove of trees; Grove has been added by some one who did not know the signification of the previous word. Both terms are descriptive of the place, and the meaning is the same.

wood; the brook Tang flows immediately in front; the hills behind shelter it from the cold winds, and the tall timber trees around give it an air of quiet solemnity.

This estate belonged to a family of the name of Spence until 1661, in which year Nathaniel Spence surrendered the same to Thomas Smith, who, by Jane, his wife, had a son, named

William, bapt. May 8th, 1664, and who, on June 18th, 1696, married Mary, daughter of William Bilton, of Clapham Green, by whom he had a son, named

Thomas, bapt. May 26th, 1700, who, Nov. 24th, 1720, married Mary, daughter of John Bilton, of Felliscliffe. Having no male issue he sold the estate to William Bilton, of Tang, in 1762, and retired to York, where he died March 1st, 1779. From William Bilton the estate descended to the late Bilton Josephus Wilson, of Hampsthwaite, who, by his will, bequeathed the same to the present owner, the Rev. Benjamin Jowett, M.A., Regius Professor of Greek in the University of Oxford, and author of the essay "On the Interpretation of Scripture," in "Essays and Reviews;" a descendant of Thomas Smith, a former owner.

Thomas Smith and Jane, his wife, had three daughters—

Mary, bapt. August 22nd, 1721, married George Clarkson, of Hampsthwaite, died July 18th, 1767.

Ann, bapt. November 14th, 1728, married John Bilton, of York, died March 20th, 1791, leaving no issue.

Elizabeth, bapt. April 11th, 1740, who, on April 14th, 1762, married Henry Jowett, of York, who served the office of sheriff for that city in 1784, and died December 3rd, 1799, leaving two daughters—

Elizabeth, who died unmarried, October 18th, 1787, aged 22;

And Ann, who married her second cousin, Benjamin Jowett, of Camberwell, by whom she had two daughters, who died unmarried, and three sons, Benjamin, Josiah, and Henry; the last of whom is father of the Rev. Benjamin Jowett, present owner of Hirst, and also, in consequence of his relationship to the late Bilton J. Wilson, is heir to some property left undisposed of in that gentleman's will.

The house is one of those antique fabrics which yeomen built for themselves about two hundred and fifty years ago,—with low side walls, and high pitched roofs, covered with thatch; the windows of many lights, divided by thick stone mullions, with small diamond shaped panes of glass, where the original glazing remains. On one pane is written, "Ann Bilton, wife of John Bilton, married 9th June, 1752."

A stone above the barn door bears, $\tau.$ ^{S} M. 1721.

Birstwith Hall is a pleasant mansion situate in a warm and picturesque spot on the northern side of the Tang rivulet.

> "It stands embosomed in a happy valley,
> Crowned by high woodlands."

Behind the house is one of the most carefully cultivated farms in the Forest of Knaresborough. This place is naturally beautiful, and art has only lent its aid as an improver in turning that beauty to use.

This house and estate formerly belonged to the family of Day, and bore the name of Day Hall. It passed from that family by sale in 1804, and, after passing through the hands of persons named Wood and Blesard, was purchased by the late John Greenwood, Esq., April 22nd, 1815, and soon afterwards it became the residence of Rawdon Briggs, Esq., for many years M.P. for Halifax, who died in 1859. By his wife, Matilda, daughter of John Greenwood, he had a son, also named Rawdon, who succeeded his father, and is the present occupier of the mansion. We believe they bear the name of Rawdon because in their veins circulates some of the blood of

Paulyn de Rawdon, a Norman warrior, who received his lands by direct gift from William the Conqueror.

Tang House is situate further up the valley, on the northern side of the stream from which it takes its name. This house and estate were held for a long time by the family of Bilton, and was occupied by them until the death of Miss Ann Bilton, August 12th, 1819; when it came into possession of the late Bilton Josephus Wilson, of Hampsthwaite.

The house is of the substantial yeoman class, and has been built at different times. Over the door of the most recent part is inscribed—

𝕿𝖍𝖎𝖘 𝕭𝖚𝖎𝖑𝖉𝖎𝖓𝖌 𝖜𝖆𝖘 𝖊𝖗𝖊𝖈𝖙𝖊𝖉 𝖇𝖞 𝕽𝖎𝖈𝖍ᵈ. 𝕭𝖎𝖑𝖙𝖔𝖓, 𝕬.𝕯. 1754.

This Richard Bilton was the son of William Bilton, and was baptized November 18th, 1698; he died unmarried, August 24th, 1769. Previous to building this house he resided at Hurst.*

Longscales is the name of a road and two or three farm-houses; one of them, of a superior class, is very pleasantly

* An old pocket book of his contains the following curious entry— "February the 18th, 1749-50:—Dear cozen Smith, remembering some discourse in Bridgefield, this shall be your directions how to proceed. In the West End of the Corn Lare, in the Hard Corn Mough, near to the North Door, against the wall, under three or four sheaves, search well, there you will find my Wigg Box, and one Old Cloath Bagg, which will supply your wants, if there be occasion for it. But I pray you to take care of my little Will, and get him some calling or business suitable to his station. Miles Bramley is Debtor to Richard Bilton Five Pounds, and no security for it, and two years' interest. The Box value is Fifty seaven pound."

We cannot remove the mystery and secrecy which hangs over this statement. It appears to indicate troublous times; and that Richard Bilton had some sufficient cause for hiding his money. The first entry in the book is the owner's name, "Richard Bilton, Hirst, 1747." Another is— "William, son of William Bilton, was born November the 15th, 1738:" whom we believe to have been his nephew. Was this the little Will mentioned above, who was then eleven years of age, and whose father had died in the same year?

situated, and commands a fine and extensive view of the country around. On the pillar of an antique sun dial in the garden is inscribed, **1678.**

The Crow Trees is the name of a respectable farm-house of the Elizabethan age, surrounded by a grove of sycamores, in which a colony of rooks make abode. This estate has been for a long time in possession of the family of Andrew. Tradition relates that the first of the name who settled here was a Scottish officer, who had been detained for some time a prisoner in Pontefract Castle, and after his release purchased a small estate here and made it his home. It is also said that a member of this family, named William, was murdered on Scotton Moor, about the year 1650, on his return from Knaresborough, at which town he had been to be sworn in constable. We find their names in the registers of Hampsthwaite as early as 1610, which is probably soon after the time of their settlement here. The owners of this estate for many generations in succession have borne the name of William; the present owner being the Rev. William Andrew, Incumbent of Trinity Church, West Hartlepool.

The western side of this township rises into high lands,—at Swarcliffe Top to 665, and near Slack Hill to 750 feet above the sea level. Here are some extensive plantations, and occasional patches of wild, rocky land; and consequently the contrast is great between the lower and higher portions of the district— the first being low, warm, well cultivated, and beautiful; the other high, cold, and comparatively barren.

The narrow arch leading across the river Nidd into Hartwith, adapted only for foot and horsemen, may be taken as a fair representative of the age when nearly all the trade of the country was carried on by pack horses.

The population of this township in 1801 was 680; in 1811, 694; in 1821, 621; in 1831, 747; in 1841, 676; in 1851, 680; and in 1861, 655.

The area is upwards of 1,800 acres. The assessment to the county rate in 1849 was £2,254; in 1859, £2,761; and in 1867, £2,999. The amount rated to property tax, in 1858, was £3,049.

MENWITH-WITH-DARLEY.

THESE two places form one township in the Pateley Bridge
Poor Law Union, and Chapelry of Thornthwaite. On the north
the boundary is formed by Darley Beck, which divides it
from Dacre; on the east it abuts on Birstwith; on the west
on Thornthwaite; and on the south on Fewston. Neither
of these places is mentioned in the Domesday survey; probably
at that time the greatest part of the district was a waste
wilderness. The first time we find them mentioned is in 1299,
in the *Inquisition* on the death of Edmund, Earl of Cornwall,
when both names are rolled into one, and it is written
Derlemonewith. In 1318, we find the names distinct, Darley
and Menwiche. The meaning of the first appears to be "the
field of deer," the second, "the stony wood,"—names
sufficiently descriptive of their state in the ancient forest day.
This township occupies the southern slope of a lateral valley,
which opens from the westward into the main valley of the
Nidd; and the stream that flows at the bottom has been
taken advantage of for manufacturing purposes—for the spinning
of flax and the grinding of corn.

A portion of this township, from Fringill eastward to the
boundary of Birstwith, is known as Holme, or the Holme. In
early times a large part of this belonged to a respectable family

of the name of Leuty. We find their names in the Hampsthwaite parish registers from their commencement, and they
resided here before that time.

In 18th Elizabeth, A.D. 1575, Richard Leuty and other
copyhold and customary tenants of the Forest of Knaresborough,
were defendants in a suit in the court of the Duchy of Lancaster
(Catherine Beckwith being plaintiff), respecting suit and
mulcture of a water corn mill, called Angram Mill, at Hampsthwaite. In the following year Wilfrid Leuty was plaintiff in a
suit, in the same court, against Thomas Beckwith; the cause
being two closes of land at Burnt Yates, and right of way
through Clint Hall Closes.

In 1597, William Leuty and one of his daughters were
cruelly murdered here. In 1655, Isabel Leuty married William
Bilton, of Birstwith, which was the second intermarriage with
that family. In 1677, William Leuty, whose wife was Elizabeth
Day, built the house here. In 1678, Susanna Leuty, of Holme,
made her will, by which she gave legacies to twenty-two
persons—two of whom were William Leuty, senior and junior,
and five of them were to her relations, the Biltons, and William
Bilton, junior, was appointed sole executor. In the Inventory
she is styled "Susanna Leuty, wid., late wife of William Leuty,
of Holme."

13th Oct., 1709. Richard Wood and Elizabeth, his wife,
surrender the half of one messuage three roods and one pole
of land "in hamletta de Menwith cum Darley, infra vill. de
Thruscross," then occupied by John Greaves, to the use of
William Lewty, of Holme, his heirs or assigns.*

20th Feb., 1716-7. Henry Rawson, sen., of Holme, "in
periculo mortis," surrenders half a messuage and two and a half
acres of land in Menwith and Darley, to the use of William

* "Knaresborough Court Rolls," vol. i., p. 63.

Lewty, of Holme, junior, and Robert Pullen, of Kettlesing, upon trust, to sell the same after the decease of the said Henry.

12th Feb., 1717-8. Robert Pullen and William Leuty, junior, surrender "dimidium unius mesuagium, et dua horrea, et quædam clausuræ, vocatæ New Field, Backside Pasture, Bridge Field, Little Close, Long Close, et Far Close, et unum parcellum, vocatum Orchard," containing two and a half acres, in Menwith and Darley (then occupied by —— Rawson), to the use of William Leuty, senior.

In 1725, Thomas Leuty built the gallery in Hampsthwaite Church, at his own charge. There is an inscription in the same church to the memory of Mary Leuty, relict of Mr. William Leuty, of Holme, Gentleman; she died December 16th, 1768, aged 76. A brass plate in the same church, that was formerly fixed upon an alabaster tomb in the churchyard, which has perished, bears the following inscription, "Here also lie interred the remains of William Leuty, of the Holm, in this parish, Gentleman, father of the above named William Leuty, who departed this life the 30th day of January, in the 61st year of his age, and in the year of our Lord 1747.

Animæ super eitheræ vivunt."

On the extinction of the family of Leuty the estate passed to that of Smithson; afterwards to that of Barstow, of Carlton, near Otley, a daughter of whom married Mr. Skelton, of Leeds, who had an only daughter now named Mrs. Blackburn, the present owner.

The house, sometimes called Holme Hall, is now occupied by Mr. Charles Pullan, whose ancestors have occupied the same for four generations; it is two stories in height in front, but only one at the back; one of the front windows is of ten lights, which appears to have lighted the principal apartment; another is of five lights; those into the upper rooms are only of four

lights each. The roof is of thatch. Over the front entrance is
inscribed, on an ornamented door head, **W.L. 1677. E.L.**[*]
The door is formed of two thicknesses of oak boards, fastened
together with wooden pins with projecting heads. Inside, all
the fittings are of oak, now dark with age; the principal living
room of the family is wainscotted with oak; over one of the
doors, on a carved pannel, is cut the date 1667. All the beams,
floors, and doors are of oak.

A large tannery was formerly carried on here by the family of
Pullan.

A short distance south of this hamlet rises a steep moorland
hill, on the summit of which a large stone bears the name
of Gallows Crag, in which are sundry holes, which appear
as though they had been made for the purpose of erecting
something above it. Tradition says that this stone obtained its
name from being the place where a gallows was fixed for
the execution of a criminal who had murdered an aged couple,
who resided in a small cottage, near the moor.

The hamlet of Holme consists of half-a-dozen houses in
a cluster, of which four are quite modern; another appears
to be of nearly equal age to the one already described, but
has not been so important in its early day.

Cinder Hills is the name of another group of dwellings
situate on the slope of the valley, about half a mile south
of Holme, near Langrill Lane, which name is derived from
their situation on hills of cinders, or iron slag, which metal
appears to have been worked and smelted here in very early
times.

Gallows Crag and Rowentree Crag are groups of rocks on
a ridge of high land near the boundary of Birstwith, where, from

[*] Over the door of an old outbuilding, on the opposite side of the road,
which also belonged to the Leutys, is inscribed, W.M.L., 1736.

the grooves and channels on many of the rocks, appears to
have been a festival fire station in the old Druidic day.

Darley is a long straggling village, with a station on the Nidd
Valley Railway.

The Society of Friends have a meeting house and burial
ground here.

A schoolroom, in which divine service is regularly held,
and a substantial parsonage for the Incumbent of Thornthwaite,
were erected here in 1846.

The Wesleyan Methodists have a chapel here, built in 1829,
which will accommodate about two hundred hearers.

The Primitive Methodists have also a chapel here, built
in 1841, which will hold about one hundred and fifty persons.

In Stumps Lane, a road which enters the main road on
the left hand, a most cruel murder was committed on the
evening of Sunday, the 1st of August, 1858, on the person
of Mary Jane Skaife, a young woman of this village, by her
professed lover, a young man named James Atkinson. They
were walking in the lane on the above evening, when in a
sudden fit of jealousy he murdered her with a knife, and left her
body lying in the lane. He was tried at York assizes for
the crime, but acquitted on the ground of insanity; but was
ordered to be kept in confinement during Her Majesty's
pleasure. A stone marks the spot where the murder was
committed.

On very high land, near the southern boundary of the
township, near a long, straight, rough road, which leads
from Birstwith towards West End, stands Turpin's Lair, or
Barn. Tradition says that it obtained its name from being
a haunt of Dick Turpin, the notorious highwayman; but this
cannot be true, as it has been built since the enclosure of
the forest; more probably from some of its owners or tenants, as

Turpin at one time was a common name in the neighbourhood. In more recent times it has been dreaded by the weak and superstitious, as a place haunted by the restless spirits of two or three of its tenants, who had chosen it as the place in which to commit suicide.

Menwith, commonly called Menwith Hill, which comprises the upper or more westerly portion of the township, consists almost entirely of detached houses, scattered at random, in the fields, and along the hill sides.

Day Ash, for many generations the home of the family of Day, of Menwith, is a comfortable looking house, sheltered by thriving plantations, situate on an eminence close to the road leading from Darley to Blubberhouses. The present building does not possess any features of antiquity, and cannot apparently be more than a century old, and has evidently been rebuilt on an old site.

Tradition states that the pedigree of the family of Day can be traced backward for twenty generations; an assertion which we have no means of proving, as we have not had access to any family papers, if indeed any such exist. As we have not the materials wherewith to compile a pedigree of this family, we shall content ourselves with giving a few facts relative thereto, gleaned from various sources. We find their names in the earliest registers of the parish of Hampsthwaite;* the

* We give a few extracts from this register—
1604. Widdow Day, buried the 3rd day of May.
Robert Medcalf and Eleanor Daye, married xxij. Julii, 1604.
1612. John Yeates and Isabel Day, married 22nd Sept.
1613. Wm. Leuty and Susan Day, marr'd 19th Octob.
1615. Francis Day and Jane Burton, marr'd 27 Jany.
1613. Wife of Wm. Day, buried 27th February.
1630. Wm., son of Francis Day, buried 22nd April.
From 1616 to 1636 many children of Francis Day are baptized.
1662. Fraunces Day, buried the 2nd of October.
1708. Christopher Yeates and Mary Day, both of this parish, were married May yᵉ first, by virtue of a license.

oldest tombstones in that churchyard also belong to them; they
formed alliances with the most respectable families in the neighbourhood; they founded a school for the use of the poor, and
gave, by will, considerable sums to be distributed in charity;
and for at least three centuries were a family of good standing
and influence on forest soil.

The following incidental notice of one of this family occurs
in the "Fairfax Correspondence."* "1641. June 18th. Upon
Monday, the 2nd of June, we taxed the two last of four sub-
sidies in Claro; and yesterday we delivered the estreat to Francis
Day and William Hardisty, whom we have made collectors
jointly."

The Rev. Francis Day was the greatest benefactor the townships of Darley and Thornthwaite ever had. He was vicar of
Topcliffe for the long term of fifty years (from 1718 to 1768).
In 1748, he founded Hookstones School; the endowment of
which he further augmented in 1757. By his will, dated 29th
December 1748, he gives to the two sons and one daughter
of his sister, Mary Yeates, each of them £80. The like sum
each to the three sons and one daughter of his sister, Hannah
Parkinson.† And, as he had already given £50 to Hannah,

1706. Stephen Parkinson, of Denton, and Hannah Day, of this parish,
were married by lycence yᵉ 14 of May.
John Day, of Hartwith, buried September yᵉ 14, 1680, in woollen
only. (This is the first entry in woollen, and there are only four more.)
1699. Hannah Day, widdow, buried April yᵉ 4.
1719. Dinah Day, wife of William Day, yeoman, buried Jany.
16th, 1719-20.
Wm. Day, yeoman, buried Feby. yᵉ 16, 1719-20.
The inscriptions on tombstones belonging to this family, will be
found in the accounts of the churches of Hampsthwaite and Thornthwaite.

* Vol. ii., p. 110.

† "Memorandum. My brother, John Day, died at Menwith-hill on
the 29th day of July, 1745, at six o'clock in the evening, and he was
buried at Hampsthwaite on Lammas Day, being the 1st day of August,
1745."—S.P.

wife of the Rev. Mr. Rayner, of Guiseley, the other daughter
of his sister, Hannah Parkinson, he only gives her an additional
£80. To John Hird and Jane Hird, his brother and sister,
each one guinea. To Mary Yeates and Hannah Parkinson, his
sisters, each two guineas. To Isabel Day, his sister, one
guinea; and to John Day, his cousin, £80. He next proceeds
to state what he has done for the endowment of the school
at Hookstones; and gives the following instructions in reference
to the master of the same school:—"My mind is that the said
trustees shall elect and choose the said schoolmaster, and if
they chuse the curate of Thornthwaite Chapell or any other
place for the schoolmaster, they shall insist on his performing
the office of schoolmaster in his own person, and not by a
deputy; and whomsoever they shall elect, they shall insist on
his performing the office of schoolmaster in his own person,
and not by a deputy; and whomsoever they shall elect, they
shall insist upon his performing the duty of his place, according
to the intent of the donour; and whatsoever fault he shall be
guilty of, if upon admonition he do not amend, to eject him."
To the poor of Menwith Hill he gave £50; to the poor of the
parish of Bolton Percy, the like sum. To the towns of Marton,
Rainton, Baldersby, Skipton, Catton, and Dalton, the sum of
£100, for the purpose of teaching a certain number of poor
children at school. To the poor of the parish of Topcliffe, £50.
The residue to William Day, of Menwith Hill, his brother, who
was appointed sole executor, and to whom administration was
granted, May 16th, 1768.

Isabel Day, widow of William Day, in 1778, further increased
the endowment of the above mentioned school, and left the
rents of certain lands to be distributed to the poor of Darley
and Thornthwaite.

In the *Award*, on the enclosure of the forest, seventeen allotments were given to this family—five in Menwith and Thruscross, and twelve in and near Day Ash.

On the death of John Day, April 22nd, 1833, the family became extinct; the estate was sold; and Day Ash was purchased by the late Mr. Bilton Josephus Wilson, of Hampsthwaite; and on his decease in 1866, according to the provisions of his will, it was again sold, and the present owner, William Sheepshanks, Esq., of Leeds and Harrogate, became the purchaser.

With this house is connected a traditional story of the civil war of the seventeenth century,—A marauding party from the king's garrison of Skipton Castle visited the forest for the sake of plunder. The owner and his family had retired to a place of safety, leaving the house and premises in charge of a steward—a man of courage and fidelity, as well as of uncommon size and strength, who dared to exchange shots with the robbers as they approached the house. They forced the door, when the defender retired upstairs; his assailants, not daring to follow him, fired repeated shots through the floor, one of which was fatal; the brave fellow fell mortally wounded upon a bed, so that those below did not hear him fall, and did not know his fate. They plundered the lower rooms, and then departed, leaving the upper protected by the dead body of their defender.

Hookstones School is a low, plain, stone building, situate on the left of the road leading to Thornthwaite. Over the entrance is inscribed—

"The Reverend Francis Day built and endowed this school in the year of our Lord 1749."

This is the original inscription, but the greater part of the fabric has since been rebuilt.

By deed, dated May 11th, 1748, Francis Day conveyed to certain trustees* a messuage situate at the high end of the village of Hampsthwaite, with a barn and orchard, the whole containing about two acres of land; also three closes, containing three acres of land, upon trust, to pay yearly the rents and profits of the same (after. deducting taxes and reasonable repairs), to a schoolmaster to be provided by the said Francis Day, for the teaching of the poor children of Menwith Hill, Thornthwaite, Padside and Darley, gratis. And by another deed, dated March 3rd, 1757, the said Francis Day conveyed to the same trustees an estate at Skierthornes and Threshfield, consisting of fourteen acres of land, upon trust (after deduction of taxes, repairs, and reasonable expenses), to pay the residue of the rents, as a yearly salary for ever, to the said schoolmaster, "for the teaching and educating, not only all the poor children whose parents reside within and belong to the several hamlets or townships of Menwith Hill, Thornthwaite, Padside and Darley, in the parish of Hampsthwaite aforesaid, but also all the children of such person and persons as were anyways of kin or related to the said Francis Day, though such person or persons did not live or reside within any of the several hamlets aforesaid; and also all the children of all and every person and persons, who then were, or thereafter should be, tenant or tenants to any of the relations or kindred of the said Francis Day,—to read and say the church catechism, if such the inhabitants, kindred, tenant, or tenants as aforesaid, should think proper to send his or their children so to be taught; and such schoolmaster being a bachelor at the time of his nomination and election, and so remaining during the time he shall continue in the capacity of schoolmaster."

* The first trustees were William Day, Edward Yates, and John Day.

By deed, dated August 16th, 1778, Isabel Day, widow of
William Day, of Menwith Hill, conveyed to the same trustees
a close of meadow ground, called Broad Ing, otherwise Crooked
Dale Close, containing seven acres, situated at Starbotton, upon
trust, to receive the rents thereof, and pay one moiety thereof
to the use of the master appointed to teach the school at
Menwith Hill.

Out of the rents of these lands the trustees pay the master
a salary of £86 a-year, and reserve the remainder to answer
the demands for repairing the school and the buildings upon
the farms.

The number of scholars on the foundation is generally twelve,
who are educated gratis, but pay one shilling each entrance
money, and two shillings a-year for firing. The master has the
liberty of taking other scholars and receiving payment for them.

The school premises consist of a schoolroom and turf-house
erected upon the waste, with about half an acre of land adjoining,
allotted to the school on the enclosure of Knaresborough Forest.

The charities consist of—a piece of land called Engleson's
Garth, containing 1a. 1r. 18p.; one other piece, called Har-
grave's Garth, containing 1a. 0r. 89p.; and Myer's Garth,
containing 1a. 1r.; the rents of which are annually distributed
to the poor.

Isabel Day, by deed, dated August 17th, 1778, gave to certain
trustees the moiety of the rent of six acres of land, situate at
Starbotton, to be distributed on St. John's Day and Whit-
Monday to the poor of Menwith Hill, Thornthwaite and Padside.

Francis Day, by his will, bearing date December 29th, 1748,
gave to the poor of Menwith Hill the sum of £50; and directed
that the interest thereof should be laid out yearly in woollen
cloth, to be distributed by the trustees of the Menwith Hill
School, at or before Martinmas, to such poor people as they

shall judge to be in need, and not in the receipt of relief from the parish.

Here is also the sum of 20s. annually, left by a person named Skaife—the time and manner unknown; and 9s., being the interest of £10, given by William Metcalfe: which last sums are distributed to poor widows at Christmas.

The population in 1801 was 554; in 1811, 637; in 1821, 648; in 1831, 742; in 1841, —; in 1851, 718; and in 1861, —.

The annual value of this township as assessed to the county rate in 1849 was £2,693; in 1859, £2,914; and in 1867, £3,651. Amount assessed to property tax in 1858, £3,178.

THORNTHWAITE-WITH-PADSIDE.

This is another township unrecorded in the Domesday survey; the whole being probably waste at that time; though the name of Thornthwaite* seems to indicate that it was settled in Saxon times. In 1299, we find it written in its present form; but Padside was then *Pateside*, showing its derivation to be the slope or side of the valley frequented by the *pate* or badger.

This is a district of undulations, hills, valleys, rocks, woods, and moorlands, forming a scene of considerable variety, extending westerly to the slopes of Greenhow, and the high lands of Thruscross.† To the geologist it offers some features

* *Thorn* appears to point to the existence of some place of strength, or fortified post, in early times, while *thwaite* might be the clearing around it.

† The following is an account of a perambulation of the boundary of this part of the parish of Hampsthwaite, made on the 14th of May, 1801, by the then officiating minister, churchwardens, and other inhabitants of the said parish—

"Beginning at a forest boundary stone, situate on Hayshaw Moor, proceeding thence N. west about two hundred yards to a spiral stone, a few yards on the south of several crags; from thence S.W. across the fence which divides Hayshaw Moor and Mr. Stockdale's allotment, to another forest boundary stone; from thence on the west side of the said fence (including a house on the east side of the boundary line, occupied by one King) to a little rivulet that divides Redlish and Bewerley Moor, turning westward on the north side of the said rivulet to an old ditch leading from the said rivulet, S. west, on to the turnpike road, near Greenhow Hill, about one hundred yards on the east of a house occupied by one Anthony ——; proceeding on the outside of the enclosures, betwixt two little huts, by two mineral boundary stones, situate on the inside of the said enclosures, at the distance of a yard, or thereabouts,

of remarkable interest. The first of which is a seam of coal of
poor quality, which here crops up to the surface, on the eastern
side of an anticlinal axis, which crosses the country from north
to south, bringing to the surface a remarkably hard kind of
stone, on which this bed of coal rests; it is very conspicuous at
Cat Crags, on the Dacre side of the valley, where it has
been much broken by the upheaval. The coal is won in the
most primitive manner, in holes called shafts, three or four
yards deep, by pick and shovel, and raised to the surface by
a rope and windlass. Near the crest of the hill is a remarkably
compact bed of gritstone, which the above mentioned eruption
has lifted up. Much stone has been lately quarried in very
large blocks—some of it sent to the new docks at Hull, some to
the royal fortifications at Spithead.

On this ridge is a large rocking stone, about seventeen feet in
length by seven feet in breadth in the widest part; the thickness
is five feet six inches. On the top are four basins, which hold
water, the largest of which is about eighteen inches in diameter
by five inches in depth; the others are smaller. This rests
on another large stone, about four feet high, sixteen feet in
length, and five feet in breadth. The rocking motion is easily
made, and is caused by the upper stone resting upon two knobs,
about four feet apart, which act as pivots. There does not
appear to be anything artificial about it. On the top of this
range of rocks, which extends for some distance northward, is

from each other, to an old ditch leading N.W., on the E. side of two
houses, situate on Greenhow Hill; from thence south, by one or two wood
posts, situate at Green Close Head, across Washburn, right up the
moor, on the south side of an old ditch, which is hardly discernable,
through a pond, to some crags, where are the dimensions of two or three
pieces of wall, standing parallel to each other; from thence S.E., to
a little stone on the north, about one hundred yards from Pox Stones;
from thence N.E., leaving the smelting mill about fifty or sixty yards
on the right hand, to a stone called Careless Stoop.

N.B.—An uncommonly fine day and dry time, notwithstanding several
horses were bogged."—*Rev. Joseph Wilson's Diary.*

a greater number of rock basins than we ever remember to have seen elsewhere. A splendid view of the country to the eastward is obtained from this ridge.

Nearly all the houses in this parish are detached—hardly two can be seen together; they are surrounded by small enclosures, and many of them sheltered by groves of sycamore trees. This tree, though not indigenous, is the most flourishing in the district, and attains to the largest size. Nearly all the old houses in the Forest of Knaresborough, prior to the enclosure, can be detected by their clumps of sycamores.

This chapelry appears to have originated from one of the chantries in the parish of Hampsthwaite. The following extract from Steven's "Monasticon"* gives all we know of its origin,—

"The Chauntry or Guilde of our Lady and Seynt Anne, within the parish of Hampsthwaite. Richard Bulland, Incumbent.

Having no foundation other than by reason of a Guilde, whereunto the said parochians, with divers others of their acquaintance, had resort unto. And had by reason thereof gathered and levyed as much money by process of tyme, as they purchased copyhold lands, held of the king's lordship of Knaresborough, of the yearly value of £6 15s., to the mayntenance of a priest to help the curate, and to visit such pore, within the said parish, as were visited with sickness; some of the parochians being five myles and above from the church.

The chantry of St. Syth,† in Thornthwayt, being a village

* Vol. i., p. 82.
† From Calendar of Pleadings in the Duchy Court, 33rd Elizabeth, we find there was a suit between Thomas Phillips, as the queen's lessee, P. and Richard Gascoigne and many others, respecting chantry lands in this neighbourhood, among which are mentioned those of "St. Osythe, or St. Sythe, chantry, Thornthwaite;"—hence we believe that such was the saint to which this church was originally dedicated. She was an English saint, born at Quarendon, daughter of Frewald, a Mercian prince. She suffered martyrdom about the year 870, during the inroads under the Danish pirates, Hinguar and Hubba. She was celebrated in the Romish Church on the 7th of October.

within the said parish, two miles and a half distant from the said church. George Redshaw, Incumbent.

Founded by the parochians for the causes above said, having copyhold lands of the lordship of Knaresborough, *ad valentiam* 46s. 5d."

In the parliamentary survey made during the Commonwealth, it was valued at only 20s. per annum, and was recommended to be made into a parish, by reason of the distance from the mother church, and the badness of the way. This has since been done by degrees. Baptismal rites were celebrated here in early times, though in the Hampsthwaite registers they are only entered distinctively in 1700. The right of burial was obtained about the middle of last century. The oldest inscription in the burial ground is to the memory of Joseph Hardacre, who died in 1758. The first marriages were celebrated in March, 1866.

By an Order of Council, dated 16th of February, 1866, the district chapelry of Thornthwaite was declared to be—"All that part of the parish of Hampsthwaite in the county of York and diocese of Ripon, which is bounded on the north by the consolidated chapelry of Greenhowhill, by the new parish of the Holy Trinity of Dacre, and by the new parish of Hartwith-cum-Winsley, all in the county and diocese aforesaid, on the east by the particular district of Saint James's, Birstwith, sometime part of the said parish of Hampsthwaite, and on the south and west by the parish of Fewston, in the county and diocese aforesaid."

The living has been augmented divers times,—as in 1744, with £200, and in 1749, with £200, both by lot; in 1765, with £200, to meet a benefaction from William Day, Gentleman, of £200; in 1808, with £200, by lot; and in 1814, from the parliamentary grant, with £600, also by lot.

In 1831, the net value was returned as £109 per annum.
On June 14th, 1866, it was further augmented by the
Ecclesiastical Commissioners with the sum of £38 6s. 8d.
per annum.

The following is the most complete list of curates we have
been able to obtain:—

Matthew Bland, curate in 1665, buried Nov. 4th, 1677.
1745. Aug. 27. Anthony Young.
1749. Sep. 24. Christopher Johnson, died Sep. 2nd, 1803, aged 83.
1804. March 5. James Mitton, died Nov. 21st, 1852, aged 82.
1848. ——— Rev. James Brittain.
Rev. Thomas Bainbridge Calvert, present incumbent.

The chapel, or church, is situate on the slope of the hill, not
far from the southern boundary of the district, near a road
which leads from Dacre. It is a plain substantial building,
without any pretensions to architectural ornament, erected in
1810, on the site of the old chapel. Within are sittings
for about two hundred hearers. The old chapel was a little low
building, the floor of which was regularly strewn with rushes,
even down to a recent period.

In 1867, one of the windows on the south side was filled with
stained glass, representing in two compartments, "The Good
Samaritan," and "The Alms Deeds of Dorcas." At the base is
inscribed, "This window was erected A.D. 1867, to the memory
of Bolland Buck, of Thornthwaite, who died May 2nd, 1866,
aged 91; and Ellen, his wife, who died May 5th, 1857,
aged 82."

In the burial ground is a tombstone—"In memory of the
Rev. James Mitton, 45 years minister of this chapel, who
died Nov. 21st, 1852, aged 82."

At the east end of the church are tombs, most of them
of the altar kind, to the memory of the following members of the
family of Day, of Day Ash, in Menwith—

Mrs. Hannah Day, of Menwith, who died June 30th, 1794, aged 83.

Mr. John Day, husband of the above, who died Nov. 21st, 1804, aged 97.

Francis Day, who died Nov. 17th, 1824, aged 37.

Mr. William Day, of Menwith Hill, who died June 3rd, 1771, aged 83. "His benefactions to this chapel, the school, and the neighbouring poor, are lasting memorials of his praise."

Sarah, widow of William Day, of Birstwith, who died October 10th, 1828, aged 66.

Mrs. Isabel Day, who died March 31st, 1789, aged 82.

Mr. William Day, nephew of the above, who died Dec. 18th, 1800, aged 52.*

John Day, of Menwith Hill, who died April 22nd, 1833, aged 47. He was the last surviving son of William Day, Esq., of Birstwith.

Mr. William Day, second son of Mr. Day, of Birstwith, died Jan. 9th, 1809, aged 22.

And here are also memorials to the following members of the family of Yeates, of Padside, who intermarried with the family of Day, of Menwith.

Christopher Yeates, of Padside, died May 22nd, 1758, aged 88.

Christopher Yeates, son of Edward Yeates, of Padside, died Sep. 16th, 1773, aged 22.

Braithwaite school was built and endowed by Edward Yeates, as a memorial of his son, the above Christopher.

---

* The following entry in the diary of the Rev. Joseph Wilson, Vicar of Hampsthwaite, describes the manner of this gentleman's death—"Mr. Day on his return from Knaresborough, about nine o'clock at night, was killed by a fall from his horse; after the fall he made a shuffling run of about 400 steps, and fell down at Thos. Lun's door, in Lunn Lane, and instantly expired."

Edward Yeates, of Padside,* died Sep. 29th, 1777, aged 78 years. He was the builder of Braithwaite school.

At Folly Gill is a large flax spinning mill, belonging to Mr. Charles Powell, of Knaresborough, driven by a large iron water wheel, the motive power of which is derived from the brook called Darley Beck.

Near High House, in this township, was found by Mr. John W. Ellis, in 1862, a stone celt, lying beneath a mass of stratified sand and clay. The length is three and three-quarters inches; breadth at the edge two inches, at the top about one inch; greatest thickness, three-quarters of an inch; circumference where thickest, four inches. It is a neat little article, has been carefully finished, fits well to the hand, and might be useful in the skinning and cutting up of animals before tools of iron were known. With this house is connected a tradition of the civil wars. When Skipton Castle was a garrison for the king it was occupied, says our informant, by a gang of felons collected from different jails, whose subsistence was obtained by plundering the country around. The farmers of Knaresborough Forest might send out their cattle in the morning to graze upon the common, but there was no certainty that they would ever see them again, as they were frequently driven away by the foragers for the use of the garrison. The soldiers were also in the habit of going out in parties to feast with the foresters at their own houses, sending word before hand to have provisions prepared ready for them. This house, then occupied by an ancestor of the present owner, had the honour of one of these visits. As resistance was out of the question they were treated with the best the house afforded. They ate and drank

* "This 28rd day of December, 1745, Edward Yates, of Padside, married one Betty Pullyne, of Timble; it was a very windy day, so I sett this for a memorandum, but no rain."—S.P.

until they were satisfied, not forgetting to select a few portable
articles to take away with them, for which they did not
even thank the real owner. They found no money, or very
little, or it would have walked away with the aforesaid move-
ables. They were making merry with the farmer's home-brewed
ale, around a fire of wood, which one of them thought was
getting rather low, when he marched off to the *wood-cast*
for a fresh supply, and brought back the chopping-block, or,
in forest phrase, the *hag-clog*, with the intention of placing it on
the fire. The master of the house seeing this (for the females
had all fled to places of safety), at once interposed to save
it from the flames. One who appeared to have some authority
over the others said, "Let the old fellah have his clog!" which
he very gladly accepted, and bore away. The reason why he
was so anxious to save the block was,—knowing the character
of his visitors, he had bored an augur hole into its centre, and
into it had dropped his gold, and then plugged up the hole
with a piece of wood, never once dreaming that his hag-clog
would be in danger: but who can tell what to-morrow may bring
forth? Such was the ending of the royalist feast at High House.

The Primitive Methodists have a chapel in this township, at
a place called Moorhouse Hill, which will accommodate about
80 hearers.

PADSIDE HALL.

This venerable building stands upon a beautiful green knoll of
land on the northern verge of the forest, commanding a fine
view of the country to the eastward. When complete it has had
much the appearance of one of those border fortress towers, once
common between England and Scotland.* The area is of a

* Sir Walter Scott, in "The Monastery," describes buildings of a
somewhat similar kind to this,—"In each village or town were several
small towers having battlements projecting over the side walls, and usually

square form, about twenty-three yards by nineteen yards. The
buildings are two stories in height around three sides of this
area, enclosing an open court in the centre; on the other
side is a strong high wall, through which is a doorway about
five feet six inches wide, the only entrance by which access
could be had into the interior. Outside, at the north-eastern
angle, has been a watch tower and small guard room, now
in ruins; in the latter is a fireplace nine feet in width; the
tower has been eleven feet square, enclosing a winding stair,
of which about twenty steps yet remain; some distance up there
is a small chamber, as if for a watchman. This tower, when
complete, would command a most extensive view of the country
round about, more especially towards the east. The windows
are all high up in the buildings, and well secured with bars
of iron. In short, everything about the place has a defensive
look with it. The hill descends rapidly down on the northern
side, clothed with a grove of tall sycamores, in which a colony of
rooks make abode. The two wings on the east and west sides
of the court are now used for widely different purposes from
those for which they were erected. The first, which has been
the kitchen, and in which a very wide fireplace yet remains,
is now used as a peat-house, in which the winter's fuel is
stored; the other is used as cow-houses. The portion extending
between them on the north is now the dwelling-house; and in
its furnishing and general appearance is much the same as
it was two hundred years ago, with the exception of the
fireplace, which was modernized about seventy years since,

an advanced angle or two, with shot holes for flanking the doorway, which
was also defended by a strong door of oak, studded with nails, and often by
an exterior grated door of iron. These small peel-houses were ordinarily
inhabited by the principal fuars and their families; but upon the alarm of
approaching danger, the whole inhabitants thronged from their own
miserable cottages, which were situated around, to garrison these points of
defence."

and a few other domestic articles. Against the walls are ranged the cupboards of carved English oak—black and hard as ebony —which have done duty for generations, and are calculated to endure for ages yet to come. In the front room is a table of oak, some eighteen feet in length, the legs turned and the framework finely carved; on the front are the initials and date, **R.W., 1671.** No absurd attempts have been made to improve the place, either internally or externally. The windows remain in much the same state as when they came from the builder's hand; and the walls have put on that venerable coating of moss and lichen which only age can give. It stands an unmutilated monument of the past—the oldest inhabited house in Knaresborough Forest.

In 1568, Sir William Ingleby, Knight, of Ripley, claimed by surrender from Peter Knaresburgh, a tenement called "Padsyde Headde."

The family of Wigglesworth having obtained it by purchase from the Inglebys, came to reside here, and have held it down to the present time; the owners' names being Robert and William, in alternate generations.*

* The name occurs in the Hampsthwaite registers, but only sparingly; they do not appear to have increased at any great rate.
1613. Robert Wigglesworth, buried 30th January.
1674. Isabell, ye wife of Robert Wigglesworth, de Padside Hall, buried July 17th.
1677. William Wigglesworth and Katherine, the daughter of John Reynard, de Harper Yeat, both of this parish, were lawfully married the 28th of March, by virtue of a licence from the Court of Yorke.
1678. George, ye sone of George Wilks, of the parish of Ripon, and Helen, ye daughter of Robert Wigglesworth, of this parish, were lawfully married, after the banns of matrimony published three several Sundays, Feby. 12, 1678.
1708. Robert Wigglesworth, buried March ye 24th, ag'ed 95.
1713. Wm. Wigglesworth, yeoman, buried Feby. 9th.
1715. John, son of Robert Wigglesworth, bapt. Oct. 12.
1720. Robert, son of Robert Wigglesworth, bapt. May 9.
1722. Tho., son of Robert Wigglesworth, whitesmith, bapt. June 15.

There are a few traditional stories connected with this place, when it belonged to the Ingleby family. One is—that at that time a squirrel could pass from Padside Hall to Ripley Castle without coming to the ground, so thick was the forest between the two places.

Another is a story of love and jealousy. Its knightly owner became enamoured of the charms of a frail beauty, whom for concealment he removed to this lonely dwelling, where he also spent much of his time to the neglect of his legal lady at home. Busy rumour soon carried tidings of her lord's doings to the said lady's ears, and she determined to seek out the place where her rival was concealed, and do—we can scarcely say what, but at the least some desperate deed. Taking advantage of her lord's absence, she ordered out the chariot and horses for the journey. Whether the driver and attendants knew their master's secret, and determined to keep it, we know not; but they either could not or would not find the place. All day long they continued driving round and round upon the rough dirty trackways of the forest, but appeared to come no nearer the object of their search. At length the shades of evening began to fall, and the lady was obliged to relinquish the useless search; the mysterious beauty and her place of concealment could not be found. How long this amour continued we know not; but we gravely suspect that as this place had been the scene of the knight's pleasures during life, it was also the place of his purgatorial penance after death—for it is well known all over the Forest of Knaresborough that a knight of that family was doomed to wander as long as the world shall endure—

"From Whalley to Selaby, to Pendle-hill end;
From Monkrigg to Blackey, to Colne town-end;
From Foxrigg to Foden, to Workisless cross;
From the Windy-wall-side to Padside i'the Moss."

Looking from the hill on which Padside Hall stands, towards

the north-east, at about a quarter of a mile distance, we see a building of stone in the middle of a small enclosure, the whole surrounded by the moor,—that is Braithwaite School, on Braithwaite Moor, founded in 1778, pursuant to the will of Edward Yeates, of Padside, who died in 1774; who endowed it with a house, twenty-three acres of land and nine cattle gaits; and made it free to all the poor children of Padside, and of all those who shall reside within twelve houses within Dacre and Bewerley—four of these houses at Deer Ings, six at the Heights, three at Holebottom, and three at the Row.

Edward Yeates resided in the house in front of the school, at the bottom of the moor. The family is extinct; and the estate is now held by that of Garth.

The boundary of the Forest of Knaresborough is the small brook which runs down the valley immediately below Padside Hall; the fence which runs along the northern side bears the name of "munk wall," and was the limit of the royal forest and the lands of the monks of Fountains. A short distance up the valley, towards the north-west, is the group of rocks called "Palley's Crags," or "The Abbot's Hand," mentioned in all the perambulations of the Forest of Knaresborough.

The population in 1801 was 229; in 1811, 291; in 1821, 309; in 1831, 304; in 1841, —; in 1851, 303; and in 1861, —

The annual value of this township as assessed to the county rate in 1849 was £1,227; in 1859, £1,577; and in 1867, £2,135. Amount assessed to property tax in 1858, £1,720.

FEWSTON.

THE parish of Fewston occupies a considerable portion of the upper part of the ancient Forest of Knaresborough, and includes within its limits the townships of Fewston, Clifton-with-Norwood, Great Timble, Blubberhouses, and Thruscross; embracing an area of upwards of 17,644 acres. The four first named townships are in the Wharfedale or Otley Poor Law Union. Thruscross is in that of Pateley Bridge.

When the Domesday survey was made Fewston was in the hands of the king, and is but very briefly described—

"In Fostune, the king, three carucates. In Bestham, four carucates. In Bestham, is only wood pasture, half a mile long, and half broad."*

The name of Bestham has entirely disappeared from the map of the parish. In the *Inquisition post mortem*, on the decease of Richard, Earl of Cornwall, in 1299, is found *Fostone-Bestaine* among the possessions which he had held in the Forest of Knaresborough.† In a survey of the forest made in 1618,

---

* "Bawdwen's Dom. Boc.," p. 17.
† In the Court Rolls of the Honour of Knaresborough, 16th Edward III. (1342), occurs the following entry, evidently referring to this place— "Fratres domus Sancti Roberti" assert that they and their tenants "infra moram de Bestayne," were accustomed "de turbis fodiendis libere, etc., a tempore domini Edmundi comitis Cornubiæ, qui quidem comes dedit in excambium Fratribus prædictæ domus Sancti Roberti villam de Rouclif, cum pertinentiis, pro terris et tenementis suis in Hameswayt, cum pertinentiis et liberis consuetudinibus, aliquo modo et aliquo tempore prius usitat, et eodem modo clamant foditionem turbaram, etc."

we find it mentioned in connection with the Roman road,—
"Beeston Leaz, with a piece between Watling Street and it;
containeth 69 acres." The next and last time we find it
mentioned is in 1688, when Richard Bannister and others
surrendered to Henry Fairfax, along with other lands, "one
messuage called Beeston Leas, and half an acre of meadow."
From the above description we are of opinion that Cragg
Cottage now stands where Beeston once stood. There are three
or four fields, through which the Roman road ran after passing
Cragg Hall, which bear the name of the Leas Allotments.

Fewston is situate about seven miles west of Harrogate.
The houses are scattered irregularly among gardens and small
garths, along the edge and slope of a rather steep hill; the
church standing pleasantly at the eastern extremity, overlooking
a fine and close prospect of the valley of the Washburn.
The builders of the village have had an eye more to the
picturesque than the solid, for they have placed many of
the houses on a continuously acting landslip; the action of
which is obvious from the edge of the hill even down to the
river. The field below the road is seamed and wrinkled all over
its surface with waves, and swells of land which have moved
from higher positions, and some of the houses near the upper
margin of the moving mass, are cracked from top to bottom, and
twisted out of shape from the same cause. This process
appears to have been going on for a long time, and is yet
in operation, depending for its speed on the rainfall; acting
with greater force during a wet than a dry season.

Of the early history of this village hardly anything is known
—if indeed there be anything to know—beyond the ordinary
commonplace events of village life. Although the country
almost immediately behind the site of the village was traversed

by the Roman road* from Isurium to Olicana, there does not
appear to have been any settlement or post of that people
within this parish. With the exception of the valley of the
Washburn, the greater part of the land lay in a state of nature;
grazed by a few hardy sheep, and the haunt of game and
wild-fowl, and seldom trod except by the sportsman and the
shepherd. Far from any town; the site of no old family
mansion, or religious house, and out of the line of any of
the great routes of traffic, it yields but little matter for the local
historian.

In the year 1640, a number of soldiers were billeted in
this parish. They formed part of that army which behaved
so disgracefully before the Scots at Newburn-upon-Tyne; and
contemptible as they were before their enemies, their pillaging
propensities made them formidable to their friends. Their
coming is thus described by Charles Fairfax, of Scough Hall,
in this parish, in a letter to his brother, Lord Ferdinando
Fairfax, dated January 6th, 1640. "Upon Christmas Eve
was brought into the parish of Fewston, Captain Langley's
company, heretofore billeted about Harrogate, but now unequally
dispersed in that parish. They had no good report before they
came, yet I hear not of any great enormity since their coming,
though they be many weeks behind with their pay, for which
they have their captain (a man of ill government, still at
Harrogate), in suspicion. The lieutenant, Captain Rouse, a
complete gentleman, who has served as major at the isle of
Rhé, has a special care and vigilant eye on them. It is much
to be feared we shall have ill neighbours in them, and when

* Like many other Roman roads, this appears to have been called Watling
Street; and the recollection is yet preserved in the name of a farmstead
called "Watling Street House," which is close to the track of the old
Roman road, as well as the present turnpike, on the left hand, between
Dangerous Corner and the Hopper Lane Hotel.

their landlord's provision fail them, that they will cater for themselves."*

At what time a church was erected here we have no certain information. In 1851, it was appropriated to the house of St. Robert of Knaresborough, and a vicarage was ordained therein; which appears not to have been thought sufficient by the parties concerned, as the appropriation and ordination were repeated in 1881.

In the *Valor* of Pope Nicholas IV. (1292), the living is returned as worth £20 per annum, and in the *Nova Taxatio*, A.D. 1318, at only £6 18s. 4d.; for even this remote place did not escape the ravages of the Scots.

In *Valor Ecclesiasticus* (1586), the rectory held by the house of St. Robert was returned as worth £11 6s. 6d. per annum, made up as follows—

	£	s.	d.
Tithe of corn and hay	7	0	0
Lambs and wool	2	0	0
Oblations	0	7	0
Small and private tithes, as in Easter book	1	19	6
	£11	6	6

At the same time the vicar received an annual pension of £5, paid by the brethren of the said house of St. Robert.

On the enclosure of the Forest of Knaresborough, when lands were awarded in lieu of tithes, the Rev. John Whinnerah received for his claims the following allotments—

	a.	r.	p.
In Clifton, at Bland Hill	580	3	32
Near Spink's Burn	21	2	16
In Timble	482	3	26
In Darley, near Mount Bank	496	3	26
	1532	1	20

The full particulars of this living are given in—"A true Terrier of all the glebe lands, messuages, tenements, portions of

* "Fairfax Correspondence," vol. ii., page 200.

tithes, and other rights belonging to the vicarage of Fewston, in
the county and diocese of York, now in the possession of
John Whinnerah, Clerk, Vicar there, taken, made, and renewed,
and prepared to be delivered in at the ordinary Visitation of the
Most Reverend Father in God, William, by Divine Providence,
Lord Archbishop of York, Primate of England, and Metropolitan,
held at Skipton, the 30th day of June, in the year of our Lord
1786. First,—One vicarage house, containing three bays of
building, about nine yards long and four yards and one half
wide, two rooms on a floor, a closet, and a milk-house, and
two chambers, built with stone, and covered with straw and ling
thatch, in the Vicar's possession. Likewise one barn, of three
bays of building, built of stone, and covered with ling thatch, in
the Vicar's possession. Likewise one piece of pasture ground,
called the Bank and Back Garth, containing about two acres and
a half, of the yearly rent of thirty shillings, in the Vicar's
possession, and abutting on the churchyard and the highway on
the north, and William Hardcastle's Toadhole on the west;
the fence belongs to William Hardcastle. Likewise one piece of
ground, arable or meadow, with a barn of two bays of building,
covered with sods and ling thatch, called Laith Close, containing
about two acres, of the yearly rent of thirty shillings, in the
Vicar's possession, abutting on William Hardcastle's pasture on
the west, and the river Washburn and a pasture of John
Petty's, tenant to Sir James Ibbetson, on the south. Likewise
a piece of meadow called Little Holme, containing about two
acres and a half, of the yearly rent of forty shillings, in the
Vicar's possession, and abutting on John Petty's pasture on the
south. Likewise one parcel of meadow or arable ground called
Long Holme, containing about three acres, of the yearly rent of
fifty shillings, in the Vicar's possession, and abutting on
the river Washburn and Sir James Ibbetson's land, now in

the possession of John Petty and William Chippendale. Likewise one piece of pasture ground called Carr Holme, with one piece of wood called Spring, containing about six acres, of the yearly rent of three pounds and ten shillings, now in the Vicar's possession, and abutting on the north and east on Sir James Ibbetson's land, now in the possession of William Chippendale. Likewise one piece of meadow or arable ground called Wheat Close, about two acres and a half, in the Vicar's possession, and abutting upon the glebe land on every side. Likewise one piece of land situated at Bland Hill belongs to the Vicar, about an acre, of the yearly rent of fifteen shillings, abutting on Sir James Ibbetson's land on the north, and Mr. Fawkes's land on the south. Likewise one allotment situated at the bottom of Fewston Bents, called the Glebe Allotment, about five acres, be the same more or less, now in the possession of the Vicar, abutting on Bramley's land on the north, on Wilson and Moon's on the west, and the highway on the east. The surplice fees belong to the Vicar. One shilling is due to the Vicar for every churching; two shillings and sixpence for every marriage by banns, and sixpence for publishing the banns. Thirteen shillings and fourpence for every marriage by licence is due to the Vicar. There is likewise due to the Vicar for every gravestone laid in the churchyard six shillings and eightpence, and three shillings and fourpence for every headstone. There is likewise due to the Vicar two shillings for every churching from any other parish, and two shillings for every burial from any other parish. The Vicar is likewise entitled to one half of an undivided moiety of two allotments. One of the allotments lies at Bland Hill, and contains 540 acres, or thereabouts, bounded by Otley road, and Hardisty's land and Bradley's on the west, and Mr. Fawkes's land on the south and east, and the high road on

the north. The other allotment lies between Watling Street and
Menwith Hill, containing about 900 acres; bounded on the
south by Watling Street, by Darley Road on the east, Menwith
Hill Road on the north, and Shann's Allotment and Meagill
Road on the west. The other half of the undivided moiety
of the two allotments belongs to the Impropriator, and these
allotments are set out, allotted, and assigned to the Vicar
of Fewston, and Impropriator in lieu of all manner of tithes,
except such tithes as are excepted in and by the act of parliament made and passed for enclosing and dividing the Forest
of Knaresborough; and such tithes as are excepted in and
by the act of parliament aforesaid, are all Easter offerings,
all moduses in lieu of tithes of corn and hay, all mortuaries
which are due and payable to the Vicar and Impropriator
yearly, and every year at Easter. And the Vicar is entitled
to one half of the Easter offerings, modus for corn and hay, and
house dues, and all mortuaries, and the other half belongs
to the Impropriator. The Vicar is likewise entitled to one
half of all moduses in lieu of the tithes of corn and hay,
the tithes of wool and lamb, pigs and geese, cows and calves,
foals and bees, in the township of Blubberhouses. The wool
and lamb, pigs and geese, to be taken in kind, if not
compounded for; and a modus is paid for cows and calves,
foals and bees,—that is, one penny for every cow in lieu
of milk, and a halfpenny for every calf under six, and one
shilling for six calves, and two shillings for seven calves,
and one penny for a swarm of bees, and one penny for every
foal. The other half of Blubberhouses tithes for wool and
lamb, pigs and geese, modus for corn, hay, cows and calves,
foals and bees, belongs to the Impropriator.

The Vicar is likewise entitled to one half of a money payment,
in lieu of tithes of several old encroachments belonging to

such persons as had no right of common before the act was passed for dividing the forest; the other half belongs to the Impropriator.

Parish Clerk's dues are paid by the inhabitants at Easter; and there is due to the Parish Clerk one penny for every christening, one shilling for a marriage by banns, three shillings and fourpence for a marriage by licence, and one shilling and sixpence for a burial.

The Impropriator and Vicar pay yearly pensions and synodals to the Archbishop of York, and pensions to the Dean and Chapter of York, jointly.

The Vicarage of Fewston is worth about thirty pounds a-year and the taxes and out payments which are paid out of it about eight pounds a year.

In witness whereof we have hereunto set our hands the 80th day of June, in the year of our Lord 1786.

J. WHINNERAH, Vicar of Fewston.

JOSEPH SMITHSON,		SAML. SMITHSON,	
JOHN HUDSON,	Inhabitants.	HENRY BRAMLEY,	Church-
NICHOLAS HOULDING,		JOHN BEECROFT,	wardens."
SAMUEL HARDISTY,		WILLIAM WATSON,	

In 1803, the vicarage was augmented with £200 by lot. In 1831, the nett value was returned as £144 per annum. The Lord Chancellor is patron.

The church, dedicated to St. Michael, or St. Mary Magdalene,* is pleasantly situate on the slope of a hill overlooking the valley. It consists of a chancel, nave with north aisle, porch,

---

* St. Mary Magdalen is the saint to whom this church is dedicated, according to Lawton (*Collecto Rerum, &c.*), and other modern authorities; but in the will of "Richard Wode, of Tymyll, gentleman," dated May 12th, 1528, he desired "to be beriede in the churche yerde of Saynt Mychaell." Also in the will of George Pulleyn, of Newhall, dated June 5th, 1557, he desires "to be buryed wythin the churche or churche-yerd of Saynt Mychaell at Fuston." The evidence of these two wills is sufficient to prove that St. Michael is the true saint of Fewston Church. —*R. H. S.*

and square tower at the west end, all modern, with the exception
of the last, the greatest part of which is old—a small portion on
the top being modern.   In the tower are four bells, which were
recast when the church was repaired, about the year 1810.

The old church has been narrower than the present one,
with a roof of a high pitch, and clerestory windows.   The roof
of the old aisle has been of the lean-to kind.*

The present fabric does not present anything remarkable.
The windows are square, generally of two lights, divided by
a transom, with the exception of the east chancel window,
which is of three lights, with perpendicular tracery in the
sweep of the arch.   Over the door of the porch is the date
1697, probably the time of the rebuilding.   Could we but
see the church as it stood before that period, how different
would it be to the present; how full of interesting inscriptions
and memorials of the past! all destroyed at that time.†   The
interior does not present anything interesting from its antiquity.
The font is of considerable age; the sittings are square pews,
chiefly of pannelled oak.   Inside one of these, in the nave,
is burnt the figure of a coronet, resting on something like
a tripod; this is said by tradition to have belonged to the
Fairfax family.   In a pew in the chancel is cut the initials
and date, **E.R.: R.T., 1714.**

The only sepulchral inscription is on a small brass, on
the floor of the chancel—

"Here lieth the body of the Revd. Mr. William Carmalt,

* Some work was going on here in 1536, as in that year Robert Beckwith, of Dacre, in his will gave "to the churche worke of Fuyston iijᵃ.
iiijᵈ.—*Memorials of Fountains*, vol. i., p. 354.
† Tradition states that the church has been twice destroyed by fire; the
last time about the end of the seventeenth century.   The date over the
entrance, 1679, indicates an extensive rebuilding at that time; the other
fire was of an earlier date.   The second fire would in some measure
account for the destruction of the tombs and monuments inside the church.

late Vicar of Fewston, who departed this life the 8rd day of November, in the year 1785."*

The earlier volumes of the register, at some period, have suffered considerably from damp, and consequently are not in good condition. The earliest legible entries are in 1594. Through the kindness of the present vicar, the Rev. John Gwyther, we have been allowed to make the following extracts—chiefly belonging to the illustrious family of Fairfax.

In 1595, the name of Pulleyne appears on the register, and never quits it from that time to the present.

"1595. John, son of William Pulleyne, was baptized on the xxj. Aprill."

"1595. Old Pulleyn wyfe was buried the xvij. of April."

This manner of recording the demise of an aged person is of frequent occurrence.

"1608. Old Beecroft's wyfe was buried the 9th of Novbr."

"1614. Old Jeffrey wyfe, of the Trees, was buried the vij. of April.

The names of Ward, Wardman, Midgeley, Gill, Jeffrey, Bramley, and Broadbelt, occur early and continue long.

A family named Slingsby was settled in the parish in early times; probably a branch of the Slingsbys, of Scriven, whose pedigree has not been traced.

"1597. Xpofer. Slingsby was buried the 7th of July."

"1684. Jannit, daughter of George Slingsbie, was baptized the 8rd of July."

"1601. William Slingsby and Anne Hardisty were married by a licence the first of February."

"1604. Richard Pulleyne and Olive Slingsby were married by a licence the xxiiij th day of May."

---

* The parish register thus records his death,—"Burials in 1785. The Revd. Mr. William Carmalt, 9ber 6, aged 95."

About this time Edward Fairfax, the poet, appears to have come
to reside at Newhall, within a quarter of a mile of this church.

"1606. Elizabeth, daughter of Edw. Fairfax, Esq., was
baptized the 8th of October."

"Mary, daughter of S⁻· Ferdinando Fairfax, Knight, was
baptized yᵉ xij. day of May, 1606."

This entry records the baptism of the seventh child of
Sir Ferdinando, afterwards Lord Fairfax, and his wife, Lady
Mary, daughter of Lord Sheffield, then residing at Scough Hall,
in this parish.

"1615. Charles, sonne of S⁻· Ferdinando Fairfax, Knight,
was baptized the 26th day of March."

This Charles was slain at the battle of Marston Moor,
July 2nd, 1644.

"1621. Anne, daughter of Edw. Fairfax, Esq., was baptized
the 12th of June."

She died the same year, as was believed, through the
influence of witchcraft.

"1621. Edward Fairfax, Esq., a child named Anne, buried
the 9th of October."

The next entry probably belongs to the Menston family.

"Charles, son of Charles Fairfax, Esq., was baptized the
22nd day of August, 1629."

There are no registers existing for the years between 1634
and 1639, and as it was in 1635 that Edward Fairfax, the
poet, died, the entry of his death would be in the missing
registers. The next entry probably belongs to the poet's family.

"Mrs. Dorothie Fairfax was buried the 24th day of
Jan., 1648."

"Mrs. Maria Fairfax, the religious and virtuous wife of
Charles Fairfax, of Menston, Esquire, was buried the 21st
day of October, 1657."

"1673. Januarie. William Fairfax, of Steeton and Newton, that noble and famous esquire, was buried the five and twentieth day.

"1673. December. Noble Charles Fairfax, of Menston, Esquire, was buried the 22nd day."

This last entry we believe belongs to the learned compiler of the Fairfax pedigree—the famous *Analecta Fairfaxiana;* thus adding another to the list of worthies sleeping in the little forest church of Fewston.*

Great was our surprise to find that one of the house of Stapylton, of Wighill, near York, had found his last resting place in this remote corner. Yet there can be no mistake about it; here he lies.

"Noble Sᵣ. Miles Stapylton, of Wighall, that quondam almost Invariable Roialist, was buried the six and twentieth day of January, 1668."

* The following sketch is by Mr. Bryan Fairfax. "Charles Fairfax was born in 1595; was barrister-at-law in Lincoln's Inn, to which society he bequeathed some excellent manuscripts. He lived many years a peaceable life; but in the unhappy civil wars was tempted to accept a commission of colonel of foot, which command he executed with great reputation, being exemplary for courage and integrity, which recommended him to the intimate acquaintance and friendship of General Monk, to whom he stood firm with his regiment in Scotland, when the rest of his army wavered. He marched into England with him; was made governor of Hull in 1659, which he resigned to Lord Bellasis, and had a pension settled by his Majesty King Charles the Second, to him and his heirs, of £100 per annum, out of the port of Hull.

He was an excellent scholar, but delighted most in antiquities, and hath left a valuable collection of that kind. He hath left a most exact pedigree of our family of Fairfax, which he calls *Analecta Fairfaxiana.* The original being in Denton Library. He died at Menston, December 18th, 1673. Ætat. 78.

In no other collection are there to be discovered such a mass of letters and documents, public and private; pedigrees, not only of the different branches of his own family, but of all the families with whom they were connected by intermarriage; seals, mottoes, arms, and the varied paraphernalia of heraldic honours. All the Fairfaxes contributed something towards this curious depositary."

"1658. Aprill. Mr. John Vavasoure, of Dog Park, was buried the first day."

One of the Weston family of that name, who resided at the now ruined tower called Dog Park Lodge.

Robin Goodfellow and his family resided in this parish early in the seventeenth century. In 1607 he had a child baptized; another in 1618; and himself was buried April 27th, 1646. A family named Munkey resided in this parish about this time.

Another name of rare occurrence—Roughcastle, is found here.

"1678. Februarie. John Roughcastle was buried the thirteenth day."

"1672. Aprill. Noble Maugeir Vavasour, of Weston, Esquire, was buried the ninth day."

"1675. March. Thomas Simpson wife, of Haverah Park, was buried on the 26th day, and he himself the 29th day."

"1668. November. William Knowles, of Beckwithshaw, being reported by his neighbours to be near one hundred and twentie years old, was buried the ninth day of the month. His funeral sermon was preached by me, Wm. Broke, Cler."

"1645. October 4th. William Wardman buried, being in the one hundred and third year of his age."

"1646. Martha, daughter of Michael Faux, Esquire, was baptized the fifth of October. Francis Gregory, Esquire, Godfather, and Mrs. Anne Gregorie and Mrs. Elizabeth Maud, Godmothers."

"1644. Christopher Briggs, and Anne, his wife, and Jane, his daughter, were altogether buried the 18th of December."

"Aprill. 1674. Alice Hurdistie, of the Nabs, that virtuous matron, was buried the sixteenth day."

"Jane, that religious and virtuous matron, and loving wife of William Barker, Clerke, was buried April ye 3rd, 1675."

Hardly any of the entries are in Latin, and from the absence of magistrates' certificates during the time of the Commonwealth, it would appear as though the ordinary rites of the church had suffered no interruption.

The following is the most complete list of the rectors and vicars we have been able to obtain—

A CLOSE CATALOGUE OF THE RECTORS OF FUYSTON.

(Torre's Archdeaconry of York, p. 206.)

4 Non. Julii, 1234.	Dom. Will. Plesitz..........Hen. III. rex.	
8 Non. Oct., 1280.	Mr. Walt. de la Mare, sub. diac...ministri	
		et fr. St. Rob.
Non. Mar., 1281.	Dom. Ric. de Eadburbury, diac..ibidem.	
2 Kal. Mar., 1303.	Dom. Will. de Thorntoft, presb...	,,
17 Kal. Julii, 1320.	Dom. Ric. de Henway, cap.	,,
10 Kal. Sept., 1320.	Dom. Joh. Wylemot............	,,
	Dom. Will. de Swynflet	,, .. per resig.
	pro ecclesia de Malberthorp.	
3 April, 1346.	Dom. Nic. Olyver, cap.	,, ...p. resig.
	pro ecc. de Briseley.	
24 April, 1347.	Dom. Will. Launeyr*	,, ...p. resig.
	pro cap. de Norton.	
20 August, 1348.	Dom. Joh. de Nessefeld, cler.....	,,

A CLOSE CATALOGUE OF THE VICARS OF FOSTON.

1 Junii, 1362.	Fr. Adam de Sukelinghall, conf. doms...min. et	
		fr. St. Rob...p. resig.
18 Maii, 1370.	Fr. Ric. de Wakefield	,, ...
	Fr. Rob. de Ebor...	,, ...p. resig.
4 Oct., 1393.	Fr. Will. de Wakefield	,, ...p. resig.
11 Maii, 1405.	Fr. Will. de Lyndsey, presb.	,, ...p. resig.
10 Feb., 1420.	Fr. Joh. de Harwood, presb.	,, ...p. resig.
5 Junii, 1423.	Fr. Will. Wyndus, presb.	,, ...p. resig.
23 Feb., 1424.	Fr. Joh. Brynsall	,, ..p. mortem.
20 July, 1444.	Fr. Joh. Hawthorne.................	,, ..p. mortem.
4 Nov., 1455.	Fr. Tho. Galway	,, ...p. resig.
6 Mar., 1462.	Fr. Will. Husworth, presb...........	,, ...p. resig.
16 Maii, 1468.	Fr. Will. Carne................... ..	,, ..p. mortem.

* "Nicholas de Launeyr, rector of Briseley, made his will 4 Kal. June 1348, at Fenwick, in dioc. Ebor: desiring burial at the Friars' Minors, Doncaster; and appointed his brother, William de Launeyr, rector of the church of Fosceton, in the diocese of York, and Will. de Synflete, rector of the church of B.M.V. of Malberthorpe, in the diocese of Lincoln, his executors. Proved 18th June, 1348."—*Reg. Zouch.* R. H. S.

9 Julii, 1494.* Fr. Tho. Parysh ......min. et fr. St. Rob...p. mortem.
14 Nov., 1515. Fr. Henr. Bell .... „ ..p. mortem.
25 Maii, 1541. Dom. Rob. Gybson, cap..assig. dom. St. Robti...p. resig.
4 Dec., 1545.   Dom. Joh. Pulleyne, cler. ....Henr. rex.....p. mortem.
2 Aug., 1583.   Henr. Pulleyne, cl...........Eliz. regina....p. mortem.
8 Junii, 1591. Nic. Smythson, cl. ....eodem.......p. mortem.
28 Sept., 1632. Will. Barker, cl., M.A. ......Chas. I. rex.

Torre's catalogue ends here. The two following names are
from the parish register—

1637. William Broke.
1675. William Barker.

ARCHBISHOP SHARPE'S MSS. *(York & W. Riding, p. 83).*

1677. Will. Hudson ....Chas. II. ....p. mort.
11 April, 1705. William Carmalt........ Queen Anne ......p. mort.
16 April, 1737. Thomas Bolland ....Geo. II. ....p. mort.
2 June, 1739. Thomas Burton............ „ ....p. mort.
1751. John Whinneray ....p. mort.
4 May, 1790. Christ. Ramshaw ....Geo. III........p. mort.
1844. John Gwyther........... ....present vicar.

The charities consist of 1a. 1r. 0p. of land, left by James
Robinson, in 1620; the sum of 12s. annually, left by Henry
Jeffray and others, about the year 1729; Paley's dole, 8s. per
annum; the Rodilholme rent charge of 2s. per annum; and
Francis Jeffray's gift, by deed, in 1756, of an annual rent
charge of £1 1s., to be equally divided among the poor of
Fewston, Clifton, and Timble.

The parish of Fewston is also entitled to one half of the rent
of a field situate at Kettlesing, let for £5 a-year, which is paid

---

* The following case, "for assaulting ye vicar during divine service,"
extracted from the Registry at York, took place during this vicar's time.
It shows a little of the spirit, as well as the language, of the age. In 1504,
one Henry Wilson, of the parish of Fewston, was suspended for not giving
a mortuary for his father. When the vicar (of Fewston) suspended him,
he said—"If thou suspend me, I sall give ye wt this axe yt thow salt
suspend me no moo, and bade me (the vicar) faste goo furthe of his sight,
false frear, and false hynsking curet yt I was, and shuke the axe at my
face." The vicar said—"Herre Wilson go furthe of the kirke, for I will
not doo devyne servis and ye be in the kirke." Henry said—"Thou art
a false curet, and hur master, and thou shalt have no preste bot one.
—R. H. S.

and distributed at Christmas. The poor of the parish of Hamps-thwaite receive the other half.

The register contains the following memorandum on this subject—

"April 24, 1687. A note of the names of all those who have given anything towards the relief of the poore of our parish of Fewston, together with the several sums, and the names of those in whose hands the money is this day.

Imprimis. Given by George Thorpe, of Gilbeck, the sum of five pounds, now in the hands of William Thorpe, his son, of the saide place.

It. Given by Anne Newell, late of Darley, the sum of five pounds, now in the hands of John Banister, Gent., within our said parish.

It. Given by John Mawson, late of Leeds, the sum of foure pounds, now in the hands of John Mawson, of Norwood.

It. Given by Richard Calvert, of Thruscrosse, the sum of one pound six shillings and eightpence, now in the hands of Stephen Gill, of Thruscrosse.

It. Given by the Right Honourable Tho: Lord Fairfax, of Denton, 20s.; and other 20s. by his reverend son, Mr. Henry Fairfax, of Newton, now in the hands of Thomas Holme, of the Gill.

Witnesses of these things—

WILLM. BROKE, Vicar.

THOMAS SIMPSON,
WILLIAM TURNER, } Church-
EDWARD GILL, } wardens.
FRANCIS BRAMBLE,

WILLM. JEFFREY,
JOHN WIGGLESWORTH, } Overseers.
THOMAS WAYTE,
WILLM. LISTER,

M^d. that there is another register booke, which begins 1592. Given by Thomas Clapham 10li for the church, and 10li for the poore. Feb. 4, 1639."

Thomas Clapham's gift is more fully described in another part of the register—

"Februarie 4th, 1689. Given by Thomas Clapham, within the township of Timble, linnen webster, the summe of ten pounds to the church of Fewston, and the yearly increase thereof to redound to the vicar thereof for the time being, and to all others successively, to the end of the world.

Given also by the said Thomas Clapham other ten pounds, and the use thereof to redound to the poore of the said parish."

The parsonage is pleasantly situated close to the west side of the churchyard. It was much enlarged and improved by the Rev. John Gwyther in 1867.

The Wesleyan Methodists have a chapel here, which will accommodate about two hundred hearers.

There are many small hamlets in the parish of Fewston, though no other collection of houses worthy of the name of a village. A few of these we shall particularize.

Cragg Hall is situate about half a mile west of Fewston, and is an Elizabethan house, pleasantly situate on the sunny slope of the valley, surrounded by a grove of sycamore trees. The front, facing the south, yet retains its mullioned windows of many lights. A square projection, near the western end, forms the entrance or porch, which is carried up to the roof, and there terminates in a small gable. The front door, from its appearance, may be coeval with the building of the house. It is of massive oak planks, studded all over with the heads of large nails. A tradition, current in the neighbourhood, relates that a body of Scotch rebels, or marauders of some kind, once halted in this neighbourhood, and committed many depredations in a most cruel and wanton manner. The owner of Cragg Hall was reported to have said that "their hearts must be as withered as Jeroboam's hand." This excited their resentment; while the information that there were certain valuable horses in his stables, equally moved their cupidity. Forewarned of their designs against himself and his horses, he hid the latter in an obscure place in the wood, by the side of the Washburn; and then having made fast his bolts and bars, betook himself to a cavity near the roof, in one of the thick inner walls of the building. The front door was first attacked by the bludgeons of the assailants, and yet bears honourable marks of the defence then made. It however withstood all their efforts; but other bolts and bars did not. An entrance was effected, and the house searched and sacked. Though the owner's cough was heard (he being affected with asthma), his hiding place could not be found. After a while the plunderers departed, and the wall gave forth its owner, and the wood his horses; neither of them having suffered harm from their uncomfortable hiding places.

In the year 1638, ".William Frankland, of Thirkilbie, in the county of York, with Henry Frankland, Knight, son and heir-apparent of the aforesaid William Frankland, and Richard Frankland de Fuiston, in the said county, gentleman," surrendered "the messuage or tenement of Upper Cragg, together with certain lands situate and existing *infra hamleto de Fuiston et villa de Timble, infra Foresta de Knaresburgh,* to the use and behoof of Henry Fairfax, of Newton Kime, in the said county, clerk."* About the same time, the

* Henry Fairfax was the second son of Sir Thomas Fairfax. He was educated at Trinity College, Cambridge, entered into holy orders, and was presented by his father to the small living of Newton Kyme. He married the pious and virtuous Mary Cholmley, a pure model of christian womanhood. During all the time of the civil wars, from 1642 to 1646, their little parsonage house was a refuge and sanctuary to all their friends and relations on both sides. From thence he removed to Bolton Percy, where his wife died in 1649, and was buried in that church. In 1660, he retired to his own house at Oglethorpe, where he spent the remainder of his life in pious solitude. His recreations were antiquities and heraldry. Thus he lived to a good old age, his conscience void of offence towards God and man; and died in April, 1665, aged 77, and was buried at Bolton Percy, near to his wife. His was the most happy and enviable career of any of the Fairfaxes.

same Henry Fairfax acquired the adjoining lands of Beeston
Leas, Lower Cragg, and Bainbridge Gate. How long Cragg
Hall continued in this family we know not. In 1681, Thomas
Goodard was the owner of it. In 1691, Marmaduke Clark
seems to have had some claim upon it. In 1713, it was
conveyed from Thomas Atkinson, of Newbridge, to John Clark,
of Pannal, who, in 1714, sold it to Edward Robinson, of
Swinsty Hall, who, on November 17th, 1716, sold the same to
Stephen Parkinson, of Denton.* The house at that time

On the death of Thomas, Lord Fairfax, the great parliamentary general,
without issue male, he was succeeded in the title by his cousin Henry,
eldest son of the above named Rev. Henry Fairfax; from whom is descended the Lords Fairfax, now of Virginia, in America.

* Stephen Parkinson, who purchased this estate, was a man of considerable learning, and it is also said was a well known "character" in his
times. From a memorandum book of his, now in the possession of his
descendant, the Rev. Thomas Parkinson, we have been favoured with the
following extracts. The notes elsewhere given with the initials S. P. are
also from the same source.—

"In the yeare 1716, I Stephen Parkinson, bought of Edward Robinson,
of Swinsty, the Cragg House, being the 12 day November; and on the
17 November, wee did . . . for it. The purchase is 600 pounds."

"Memorandum. In the year 1730, I sett 20 apple trees, and three
cherry trees; and in the yeare 1731, I sett 13 apple trees."

About 1740, he gives the following list of his family,—John, Thomas,
Francis, Stephen, sons; and Jane, his daughter. Thomas was married with
Mary Pulyen, of Timble, June 28th, 1740: Stephen to Anna Wilks, Jan. 19,
1743-44. On July 14, 1744, the house at Hardisty Hill was reared for the
dwelling of the said Stephen and Anna. The following entry has reference
to a custom now nearly obsolete.—"In the year 1741, and the 26 day of
January, John Tiplady of Blouberhouses was married. Our Stephen did
ride for the bride, and did win." The following two entries are highly
interesting.—"Denton, May the 18th day, 1716. Memoriall. My Lord
Fairfax sould his estate at Denton and Askwith to one James Ibbotson, of
Leeds; and he sould a place called Billborough, neare Yorke, to six men,
Captain Fairfax, Barnard Banks, Nathanill Hird, and one Smith, and one
Ma—kes, and one Roodman of Yorke. They took possession of it the
day and year above written. James Ibbetson took possession, and all set
their hands to a paper and paid sixpence. All the tenants paid sixpence as
before mentioned, to James Ibbetson of Leeds."

"For a memorandum. On Aprill 26th day, att night happened a fire in
Denton Hall, which burnt all down. This was in the year 1734. One
Samuel Ibbetson owned it then, and lived in it. At this time it was the
fairest hall that was within the dale. This was sett down by Stephen
Parkinson, at Cragg Hall, in the Forest."

was described as "a messuage called Over Cragg Hall." This family has held possession of it ever since, along with other estates adjacent, as well as in Pannal, Beckwithshaw, and Timble.

Stephen Parkinson died in 1763, at the ripe age of fourscore and six, leaving, by his will, the estate at Cragg Hall between his sons, John and Thomas; specifying the portions of the house, and the parcels of land to go to each. In 1776, John Parkinson sold his share to his brother, who thus re-united the estate. On the death of the said Thomas, in 1779, at the age of 70, he bequeathed Cragg Hall to his son, also named Thomas, who held it until his death in 1816, considerably increasing the family estate by additional purchases. On his decease, in the above year, he left the estate, by will, between his sons, Thomas and Joseph. In 1819, they divided it, Thomas taking the hall, and lands thereto appertaining, which he held until his decease in 1846, when he disposed of it, by will, to his son, the present owner, the Rev. Thomas Parkinson, now Vicar of Clare, in the county of Suffolk.

One peculiarity in the bequests dividing the estate is the division of the ovenhouse; by which both parties had an equal right to the use of that necessary article of household economy—the large brick oven, ·in which the family bread was baked.

How enviable appears the lot of those substantial yeomen! well provided with all the conveniences of life, closing their eyes in death on the same spot in which they first opened them at birth, and then their bones were laid beside those of their fathers in the quiet village churchyard.

The huge grey crag which gave name to the hall and adjacent homesteads, still peers out of the steep hill side, close to the road leading to Fewston,

2G

At Busky Dike, a place between Cragg Hall and Fewston, according to the report of tradition, there once existed a Druidical altar; and the same venerable authority declares that the same place is the haunt of a "Barguest;" and many of the country people yet tremble as they pass that place in the dark, for fear they should meet that strange and terrible beast.

The well known and pleasantly situated Hopper Lane Hotel is situate on the right of the road leading from Knaresborough to Skipton. It has been kept for two generations by the family of Ward, previous to whose coming it was a small roadside inn, kept by a person named Tiplady. In 1775, Thomas Ward came to reside here. He afterwards purchased the premises, and built the present house. On his decease, in 1823, he was succeeded by his eldest son, Thomas Ward, the present owner. The family of Ward is of considerable antiquity in this parish. Previous to their coming here they resided at Fewston, and before their residence there, they were settled at Great Timble for many generations.

Hardisty Hill is another hamlet in this parish, overlooking the valley of the Washburn. It is said to have derived its name from the family of Hardisty, which settled here, and by whom the lands around were owned for many generations. They formed alliances with the Wardmans, Wards, and other respectable families in the neighbourhood.

William Hardisty, of Hardisty Hill, yeoman, married Mary, daughter of William Wardman, of Blubberhouses Hall, by whom he had, besides three sons who died in infancy, one son named Joseph, who died before his father, unmarried, and three daughters—

Anne, married to Thomas Metcalfe, of Leeming Stile, who died in 1841.

Hannah, married to Thomas Skaife, of Braisty Woods, by whom, among other issue, she had a son named Joseph, who married Elizabeth Davies, of York, by whom he had one son Robert Hardisty Skaife, one of the most pains taking of antiquaries and geneaologists; and

Susanna, married to Jonathan Ward, who became in consequence owner of the estate here, sometimes called Hardisty Hall. He sold part of the estate to Messrs. Colbeck, Ellis, Wilks, and Co., on which the large manufactory at Westhouses was built. He died July 28th, 1834, aged 80.

Here is a small Wesleyan Methodist Chapel, built in 1841, which will accommodate about one hundred hearers.

Westhouses is the name of a hamlet and large manufactory situate close to the river Washburn, where it is crossed by the Knaresborough and Skipton turnpike road. The manufactory was first erected for the spinning of flax, by Messrs. Colbeck, Ellis, Wilks, and Company, about the year 1806. The land was purchased from Jonathan Ward, of Hardisty Hill, being part of the estate which he had received with his wife, Susanna, daughter of William Hardisty. At that time it was a scene of active industry on a large scale—both manufacturing and agricultural. Large quantities of waste land were enclosed, cultivated, and ornamented with plantations in suitable places; many new buildings were erected for the accommodation of the work people; and the number of apprentices employed in the works, and maintained on the premises, was frequently upwards of two hundred.* Two enormous water wheels gave motion to the long lines of machinery; and a more busy, bustling, apparently prosperous place, was not easily to be

---

*This system was the means of introducing great numbers of poor people, who obtained settlements; and on the failure of the firm, 1,400 of them became chargeable to the township of Fewston.

found. The day of misfortune came; the establishment was broken up; the work people dispersed; and the huge water wheels and long lines of polished machinery became still; and silence for some years settled over the busy scene. Not having the facilties of railway transit, it is not likely to ever resume its former importance.

The spinning of silk was afterwards substituted for that of flax, by Messrs. Crowther. This mill and all its water rights has recently been purchased by the Corporation of Leeds, in furtherance of their scheme for supplying that town with water from the valley of the Washburn.

The population in 1801 was 526; in 1811, 823; in 1821, 610; in 1831, 688; in 1841, —; in 1851, 399; and in 1861, 496. The annual value of this township as assessed to the county rate in 1849 was £1,469; and in 1859, £2,174. The amount assessed to income tax in 1858 was £2,898.

GREAT TIMBLE.

THIS township is bounded on the north and north-east by Little Timble; on the south-east and south by Weston and Denton; and on the west by Blubberhouses. The whole area is 1,566 acres.

At the time of the Domesday survey this place was in the hands of the king, but no quantity or value is given.

Forming a part of the Forest of Knaresborough, it always passed along with that fee. In 1299, we find it called Timble Percy; and also in 1802, when, in the enumeration of the knights' fees in Yorkshire, it is stated that the king held Tymble Percy for the eighth part and the sixteenth part of one fee.*

The family of Hardisty appears to have settled here in very early times, as in the Poll Tax Roll, 2nd Richard II. (1878-9), we find in *Villa de Tymble*, Knaresborough Liberty, "Johannes de Hardolfsty, iiij^d," and "Stephanus de Hardolfsty, iiij^d." Again, in the Subsidy Roll, 40th Eliz. (1597-8), occurs, under Tymble-cum-Fuyston, "Stephanus Hardistie, in terris, xx^s· iiij^d·" The name is now extinct here, though found abundantly in other parts of the forest.

The village is situate on high ground, from 720 to 750 feet above the sea level, and consists of a cluster of good substantial farm-houses and cottages, well sheltered by lines of sycamores.

* "Surtees' Soc.," p. 211, 1866.

Wise and prudent were the men who planted them, for no tree thrives so well in high situations. Notwithstanding its height the soil is generally good, and slopes pleasantly down towards Timble Gill, on the south.

Here is a Wesleyan Methodist Chapel and a school, to the latter of which a small endowment in land was attached, which the overseers very improperly sold for £10, about the year 1813.

On the enclosure of Knaresborough Forest 2a. 1r. 5p. of land were awarded to the poor of Fewston and the school at Timble.

The population in 1801 was 172; in 1811, 201; in 1821, 288; in 1831, 218; in 1841, —; in 1851, 184; and in 1861, 224.

The annual value of this township as assessed to the county rate in 1849 was £997, and in 1859, £1,065. The amount assessed to property tax in 1858 was £1,161.

NORWOOD.

This township is sometimes called Norwood-with-Clifton, sometimes Clifton-with-Norwood. Why we know not, as there is no place of the name of Clifton within its limits, and it has no connection with Newhall-with-Clifton, near Otley, which is in another parish. However the appellation may have been given, the fact is certain, Clifton has formed part of the name from the earliest times. It is mentioned in Domesday survey, among the lands of the king, who had in "Elsword-Clifton and Timble, five carucates and a half of land."* In the *Inquisition* on the death of Richard, Earl of Cornwall, in 1299, it is styled "Clifton-Elsworth." In the Court Rolls of the Honour of Knaresborough, 16th Edward III., "Johannes Taillur, de Ellisworth," occurs. In 1558, the name of the township, as entered on the rolls, is "Clyfton-cum-Norwoode, *alias* Ellisworthe." The name of Norwood also occurs in early times, as in 16th Edward III., Evorta, widow of John Vavesur, de Norwoode, was living. No such place as Elsword, or Elsworth, is now to be found in the township. The term appears by some unaccountable process to have changed into Norwood.

On the west this township is bounded by the river Washburn and the township of Fewston; on the south it touches Farnley,

* "Bawdwen's Dom. Boc.," p. 256.

Lindley, Stainburn, and Pannal; on the east it abuts on
Haverah Park; and on the north Felliscliffe and Darley form
the boundary.*

Large quantities of stirrups and bridle bits were formerly
made in this township; the whitesmiths living in cottages on

* The boundary of Clifton-with-Norwood, which was perambulated in
the year 1829, by Mr. John Moorhouse, churchwarden.—"Beginning at
Fewston churchyard gate, thence proceeding eastward along William
Bramley's Lane to the corner, then by John Moorhouse's Lane to opposite
John Bramley's field bottom, when it goeth over John Moorhouse's field
to the aforesaid John Bramley's field bottom; and then by lands of John
Bramley, Henry Bramley, and John Bramley, senr., to Spinksburn beck;
then up the said beck to Whydraw bridge; there are certain small pieces
betwixt the fence and the beck, but the boundary appears to go by the
fence; thence round Samuel Dennington's field to the beck, then by the
said beck to the old enclosure of George Spence, a little above Bedlam
bridge; whence it proceeds up the outside of the old land of George Spence
to a stoop in a field a little above a turn in the lane; (at this place the
boundary is very crooked, owing to the old fence of George Spence, part of
which is now taken away and altered,) from this post it proceeds straight
to a post upon Skipton road, a little below Dangerous corner; and then
straight forwards, crossing the Black dike; (note—the distance from Darley
road is more than at Dangerous corner;) thence it goeth straight to the
corner of the hill, to a small dike at the foot of the hill, then up the said
dike to a post on the road leading from Darley to Norwood; and from the
said post to another post standing in Nesfield Close; thence to a post
standing on Skipton road, and then straight to Constable Ridge, where
there is a post, but it appears to be rather too high; it then twineth a little
across the allotment of the Rev. T. M. Shann, to the old enclosure of Penny
Pot House, where it leaves out a small corner, and thence proceeds straight
forwards, crossing the road aslant to a post in William Todd's field, opposite the old enclosure; thence to the old Park wall (Haverah Park), by
which it is bounded until it meets the Broad Dub beck, at the corner of
the pasture known as William Turner's out pasture; then up the said beck
to Sandwith bridge stone; (note—the beck is altered here, the old beck
was very crooked, not so far out as the new beck;) then up the said beck
to the Rev. C. Ramshaw's allotment, and then turns to the right on the top
of the said allotment to Oacken Well, and then turns to the left right down
to Sunderland beck; thence right down Hopkinson Gill to Otley road;
then down the said road to a post, where Farnley meets the said township
(Norwood), and then turns to the right to a turn in Washburn; whence it
is bounded by the river Washburn to Joshua Rowlinson's holme, where
there is a piece in Farnley (part of the posts are yet standing, but some
are taken up); then by the outside of the river Washburn to Dog Park
bridge, then by the said river to the bottom of the Rev. C. Ramshaw's
holme; thence by land of the said Rev. C. Ramshaw to Fewston churchyard gate, where the boundary began."

the edge of the common. The business began to decline about the year 1800, and in 1840 had entirely ceased.

The most remarkable work of man in this township is an ancient earthwork, known by the name of Bank Slack, and marked on the ordnance maps as an old camp, to which it bears not the most remote resemblance. The country people believe it to have been made for military purposes, and relate that Oliver Cromwell's cannon was planted here when he battered down the walls of John o' Gaunt's Castle, on the opposite side of the valley. The probability is, that it is of British origin, and has formed the town or home of a clan or family at a very early period of our history; probably two thousand years ago.

It is situate on the northern side of a small valley; the water from which flows in two directions—that from the eastern end, down Haverah Park into the Nidd; that from the western, into the Washburn. The main work consists of a trench, about ten yards in width by about three yards in depth, varying considerably in size in different places; keeping always on dry ground, and running along the hill side, very crookedly, for upwards of a mile; extending from the upper part of Haverah Park to a piece of waste ground called Worstall Crags, though not continuously, there being two or three gaps or interruptions during the course, caused by slight valleys or undulations of the ground. A cart road runs along, about half its length, and two farm-houses are built upon, or immediately adjoining, to it. Its general direction is east and west, until the valley opens to the westward and the land bends northward, when it also turns towards the north, cutting through the shoulder of the hill. At this point it is the deepest and least obliterated, and has been delved into the rock, which here consists of a stratum of fossilized shells of great hardness, in thin beds, with numerous joints,—a kind of transition limestone. An old fence, partly hedge, partly wall, is carried along the trench—sometimes at the bottom—sometimes on one side. After passing this hill the trench is interrupted by a natural break in the ground, down which passes an old trackway, and a footpath laid with grit flagstones. About one hundred yards across this old road the trench again commences, not quite so deep as before, curving with the bendings of the hill for three or four hundred yards further, when it suddenly terminates. It has evidently been made at a great cost of time and labour, and we believe for places of residence, not for a place of defence, for which it is not at all adapted. The greatest part of it is situate midway the slope of the hill, overlooked by higher land; and only at one point, where it bends northward, does it assume any dominant position with respect to the surrounding country; and from that point there is certainly a close, interesting, and most beautiful view of the country to the south and west, and by a slight change of position to the east.

Near this trench we should be inclined to place Straling, a hamlet mentioned in Ogilby's survey, in 1674, though the name is not at present known. The "long stoop" mentioned by him yet exists, close to a modern farm-house, called Long Stoop Farm. The road leading from Harrogate to Fewston is called Penny Pot Lane. Unfortunately for the thirsty soul the Penny Pot House is deserted, and a ruin now, where in good old times ale was sold at *a penny a pot.*

The Roman conquerors of Britain appear to have wandered into this township with money in their pockets, and forgotten to to take it away again. About the year 1830, a farmer ploughing in a field near Lindley Wood, turned up what he at first deemed some rust of iron, but on kicking it with his foot, he observed some small copper coins, about as many as would fill a pint measure. They appear to have been enveloped in a leathern purse; many of them were much corroded; the inside ones were more perfect. They proved to be Roman coins, chiefly of the Emperors Gallienus, Hadrian, Tetricus, Victorinus, Aurelianus, Diocletianus, Constantius, and Constantine.*

East End Houses form a small scattered hamlet near the eastern boundary of the township, adjoining Haverah Park. The residence of Mr. John Bramley here is an old respectable building, such as the better class of yeomanry built for them-selves two hundred and fifty years ago. It is of a square form, with a projecting porch, which is carried up to the height of the roof, where it terminates in a neat gable. Over the door are the initials and date, **R.A., 1625.** At either end is a large projecting, buttress-like chimney, decreasing by regular steps towards the top, yet occupying nearly half the gable.

This house and estate belonged to Robert Parker, whose daughter, Ann, married John Bramley, of Fewston, and having no sons of his own, on his decease, in 1768, he bequeathed the same to his grandson, Robert Bramley, whom he had brought up from the age of two years.

Robert Bramley, who married Mary, daughter of Mr. John Robinson, of Swinsty Hall, held the same until his decease in 1817, at the age of 72, when he was succeeded by his son, John Bramley, to whom Samuel Carr, his uncle, bequeathed the other moiety of the Swinsty Hall estate. He also much improved his estate by the erection of good substantial farm buildings, as well as increased it by his judicious purchases. He married Ann, daughter of Thomas Simpson, of Felliscliffe, by whom he had one son and two daughters. On his decease in 1858, he was succeeded by his only son, John Bramley, of East

* "Shaw's Wharfedale," p. 116.

End House and Swinsty Hall, who married Mary, youngest daughter of Simeon Moorhouse, of Gill Bottom, by whom he has a family of four sons and four daughters.

At Brown Bank, not far from East End, is a Wesleyan Methodist Chapel, founded by Robert Bramley, of Norwood, about the year 1828. He transferred the same to the Wesleyan Conference. It will accommodate about one hundred hearers.

Brame Lane is the name of the road passing through this township from north to south, leading from Pateley Bridge to Otley, almost close to which, on the left hand, is Brame Hall, an antique farm-house, though evidently at some period a dwelling of importance. It formerly belonged to a family of the name of Ellill.

At Fox Crag, on the southern side of this township, on a ridge of high land 950 feet above the sea level, are two very remarkable rocks, of a square form and of large bulk, the upper surfaces of which are deeply indented with artificial channels and rock basins, pointing them out as places where the Druids had lighted their fires on the great festival days,—so that they may be styled, in more senses than one, the "high places" of the earth.

Gill Bottom, near the Gill Beck, almost hid by a grove of trees, is the residence of Mr. John Moorhouse; a warm, comfortable situation, which has been held by the same family for many generations. Brian Moorhouse, about the middle of the seventeenth century, purchased the farm on which he was then residing from one of the Fairfax family. Brian was succeeded here by his son, Simeon Moorhouse, who has left behind him the reputation of being a very learned man—an adept in astrology, and a skilful penman. He collected an extensive library of books on his favourite studies, and on his decease, in 1769, was succeeded by his son, John Moor-

house, who dying without issue, in 1798, was succeeded by his
nephew, Simeon, son of Simeon Moorhouse, of Clint, who held
the same until his decease in 1826, when he was succeeded
by his only son, John Moorhouse, the present owner and
occupier.

A family of the name of Smithson also resided at Gill Bottom;
and the road leading hence to the turnpike bears the name
of Smithson Lane. At one time this was considered to be
the wealthiest family in the Forest of Knaresborough. They
were possessed of large estates in land, and carried on a considerable business as maltsters. The ruins of their malt kiln are
yet standing, but the business ceased on the death of Joseph
Smithson, the last of the family, who died in 1787, leaving
an only daughter, named Sushannah, who married Jacob Wilks,
of Darley, linen manufacturer. She sold the estate in Norwood,
in 1829. Folly Hall also belonged to them, but was sold
by William Smithson, of a younger branch of the family.
Lacon Hall, near Dacre Banks, also belonged to them, and was
sold to Sir John Ingilby, of Ripley Castle, by the above
Sushannah. One half the great tithes of Fewston parish
belonged to them, and were sold to Messrs. Hill and Shann, of
Tadcaster, for 700 guineas. The money was paid at Fewston,
and Sushannah carried the same home, folded in her blue linen
apron. Joseph Smithson went out of his house in the evening
to attend to his cattle, not returning in due time, search was
made, and he was found dead between the house and
the barn; being a frost, and ice where he was found, it was
supposed he had fallen and been killed. His son had previously
been found drowned at Rowton Wath, in the river Washburn.

Further southward, along Brame Lane, is the Norwood
School, a small unpretending stone building. The small
endowment to which was left by John Jeffrey, in 1716, for the

teaching of four poor children. Timothy Ellill, in 1769, gave a sum of money, the interest of which was to be applied towards the instruction of eight poor children of this township. No school is specified in either of these bequests, at which the said children were to be taught. The master at present receives one-half of the rents of the poor's lands, or charities, for which he teaches eight free scholars.[*]

Scough Hall is situate between the river Washburn and the turnpike road, in a slight hollow, open to the south and south-west, and sheltered on the north by a ridge of land, which at a very short distance rises above the highest part of the house.

It was probably built by some one of the family of Breary, by whom it was occupied during some parts of the sixteenth and seventeenth centuries. A daughter of John Breary,[†] named Maria, married Charles Fairfax, the learned compiler of *Analecta Fairfaxiana*, and by that means the estate passed into the Fairfax family. The mother of Dame Maria Fairfax appears to have had some claim to dower, or an interest of some kind in the estate, for the learned Charles writes to Lord Ferdinando,

---

[*] We have no direct information as to the time when this school was built; it was however previous to 1757, as in that year there is an entry in the accounts of George Walker, Constable of Clifton Hamlet, of 8s. 6d. "paid to William Hobson, for mason work at the school." It was afterwards used for many years for town's meetings and parochial purposes. It was enlarged in 1835.

[†] Breary, or Brearhaugh, near Bramhope, was the original home of this family, from which they took their name, and where they flourished in very early times. Thoresby says, "Alan de Brearhaugh was great-grandfather to William, who died in the 8th of Edward III."
The following memoranda of their residence here are from the register of Fewston—
"1596. Samuel, son of John Breary, was baptized ye 24th of August."
"1604. John, a son of John Breary, was baptized the 10th of August."
"1608. John Breary was buried the 3rd of September."
An old gritstone altar tomb in Fewston churchyard has cut upon it, lengthways, in large letters—"Jhon Breary, died 1613." The inscription has evidently been put upon the stone after a former one had been partially worn out, and there may be a mistake in the date.

in April, 1640, when a rather heavy subsidy was about to be assessed upon his estates here and elsewhere,—"My mother-in-law never before now admitted me to an estate at Scough;" implying that she was willing to admit his claim when payments were to be made, but at no other time; which proceeding indicates a considerable degree of worldly wisdom in the old lady.

This estate passed from Charles Fairfax, Esq., to Lord Thomas Fairfax, as is shown by the following extract from the Knaresborough Court Rolls—"Charles Fairfax, of Mensington, *als.* Menston, surrenders into the hands of the Lady of the Manor, the Dowager Queen, Henrietta Maria, all that capitall messuage called Scoughe, six other messuages, with edifices built thereon, and also seventy-three acres of land, meadow and pasture, with all thereto belonging, to the use and behoofe of the very noble Sir Thomas Fairfax, of Denton, Baron Fairfax, of Cameron, and to Henry Arthington, Henry Fairfax, of Ogle-thorpe, George Smithson, of Newton, and George Rawdon, of Rawdon, Esqrs., their heirs and assigns."

Sir Ferdinando Fairfax resided for some time in this house; and here on the 22nd of March, 1614, was born his son, Charles Fairfax, who was christened at Fewston on the 26th of the same month. Sir Guy Palmes, of Lindley, and Walter Hawksworth, Esq., of Hawksworth, were the godfathers; and Mistress Douglass Sheffield, aunt to the said child, was god-mother. What a gathering of notables in this now neglected spot! The child who first saw daylight here, and received his name at the antique font of Fewston, grew up, became in early life a soldier, served in the Low Countries, returned home on the breaking out of the civil war in England, was made a colonel of horse in the service of Parliament, was mortally wounded at the battle of Marston Moor, July 2nd, 1644, and died five days afterwards. In what a few short words the story of a life is told!

This estate, with other houses and lands adjoining, afterwards became part of the possessions of the family of Wilkinson, of Newhall-with-Clifton, near Otley, with whom it continued until about the year 1788, when it passed to the family of Fawkes, of Farnley, by the marriage of Francis Fawkes, Esq., with Christiana Wilkinson, and was held by that family until it was purchased by Mr. Edward Taylor, the present owner and occupier.

Scough is probably the oldest of the old halls in the valley of the Washburn; it also exhibits most symptoms of ruin and decay. It is a low, rather long building; two stories in height in front, but only about five feet high at the back. The original windows yet remain; those in the upper story of three lights each—those in the lower of five. The walls are of large carefully dressed stones, about a foot in thickness. The back part of the roof, upon the slating, is overgrown with masses of stonecrop and fern. In what has been the kitchen, now used as a cowhouse, is a large fireplace, at least fifteen feet wide; the opening is about six feet in height, when the chimney rises from a remarkably flat arch. These old fireplaces give us ideas of the huge masses of meat which have hissed, crackled, and roasted before them. Times have changed sadly with Scough since the fat sirloin revolved and emitted its savoury scent before the blazing fire on this ample hearth. Popular report says there is a public road through this house, which can neither be stopped nor diverted, and that it goes through the passage in the centre; and that an old forester, a stickler for the rights of olden times, up to no very remote period rode through the passage once a year to keep the right of road inviolate.

Jack Hill is a hamlet a short distance south of Scough Hall, clinging to the slope of the hill. It has a deserted and somewhat lonely appearance, like a place that has seen better days. Indeed some of the farm-houses bear witness that such has been the case. One in particular, of considerable age, has evidently been built by some one with good taste and ample means. A branch of the family of Hardisty has been settled here for many generations. In the Subsidy Roll, 40th Elizabeth (1597-8), we find in "Clyfton, Will. Hardistie, in terris, xx⁸· iiijᵈ·," and "Johannis Hardistie, in terris, xx⁸· iiijᵈ·" On the enclosure of the Forest of Knaresborough, twenty-one allotments, chiefly in Norwood, were awarded to Joshua Hardisty. Joshua was a favourite name with them, and borne by the eldest son for many generations. The family yet exists, holds its lands, and resides here.

The charities of this township, arising from lands and the interest of money, amount to upwards of £30 annually, which is equally divided between the poor and the schoolmaster.

In 1716, John Jeffrey, of Trees, surrendered to certain trustees three closes of land, containing, by estimation, three acres, in the hamlet of Clifton; one-half of the yearly rents thereof to be given at Easter and Christmas to the poor of Clifton hamlet; the other half for the teaching of four poor children of the said hamlet at school, and buying each of them a cap. On the enclosure of the forest an allotment was awarded to the aforesaid premises, which now comprise 6a. 2r. 23p. of land.

In 1784, William Jeffrey, of Brown Bank, surrendered to certain trustees, "one antient building, one barn, and a parcel of arable, meadow, or pasture ground, thereto belonging, containing by estimation one acre." The yearly rent of the same to be given to the poor of this township for ever. On the

2H

enclosure of the forest an allotment was awarded to the same premises, which now comprise 8a. 1r. 22p. of land.

On the enclosure of the forest in 1778, the commissioners awarded to the poor of this township two pieces of land, one of them situate at Brass Castle, containing 5a. 1r. 21p., the other near Brame Lane, contains 1a. 2r. 28p.

In 1769, Timothy Ellill, of Brame, surrendered to a trustee, and if he failed to act, to the churchwardens of the township, one messuage and one piece of land (1r. 16p.) known by the name of Snell Hole. One half of the yearly rent to be laid out in bread, to be dealt yearly and every year to the poor of Clifton hamlet, at the parish church of Fewston, on Christmas day; the other half to be dealt with after the same manner, at the same place, on Whit-Sunday, yearly, and every year for ever. This was not the only benefaction of Timothy Ellill to the poor of this township.

Copy of a Record in the Parish Church of Fewston— "Donation. Be it remembered that Timothy Ellill, late of Brame Hall, in this parish, gave to the poor of Clifton hamlet one field of land situate at Brame Lane, called Snell Hole, the rents and profits thereof to be dealt yearly to the poor for ever. He likewise gave twenty-four pounds into the hands of the Vicar of Fewston, together with the churchwardens and over-seers of the poor of Clifton-with-Norwood; the interest thereof, yearly, for ever to be applied towards instructing eight poor children in the English tongue, in such manner as is expressed by a writing lodged among the records of this parish."

The £24 above named were in the hands of John Hill until the 24th of May, 1835, when the same was paid into the hands of trustees, when it was lent to the township of Clifton-with-Norwood, due interest to be paid therefore; which money was laid out in the enlargement of the school.

This township receives one-eighth of the £5 yearly, which is divided between the parishes of Hampsthwaite and Fewston.

The population in 1801 was 408; in 1811, 415; in 1821, 420; in 1831, 415; in 1841, —; in 1851, 474; and in 1861, 864.

The annual value of this township as assessed to the county rate in 1849 was £2,398, and in 1859, £2,604. The amount assessed to property tax in 1858 was £2,891.

BLUBBERHOUSES.*

THIS township occupies the south-western angle of the Forest
of Knaresborough; and is bounded on the north by the river
Washburn, which divides it from Fewston, and Redshaw Gill
Beck, which forms the boundary towards Thruscross; on the
east by Great and Little Timble; on the south by Middleton
and Nessfield; and on the west by Beamsley and Hazelwood.
It presents great variety of soil and surface, and includes a large
quantity of uncultivated moorland. The total area is 8,736 acres.

William de Stuteville, when lord of the Honour of Knaresborough, granted lands in this township to Robert le Forester
and his heirs.

Robert Forester gave lands in this place, as described by the
boundaries, to the Prior and Canons of Bridlington.

Maude, daughter of Robert Forester, widow, gave to the same
canons one oxgang of land here.

John, son of Robert Forester, confirmed his father's grant;
and Ralph, brother of the said Robert, did the same, in the
presence of Alan and William, his sons.

* Hargrove, in his History of Knaresborough, derives this name from
the whortleberry, or *blueberry*, with which the neighbouring hills abound.
Another etymology is from *Blue Boar*, the sign of an inn here in former
days,—hence, *Blueboarhouses*. Neither of them admissible. In early
documents we find the name written *Bluburgh*, *Bluburrow*, and *Blubur-
house*. From the term *burgh* it is probable that some fortified post existed
here in early times and gave name to the township.

Richard, son of Richard de Goldesburge, in the reign of King
John, before A.D. 1217, quit claimed all the land here; and
Henry de Scriven did the same, before Brian de Insula, the
constable of Knaresburgh.

John, son of John de Walkingham, gave leave to the canons
to inclose, plough, and sow, the twenty acres of land here, given
by Robert Forester; and also to dig iron ore, and make forges
within the said division; and Robert, son of Huntobrith of
Killinghall, did the same; Robert de Stainley and Henry Turpin
de Killinghall did the same.

Henry, eldest son of the King of the Romans, in 51st Henry
III., A.D. 1267, ordered all his bailiffs of Knaresburgh to permit
the Prior and Convent of Bridlington, and their men, peaceably
to enjoy their manor of Blubberhouses, with common of pasture
in Thorescrosse.

The contest between Hubert, prior, and the Convent of Bridlington, on the one part, and Brian de Insula and Robert de Percy
on the other part, about common of pasture at Tymbel and
Blubberhouse, was agreed in 2nd Henry III., A.D. 1227.

Richard, Earl of Poictou and Cornwall, confirmed what the
canons had in this place. He also, in A.D. 1229, disafforested
their wood of Blubberhouse.

The contest between John, Prior of Bolton, and Gerard,
Prior of Bridlington, about the common of pasture in Blubberhouse, was ended in A.D. 1297, at York, when Gerard, Prior,
and the Convent of Bridlington, agreed that John, Prior of
Bolton, &c., should have common of pasture in Blubberhouse,
for all their cattle of Bolton, in Bethmesley, and their tenants
in villenage in the same place, as they were wont to do of old;
saving to the said prior of Bridlington, &c., all kinds of improvements, as well in the house as in the enclosures, in the moor

and pasture of Blubberhouses, made and to be made when and as they please.

And the said Prior of Bolton, &c., granted to the said Prior of Bridlington, &c., common of pasture for all sorts of their own or their tenants' cattle, of Blubberhouse, in Bethmesley, as they used to do of old; saving to the said Prior of Bolton, &c., all kinds of improvements, as well in house and enclosures as in the moor and pastures of Bethmesley, made or to be made.

At the *Inquisition* held at York Castle, A.D. 1535, the manor of Blubberhouse was stated to be of the annual value of £10.*

On the 16th of July, 5th of Elizabeth, A.D. 1562, Thomas Wood, gentleman, and William Frankland and his heirs, had a grant of the lordship of Blubberhouse, and Scite and mansion of Blubberhouse Hall, parcel of the lands of the late dissolved monastery of Bridlington.† William Frankland, Esq.,‡ was of Rye, in the parish of Standstead Allot, in the county of Hertford; and on the 19th of August, in the year 1574, he gave to his brother, Richard, and his son, Hugh, the manor of Blubberhouses, and all his lands there and at Fewston. These were the ancestors of the family of Frankland of Thirkleby

---

* "Burton's Monasticon Eboracense."
† "Cal. Rot. Pat.," p. 6.
‡ William Frankland, by will, dated Aug. 19th, 1574, gave to the master and four wardens of the guild or fraternity of the mystery of clothworkers in London, two tenements in Thames Street, over against Fryer Lane, in London, upon condition to pay 20s. a-year for the purposes therein mentioned; and also £3 a-year to the poor people inhabiting in Somerscales, Hazlewood, and the Storriths, in the parish of Skipton, when any of them or their deputies should demand it. This sum of £3 is regularly paid by the clerk of the Clothworkers' Company, about the month of January in every year, to the agent of the Frankland family, and by him distributed to the poor of the places above mentioned. The said William Frankland died Aug. 19th, 1576.
In 33rd Eliz., John Franckland and John Pulleyne were defendants in a lawsuit in the Duchy Court of Lancaster, against the complaint of Thomas Douglass, respecting a halfpennyworth and a pennyworth of land situate in Keskill, Timble township, Knaresborough Forest.

Park, near Thirsk, and who have been owners of the same lands from that time to the present.

In 1856, Lady Frankland Russell built a church here. It is a small building in the early English style, consisting of a nave and chancel, with a tower and spire at the north-west corner. It was consecrated Sept. 24th, in the above year, by Dr. Longley, then Bishop of Ripon, and was the last building set apart by him for divine worship before his translation to the see of Durham, and completed the number of 150 churches consecrated by him during the twenty years which he presided over the see of Ripon. Her ladyship also endowed it with £80 per annum.

The valley of the Washburn at this point—within its frame of hills, moors, and woods, with its winding river, its church, factories, villas, and houses—presents a beautiful and interesting picture when viewed from the hill on the south side, a short distance above the church.

The Manor House, situate on the hill on the right of the Otley road, is a large respectable building, surrounded by a grove of trees. It has been for many generations the abode of the family of Pullan.

Blubberhouses Hall is situate on the right of the turnpike road leading to Skipton, and was rebuilt on the old site, in the Elizabethan style, in 1846. During the last century a family named Wardman resided here, of whom William Wardman died in 1699, and was succeeded by his son, named Thomas, who died in 1742. He had a son named William, and three daughters, Anne, Elizabeth, and Faith. William died during his father's lifetime, leaving a son, named Thomas, and two daughters, Faith and Mary. Thomas Wardman died without issue in 1751. Mary married William Hardisty, of Hardisty Hill, and had a numerous family, of whom Susanna, the third

daughter, married Jonathan Ward, of Hardisty Hill, whose
daughter, Jane, married John Gill, who, on the rebuilding
of Blubberhouses Hall, went to reside there. He died in 1864,
and was succeeded by his only son, Matthew Gill, the present
occupier.

The turnpike road from Knaresborough to Skipton passes
through this township, winding up a narrow ravine until it
attains the heathy heights of Kexgill Moor. This glen has
evidently been torn asunder by some violent natural convulsion,
as the indentations on the sides exactly correspond, and could
they be brought together would fit into each other. A small
affluent of the Washburn flows, or rather tumbles, down this
glen. On the north side is a range of rocks, in a plantation of
larches, which have been supposed to have been used by the
Druids, but which a close examination will not warrant. A
vein of lead ore is now being worked in this rugged and
romantic valley. The highest land in the township is on
the moor, a short distance south of this glen, which rises to the
height of 1,832 feet above the level of the sea.

On the northern side of Blubberhouses Moor are Brandrith
Crags, a fine range of Druidical rocks, overlooking the valley
called Redshaw Gill. The whole range is about three hundred
yards in length, divided into three groups. The most westerly
of these is about forty yards in length, thirty feet in height,
and sixty feet in breadth. Many of these rocks bear marks on
their summits of their dedication to fire worship. The middle
group is about 150 yards east of the last named, but is much
smaller in size, but similar in kind. The most easterly is
about 100 yards from the last, and is the longest, the highest,
and the most interesting of the whole series. The rocks on
the western end are marked with a series of rock basins, cups,
and a network of crooked channels leading from them down

both sides; these channels are generally about three inches wide
and as many deep. The eastern end is the most remarkable,
and on the highest part is a large cavity in the rock of a most
singular kind; it is about five feet ten inches in length, by three
feet six inches in breadth, and about sixteen inches in depth,
of an irregular oblong shape. On the northern side is a breakage
through the rim, so that it will not hold above four or five
inches of water at the bottom. All around the main cavity are
a series of smaller basins and cups, of various shapes and sizes;
the most remarkable being near the north-east corner, which
is eleven inches in diameter and six inches in depth, quite
perfect. This has probably formed the holy water stoup of
some Druidic priest.

Nothing gives us greater pleasure than being able to point
out the birth-places of men who have distinguished themselves
in art or literature; and Blubberhouses may be justly proud of
one of its children—the Rev. Robert Collyer, who was born
at this village early in the year 1824. The little school education he received was at Fewston, under the tuition of Willie
Hardie, and which was completed before he was eight years
of age. At fourteen he went to Ilkley, where he worked as
a blacksmith with a man named Birch, a native of Lofthouse,
in Nidderdale. In 1850, he emigrated to America, and arrived
at Chicago in 1859, where at present he is pastor of Unity
Church, one of the largest in that city.* In 1867, he published

* The *Chicago Republican*, of June 20th, 1869, contains an elaborate
account of the completion and opening, in that city, of a Unitarian church,
of which the Rev. Robert Collyer is the pastor. About sixteen years ago
Mr. Collyer was a blacksmith at Ilkley, and since then his name has
become famous among the Unitarian body in the United States. Last
year an American gentleman visited Ilkley, and took away with him the
anvil at which Mr. Collyer stood, and the sledge hammer he worked with
when a blacksmith; and in Mr. Collyer's new study these articles have
been placed by his congregation. The new church was opened on the 20th

a small volume of sermons, which ran through eight editions in
sixteen months. A successful career like his would be highly
creditable to a person with the advantages of education and
station to assist him, how much more so to the almost illiterate
blacksmith's boy! What difficulties he must have met with
and overcome! and what a fine example he presents to working
men—but more especially to those of his native village.

The population in 1801 was 120; in 1811, 129; in 1821,
120; in 1831, 118; in 1841, —; in 1851, 83; and in 1861, 87.

The value of this township as assessed to the county rate
in 1849 was £601, and in 1859, £655. The amount assessed
to property tax in 1858 was £702.

---

of June, and at the close of the sermon the offertory that was taken
reached 70,000 dollars, said to be the largest church collection ever made
in the United States.

From a speech of his delivered in London, on the forty-sixth anniversary
of the British and Foreign Unitarian Association, and reported in the
Inquirer of June 3rd, 1871, we obtain some glimpses of the feelings of the
great popular preacher. He said, "There has never been a moment in the
twenty-one years that I have been absent from this land when it has not
been one of the proudest recollections and convictions, that I came of this
grand old English stock, that, as I said this morning, my grandfather
fought with Nelson at Trafalgar, and my father was an Englishman too,
and my mother was an Englishwoman—that, so far as I can trace my
descent back and back, and that is just as far as my grandfather, we are
all English, every one of us. Well, there is not a day when I stand on the
lake shore that I do not see the moors that were lifted up about my
old habitation, and a little stone cottage nestling in among the greenery,
and the glancing waters, and the lift of the lark, with his song, up
into heaven, until you cannot see him, and a hundred other things beside
that belong to this blessed place of my birth and breeding."

THRUSCROSS.

THIS township occupies the highest part of the valley of the Washburn, and also the highest land in the Forest of Knaresborough, of which it forms the north-western corner. It is bounded on the south by Blubberhouses; on the east by Thornthwaite and Menwith-with-Darley; on the north by Bewerley; and on the west by Burnsall and Bolton. The area is 6,840 acres.

No part of this township is mentioned in the Domesday survey; and the first time we have seen the name in any document is in 1299, in the *Inquisition* on the death of Richard, Earl of Cornwall, where it is styled Thorescross.

In the 4th of Edward II. (A.D. 1810), Thomas de Walkingham held two oxgangs of land in Thores Cross.*

From this form of writing the word we might easily infer that it was derived from the northern god *Thor*, whose worshippers amid these rugged wilds upreared "the stone of his power;" and as the whole of this district received a large number of Danish and Norwegian colonists, the supposition is not improbable that here the Northmen

> "Reared high their altar's rugged stone,
> And gave their gods the land they won."

The term *cross* might be added after the inhabitants were converted to christianity.

* *Inquis. post mortem.*

The rapid descent of the water from the hills, on the formation of the factory system, was taken advantage of for manufacturing purposes, and a number of flax spinning mills arose by the sides of the streams—some of them in romantic and beautiful spots; and at that time this remote region might be styled a hive of industry. The general application of steam as a means of transit has given other places an advantage over this, and the consequence has been that some of the mills have become ruins, others are standing idle, and not more than one is regularly at work.

The houses are scattered around the sides of the valleys, and over the hills—by rapid brooks, and in quiet corners, or in hamlets known as Bramley Head, West End, Low Green, and Thruscross Green.

In a narrow part of the valley, almost close to the stream, and always within hearing of its music, sheltered by a steep hill on the northern side, and nearly surrounded by high lands and woods, stands the parochial chapel of Thruscross. The situation is romantic, but the building is plain, tasteless, and somewhat dilapidated, shewing either a poverty of endowment, or lack of zeal in the establishment to which it belongs. In the Parliamentary survey made during the Commonwealth it is stated—"There is a chapel supplied with a preaching minister,* who hath no maintenance but a voluntary contribution; which chapel we think should be made a parish church." As it was then so it is now as far as endowment is concerned, but the building is evidently of a far more recent date. There is a cottage and an acre of land belonging to it, subject to the payment of 5s. yearly to the poor.

* The following entry in the Fewston register may have reference to this minister—"1668. Januarie. Mr. John Umplebie, late minister of the chapell, was buried the 16th day."

The charities consist of the above 5s. and 16s. yearly, being a rent charge left by Francis Jeffrey, in 1756.

The Wesleyan and Primitive Methodists have both chapels in this township. The latter, built in 1829, is situate near the Low Mills, and will accommodate about one hundred and twenty hearers.

Many inhabitants of this district have attained to extreme old age, from whom we select the venerable John Demaine, a small farmer, near West End, in this township, who died in 1820, at the age of 110. In his youth he was a tall active man, and a remarkably swift runner. The great amusement of his life was following the hounds, which he pursued on foot till within the last five years of his life. He was never known to change his dress after those days of severe exercise, though frequently drenched with rain; nor did he ever experience a day's confinement from illness during the course of his long life. At the age of 97 he could mow an acre of grass in one day,—a task sufficient for most young men. After he had attained his hundredth year he complained that he felt he was growing old, as he could not leap the walls, hedges, and ditches as he used to do. After struggling against the growing infirmities of age, which impeded his favourite amusement, at the age of 105 he fairly gave it up, and acknowledged himself an old man. He was quick of sight and hearing to the last.

Amongst the allotments awarded in this township on the enclosure of the Forest of Knaresborough were, one to Lady Frankland of 84a. 1r. 4p., freehold, at Willow Bog. One of 1,614 acres to the king, at Bramley Head. This is on the western side of the valley, and must form part of the lands called Roggan Hall Moor. Another was to Sir Cecil Wray, Bart., 2,751 acres, at Hanging. This is the ridge of uncultivated moor on the eastern side of the Washburn, extending from the neighbourhood of Hardisty Hill to Stone House; and John Metcalfe, bit maker, had seven allotments in Thruscross.

Roggan Hall, or Rocking Stone Hall, is the name of a shooting box belonging to his grace the Duke of Devonshire, situate on the moor between the upper springs of the Washburn and Wharfedale, at an elevation of 1,818 feet above the sea level. Around it is a piece of land about two acres in extent, enclosed from the surrounding moor with high walls of stone. The hall is in the centre of this enclosure, and consists of a centre and wings; the centre being two stories in height—the wings are only of one. The front is towards the east, and over the arch of the door is the figure of a large human face carved in stone. Behind are kitchens and other offices.

The rocking stone which has given name to the place is situate between the hall and the kitchen; though it does not rock now, it has done so within living memory. This rock—a genuine relic of the Druidical day—is eleven feet in length, seven feet six inches in breadth, and two feet six inches in thickness. The whole of the upper surface is thickly indented and grooved with cups and channels; the artificial character of which can be easily seen by any one. This logan rests upon a lower rock, the upper surface of which is about three feet above the ground, fourteen feet in length, and nearly the same in breadth.

At the north-west corner of this township is some of the highest land in the neighbourhood—indeed the highest in the millstone grit series east of the Wharfe. Of this the loftiest points are Simon's Seat (1,598 feet), Lord's Seat (1,585), and Poxstones (1,517), all forming part of one mountain, or ridge of land. These names are given to groups of rock—all worn and crannied by elemental action, and when seen in *situ*, all dipping south-easterly, as if the beds had been broken and bent

by the upheaval of the mountain limestone of Greenhowhill and
the Craven region. Some of the highest of these rocks bear
cuplike indentations, rock basins and grooves, all indicative
of the fire worship of the Druids. From their situation, fires
lighted on these summits would be seen at a great distance, and
on a clear day the view from these rocks is most extensive and
various, extending for miles upon miles in all directions.
Notwithstanding the height of this eminence, its grit formation
and peaty surface, there is much grass among these rocks and
all around the hill; and for a considerable distance there is
but little ling; bent, in two or three varieties, being the
prevailing plant. The whole surface of this moor, about the
year 1790, was much improved by a series of drains cut across
it, which carry away the surplus water, and make the ground
sounder and better for pasturage.

The Washburn may be said to be the child of this region,
deriving its first waters from the high lands around Greenhowhill, it flows down a shallow lonely valley past Hummerston
Bank and Thruscross Green to West End, where it receives
a considerable affluent from the right, called Cappishaw Beck,
which drains the long slopes extending beyond Bramley Head
and Roggan Hall. Further down, Redshaw Beck also enters
from the right, and thence downwards, after filling the enormous
reservoirs of the Leeds Corporation Waterworks it empties
itself into the Wharfe at Leathley.

The population of this township in 1801 was 467; in 1811,
610; in 1821, 600; in 1831, 601; in 1841, —; in 1851, 839;
and in 1861, 868. This variation in numbers is entirely due
to the state of trade. Now the population has nearly all become
agricultural.

The annual value as assessed to the county rate in 1849 was
£1,592, and in 1859, £2,088. The amount assessed to property
tax in 1858 was £2,246.